BECOMING A HISTORY TEACHER

Sustaining Practices in Historical
Thinking and Knowing

Edited by Ruth Sandwell and Amy von Heyking

A revolution in history education is propelling historical thinking and knowing to the forefront of history and social studies education in North America and beyond. Teachers, teacher education programs, schools, and ministries of education across Canada are embracing the idea that knowing history means knowing how to think historically.

Becoming a History Teacher is a collection of essays by history teachers, historians, and teacher educators on how to prepare student teachers to think historically and to teach historical thinking. Exploring teachers' experiences before, during, and after formal certification, this volume presents a wide range of resources for teachers and educators, including information on the latest research in history education and examples of successful history teaching activities.

RUTH SANDWELL is an associate professor in the Department of Curriculum, Teaching and Learning at the Ontario Institute for Studies in Education, University of Toronto.

AMY VON HEYKING is an associate professor in the Faculty of Education at the University of Lethbridge.

Becoming a History Teacher

Sustaining Practices in Historical Thinking and Knowing

EDITED BY RUTH SANDWELL
AND AMY VON HEYKING

UNIVERSITY OF TORONTO PRESS
Toronto Buffalo London

© University of Toronto Press 2014
Toronto Buffalo London
www.utppublishing.com
Printed in the U.S.A.

ISBN 978-1-4426-4901-9 (cloth)
ISBN 978-1-4426-2651-5 (paper)

Printed on acid-free, 100% post-consumer recycled paper with vegetable-based inks.

Library and Archives Canada Cataloguing in Publication

Becoming a history teacher : sustaining practices in historical thinking and knowing /
edited by Ruth Sandwell and Amy von Heyking

Includes bibliographical references
ISBN 978-1-4426-4901-9 (bound)   ISBN 978-1-4426-2651-5 (pbk.)

1. History teachers – Training of – Canada.   2. History – Study and teaching –
Canada.   3. Canada – History – Philosophy.   4. Canada – History – Study and
teaching.   I. Sandwell, R.W. (Ruth Wells), 1955–, author, editor   II. von Heyking,
Amy J. (Amy Jeanette), 1965–, author, editor

D16.4.C3B42 2014   907.1'071   C2014-903496-2

This book has been published with the help of a grant from the Canadian Federation
for the Humanities and Social Sciences, through the Awards to Scholarly Publications
Program, using this and other funds provided by the Social Sciences and Humanities
Research Council of Canada.

University of Toronto Press acknowledges the financial assistance to its publishing
program of the Canada Council for the Arts and the Ontario Arts Council, an agency
of the Government of Ontario.

Canada Council   Conseil des Arts
for the Arts   du Canada

University of Toronto Press acknowledges the financial support of the Government of
Canada through the Canada Book Fund for its publishing activities.

Contents

List of Tables and Figures   ix

Acknowledgments   xi

PART I: Introduction

1 Introduction   3
RUTH SANDWELL AND AMY VON HEYKING

2 Moving from the Periphery to the Core: The Possibilities
for Professional Learning Communities in History Teacher
Education   11
ALAN SEARS

3 "The Teacher Is the Keystone of the Educational Arch": A Century
and a Half of Lifelong Teacher Education in Canada   30
PENNEY CLARK

4 The Poverty and Possibility of Historical Thinking: An Overview
of Recent Research into History Teacher Education   60
SCOTT A. POLLOCK

**PART II: Nurturing Historical Thinking before Entering
a Teacher Education Program**

RESEARCH AND REFLECTION

5 On Historians and Their Audiences: An Argument for Teaching
(and Not Just Writing) History   77
RUTH SANDWELL

6 Canadian History for Teachers: Integrating Content and Pedagogy in Teacher Education   91
   AMY VON HEYKING

PART III: History and Social Studies Teacher Education Programs in Canada

RESEARCH AND REFLECTION

7 What Is the Use of the Past for Future Teachers? A Snapshot of Francophone Student Teachers in Ontario and Québec Universities   115
   STÉPHANE LÉVESQUE

8 Through the Looking Glass: An Overview of the Theoretical Foundations of Quebec's History Curriculum   139
   CATHERINE DUQUETTE

9 Troubling Compromises: Historical Thinking in a One-Year Secondary Teacher Education Program   158
   PETER SEIXAS AND GRAEME WEBBER

10 Engaging Teacher Education through Rewriting That History We Have Already Learned   175
   KENT DEN HEYER

11 "Walking the Talk": Modelling the Pedagogy We Profess in History and Social Studies Methodology Courses   198
   ROLAND CASE AND GENIE MacLEOD

STRATEGIES AND PRACTICES

12 Teaching Student Teachers to Use Primary Sources When Teaching History   214
   LINDSAY GIBSON

13 Learning to Learn in New Brunswick Teacher Preparation: Historical Research as a Vehicle for Cultivating Historical Thinking in the Context of Social Studies Education   226
   THEODORE CHRISTOU

14 When in Doubt, Ask: Student Teacher Insights into Research
and Practice   235
JOHN JC MYERS

PART IV: Boundary Work: Sustaining Communities of Practice

RESEARCH AND REFLECTIONS

15 Can Teacher Education Programs Learn Something from
Teacher Professional Development Initiatives?   249
CARLA L. PECK

16 On the Museum as a Practised Place: Or, Reconsidering
Museums and History Education   269
BRENDA TROFANENKO

STRATEGIES AND PRACTICES

17 Teaching History Teachers in the Classroom   283
JAN HASKINGS-WINNER

18 Engendering Power and Legitimation: Giving Teachers the
Tools to Claim a Place for History Education in Their Schools   291
ROSE FINE-MEYER

19 Telling the Stories of the Nikkei: A Place-Based History
Education Project   303
TERRY TAYLOR AND LINDA FARR DARLING

20 Conclusion   313
AMY VON HEYKING AND RUTH SANDWELL

Bibliography   321

Contributors   339

Tables and Figures

Tables

3.1   Establishment of Normal Schools in Canadian Provinces
15.1 Knowledge of HTCs at Beginning of Project
15.2 Knowledge of HTCs at End of Project

Figures

2.1   Participants in Communities of Practice
3.1   Normal School, London, Ontario ca. 1920. Albertype Company
      fonds/ Library and Archives Canada PA-03180. Copyright
      expired.
3.2   Frontispiece from *The Child-Centered School: An Appraisal of the
      New Education* by Harold Rugg and Ann Shumaker
3.3   Ottawa Normal School students reading *Our Canada* in the
      library, 1950. Digital Image Number: I0021762.JPG. Ref. Code:
      RG 2-251. Courtesy of Archives of Ontario.
3.4   Manual arts project — "Holland." Primary Grade Coarse [sic],
      Summer School, Victoria, BC. This project was displayed in the
      closing exhibition of student teachers' work, 10 August 1922.
      British Columbia Department of Education, *Annual Report
      of the Public Schools, 1922* (Victoria: Author, 1922), np.
3.5   An example of an enterprise in action in BC Schools. From
      Rita D. Bowyer [sic], "Indian Life," *British Columbia Schools* 1
      (February 1946), 43.
7.1   Ethnic origins (in percentage by subgroup)

7.2   Number of postsecondary history courses (in percentage by subgroup)

7.3   Uses of the past (activities done in the last twelve months in percentage)

7.4   Frequency for uses of the past (in percentage per category)

7.5   Interest in various types of history (in percentage by option)

7.6   Trustworthiness of sources about the past (in percentage)

7.7   Rationale for history in Canadian schools (in percentage)

7.8   Historical competencies to develop in school history (in percentage)

7.9   Fields of study in school history (in percentage)

7.10 Preferred teaching strategies in school history (in percentage)

7.11 Most pertinent teaching resources (in percentage)

7.12 Knowledge of history (in percentage by subgroup)

7.13 Level of confidence in teaching history to students (in percentage by subgroup)

8.1   The historical method of research as viewed by the MELS

8.2   Synthesis of historical thinking as understood by the Quebec curriculum

8.3   Comparison of the historical thinking model emerging in francophone research and the Quebec history curriculum

8.4   Comparison of the model proposed by The Historical Thinking Project and the model found in the Quebec curriculum

10.1 An example of intersecting narrative trajectories

Acknowledgments

The editors gratefully acknowledge the direct and generous support of The History Education Network/Histoire et éducation en réseau (THEN/HiER), and in turn the Social Sciences and Humanities Research Council (SSHRC) who provided THEN/HiER support through their Strategic Knowledge Clusters Grant. This collection is the third major scholarly publication of the Network. This collection of essays, like the two earlier volumes, benefited not only from the organization's financial support, but from the encouragement, knowledge, and enthusiasm provided by the THEN/HiER's executive board: Margaret Conrad, Anne Marie Goodfellow, Jan Haskings-Winner, Kevin Kee, Jocelyn Létourneau, Stéphane Lévesque, Alan Sears, and Peter Sexias. We would like to extend an especially warm thank you to THEN/ HiER's Director, Dr Penney Clark. She provided us with the inspiration for this volume, as well as a fine example of how to go about creating a work of collaborative scholarship appropriate for the Network. THEN/ HiER's other edited collections are *New Possibilities for the Past: Shaping History Education in Canada* (UBC Press, 2011), and *Pastplay: Teaching and Learning History with Technology* (University of Michigan Press, 2014). These have set a standard to which all of us who care deeply about history education can only aspire.

The editors would also like to thank The History Education Network/ Histoire et éducation en réseau and the Office of the Dean, Faculty of Education, University of Lethbridge for their support for the symposium which launched this collection. Research that formed the basis of individual chapters in this volume was funded by: SSHRC (Chapter 13); the University of Alberta Support for the Advancement of Scholarship Fund (Chapter 15); the Canada Research Chair Secretariat and the

Acadia University (Chapter 16); and THEN/HiER's Small Project Grant; Office of Eleanor Rix, Professor of Rural Teacher Education; Arts Starts Artists in the Classrooms; and Lucerne Elementary-Secondary School (Chapter 19). The editors would like to thank all of these organizations for their support of this important research.

We would like to thank the editors at the University of Toronto Press, particularly Douglas Hildebrand, who worked closely with us through the review and editing process. The anonymous reviewers provided detailed, thoughtful, and even inspiring commentary for all of the authors. Margaret Beintema at the University of Lethbridge provided invaluable technical and administrative assistance. Finally, we would like to thank all of the contributors for their hard work and unerring support as we worked together to create this volume, and their families, who suffered and supported along the way.

PART ONE

Introduction

1 Introduction

RUTH SANDWELL AND AMY VON HEYKING

Any fool can make history, but it takes a genius to write it.

– Oscar Wilde

A revolution in history education in recent years is propelling historical thinking and knowing to the forefront of history and social studies education in North America and beyond. Teachers, university teacher education programs, schools, and ministries of education across Canada are among those embracing a newly championed approach to history teaching and learning, one that promises to supplement the wide range of pedagogical strategies and practices that experienced teachers have in their history-related repertoire, and to replace what many critics believe is an overreliance on rote learning and memorization with the richer and deeper disciplinary understanding that comes from knowing how history is made. At the centre of the new approach is the supposition that knowing history means knowing how to think historically. Students are introduced to the kinds or procedures of knowing that historians engage in, including evaluating significance, assessing cause and consequence, exploring the varied perspectives of people in the past, and probing the ethical dimensions of history. Many educators are demonstrating that it is by actively engaging in "doing" history that students experience, and come to know, historical thinking: the complicated, nuanced process of evaluating the meanings and significance of often-conflicting evidence (generated during the time in question as primary sources, and from more recent evaluations or histories) in the best way possible.

Or that is the hope. While this approach to history and social studies education has been taken up enthusiastically, it is not, unfortunately, entirely clear where history and social studies teachers are finding the knowledge and expertise they need to convey this deeper and richer disciplinary understanding to their students in secondary and elementary schools. Evidence suggests that this lacuna in teacher education and understanding may be of key importance if history classrooms are indeed going to change, and in a lasting way. Historians of education have pointed out that different iterations of "document-based learning" and "doing history" have been championed by history educators on several occasions over the last century.[1] While excellent history teachers have *long* taught in a variety of ways, often inspired by the promise of "doing history," history teaching has never succeeded in completely dislodging some of the most disparaged of pedagogical strategies, particularly the "kill and drill" history so often blamed for the generally low popularity of history and social studies courses among secondary students – and these students' poor historical understanding.

Alan Sears frames the problem this way in his essay in this volume: "If I am correct that most history teachers work on the margins of the discipline, they often understand themselves as passive recipients of history, not active makers of it." Identifying history with facts, and history teachers with fact transmission, Sears argues, is particularly problematic because cognitive research has been demonstrating for some time that active engagement is central to the construction of knowledge. Teaching and learning more history, therefore, means learning to think better historically, and "in order for teachers to understand history as a discipline and be able to teach it that way, they will have to engage it as a verb – they have to *do* it." But teachers need to not only change their minds about what history as a discipline *is* and develop new strategies for teaching it: Sears argues that they will also need to develop a *new identity* to fully embrace this new knowledge of both history and of teaching. This is not going to be a quick or easy process. More about this below.

Symposium to Book

The essays in this collection grew out of conversations among Canadian history teacher educators about how best to prepare our teachers to add yet another pedagogical strategy, and perhaps even change the way they think about history, by explicitly nurturing historical thinking in their classrooms. In Calgary, Alberta, in April 2011, nineteen history education researchers and teacher educators (including university professors and instructors, historians, secondary school teachers, and both graduate students and student teachers) gathered at a symposium sponsored by The History Education Network/Histoire et éducation en réseau (THEN/HiER). The organizers initially imagined that the symposium would provide an opportunity for participants to share examples of best practices from their work with student teachers, and share the results of research they were conducting on effective history teacher preparation. What emerged were research projects, reflections, and descriptions of exemplary teaching activities that reflected the diverse, intellectually rigorous, and creative initiatives that scholars across Canada were experimenting with in order to help students, teachers, and university educators improve their history instruction. Perhaps even more significantly, these history educators shared the ways in which they had struggled to identify what, exactly, was intervening between research, scholarship, and effective teaching in history and social studies classrooms.

The call for proposals for the symposium had asked participants, most of whom work in postsecondary teacher education settings, to present research papers or to conduct short workshops illustrating their teaching strategies. The goal of THEN/HiER has always been to bridge the theory and practice divide and facilitate collaborations among all stakeholders engaged in history teaching and research into history teaching. The organizers, therefore, sought to organize the symposium in a way that would truly reflect the research-informed practice we are all striving for. Once nineteen papers and workshop presentations had been selected, the participants were asked to complete drafts of their papers and presentations and post them to the symposium website. Participants were asked to review all the drafts prior to the symposium; they were assigned one paper or presentation to review critically and in detail.

Over the two days of the symposium, participants presented their papers and teaching strategies workshops. The organizers had categorized the papers and presentations, and organized the symposium, according to themes that had emerged in the proposals: frameworks for problems and solutions, research in history education, and classroom strategies for history teacher educators. Participants were given limited time to present their papers in order to provide ample time for the assigned respondent's remarks and a constructive, collective roundtable discussion. The final afternoon was used to summarize the themes and issues that had emerged over the course of the sessions.

In holding a symposium that was meant to comprise an important stage in writing a collaborative edited collection, organizers had followed on the examples set by Penney Clark and Kevin Kee in their books for our THEN/HiER series.[2] Each benefited from holding a symposium, whose purpose was to bring together the authors in a fairly structured way to comment on one or two draft chapters that they had been asked to read in advance, and to discuss the collection as a whole. Like Clark and Kee, the editors of this collection had hoped that the critique and discussions among the participants would create something more than the sum of the individual parts that we brought to the symposium. By presenting the papers at the symposium, authors would, we hoped, provide both context and information to other contributors that would give the collection more coherence, and at the very least avoid repetition. But we also thought there was a good chance that the dialogue occurring within the symposium itself just might transform the book from the one we had imagined when we were initially planning the book. We were not disappointed: the dialogue among the authors that emerged over our two-day symposium caused us to rethink what this project was about, and its larger purpose.

The symposium convinced us to rethink and restructure the book in three key ways. Originally we had organized the symposium by sessions that focused on particular themes, issues, and approaches to history teacher education. As a direct result of the stimulating discussions among the participants during the symposium, however, the editors developed a structure that we felt more fruitfully reflected the issues, concerns, and hopes expressed by the contributors. Rather than organizing the book in clearly separated categories of issues, concerns, research, and practice, we incorporated into the very structure of the book a point of discussion that came up over and over again throughout the symposium – history teacher education is not simply what happens within the formal structure of teacher education programs. Instead, it begins before this formal process, and must continue long after the teacher certificate is obtained. The book is now, accordingly, divided not by issues, concerns, and methods, but instead into the three key chronological phases of a history teacher's life – before, during, and after a teacher receives formal certification.

This change of organization necessarily led to a second key change in structure between symposium and book: the organization of essays within each of these sections. Within the new chronological structure of a history teacher's life, chapters could no longer be clustered by the issues, themes, or approaches we had originally envisaged. Again, the active discussions during the symposium itself gave us direction. One of the key issues that had emerged in every part of our two-day symposium (itself organized by categorizing history teacher education in terms of problems, solutions, research, and practice) was the problematic and indeed actively harmful nature of the "theory/practice divide" within teaching generally, and history teacher education in particular. In inviting not only researchers and history teacher educators to the symposium, but also teachers and students, we thought that we had met our goal of including the multiple voices of the history teacher education community. By the end of the second day, however, we had come to understand (rather painfully!) that the structure we had created for the symposium exemplified exactly the kind of theory/practice divide that – as all participants in the symposium agreed – was one of the most significant obstacles to improving history teacher education. The editors decided, therefore, to respond to this key issue once again by using the structure of the book itself to bring together chapters on reflection, research, and practice in history teacher education into the sections representing each of the three stages of a history teacher's life.

The three main sections within this book – "before, during, and after" teacher education programs – each include two different kinds of chapters: first, research or research-based reflections on learning and teaching historical thinking and knowing. We will return to those essays in a moment. Each section also includes a second, shorter, and more highly structured chapter that illustrates specific strategies, practices, or activities that can create and sustain new environments of teaching and learning historical thinking. After the symposium, we asked the authors of these chapters – in the interests of coherence across the volume, and of keeping the volume to a manageable length – to structure (or restructure, in most cases!) their original chapters/presentations around the following questions:

1 What problem or problems did this course/lesson/approach seek to address in history teacher education in general, and the problem or issue of teaching historical thinking in particular?
2 What is the structure of the history curriculum in your province, and what is the structure of history teacher education?
3 How exactly did you address the problem that you identified? (What was the course name? How did it fit into which curriculum?

Was it compulsory or not? How many students participated, and what kind of students? Please provide an overview of the lesson or course, being sure to articulate just what the students were required to *do*, and with what kind of support from the instructor, from each other, and/or from other sources. What kind of assessments did you use?)

4   How successful was the course or lesson, and how do you know?

The editors were delighted that the authors were not only willing to make considerable changes to their original papers to accommodate this restructuring, but did so with the same enthusiasm and professional grace that had characterized their participation in the symposium.

If the symposium discussions significantly altered the structure of the book and the structure of each section within the book, there was an even more significant shift in the exact focus of the book. During the symposium, participants kept referring back again and again to Alan Sears' essay, in which he had clearly articulated some key challenges for history educators, as they discussed and explained the problems and promise of their own work in history teacher education. And Sears' insistence during the symposium that each author address the factors that have allowed (and in some cases encouraged) history teachers to linger on the periphery of the profession, rather than moving to the core, became a key point of discussion – and not always a comfortable one! After the symposium, we wrote to each of the participants as follows:

> In order to give even greater focus and force to the discussions about history teacher education in our collection (while remaining "true" to the varied contributions on this subject that comprise it) we are asking all contributors to do something a little unusual as they move ahead with the revisions to their individual papers. We are inviting everyone to articulate explicitly just how your own chapter reflects, responds to, or contradicts Alan Sears' framing of "the big problem" in history teacher education – that most history teachers have neither the expertise nor the interest in history that they need to be at the core of their profession – and his proposed solution to this dilemma: ensuring that history teachers learn to think and know historically.

We went on to explain that the editors had been struck by the fact that all of the authors were *already*, in an important sense, responding to the key issues identified so clearly in Sears' chapter. With the goal of providing more focus to the manuscript, and in the spirit of moving dialogue forward from our symposium and into the book, we invited all of the authors to take the additional step of addressing explicitly how their own research, practice, or reflections on being and becoming a history teacher reflected the distinction Sears was making between teachers being at the core or at the periphery of the profession.

More specifically, we invited reflection on Sears' contention that too many history teachers continue to occupy positions on the periphery of a *community of practice*, rather than at the core; "they have little or no experience even learning about and observing the practice of history" and "really cannot be expected either to adapt their practice to new situations or to teach others to engage in practice in anything beyond mechanistic forms." Drawing particularly on the work of Wenger, Barton and Levstik, and Gardner, Sears goes on to suggest that the solution to this key problem is to engage history teachers, and history student teachers, in "boundary practices" with historians in a range of settings. Literature from "the cognitive revolution" stresses the important relationship between learning and identity, leading Sears to the conclusion that history teachers not only need to change their minds about what the discipline is, but also develop a new sense of who they are and what their role is. He concludes by noting that this must necessarily be a long and difficult task, and not one that can be completed in a single class, course, or program. By the end of the symposium, as we reminded the authors, we were *all* expressing the need for history education researchers and teacher educators to take up Sears' challenge to explore how to provide teachers, and future teachers, with the *sustaining environments* that they need before, during, and after their formal teacher education programs in order to know and teach history differently, with an emphasis on historical thinking.

Notwithstanding the shift in direction between what we had originally planned, what people originally wrote, and what this volume finally looks like, the editors were delighted that all of the authors responded enthusiastically to this invitation to draw on their own work to give more focus to this collective volume.

In this final iteration, the essays in this volume reflect the different regions of Canada, and the diversity of history and social studies curricula and history teacher education in each. The essays also, we believe, reach out to include the kinds of issues and challenges that have been articulated in other parts of the world. The book begins with three chapters that provide introductions to various aspects of history teacher education. As a whole, the book emphasizes that the process of becoming a history teacher takes a lifetime, and the structure of the next three sections of the manuscript reflects this life course approach. The first section explores appropriate learning environments before formal teacher education programs, while the second (and largest) section explores various elements of history teacher education programs. In the final section, a number of authors posit the important role of "boundary work" for history teachers after they have completed their professional training and formal education, wherein history and social studies teachers can find sustained (and sustaining) communities of practice both inside and outside the school system to support their ongoing work. As well, each section includes broad-ranging reflections on teachers' and student teachers' encounters with history education in general, and historical thinking in particular, and/or examples of theoretically-informed research in the field of history teacher education. Finally, each section also includes shorter essays that articulate one or more specific strategies and practices of the kind needed to create new environments of teaching and learning historical thinking at various points in the life course of a history teacher. It is our hope that you find these essays as informative and thought-provoking as we have.

NOTES

1 For a full description of the "debate" about teaching history by doing history, see Ken Osborne, "Teaching History in Schools: A Canadian Debate," *Journal of Curriculum Studies* 35, no. 5 (2003): 585-626.
2 Penney Clark, ed., *New Possibilities for the Past: Shaping History Education in Canada* (Vancouver: UBC Press, 2011); Kevin Kee, ed., *Pastplay: Teaching and Learning History with Technology* (Ann Arbor: University of Michigan Press, 2014).

2 Moving from the Periphery to the Core: The Possibilities for Professional Learning Communities in History Teacher Education

ALAN SEARS

Introduction: Getting in the Game

Imagine you have signed up for a course titled Hockey 101. You show up at the first class with your skates, hockey stick, and a genuine enthusiasm to get started. The instructor gives you a strange look and asks why you have brought this paraphernalia to class. Stunned, you respond that you are eager to begin playing the game. The instructor smiles at your naiveté and explains rather condescendingly that you won't be playing hockey in the class but rather learning about hockey: studying the development of the game over time, learning the rules, and reading biographies of the best players and accounts of the greatest games. The course is about studying hockey, not playing it.[1]

Sound incongruous? Perhaps it is, but I submit something like this is standard procedure in many history classes from kindergarten through to a bachelor's degree. Students spend years in history class reading about history, historical processes, and even great historians, but never actually doing any history. Almost thirty years ago, Shirley Engle described the transformation of the historian between the archives and the classroom:

> For reasons I have never fully understood, most history professors completely change their colors when they step out of their role as research scholars and take on the mantle of "herr" professor. As scholars they hold truth in great tenuousness; they are not all of one mind; their disciplines are hotbeds of controversy; they are forever correcting one another's errors. But once they have laid aside their research eyeshades and donned

their teaching robes, they become authorities whose mission is considered to be the transmission of their superior knowledge to students.[2]

Unfortunately, in speaking with the pre-service teachers I meet today, little seems to have changed. Many, even those with majors in history, have little or no first-hand experience with the processes of doing history. They haven't struggled to define a "significant" and unexplored (or underexplored) question about the past to study, sat with a pile of diverse sources trying to weigh their relative merits and build an argument, or tried to make judgments about the moral actions of historical agents in particular times and places. They haven't, in other words, had to think historically, but rather have been relatively passive observers of others' attempts to do so.

This has serious implications for the preparation of teachers to be able to teach historical thinking in at least two ways: the candidates have little or no actual experience with the processes they will be teaching and, therefore, probably aren't very good at them themselves; as well, in my view much more importantly, the candidates have a strong cognitive frame that history teaching essentially involves the passing on of historical information and not the fostering of historical thinking. In this paper I will draw on scholarship in both professional learning communities and cognition to examine these implications in more depth and explore possibilities for structuring pre- and in-service learning opportunities that will help move history teachers from observers on the margins of the discipline towards being practitioners at the core.

History Teachers on the Margins

In the seminal and later work on professional learning communities, Etienne Wenger and his colleagues describe a range of actors within any sphere of practice, from those at the centre of the enterprise, shaping both its knowledge base and practices, to those on the fringes who, while they may engage in the mechanical processes of the venture, neither really understand nor shape it.[3] The core group at the centre of the enterprise provides leadership and is composed of the key actors in shaping community practices and standards. Active members participate regularly but "without the intensity of the core group."[4] The majority of members are peripheral, engaging in essential dimensions of the community of practice but keeping largely to the sidelines because they feel they have little to contribute to shaping the enterprise, or time constraints and other responsibilities limit their participation. Finally, there are marginal members and interested outsiders. These are content to operate on the margins; they are interested neither in learning more and moving towards the core areas of practice, nor in moving on and leaving the field altogether (Figure 2.1 illustrates this). Marginal players and outsiders, Wenger argues, are on one of two trajectories: inbound towards the core or outbound, often all the way to non-membership in the particular community of practice. Effective communities of practice design activities to allow peripheral members to feel like full members of the community and set marginal members on inbound trajectories to more engaged participation. They also "build benches" from where interested outsiders can observe the community in operation and perhaps develop interest in joining.[5]

In terms of the disciplinary practices of history, most teachers are very much at the margins or are even outsiders. This is true of specialist teachers with university majors or minors in history, and even truer of nonspecialists who may not even be at the margins as they have little or no experience even learning about and observing the practice of history. Wenger argues that those at the periphery or margins of a community of practice might be able to employ appropriate practices in a mechanistic way – what he calls compliance – but he goes on to make the point that "compliance does not require understanding."[6] Further, those who comply in this way really cannot be expected either to adapt their practice to new situations or to teach others to engage in practice in anything beyond mechanistic forms. They cannot, in other words, teach others to understand what they do not understand themselves.

If a central function of history teaching is to teach the disciplinary processes of history, which are at the heart of work in historical thinking, then a key role for teacher education should be to set teachers on an inbound trajectory, to nurture them as practitioners of the discipline themselves. This does not necessarily mean making them historians but rather engaging them in "boundary practices" with historians in a range of settings.[7] For Wenger, communities of practice are tightly bound systems with well-established (although ideally fluid) bodies of knowledge and practice and clear boundaries. They cannot, however, "be considered in isolation from the rest of the world, or understood independently from other practices."[8] Different communities of practice often interrelate and overlap and "interacting across practices

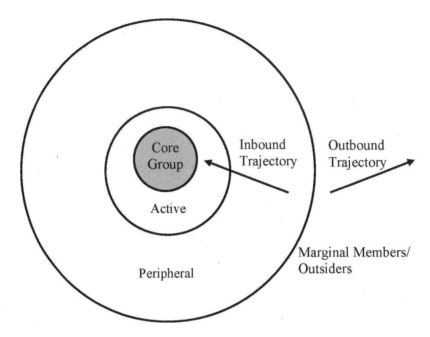

Figure 2.1: Participants in Communities of Practice

forces members to take a fresh look at their own assumptions. As a re-sult boundary crossing can be the source of a deep kind of learning."[9]

History teachers and historians constitute two related and overlap-ping communities of practice, and productive "boundary practices" between them could help move teachers towards the core of historical practice and help historians become better teachers. Wenger argues that a key role in this process is that of brokers, who understand the work of both areas and "are able to make new connections across communities of practice, enable coordination and – if they are good brokers – open new possibilities for meaning."[10] This kind of broker-ing ought to be a key function of those of us involved in the scholar-ship of history education and the education of history teachers. Later, I will sketch out some principles and preliminary ideas for playing this role, but first I will explore how lessons from the cognitive revolution make it abundantly clear just how big a challenge it will be to move history teachers towards significantly new ways of understanding themselves and their role.

Being Made New

In their book, *Teaching History for the Common Good,* Keith Barton and Linda Levstik begin one of the chapters with a vignette about two "pedantic blowhards" who dominated a history class by rudely calling out answers before anyone else could respond and brashly correcting others' mistakes when they did get a word in. They argue this "Trivial Pursuit" approach to history is far too common among those who choose to teach it. People with this orientation have always enjoyed history as the quest for interesting bits of information and see it as their role as teachers both to demonstrate their superior knowledge of the subject and to have their students inculcate similar collections of "discrete factual details."[11] While most teachers are probably not as irritating as the two described by Barton and Levstik, the view of history as a collection of facts and stories to be memorized and recalled intact when necessary is, I believe, far more prevalent than not among history teachers. If true, this cognitive frame will prove a powerful inhibitor to developing teachers disposed to fostering historical thinking in their students.

I have written at length elsewhere about the cognitive revolution of the twentieth century and its implications for history and social studies teachers, but here I want to focus on one of those lessons in particular: "prior knowledge matters."[12] A central tenet of research in cognition is that people come to any learning situation with a set of cognitive structures that filter and shape new information in powerful ways. Howard Gardner calls these structures "mental representations" and argues they underlie the fact that "individuals do not just react to or perform in the world; they possess minds and these minds contain images, schemes, pictures, frames, languages, ideas, and the like."[13] The literature uses a range of terms but generally refers to this phenomenon as prior knowledge, meaning the knowledge learners bring with them to the classroom or any other learning situation.

Research demonstrates not only that learners bring mental representations or schemata with them to learning situations, but that these filter and shape new learning. These are sometimes substantial and sometimes charming, but "many are simply wrong."[14] When presented with information that does not fit existing frameworks, learners will often distort it or discard it completely rather than doing the difficult work necessary to restructure their frameworks. Research on prior knowledge consistently shows cognitive schemata to be persistent and resistant to change. As Gardner puts it, "Minds, of course, are hard to change."[15]

Among those involved in social education generally, no group knows this better than history educators. Keith Barton's research on the understandings of national history held by students in the United States and Northern Ireland, Jocelyn Létourneau's work on young Quebecers' understandings of their province's place in Canada and North America, and Carla Peck's study of how ethnic identity shapes Canadian students' understanding of their nation's past are just a few examples of a very large body of work on the cognitive frames students bring with them to the study of history.[16]

Barton and Levstik provide a clear example from their research on children's understandings of history of how pre-existing frameworks shape new knowledge. A large body of work in this field demonstrates that American students have a conception of the history of the United States as framed by the twin themes of freedom and progress. This view allows for slight deviations from the nation's commitment to freedom or minor setbacks on the road to progress in the American story, but the overall direction of American history is towards greater freedom as well as social and economic progress. As part of their work, Barton and Levstik exposed students to historical material that countered these preconceptions and found "so powerful was the narrative of progress that it led students to distort the historical evidence to fit their preconceptions."[17]

The irony is that while we have paid close attention to the cognitive frames of students in history class, scant consideration has been given to the frames of those who teach them. A clear lesson from the cognitive revolution is that teachers come to the teaching of history with preconceived and powerful ideas of what the discipline is and how it should be taught, and any approaches advocated in pre-service methods courses or in-service educational opportunities will be filtered through those frames. If, as we have seen, the cognitive frames of young children are powerful shapers of new knowledge and resistant to change, we can be sure these challenges will be multiplied for those who are older and have much longer experience with the dominant approaches to history teaching described above. As Gardner points out, "While it is easy and natural to change one's mind during the first years of life, it becomes difficult to alter one's mind as the years pass."[18]

Wenger argues, "there is a profound connection between identity and practice."[19] In other words, professional practice depends not only on what we know and can do but also on our sense of identity – on who we are. If I am correct that most history teachers work on the margins of the discipline, they often understand themselves as passive recipients of history, not active makers of it. Researchers who do not see the need to disseminate their findings in forms or forums frequented by teachers can reinforce that perception. This sense of identity manifests itself in how some history teachers understand and carry out their role: passing on historical information rather than fostering historical thinking. In order for this to change, it is necessary that both teachers and historians think differently about the relationship of teachers to the discipline of history. Teachers need to grow in understanding of both disciplinary processes and new scholarly work, and researchers need to acknowledge the value of working with teachers in cross-boundary partnerships designed to enhance teacher participation in the discipline and, through that, teaching practice in classrooms.

As if the challenges presented by the prior knowledge of history teachers and teacher candidates and the consequent resistance to new ideas were not enough, Howard Gardner raises another. He affirms in the strongest terms the general direction of the historical thinking movement to foster the development of disciplinary understandings in students, arguing, "The disciplines represent the most advanced ways to think about issues consequential to human beings."[20] He goes on to make the point, however, that cognitive science demonstrates that "both disciplinary content and disciplinary habits of mind may be *deeply* counterintuitive."[21] As Sam Wineburg suggests, it seems historical thinking is indeed an "unnatural act."[22]

All of this is not to suggest that changing the cognitive frames of teachers and teacher candidates with respect to history and history teaching and developing in them enhanced disciplinary understandings and skills is impossible. It is simply to recognize this will be a long and difficult task, not something that can be accomplished in a single methods course in a faculty of education or in half-day workshops during professional development days. As Gardner contends, "we need to devote years to educating students in the arcana of the disciplines."[23]

This is where Wenger's work on professional learning communities intersects with lessons from the cognitive revolution. For Wenger, understanding develops "as social participation" in communities defined by three features – "mutual engagement," "a joint enterprise," and a "shared repertoire." Over time, engagement in these communities shapes understanding, processes, and identity.[24] When the communities include intentionally reflective elements, they foster what Vygotsky called interpersonal and intrapersonal dialogue and can move learners to profoundly new ways of understanding and operating in the world.[25] I believe the tactic of engaging teachers in communities of practice that actually do history and reflect on the implications of that for teaching has the greatest potential to break down the resistances of long-standing cognitive frames and develop the kind of complex disciplinary understanding necessary for fostering historical thinking. The next section sets out some principles for establishing these kinds of communities of practice that include work across boundaries with related communities and some specific examples of how to operationalize these principles.

Doing History to Learn about Teaching History

Principle 1 – Identity Formation Is Central to Teacher Education

As Ruth Sandwell points out, "history is a verb."[26] In order for teachers to understand history as a discipline and be able to teach it that way, they will have to engage it as a verb – they have to *do* it. But doing it alone is not enough. Teachers will have to develop an identity as a participant – at least in the peripheral sense – in a professional learning community of history education. They have to understand themselves as not only observers and practitioners but as shapers, or potential shapers, of the field. They have to develop a new identity.

Perhaps an example will help clarify this. Before becoming a faculty member, I spent eleven years as a teacher. Before and during my time as a teacher, I wrote a considerable amount. As both an undergraduate and graduate student, I wrote papers of various kinds; in my professional life, I wrote lesson and unit plans, assessments of curricula and materials, reports to administrators, peers, and parents; and in my personal life, I wrote letters, reports, and talks for volunteer groups, et cetera. I wrote a lot but never thought of myself as a writer. Writing was something I did but not something I thought I had much part of as a craft or much control over. I followed conventions set by others and did the work technically well but never felt it was truly mine.

As a professor, writing became a part of my life in a much richer way. I was not only expected to write articles, chapters, and books, I was charged with fostering writing in others: students, colleagues, and other authors for whom I served as peer reviewer. It became part of my job to set the standard for others to pass a course or to get published in journal. Over time, I began to feel freer in my own work to take risks and write in different styles for a range of audiences. I knew the conventions and could work in them, but I also felt like I could experiment with alternative styles and thereby try to shape conventions as well. Recently, I was invited to give a workshop for university faculty on academic writing, and in preparing for that, it occurred to me that my sense of identity had changed; I not only write, I am a writer.

Central to what happened to me was a rebalancing of processes Wenger describes as "reification" and "participation." Reification is the establishment, usually by an academic or professional community, of codified standards of knowledge and practice.[27] It is, Wenger argues, absolutely essential because it provides the framework in which new work can be done and its quality judged. Members of a community are expected to conform to the standards set by the field. The framework of six concepts outlined by The Historical Thinking Project is an example of reification in the field of history education. It sets out a widely accepted (in Canada, at least) approach for teaching and learning in history classrooms and is explicitly intended as a means of judging progress in both areas.

Within most complex and changing fields, including historical scholarship, standards frequently shift. Participants in communities of practice in these fields not only adhere to them, but core and active members participate in challenging and reshaping them. This kind of participation is essential for maintaining the vitality and relevance of the field but also in more deeply engaging those involved in it. Wenger argues that the tension between reification and participation has potential to transform the identities and practices of fields and those of the people who work in them. He writes, "participation in social communities shapes our experience, and it also shapes those communities; the transformative potential goes both ways."[28]

My experience as a writer highlights the pedagogical potential of the tension between reification and practice. As a marginal participant, I conformed as nearly as possible to the standards but felt very much an outsider to the community of writers. With the help of dedicated mentors and sustained practice, I grew in knowledge of the conventions and skill at applying them. I also developed a sense of the conventions' constructed nature and felt that I could adapt and even challenge them at times. Wenger would say that through the processes that fostered this transition, I had been educated "in the deepest sense." For him, that kind of education "concerns the opening of identities – exploring new ways of being that lie beyond our current state."[29] That is exactly the kind of education necessary to move teachers from the margins of the community of history teachers towards the core. In order to reshape powerful cognitive frames and foster new identities, students require "deep transformative experiences" repeatedly, over time, and across contexts.[30]

Principle 2 – Taking the Long View of Teacher Education

We need a significant rethinking of what we mean by teacher education to include much more than the period of time people are enrolled in undergraduate teacher preparation programs. Colleagues and I have argued that teacher education should be thought of "as a three-stage process: the learning and experiences that occur prior to the professional program; the actual teacher education program itself; and, finally, ongoing in-service teaching and professional development."[31] Focus for teacher educators has been on the brief period of time pre-service teachers are in undergraduate education programs, which, as Peter Seixas and Graeme Webber point out in this volume, are generally overcrowded with requirements that have little or nothing to do with teaching and learning in particular disciplines. Some teacher educators involve themselves heavily in professional learning programs for in-service teachers (both The Historical Thinking Project and THEN/HiER are important examples), but there is often little recognition or reward for university faculty who work in this area. Teacher educators almost never account for pre-teacher preparation experiences in any serious way, but, if the work on cognition described above is right, they may be the most important shapers of teacher identity of all.

Taking the long view of teacher education is consistent with findings from research in both cognition and professional learning communities. In the case of the former, for example, Gardner argues that persistent and incorrect "scripts or stereotypes" in the humanities can only be changed by "Christopherian encounters." That is, just as

Christopher Columbus challenged the way people thought about the world, teachers have to challenge students' assumptions. As Gardner writes, "Christopherian encounters have to happen over and over again."[32] Similarly, Wenger contends that induction into a professional learning community takes time and multiple opportunities to engage in the practices of the community in various forms. Newcomers, he suggests, should be closely mentored through many well-scaffolded opportunities to engage in core professional and disciplinary practices. We often seem to take the view that one methods course or one workshop will suffice in reframing teachers' understandings of history and history teaching, but all the evidence indicates this is simply naive.

A lifespan view of teacher education should include attention to all three stages (pre-program, teacher preparation program, professional practice) of teachers' professional lives rather than concentrate on the shortest (and arguably least effective) aspect. Explicitly doing this will relieve the pressure of "covering" everything during packed teacher education programs and will mean rethinking what is done in those programs to take into account the prior knowledge students bring with them and to lay the foundation for ongoing professional learning beyond initial teacher education.

Principle 3 – Communities of Practice Provide a Substantial Context for Teacher Education

If there is any truth at all in the contentions made in this essay that significant changes in mind and practice are difficult to achieve, post-degree education for teachers (what is commonly called professional development) must be completely rethought. The usual short-term workshop sessions are not adequate to prompt or sustain substantial professional growth.

Two Canadian projects in the field of social education transformed curricula and teaching across the country: the Canadian Studies Foundation, which ran from 1970 to 1986, and the Global Education Centres established in most provinces by the Canadian International Development Agency (CIDA) in the late 1980s and early 1990s. Several studies document the effect of the CSF on changing what was, and is, taught in Canadian social studies classrooms, and some of my own work demonstrates the ubiquitous presence of global education as a theme in curricula by the mid-1990s.[33] Both these initiatives focused on two related programs of work: teacher professional education and the production of quality teaching materials. Both projects merged these two strands by developing communities of practice consisting of academics from humanities and social science disciplines and teacher education, and classroom teachers. Teachers worked collaboratively with their university-based colleagues in both the development of materials and providing in-service education to other teachers. A range of teaching materials was developed in both projects and widely disseminated and used in classrooms. John Grant argues that one of the most significant contributions the CSF made to Canadian education was the training of thousands of teachers in the area of Canadian Studies. According to Grant, the foundation involved some 1,300 teachers directly in curriculum development projects and sponsored in-service programs for 30,000 others.[34] Grant goes on to contend that many of the 1,300 teachers involved in the development teams went on to become leaders in social studies education in Canada.

Both The Historical Thinking Project and THEN/HiER have fostered and are working to sustain similar cross-boundary teams of professors, public historians, and teachers. These teams are engaged in a range of activities related to history teaching, including developing materials, providing in-service education, and working to rethink and reshape disciplinary and professional practices in history and teaching. This is the kind of approach that will help develop inward trajectories moving teachers from the margins of disciplinary practices towards the core. A key part of initial teacher education should be to induct students to similar kinds of cross-boundary teams to both facilitate their own rethinking of what it means to teach history and lay the groundwork for future collaboration. This sort of long-term approach rooted in professional learning communities holds far more promise for professional development than the occasional workshop.

Beginning Ideas for Moving Forward

The following specific ideas are initial suggestions for ways of operationalizing the above principles across the three stages of teacher education. Although by no means exhaustive, these examples might provide a platform for refinements, extensions, and new ideas.

1. We should work to map the cognitive frames of beginning history teachers and take those into account in planning for teacher education. This could begin in the selection processes for teacher education. A preliminary look at these processes in Canada and elsewhere identified a

range of approaches for vetting potential teacher candidates, from minimalist to maximalist. Minimalist approaches use a fairly standard array of documents, including university transcripts for previous degrees, a short statement outlining why the applicant wants to be a teacher, several letters of reference, and a record of previous experience working with children and young people. Maximalist approaches usually incorporate these elements but add other things such as interviews, demonstration lessons, and structured group activities. My colleagues and I argue that virtually none of the processes make a serious attempt to map the cognitive frames of applicants to uncover the structure of their ideas about teaching and learning. Even in maximalist approaches, the emphasis is on more tangible (some might say more superficial) elements such as level of comfort working with children and peers, or technical aspects of lesson delivery such as organization of material, pacing, and voice modulation. Candidates are sometimes asked about their conceptions of teachers and teaching, but this evidence seems to be treated anecdotally and has not been analysed systematically for what it might reveal about the cognitive schemata of applicants. This is curious given the fact that academics in history education around the world seem to have largely accepted key findings from the "cognitive revolution" of the twentieth century, including the compelling evidence that "prior knowledge matters."[35]

Most of the required activities from either minimalist or maximalist approaches to vetting applicants could be tweaked to help lay bare aspects of prior conceptions related to history as a discipline and the appropriate processes for teaching it. Building on the pervasive idea from research in cognition that good teaching necessarily pays attention to existing cognitive frameworks, this information could be immensely valuable in planning for the kind of "Christopherian encounters" that enhance students' experiences.

2. Historians need to be explicit about their own efforts to do history both in their writing and undergraduate teaching. In recent years I have had the good fortune to encounter a number of popular but serious books on ancient history that reflect ongoing struggles in the field to sort out issues of significance and make sense of available sources (and the often-frustrating lack of sources). Barry Strauss of Cornell University, for example, has written three popular books on Greek and Roman history dealing with the Trojan War, the battle of Salamis, and the Spartacus War.[36] All of these make explicit arguments related to debates about the significance of the events chronicled, detail how historians use a range

of sources (including studies of architecture, topography, and comparative sources from other regions) to piece together accounts, and clearly discuss the limitations imposed by the relatively scarce nature of sources from the ancient world. Peter Krentz's recent study of the Battle of Marathon provides a rich discussion on how new source evidence led him to challenge accepted scholarship on the nature of hoplite armour and therefore significantly rethink how the key opening charge of the battle might have unfolded. Readers are introduced to new evidence, as well as brought right into debates about how to reinterpret long-accepted sources.[37] Finally, Bettany Hughes' new book on the life of Socrates presents a similarly rich description of recently discovered sources and how they have contributed to a rethinking of accepted tenets about the philosopher himself and the vibrant, democratic city in which he lived and died.[38] All of these historians have taken seriously ordinary readers' ability to engage history as a contested and contingent disciplinary field. We need much more of this kind of historical writing, particularly for undergraduate students of history and history teachers.

3. Similarly, undergraduate history courses should give greater attention to the disciplinary aspects of history in addition to historical content. In other words, students should, in the words of Engle cited above, be exposed to the historical fields they study as "hotbeds of controversy" and introduced to the mechanisms historians use to engage those controversies around issues of significance, cause and consequence, historical perspective, evidence, and the like. Students should also have the opportunity to do some history themselves and grapple directly with making sense of evidence and other elements of historical thinking.

Michael Smith details his attempts to do just this in an undergraduate course titled "The History of American Environmental Thought," which he teaches at Ithaca College in rural New York State. Smith felt it important to engage his students with a nearby museum and archive in doing a focused local history project as a vehicle for providing a deeper and localized understanding of the issues covered in class but also for fostering a more nuanced disciplinary understanding of history. He uses evidence from student reflections and assignments to demonstrate that students learned significant historical information as well as significantly changed their perspectives on history as a discipline.[39]

4. Professors of history and history education should work together to create boundary projects that will help students think more deeply

about learning and teaching history. In this volume, Amy von Heyking provides an example of just such a boundary project in the form of a course she developed and co-taught with a colleague in history.

As von Heyking's example demonstrates, this kind of course should focus both on teaching the history of particular eras or events and how that history should be taught. A course on Confederation in Canada, for example, could include the consideration of questions such as: What topics or events are the most significant in understanding Confederation? What primary and secondary sources might be useful in helping students construct explanations for the readiness or reluctance of some colonies to consider a merger? How might students be engaged in considering the consequences of the British North America Act for subsequent political, economic, and social development in Canada? Consideration of questions like these would lead to a deeper understanding of the history involved, as well as helping foster a more complex sense of how that history might be taught. It would, I believe, be just as valuable for students of history who were not intending to teach as for those who were (not to mention that some of those not intending to pursue school teaching as a career might end up in graduate school and subsequently teach at the university level).

5. Cross-boundary teams should be created to engage teachers in long-term work with academic and public historians in developing materials and approaches for use in classrooms. Several examples of these kinds of projects are highlighted in this volume. Another is the "Lest We Forget Project" of Library and Archives Canada. Blake Seward, a history teacher from Smiths Falls, Ontario, developed the project for his own classes, and it grew to a national collaboration involving teachers, Library and Archives Canada, academic historians from several universities, and site-based historians at Canadian battlefield memorials in Europe. The project engages both teachers and students in an investigation, using primary sources, of local citizens who participated in World Wars I and II. It has grown to include battlefield tours for teachers designed to "push teachers out of the practice of content regurgitation and into the arena of developing historical significance and perspective."[40]

6. Finally, history educators and history teachers should be encouraged to engage in the cross-boundary work of practicing history, and historians should be encouraged to engage in work related to pedagogy. Ken Osborne and Peter Seixas, for example, are education profes-

sors who regularly engage with historians on the latters' academic turf at conferences and in journals. Conversely, Jocelyn Létourneau and Margaret Conrad are well-regarded academic historians who have engaged with educators in thinking, writing, and presenting about teaching history. Finally, Paul Bennett is an example of a history teacher who writes about both history and history education. This kind of cross-boundary work strengthens all the fields involved.

Conclusion

Wenger concludes his work on professional learning communities with a reflection on the transformational nature of education. He writes, "Education in the deepest sense and at whatever age it takes place, concerns the opening of identities – exploring new ways of being that lie beyond our current state." In other words, "education is not merely formative – it is transformative."[41] History teacher education is not solely about learning new concepts and skills, it is about becoming history teachers: teachers who not only know historical information and can describe historical processes but teachers who are practitioners and shapers of the field itself. There are no magic potions to instantaneously make this transformation – and that includes the preliminary ideas presented here. As Gardner points out, a key lesson of the cognitive revolution is that this kind of learning must involve learners "struggling with the ideas [they] resist" over time using a variety of approaches in a range of contexts.[42] Teacher education of this sort must begin long before students show up in BEd programs, continue long after initial teacher education, and engage learners in "experimenting and exploring possibilities, reinventing the self, and in the process reinventing the world."[43]

NOTES

1 See Chad Gaffield, "Towards the Coach in the History Classroom," *Canadian Issues Thèmes Canadiens* (October/November 2001): 12-14 for a similar sports analogy.

2 Shirley H. Engle, "Late Night Thoughts about the New Social Studies," *Social Education* 50, no. 1 (1986): 21.

3 Etienne Wenger, *Communities of Practice: Learning, Meaning, and Identity, Learning in Doing* (Cambridge, UK: Cambridge University Press, 1998);

Etienne Wenger, Richard A. McDermott, and William Snyder, *Cultivating Communities of Practice: A Guide to Managing Knowledge* (Boston: Harvard Business School Press, 2002).

4 Wenger, McDermott and Snyder, *Cultivating Communities of Practice*, 56.
5 Ibid., 57.
6 Wenger, *Communities*, 39.
7 Ibid., 114.
8 Ibid., 104.
9 Wenger, McDermott, and Snyder, *Cultivating Communities of Practice*, 153.
10 Ibid., 109.
11 Keith C. Barton and Linda S. Levstik, *Teaching History for the Common Good* (Mahwah, NJ: Lawrence Erlbaum Associates, 2004), 113.
12 Alan Sears, "Children's Understandings of Democratic Participation: Lessons for Civic Education," in *Civic Education and Youth Political Participation*, edited by Murray Print and Henry Milner (Rotterdam/Boston/Taipei: Sense, 2009), 145; see also Alan Sears, "Making Room for Revolution in Social Studies Classrooms," *Education Canada* 49, no. 2 (2009): 5-8 and Alan Sears, "Historical Thinking and Citizenship Education: It Is Time to End the War," in *New Possibilities for the Past: Shaping History Education in Canada*, edited by Penney Clark (Vancouver: UBC Press, 2011).
13 Howard Gardner, *The Development and Education of the Mind: The Selected Works of Howard Gardner*, World Library of Educationalists Series (London and New York: Routledge, 2006), 76.
14 Howard Gardner. *Changing Minds: The Art and Science of Changing Our Own and Other People's Minds* (Boston: Harvard Business School Press, 2006), 54.
15 Gardner, *Changing Minds*, 1.
16 Keith Barton, "A Sociocultural Perspective on Children's Understanding of Historical Change: Comparative Findings from Northern Ireland and the United States," *American Educational Research Journal* 38, no. 4 (2001): 881-914; Keith Barton, "'You'd Be Wanting to Know about the Past': Social Contexts of Children's Historical Understanding in Northern Ireland and the USA," *Comparative Education* 37, no. 1 (2001): 89-106; Jocelyn Létourneau and Sabrina Moisan, "Young People's Assimilation of a Collective Historical Memory: A Case Study of Quebeckers of French-Canadian Heritage," in *Theorizing Historical Consciousness*, edited by Peter Seixas (Toronto: University of Toronto Press, 2004); Jocelyn Létourneau, "Remembering Our Past: An Examination of the Historical Memory of Young Québécois," in *To the Past: History Education, Public Memory, and Citizenship in Canada*, edited by Ruth Sandwell (Toronto: University of Toronto Press, 2006),

71-87; Carla Peck, "'It's Not Like [I'm] Chinese and Canadian. I Am in Between': Ethnicity and Students' Conceptions of Historical Significance," *Theory and Research in Social Education* 38, no. 4 (2010): 575-617.

17 Barton and Levstik, *Teaching History*, 170.

18 Gardner, *Changing Minds*, 17.

19 Wenger, *Communities*, 149.

20 Gardner, *Changing Minds*, 138.

21 Ibid., 138. Emphasis in the original.

22 Samuel S. Wineburg, *Historical Thinking and Other Unnatural Acts: Charting the Future of Teaching the Past* (Philadelphia: Temple University Press, 2001).

23 Gardner, *Changing Minds*, 139.

24 Wenger, *Communities*, 4, 73.

25 See Lev S. Vygotsky, *Thought and Language* (Cambridge, MA: M.I.T. Press, 1962); Lev S. Vygotsky, *Mind in Society* (Cambridge, MA: Harvard University Press, 1978).

26 Ruth W. Sandwell, "History Is a Verb: Teaching Historical Practice to Teacher Education Students" in *New Possibilities for the Past: Shaping History Education in Canada*, edited by Penney Clark (Vancouver: UBC Press, 2011), 224-42.

27 For a discussion of how history as a community of practice operates to set such standards, see Peter Seixas, "The Community of Inquiry as a Basis for Knowledge and Learning: The Case of History," *American Educational Research Journal* 30, no. 2 (1993): 305-24.

28 Wenger, *Communities*, 57.

29 Ibid., 263.

30 Ibid., 268.

31 Mark Hirschkorn, Alan Sears, and Elizabeth Sloat, "The Missing Third: Accounting for Prior Learning in Teacher Education Program Admissions," in *ATEE Annual Conference 2011: Teachers' Life-cycle from Initial Teacher Education to Experienced Professional* (Riga, Latvia, 2011).

32 Gardner, *Development and Education of the Mind*, 140.

33 George S. Tomkins, "The Social Studies in Canada," in *A Canadian Social Studies*, edited by Jim Parsons, Geoff Milburn, and Max van Manen (Edmonton: Publication Services, Faculty of Education, University of Alberta, 1983); Ken Osborne, "'To the Schools We Must Look for Good Canadians': Developments in the Teaching of History in Schools since 1960," *Journal of Canadian Studies* 22, no. 3 (1987); Alan Sears and Andrew S. Hughes, "Citizenship Education and Current Educational Reform," *Canadian Journal of Education* 21, no. 2 (1996): 123-42.

34 J. Grant, "The Canada Studies Foundation: An Historical Overview," in *The Canada Studies Foundation*, edited by J. Grant et al. (Toronto: Canada Studies Foundation, 1986).

35 For an extended discussion of this, see Hirschkorn, Sears, and Sloat, "The Missing Third."

36 Barry S. Strauss, *The Trojan War: A New History* (New York: Simon & Schuster, 2006); Barry S. Strauss, *The Battle of Salamis: The Naval Encounter That Saved Greece – and Western Civilization* (New York: Simon & Schuster, 2004); Barry S. Strauss, *The Spartacus War* (New York: Simon & Schuster, 2009).

37 Peter Krentz, "The Battle of Marathon," in *The Yale Library of Military History*, edited by Donald Kagan and Dennis Showalter (New Haven: Yale University Press, 2010).

38 Bettany Hughes, *The Hemlock Cup: Socrates, Athens and the Search for the Good Life* (London: Jonathan Cape, 2010).

39 Michael B. Smith, "Local Environmental History and the Journey to Ecological Citizenship," in *Citizenship across the Curriculum*, edited by Michael B. Smith, Rebecca S. Nowacek, and Jeffrey L. Bernstein (Bloomington, IN: Indiana University Press, 2010), 165-84.

40 Blake Seward, personal communication.

41 Wenger, *Communities*, 263.

42 Gardner, *Changing Minds*, 126.

43 Wenger, *Communities*, 273.

3 "The Teacher Is the Keystone of the Educational Arch":[1] A Century and a Half of Lifelong Teacher Education in Canada

PENNEY CLARK

This chapter provides historical context as a means to situate other chapters in the collection, most of which examine specific programs and initiatives in particular provinces from a contemporary perspective. Due to the provincial autonomy over education granted in the British North America Act of 1867, approaches to teacher education vary province by province, although there are also commonalities. This chapter will explore pre-service and in-service teacher education, using examples from all provinces, but particular emphasis will be placed on Ontario and British Columbia.

Pre-Service Teacher Education

As provinces established their government infrastructures, including educational bureaucracies, teacher preparation moved from ad hoc approaches to formalized programs with standards and performance expectations. Ontario and provinces in the Atlantic region (with the exception of Newfoundland) established normal schools for the education of future teachers in the second half of the nineteenth century. Normal schools in the western provinces and Newfoundland were established later. Post–World War II, provinces began to move teacher preparation programs into the universities, concurrently increasing entrance standards and time required to achieve certification.

In 1979, educational historian Robert Patterson identified some of the perennial questions that have guided deliberations around pre-service teacher education:

> What is the place and relationship of theory and practice in teacher education? Should preparation deal more with improving the academic

qualifications and general education of the prospective teacher or focus upon pedagogical techniques or gimmicks for use in the classroom? Is there a type of preparation which will heighten both the immediate and the long-range effectiveness of the teacher? Are there general principles which can be identified and employed in teaching or does the teaching of each subject represent such a unique experience that a form of preparation emphasizing the specific is more valuable? Is teaching more of an art than a science?[2]

This chapter does not attempt to tackle these questions head-on, but acknowledges that they lie behind the approaches to pre-service teacher education discussed here and in other chapters in this collection.

Normal Schools and Model Schools

The establishment of normal schools was the first attempt to formalize teacher preparation. As Paul Axelrod has pointed out, "The normal school signaled an interest by educators internationally in bringing state control, regulation, and uniformity to teacher training."[3] "Normal" originates in the French "normale" and refers to the values and norms of society. At its heart the term implies that students were expected to pass on these values and norms to their own students.

Admission requirements were very low in early normal schools. A minimum age of sixteen; basic reading, writing, and arithmetic skills; a certificate from a clergyman attesting to one's moral character; and a written declaration of an intention to continue in the teaching profession were often all that was expected. However, one or two years of high school education quickly became mandatory.

Before the turn of the twentieth century, most teachers did not attend normal schools. In 1850, only 291 of 3,476 certificated teachers in Ontario were normal school graduates.[4] In 1877, fifty county model schools were established in Ontario in order to meet a growing need for teachers and to increase opportunities for prospective teachers in rural areas. Until these schools were closed in 1900, most of the teachers in Ontario were trained in them. The model schools were less costly for the province to run than the normal schools, because they used existing public schools. A student teacher, after a period of observation and practice teaching (originally eight and then fifteen weeks), primarily under the supervision of the school principal or local school inspector, earned a third class certificate, rather than the first or second class certificate which could be earned at the normal schools. These certificates were

Table 3.1 Establishment of Normal Schools in Canadian Provinces

Province*	City	Year
Canada East**	Montreal	1836
Canada West	Toronto	1847
New Brunswick***	Saint John	1848
Nova Scotia	Truro	1855
Prince Edward Island	Charlottetown	1856
Canada East	Montreal	1857
New Brunswick***	Fredericton	1870
Ontario	Ottawa	1875
Manitoba	Winnipeg	1882
Saskatchewan	Regina	1893
Ontario	London	1900
British Columbia	Vancouver	1901
Alberta	Calgary	1906
Ontario	Hamilton	1909
Ontario	Peterborough	1909
Ontario	North Bay	1909
Ontario	Stratford	1909
Saskatchewan	Saskatoon	1912
Alberta	Camrose	1912
Manitoba	Brandon	1914
British Columbia	Victoria	1915
Alberta	Edmonton	1921
Newfoundland****	St. John's	1923
Saskatchewan	Moose Jaw	1927

* Some schools of particularly short duration have not been listed.
** The Montreal school lasted only six years.
*** A school opened in Fredericton in 1848, but closed in 1850. The Saint John school closed in 1870, the same year a new school opened in Fredericton.
**** Newfoundland's normal schools were established much later than those in the rest of the Atlantic region because it was not yet a province, and did not have the same administrative structures in place. It was also more remote and more sparsely populated.

valid for three years in the county in which they were issued, and were renewable only on the recommendation of the county inspector. Not everyone was in favour of model schools. According to J.C. Althouse, Chief Director of Education, Ontario, "The effect ... upon the status of the profession was devastating ... the Model Schools accelerated, rather than checked, certain tendencies which were threatening to lower the standing of teachers in the Province."[5] When the county model schools were closed, provincial model schools were established in some remote northern areas of the province. This "travesty of teacher education"[6] was in place until 1924.

In 1906, Ontario transferred responsibility for preparation of high school teachers to new faculties of education at the University of Toronto and Queen's University. The province maintained control over teacher preparation by reserving the right to approve the courses of study. Applicants had to be British subjects, possess a university degree in arts or agriculture, as well as a Certificate of Entrance to the Faculty of Education, and agree to teach in Ontario schools for one year.[7] Elementary teacher preparation remained the preserve of the normal schools.

Ontario's normal schools – like its school system and selection of authorized textbooks – became the model for those in other provinces. This was largely because it was men who were trained in Ontario who later established schools elsewhere. For example, David Goggin, the first principal of the normal schools in Winnipeg and Regina, was educated in Ontario, as was S.P. Robins, the principal of the McGill Normal School in Montreal.

Between the establishment of its school system in 1872 and the opening of its first normal school in 1901, British Columbia certified teachers through examining their knowledge of history, geography, English literature, arithmetic, algebra, bookkeeping, and English composition. In the 1874 exam, history knowledge concerned "English, Scottish, and Irish constitutional and economic history, Catholic Emancipation, the Reform Bills, Britain's 14th century loss of possessions in France excepting the Channel ports, the Edict of Nantes, the American War of Independence and the War of 1812, early North American colonization, and the union of Upper and lower Canada."[8] As historian John Calam concludes, "Clearly, an assumed central responsibility of the qualified British Columbia teacher was to keep alive a very broad western tradition reaching back to the ancients. The Board took no chances on popularized localisms."[9] He also notes differences in questions posed to male and female candidates. In 1874, the men were asked to write on how the California and Australia gold rushes influenced civilization, and the women were asked to discuss the positive results that might emerge from agitation for women's rights. Calam comments, perhaps facetiously, that the latter may have been deemed too controversial a question, because in 1876, women were asked to write about manners

Figure 3.1: Normal School, London, Ontario ca. 1920. Albertype Company
fonds/Library and Archives Canada PA-03180. Copyright expired.

instead.[10] Candidates were awarded first class (valid until revoked by
the Board of Education), second class (three-year), or third class (one-
year) certificates based on performance on the examinations.[11]

The emphasis on Canadian history increased as time went on. The
questions on the 1913 history exam at New Brunswick's provincial normal school were evenly divided between British and Canadian history:

1. Explain the connection of the following with English History: Cranmer,
Monmouth, Phillip II [sic] of Spain, Napoleon Bonaparte, Gaveston, Lady
Jane Gray [sic], Huskisson, Wat Tyler, Disraeli, St. Augustine. 2. Relate the
circumstances which led to the (1) taking of Calais by the English, and (2)
its loss. 3. Write a paragraph on the efforts of James II and his descendants
to regain the throne of England. 4. Write notes on the following: The
Massacre of Lachine, Founding of Halifax, Quebec Act, Sir Wm. Phipps,
Exile of the Acadians. 5. Enumerate the causes in Upper Canada and
Lower Canada which led to the Rebellion of 1837. 6. Describe "The Times
of Frontenac." [12]

Normal school hours of instruction were typically long. For example, in British Columbia's 1928–9 school year the program was organized around seven periods, each 45 minutes in length, per day. History and civics education (combined) were allotted 50–60 periods over the year. To put this into perspective, 100–120 periods were devoted to grammar, writing, reading, composition, and spelling, and 60–70 periods to music and voice-training. Subject matter content was emphasized in early normal schools because students were viewed as being woefully inadequate in the knowledge they needed to impart to their own future students. Reference books for history and civics were a mix of public and high school textbooks, for transmitting content, and teacher preparation texts about pedagogy.[13] Lecture was the main mode of instruction.

The history course content for a second class certificate in Saskatchewan in 1928 consisted of "the educational value of history; the nature of primary history; methods suitable to the material and the age of the child; the sequence of the courses; the organization of a unit of history for teaching; methods of teaching; use of the text book; the use of the assignment; means of vitalizing the teaching of history; practical work in the classroom."[14]

Acquiring teaching experience was a central aspect of the normal school program. Many normal schools had model classrooms attached, with actual students and teachers, where the normal school students could both observe and do a little teaching of their own. Students also taught in local schools. E.W. Coffin, principal of the Calgary Normal School, remarked that "practice teaching is, of course, the *sine qua non* of the course whatever else has to be omitted or condensed."[15] A perennial criticism of the practicum, and the normal school experience more broadly, was that they did not prepare students to teach in rural schools. This was ironic, since most normal school graduates began their teaching careers in rural schools, where they had to face the enormous challenge of planning for and teaching multiple grades at once. As one school inspector put it: "the work of the inexperienced teacher in a rural school would be made much more efficient if the teachers in training at the normal schools could obtain more practical knowledge of conditions similar to those which they must actually face in their first schools."[16]

Move to the Universities

Following World War II, secondary school teachers were typically required to have a bachelor's degree and a one-year post-baccalaureate program leading to certification. Elementary teachers were normally expected to have only a high school graduation certificate and to have completed a one-year normal school program. Saskatchewan, Manitoba, Ontario, New Brunswick, and Nova Scotia chose to call their normal schools "teachers' colleges," although this change was not accompanied by an alteration in fundamental pedagogical approach. Alberta, in 1942, was the first to transfer its elementary teacher training programs to the university. Newfoundland was next, in 1949 – the same year it joined the nation as a province. The University of Saskatchewan began a four-year degree program, which was recognized by the Department of Education in 1952 for the training of both elementary and secondary teachers. The province left the teachers' colleges as an alternative route for elementary teachers until 1964. British Columbia closed its normal schools in 1956, placing all teacher education under the aegis of the University of British Columbia and its affiliate, Victoria College, which became the University of Victoria in 1963. Manitoba moved elementary teacher education to the University of Manitoba in 1965 (its Faculty of Education was established in 1935).[17] McGill University established its education faculty in 1965, the University of Prince Edward Island in 1969, and the University of New Brunswick in 1973. In Nova Scotia, Acadia University has had a School of Education since 1949, and Dalhousie University began a four-year undergraduate program in 1968. At present, Nova Scotia has four institutions which grant bachelors of education: Mount Saint Vincent University in Halifax, St Francis Xavier University in Antigonish, Acadia University in Wolfville, and Cape Breton University.

Ontario began to move its elementary programs into the universities in 1968. These programs were initially two years and then four. The Faculty of Education at the University of Toronto, which had been renamed the Ontario College of Education in 1920, was again renamed the Faculty of Education at the University of Toronto (FEUT) in 1972. It merged with the Ontario Institute for Studies in Education (OISE), which had been mostly a graduate and research institute, in 1996.[18] A number of new universities were established in Ontario during the 1960s in order to meet the needs of the baby boom generation. They generally established their faculties of education over the following decade. Brock University in St Catharines opened its College of Education in 1971; York University in Toronto and Trent University in Peterborough (in partnership with Queen's University) established their faculties in 1972 and 1973 respectively.[19] North Bay Teachers' College – which, unlike Brock, York, and Trent, was established in 1953 from normal school (established 1909) roots – became the Faculty of Education at Nipissing University College in 1967.[20]

The three territories offer teacher education programs for Aboriginal students, all with an elementary focus: Nunavut Arctic College and Yukon College, in conjunction with the University of Regina, and Aurora College in the Northwest Territories, in conjunction with the University of Saskatchewan. These programs incorporate Aboriginal cultural perspectives and allow Aboriginal students to be educated in their own communities.[21]

At present, most faculties of education offer one- or two-year after-degree (often referred to as consecutive) teacher education programs. The University of Alberta, the University of Saskatchewan, OISE/UT, and McGill are among those that offer four-year concurrent degrees, although Alberta and OISE also offer after-degree programs. Grade point average requirements for entrance range from 65 per cent to high 70s, although this varies in practice according to the number of applicants. Most institutions stipulate that applicants have some experience working with children. Interviews and letters of reference are usually required only in smaller programs. Some institutions require a writing sample. Disciplinary preparation requirements show considerable variation. Academic background for history or social studies majors can include courses in Canadian studies, business studies, economics, geography, philosophy, political science, sociology, religious studies, Native studies, cultural studies, African Canadian studies, and Mi'kmaq studies. It is not surprising that many history teachers have little academic background specific to the discipline.

As in the normal school programs, the universities have made the practicum a central part of teacher education. It has gradually increased in length, with a 13–16 week extended practicum typical at this time, often accompanied by other school-based experiences, such as regular weekly observations, followed by debriefing sessions at the university.

With the move from normal school to university, the institutional mandate became less clear. As Marvin Wideen points out: "As free-standing institutions [normal schools] enjoyed a clear mandate for the preparation of teachers for the schools. The move to universities, however, meant that this central mission became only one concern of those who educated teachers. Not only do faculties of education find themselves in competition for resources with other departments in the university setting, but many of their faculty have developed interests that have little bearing on the preparation of teachers."[22] Nancy Sheehan and J. Donald Wilson have presented an alternative view, contending that the transfer of all teacher education to the universities helped both teacher education and professional development. They see three benefits: 1. Because almost all teachers now have degrees, they have both a broad liberal education and a grounding in the professional aspects of education. 2. Research, which is integral to the university setting, is having an influence on teacher education programs, policy decisions at the ministry level, and the development of curricular and resource materials. 3. Graduate studies have helped develop a range of specialists, from administrators to counsellors to curriculum developers. The theoretical knowledge base, professional understanding, and skill levels attained have enhanced the professional status of teachers in the eyes of parents and the public generally.[23]

History Teacher Education

This section relies on teacher education program methodology textbooks to trace the approaches used in history and social studies teacher education courses. Pre-service textbooks reflect prevailing educational philosophies and provincial school curriculum emphases. Their content reveals views on history education among university teacher educators and curriculum developers, although not necessarily teachers in the field, parents, or the public at large. It is also worth noting that history and social studies methodology textbooks have been primarily aimed at elementary teaching and, as has been the case with school textbooks, there has been a strong preference for books of Canadian authorship.

Since the prime mandate of early normal schools was to fill the knowledge gaps present in a student teacher population with little schooling, history classes were predominantly concerned with imparting historical information. To that end, public and high school student textbooks were used. For example, W. Stewart Wallace's *A New History of Great Britain and Canada* was used in British Columbia normal schools, along with methodology textbooks.[24]

History does not seem to have had an important place in early normal school methodology textbooks. For example, *Notes on Education* (1888) by J.B. Calkin, principal of the normal school at Truro, Nova Scotia, includes sections on the teaching of reading, spelling, composition (called "language" in the text), grammar, geography, and arithmetic, but nothing on history.[25] By 1913, *Public School Methods*, by Toronto

Chief Inspector of Schools James L Hughes and coauthors, provided six reasons why students should study history: imparting of information, training of reasoning powers, and developing patriotism, reading skills, a love of historic literature, and character. Like school textbooks, normal school texts treated history as a source of stories about heroic adventures, which could be used as a means to inculcate values. As Hughes et al. put it, "Through the study of history the pupil lives in imagination with the good and great of the past. He learns by what qualities they succeeded, how they extolled virtue and condemned vice, and that because of their heroic struggles for truth and liberty we enjoy the privileges under which we live. Consciously or unconsciously, he is influenced by the lives of these men, and thereby his character is strengthened."[26] In fact, the text went so far as to state, "The success of the teacher depends upon her ability to tell stories."[27] However, the reader was cautioned to avoid "side issues ... One of the most important requisites is that a teacher shall know when to say no more."[28]

In the 1920s and 1930s, some normal school methodology textbooks reflected the New Education movement, with its child-centred views. For example, *The Child-Centered School: An Appraisal of the New Education*, by American educators Harold Rugg and Ann Shumaker, was used in Canada. It discussed creative self-expression, personality, and social adjustment, and units of work or centres of interest versus school subjects. It also focused on music, art, dance, theatre, and creative writing, while more traditional academic subjects such as history were not mentioned.[29] The two photographs on page 41, and the delightful caption, capture the authors' message at its core.

In the same period, the 1928–9 British Columbia Normal School curriculum lists seven textbooks on the teaching of history. There was still a concern about history content mastery. One book, *Canadian History: A Syllabus and Guide to Reading*, was a detailed content guide for course planning.[30]

The most widely used textbook in the 1940s was *The Enterprise in Theory and Practice* by Donalda Dickie,[31] who taught at all three of Alberta's normal schools and has been called "one of Canada's most influential educational leaders during the first half of the twentieth century."[32] Dickie's 1940 textbook, which sold 3,530 copies,[33] captured the progressive education spirit and was used in many provinces to help future teachers better understand how to implement progressive ideas in the new elementary curricula. "Enterprise" was defined as "the co-operative achievement of a social purpose that a teacher presents to her class with a view to having them use it as an experience in intelligent social behavior."[34] Ideally, the students themselves suggested a practical problem with a social component. The point was to have them work out a plan for investigating the problem, carry out that plan, share their findings, and then evaluate the effectiveness of the process used. This text devotes almost no attention to the teaching of history, which is somewhat surprising, given that Dickie possessed a PhD in the discipline and was a prolific history school textbook author. The message in *Enterprise* is that history is important only to the extent that it is useful to achieve the purpose of a particular enterprise. She provides the example of an enterprise involving a class plan to take a trip to Aklavik by air, mentioning that "the enterprise presents a practical purpose which integrates groups of facts from each of several subjects."[35] "Historical information may include the story of aviation; the discovery, exploration, and settlement of Northern Canada, an account of the Eskimos."[36]

In spite of an emphasis on progressive approaches in many teacher education programs, most research on the progressive education era has concluded that progressive, child-centred approaches were not widely implemented in schools.[37] Amy von Heyking has recently provided compelling evidence to the contrary in Alberta, although she concedes that the response was varied.[38]

Textbooks used in the late 1960s and 1970s were heavily influenced by the work of psychologist Jerome Bruner and his "structure of the disciplines" approach.[39] *Teaching the Subjects in the Social Studies*, by Evelyn Moore of the University of Calgary and Edward E. Owen of the University of Victoria, turned away from the integrated, activity-oriented, child-centred approach found in Dickie's text, with its emphasis on democratic decision making around student-initiated projects.[40] The Moore/Owen book carefully elucidated the principles behind the disciplines-based approach, and urged teachers to compile collections of significant historical documents and artefacts for students to use as a basis to form hypotheses to explain historical events, followed by systematic investigations and the writing of historical accounts.

While new graduates from teacher education programs in this period no doubt employed some primary sources in their teaching, the empirical evidence points to the predominance of other approaches to the teaching of history. A.B. Hodgetts and his team spent two years interviewing teachers and observing activity in 847 classrooms across the country. In the 1968 report of the findings of his National History Project, *What Culture? What Heritage? A Study of Civic Education in*

Above: Freedom! Pupil initiative! Activity! A life of happy intimacy – this is the drawing-out environment of the new school.
Below: Eyes front! Arms folded! Sit still! Pay attention! Question-and-answer situations – this was the listening regime.

Figure 3.2: Frontispiece from *The Child-Centered School: An Appraisal of the New Education* by Harold Rugg and Ann Shumaker.

Figure 3.3: Ottawa Normal School students reading *Our Canada* in the library, 1950. Digital Image Number: I0021762.JPG. Ref. Code: RG 2–251. Courtesy of Archives of Ontario.

Canada, he concluded that high school students were "bench bound listeners" rather than the active investigators promoted in teacher education programs.[41]

A parallel influence in the 1970s stemmed from the work of the American progressive educator, curriculum theorist, and textbook series developer Hilda Taba. Taba's *A Teacher's Handbook to Elementary Social Studies* found its way into teacher education programs in Canada.[42] Taba's work was empirically based, documenting the processes children use to develop concepts. She identified the key factors influencing education as the explosion of knowledge, the obsolescence of knowledge, the variety of knowledge, the range of student abilities and sophistication that exists within any classroom, and both cognitive and affective development.[43] This book and the teaching strategies in it, such as those associated with concept development and concept attainment, are still frequently referenced in history teacher education courses.

The most widely used methodology textbooks over the past thirty years have been written by western Canadian academics, and have had a social studies, rather than history, orientation, in keeping with the emphasis in provincial curricula. The book with the greatest longevity has been *Elementary Social Studies: A Practical Approach to Teaching and Learning* (2010) by Ian Wright, a retired social studies educator from the University of British Columbia.[44] This textbook, which was first published in 1980, is now in its seventh edition (with David Hutchison, Professor of Education at Brock University, as coauthor). It takes an inquiry approach to social studies education, presenting the reader with problems and activities. There is little attention to history education. Another textbook in use at the present time is *Teaching Social Studies in Elementary Schools: A Social Constructivist Approach* (2009) by Susan E. Gibson of the University of Alberta. This text treats history as only one of the social sciences present in the content of social studies, although acknowledges that it is "the most influential."[45]

In the last decade, a number of methodology textbooks that include, or indeed focus on, history teaching and learning have been published. *The Anthology of Social Studies: Issues and Strategies for Secondary Teachers* (2008) and *The Anthology of Social Studies: Issues and Strategies for Elementary Teachers* (updated edition, 2013), both edited by Roland Case of the Critical Thinking Consortium and Penney Clark from the University of British Columbia,[46] advocate a critical disciplinary approach to the teaching of history, which promotes active engagement with history through use of second-order (distinct from substantive) historical thinking concepts: significance, evidence, continuity and change, cause and consequence, historical perspective-taking, and ethical dimensions.[47] Another book currently in use, and which supports the two anthologies in its approach to the teaching of history, is *Teaching about Historical Thinking* by Roland Case and retired secondary school social studies teacher Mike Denos.[48] The most recent text is *The Big Six: Historical Thinking Concepts*, coauthored by Peter Seixas of the Centre for the Study of Historical Consciousness at the University of British Columbia and retired social studies teacher Tom Morton.[49]

The historical thinking framework advocated in the above books is beginning to be evident in new provincial curricula and authorized school textbooks, as well as in teacher education programs and the methodology textbooks used in them. What remains to be seen is the extent to which these ideas will be taken up by new teachers once they enter their own classrooms.

Pre-service teacher education has not reached a place where it can provide definitive answers to Robert Patterson's questions listed at the beginning of this chapter. Perhaps what is more important is that we continue to consider them as circumstances and contexts change.

In-Service Teacher Education

Historian Charles Phillips remarked that "the licensing of teachers with very low qualifications had one good effect: it established the custom of inservice improvement."[50] The 1925 British Columbia provincial inquiry, *Survey of the School System*, described the teaching profession in these dismal terms:

> Too many unmarried male teachers; the immaturity of the teachers, especially in rural schools; lack of vision and professional pride; deficient academic and professional qualifications, unwillingness to take additional professional training beyond the legal minimum; lack of experience; inability adequately to profit from experience; tendency to change schools too frequently.[51]

Clearly, this indicated a need for in-service education. In 1950, M.E. Lazerte, former dean of the Faculty of Education, University of Alberta, reported on a cross-Canada survey on teacher education. On the topic of in-service education he commented:

In-service training ... is provided in all provinces by the Departments of Education. Professional libraries are circulated, supplements to the courses of study are distributed, reference materials in social studies and other subjects are compiled and mailed to all teachers – these and other means of helping the teachers are used. Thirteen principals of training schools reported the following activities of their staffs: all staffs instruct in summer sessions; many assist teachers with institutes and conventions; a few publish articles in the teachers' journals; two give evening courses of lectures; and several visit and assist rural teachers during the spring months following the close of the training session.

Supplementing the work of the training schools, inspectors and superintendents of schools meet with the teachers in institutes and conventions at regular intervals throughout the year.[52]

I will discuss four approaches to in-service teacher education or ongoing professional development: teacher institutes and conferences, summer school courses offered at universities, professional journals, and teacher supervision. There are, of course, many other opportunities, both formal and informal, for teachers to engage in professional development activities. These include collaborative planning with other teachers; in-service opportunities offered through local school districts, provincial and federal government departments, private organizations, and foundations; and personal reading selections.

Teacher Institutes and Conferences

Historian John Calam described teacher institutes in British Columbia as "an early sort of in-service training which helped ensure 'uniformity of method' and stimulate discussion on such subjects as 'timetabling, curriculum, and methods of teaching' ... they were department-sponsored until the end of the First World War when the teachers petitioned the Department to establish their own organization, the British Columbia Teachers' Federation."[53]

In moving from department of education sponsorship to teachers' professional association control, British Columbia was repeating events in Ontario. Ontario's first chief superintendent of education, Egerton Ryerson, took up the idea of institutes enthusiastically, organizing twenty institutes around the province in 1850. The program consisted of lectures delivered by normal school staff members, group activities followed by discussion, and model lessons. The institutes were not well received by teachers, some were not particularly well attended, and Ryerson was noticeably less enthusiastic about them in following years. J.G. Althouse, who was to become chief superintendent of education for Ontario, contended their lack of success was due to the autocratic way the department organized the institutes, as the department did not allow for any input on the part of the teachers whom it wished to attract.[54]

As Patrice Milewski points out, "pedagogic reform, consolidation of centralized state control and revisions to the regulations ... created the statutory framework that made teachers' institutes a regular feature of the school year until 1939."[55] Attendance became compulsory in 1884, and the range of topics expanded considerably. In 1913, over two hundred topics were offered, ranging from hygiene in the schoolroom and the training of memory, to sessions about the testing of pupil "mentality." Previously, four or five topics in a day were a typical offering. Milewski concludes by saying: "In one of its aspects, the professionalization of teaching was attended by a proliferation of knowledge about teaching, learning and children. This was no more apparent than in the teachers' institute programs of the twentieth century."[56]

This approach to professional development, in the sense of full-day sessions often extending over several days to a week, continues to the present. However, they are offered by a variety of organizations and are no longer the sole responsibility of a department of education. For example, week-long summer institutes, organized around a theme and offered in various provinces, were a feature of the approach practised by Historica, a national organization formed in 2000 for the purpose of promoting Canadian history education.[57] More recently, The Historical Thinking Project (called Benchmarks of Historical Thinking until 2011), situated in the Centre for the Study of Historical Consciousness at the University of British Columbia, has taken the same approach, offering institutes in different Canadian cities each summer since 2010. These are a blend of theory and practice, culminating in collaborative development of teaching materials, which emphasize application of second-order historical thinking concepts. Historica and The Historical Thinking Project have had a pan-Canadian emphasis, but other institutes have been sponsored by departments of education and universities. For example, in the summer of 2011, the University of Winnipeg's Department of History, in collaboration with the Manitoba Department of Education, offered "Oral History, Story Telling, and Literacy." The Nova Scotia Department of Education offered a one-day institute called "Being a History Detective

– Learning with Objects and Artifacts." The University of Manitoba offered "Social Justice: Teaching the Ukrainian Famine – Genocide and Ukrainian Canadian Internment."

Annual conferences sponsored by provincial specialist teachers' associations are another form of professional development, and the one in which most teachers typically engage. All provinces, with the exception of New Brunswick and Newfoundland, have history, social science, or social studies teachers' associations (depending on the provincial curriculum orientation). Departments of education typically provide a non-instructional day when all teachers are expected to attend a provincial teachers' conference. Subject-area conferences are devoted to a broad range of topics, which could be categorized as ideological, policy-related, and practical. There is often a strong emphasis on history topics, even in cases where the provincial curriculum is based on social studies or social sciences. The 2011 conference of the Saskatchewan Council of Social Sciences gives a sense of this. The conference theme was human rights, but there was a distinct historical emphasis, with conference sessions including presentations by Veterans Affairs Canada, the Great Unsolved Mysteries in Canadian History project, the Hong Kong Veterans' Association, and the Benchmarks of Historical Thinking project.

Peter Seixas is in demand as a keynote speaker, presenting on The Historical Thinking Project at both the British Columbia Social Studies Teachers' Association Conference and a joint conference of the Ontario History and Social Science Teachers' Association and the Association for Canadian Studies in the fall of 2012. Again, the extent to which teachers are employing historical thinking concepts in their own classroom practice is not yet known.

Summer Schools

An instructor at the Ottawa Normal School observed in 1916 that preservice teacher training was insufficient for a lifetime of teaching. He suggested that new teachers be required to participate in a summer school for six weeks a year for the first few years of their careers, presumably at the expense of the department of education.[58] Unfortunately, this suggestion has never been incorporated as a requirement of ongoing teacher certification.

The first summer school was offered at the University of Toronto in 1905, and by 1939 every province except Prince Edward Island provided them. Courses tended to reflect prevailing educational philosophies and the curriculum being implemented at a particular time. For example, in 1913, during the era of the New Education movement, disciplinary subjects took a backseat at the University of Alberta to an array of courses with vocational content. Courses included agriculture, school gardening, nature study, manual training, woodworking, methods in art, design, drawing and painting, household art, household science, and physical training. This trend continued for some time, as can be seen from the 1922 Victoria example on page 49.

Summer school courses have been particularly popular when new curriculum is introduced. For example, in the summer of 1936, just as the new elementary "Enterprise" curriculum was being introduced, Alberta teachers flocked to summer school sessions offered jointly by the provincial department of education and the University of Alberta.[59] The 1937 summer school calendar for the British Columbia department of education stated the purposes and described the activities very well: "Each summer an increasing number of teachers are turning to Universities and Summer Schools of Education for intellectual and cultural stimulation and for professional preparation in new fields. These teachers listen to lectures, participate in class discussions, and read professional and general literature more intensively than is possible for them when they are absorbed in their regular work. Broadened by their summer experiences, they return to their class-rooms better able to discharge the great responsibility which is theirs."[60]

Summer schools, offered first by provincial departments of education and later by faculties of education, have been a popular choice for professional development, for upgrading of teacher certificates, for earning diplomas in specialty areas, and for accumulating credit towards university undergraduate and graduate degrees.

Professional Journals

A Prince Edward Island school inspector remarked in 1899 that "a good educational periodical is as necessary to the teacher as the market reports are to the merchant or trader."[61] Some early Ontario journals of note were *Canada Educational Monthly* (1879–1908), *The Canada School Journal* (1877–87), and *The Educational Journal* (1887–97). *The School*, published from 1912 to 1947 by the Ontario College of Education, was the most widely accessible and was read in every province.[62] Separate elementary and secondary editions were produced from 1935 onwards. Articles ranged from discussion of broad policy issues, such as

Figure 3.4: Manual arts project – "Holland." Primary grade Coarse [*sic*], Summer School, Victoria, BC. This project was displayed in the closing exhibition of student teachers' work, 10 August 1922. British Columbia Department of Education, *Annual Report of the Public Schools, 1922* (Victoria: Author, 1922), np.

the movement to larger administrative units, to the problems of rural schools and classroom issues, such as classroom management or provision of teaching plans in every school subject. There were many articles on the teaching of history. For example, the secondary edition for the 1937–8 school year included these articles: "The Norse Discovery of America," "Supplementing the Text-Book in British History," "British Immigration to Canada in the Eighteenth Century," "The Pnyx, The Seat of Athenian Democracy," "The Application of the Unit Assignment Method to History," "Writing the Canadian History Examination," "Isle St Jean and the Seven Years' War," and "Visual Aids in the Teaching of History." The elementary edition included: "Making History Meaningful," "A Meaningful Study of the North American Indian," "Indian Life, an Enterprise for Grades I and II," and "The Norse Discovery of America." Contributors to the more practical, classroom-based articles were mainly classroom teachers, who described their own plans and recounted their experiences in teaching the topics. Many prominent educationists such as Donalda Dickie also contributed.[63] Contributors in this particular year (1937–8) included Maxwell A. Cameron, later head of the department of education at the University of British Columbia and author of the 1945 Cameron Report on educational costs; C.B.

Conway, head of the British Columbia Department of Education's Division of Tests, Standards, and Research from 1938 to 1974; George A. Cornish, textbook author and professor at the Ontario College of Education; A.R. Lord, school inspector and principal of the Vancouver Normal School; and Peter Sandiford, eminent educational psychologist. In future years, the history (and geography) sections were replaced by sections on social studies, in keeping with curricular trends. For teachers lacking references and without a great deal of training, this journal must have been a highly useful resource.

Journals were particularly important for teachers in isolated rural schools. The journal *British Columbia Schools* was originally produced by the BC department of education in the 1930s and sent to rural teachers because they did not have the same access to professional development as did their urban counterparts. It proved to be so popular that urban teachers demanded it as well, and its circulation was increased accordingly. Its aim was to provide teachers, and rural teachers in particular, with practical strategies for curriculum implementation, mostly by encouraging them to share their own ideas through the medium of the journal.

Teachers' association journals have also provided instructional assistance to their members. During implementation of the new enterprise curriculum in Alberta, the *A.T.A. Magazine* introduced a column called "Our Teachers' Helps Department," edited by W.D. McDougall of the normal school in Edmonton. McDougall included practical suggestions as well as summaries of useful books and articles about progressive education. He encouraged teachers to seek help through the journal: "Our Teachers' Helps Department is your department, too. If you are meeting with difficulty in organizing your Enterprise, in integrating widely separated fields of subject matter, in stimulating a desirable type of response, or in controlling it after it is stimulated, communicate with this Department and your problems will be passed over to an experienced teacher for solution."[64] The magazine also included reprints of lectures given by school inspectors on new classroom procedures and keynote addresses delivered by prominent American progressives at teachers' conventions.

At the present time, all provincial associations with a connection to history education (with the exception of the Nova Scotia and Prince Edward Island) have an online journal. In addition, the journal *Canadian Social Studies: Canada's National Social Studies Journal* (formerly *The History and Social Science Teacher* and before that the *Canadian Journal of*

Indians, Indians, tall and red
With arrows and spears of very sharp head
Dressed in fine feathers...

Miss Rita Boyer's class at Westridge School No. 2 really
learned how Indians lived.

Figure 3.5: An example of an enterprise in action in BC Schools. From Rita D. Bowyer [*sic*], "Indian Life," *British Columbia Schools* 1 (February 1946), 43.

History and Social Science), which has been in existence since 1965, is available online.[65]

Teacher Supervision

Provincial departments of education were responsible for teacher supervision until the mid-twentieth century. This approach was not particularly effective. Rural school inspectors, in particular, were taxed to the extreme, having to make their way across challenging terrain during the ten months of the school year, including the difficult winter months.[66] Given the large expanses they had to cover, the limited transportation options, and their other duties, most rural schoolteachers could reasonably expect to have a visit from the inspector only once a year. For the most part, their visits were not viewed by teachers as opportunities for professional development, but rather as dreaded times of assessment. Historian Robert Patterson talks of the "showy projects" some teachers left on display from one year to another, in order to impress the inspector with the cooperative group activities in which their students were supposedly engaged.[67] On those few occasions when some teachers had the temerity or sense of desperation to ask the inspector for help, they did not necessarily receive it. As one teacher summarized, "Not one ever said, 'Can I help you?'" She explained that while she had asked explicitly for instruction in her first year of teaching, even admitting to the inspector that she did not have "a clue how to do this and I can't afford to go to summer school," the inspector "wrote right back to say, 'Neither have I. But do it anyway for this year and next year I will get you a grant to go to summer school.'"[68]

Supervision has devolved to local school districts and schools (although provincial examinations could be considered a form of teacher supervision). Ontario, for example, removed responsibility for inspection from its department of education in 1968. Today, it is school administrators who are normally responsible for monitoring adherence to provincial curriculum requirements and quality of instruction.

Concluding Thoughts

To use a set of second-order historical thinking concepts – continuity and change – one can ask what has changed since the establishment of formal teacher education programs in Canada, and what has stayed the same. In terms of continuity, from the beginning of formalized teacher preparation in Canada, it has been conceptualized as a lifelong process involving three stages: disciplinary preparation, pre-service education, and ongoing accessible professional development opportunities. In terms of change, efforts have been made to address each of these in different ways at different times.

As Alan Sears points out in Chapter 2 of this collection, researchers of historical thinking have made the cognitive frames of school students central, largely ignoring the cognitive frames of teachers. Pointing to the folly of this way of thinking, Sears notes that Howard Gardner argues the opposite position – that it is harder to change people's minds as they age. This view has implications for approaches to all three stages of teacher preparation.

Expectations for disciplinary preparation have increased over time. This is to be expected. As a university degree became more accessible to a greater number of people, it became easier to make it a requirement for entrance into teacher education programs. Even so, student teachers can enter history or social studies teacher education programs with a wide range of disciplinary backgrounds, which do not necessarily provide them with a rich understanding of history. One improvement in this regard is that students enrolled in such programs are more likely to have encountered at least one undergraduate history course in which they engaged with primary source evidence.[69]

With respect to pre-service teacher education, the framework of formal theory and methodology classes, accompanied by an extended practicum experience, has continued since the days of normal schools. Perhaps the most intriguing of new approaches are boundary practices and communities of inquiry. Amy von Heyking discusses the crossing of boundaries and her experience working with an historian teaching a Canadian history undergraduate course in Chapter 6.[70] It would be useful to seek out opportunities to engage in such boundary practices in teacher education programs. We could also consider crossing boundaries during the practicum experience. For example, we might consider providing history teaching experiences in nontraditional settings, such as museums or historic sites, in addition to classrooms. Terry Taylor and Linda Farr Darling explore their experience with such an experiment in Chapter 19 in this collection.

Some teacher education programs, including those at the University of British Columbia (described by Lindsay Gibson, and by Peter Seixas and Graeme Webber, in Chapters 12 and 9 respectively in this volume), OISE (University of Toronto) and the University of New Brunswick (described by Theodore Christou in Chapter 13)[71] are taking deliberate steps towards a student inquiry orientation. There is promise in this direction because it involves a (limited) devolution of ownership of the program from the institution to the students. We have seen time and time again that people perform at a higher level when they take ownership and responsibility for the outcomes of their work. Communities of inquiry might include student teachers and history education scholars, along with historians and museum educators who are interested in what is happening in school classrooms. This book itself involves a community of inquiry, with its authorial representation from many of the constituencies that are interested in the betterment of history education.

There is an array of professional development opportunities for those teachers who have a commitment to lifelong learning; however, it must be acknowledged that these opportunities are more readily available for teachers in urban settings. It is not reasonable to expect that student teachers will leave a teacher education program, which might involve one history or social studies methodology course followed by a practicum experience, with a sound grasp of how to teach history in a rich and thoughtful way. Carla Peck's description in Chapter 15 of the challenges involved in leading a long-term professional development workshop is evidence of this. It took the teachers a great deal of time, as they tried out and refined new approaches, to develop deep understandings of the purposes and possibilities of teaching historical thinking – and strategies for teaching this kind of thinking. Jan Haskings-Winner describes in this volume two other experiments in ongoing history teacher education that have proved effective in the Ontario context.

Professional development opportunities include teacher institutes offered by pan-Canadian organizations, provincial departments of education, and university history departments and education faculties; conferences offered by provincial social studies, social science, and history teachers' associations; university summer school courses taken in order to earn certificates, diplomas, and undergraduate or graduate degrees; professional journals; and teacher supervision. Opportunities could also include professional development days spent engaging in collaborative planning or attending in-service sessions offered by local school districts, provincial and federal government departments, or private organizations and foundations. One approach to professional development that was not discussed in this history of history teacher education chapter, because it does not receive significant attention in practice, is the induction phase of ongoing teacher education. This is the first phase beyond the formal teacher education program. It could involve having experienced teachers mentor new teachers for a one- or two-year period following hiring by a school district. It could also involve giving new teachers less than a full-time teaching load to allow for periods of reflection and inquiry into better teaching practices, and might incorporate time spent back on campus, where they could share and discuss their experiences with other new teachers – the community of inquiry once again.

Teacher education is a lifelong process, and it has been viewed this way since provincial bureaucracies were put in place and educational infrastructures were established. It does not begin the first day of a history methodology class, nor does it end as the student teacher walks across the stage with a bachelor of education degree.[72]

NOTES

1 Ontario, *Report of the Royal Commission on Education in Ontario* (Toronto: King's Printer, 1950), 564.
2 Robert S. Patterson, "History of Teacher Education in Alberta," in *Shaping the Schools of the Canadian West*, edited by David C. Jones, Nancy M. Sheehan, and Robert M. Stamp (Calgary: Detselig, 1979), 202.
3 Paul Axelrod, "Normal School," in *The Routledge International Encyclopedia of Education*, edited by Gary McCulloch and David Crook (London and New York: Routledge), 406.
4 Ontario Department of Education, *Annual Report of the Chief Superintendent of Education, 1850*, 118.
5 Quoted in Albert Fiorino, *Teacher Education in Ontario: A History, 1843-1976*, unpublished paper commissioned by the Commission on Declining School Enrolments in Ontario, April 1978.
6 F. Henry Johnson, *A Brief History of Canadian Education* (Toronto: McGraw-Hill, 1968), 157.
7 Martin L. Friedland, *The University of Toronto: A History* (Toronto: University of Toronto Press, 2002).
8 John Calam, "Culture and Credentials: A Note on Late Nineteenth Century Teacher Certification in British Columbia," *BC Historical News* 14, no. 1 (Fall 1980): 13.
9 Ibid.
10 Ibid., 14.
11 Ibid.
12 http://museum.nbta.ca/teachereducation.htm, accessed 19 March 2014.
13 BC Department of Education, *Regulations and Courses of Study for Provincial and Normal Schools, 1928-29* (Victoria: Kings Printer, 1928), in *The Homeroom: British Columbia's History of Education Web Site*, edited by Patrick A. Dunae. Available at www.viu.ca/homeroom/content/Topics/Programs/Curriculum/nschool.htm.
14 Province of Saskatchewan Department of Education, *Regulations and Courses of Study for Provincial Normal Schools* (Regina: J.W. Reid, King's Printer, 1928), 13.
15 Quoted in K.A. Hollihan, "'Willing to Listen Humbly': Practice Teaching in Alberta Normal Schools, 1906-44," *Historical Studies in Education* 9, no. 2 (Fall 1997): 238.
16 Quoted in Patterson, "History of Teacher Education in Alberta," 200.
17 See http://umanitoba.ca/libraries/units/archives/UofM_history/um_year.shtml.

18 Friedland, *The University of Toronto*. I also acknowledge the assistance of Corinne Pask-Aube, Senior Institutional Research Analyst, Government, Institutional and Community Relations, U of T.

19 Trent established its own faculty in 2003.

20 Information about establishment of faculties of education was obtained from university websites.

21 See http://arcticcollege.ca/en/education-programs/item/4415-nunavut-teacher-education-program-ntep; http://www.yukoncollege.yk.ca/programs/info/yntep; http://www.auroracollege.nt.ca/live/pages/wpPages/ProgramInfoDisplay.aspx?id=41&tp=PRG.

22 Marvin Wideen, "Teacher Education at the Crossroads," in *Changing Times in Teacher Education: Restructuring or Reconceptualization?*, edited by Marvin F. Wideen and Peter P. Grimmett (London and New York: RoutledgeFalmer, 1995), 14-15.

23 Nancy M. Sheehan and J. Donald Wilson, "From Normal School to the University to the College of Teachers: Teacher Education in British Columbia in the 20th Century," *Journal of Education for Teaching* 20, no. 1 (1994): 28.

24 W. Stewart Wallace, *A New History of Great Britain and Canada* (Toronto: Macmillan, 1928); and Dept. of Education, *Regulations and Courses of Study for Provincial Normal Schools* (Victoria, BC: King's Printer, 1934), 22. Note that the textbook is incorrectly called *A Short History of Great Britain and Canada* here.

25 J.B. Calkin, *Notes on Education: A Practical Work on Method and School Management* (Truro, NS: D.H. Smith, 1888).

26 James L. Hughes et al., *Public School Methods*, vol. 5 (Toronto: School Methods Co., 1913), 167.

27 Ibid.,170.

28 Ibid.,171.

29 Harold Rugg and Ann Shumaker, *The Child-Centered School: An Appraisal of the New Education* (Yonkers-on-Hudson, NY: World Book Company, 1928).

30 Reginald George Trotter, *Canadian History: A Syllabus and Guide to Reading* (New York: The Macmillan Company, 1926).

31 Donalda Dickie, *The Enterprise in Theory and Practice* (Toronto: W.J. Gage, 1940).

32 Rebecca Priegert Coulter, "Getting Things Done: Donalda J. Dickie and Leadership Through Practice," *Canadian Journal of Education* 28, no. 4 (2005): 670.

33 Robert S. Patterson, *Progressive Education: Topics in the History of Education in Western Canada: A Skill Centred Approach* (Edmonton: Faculty of Education, University of Alberta, nd).

34 Dickie, *Enterprise*, 125.
35 Ibid., 100.
36 Ibid., 101.
37 See Robert S. Patterson, "The Canadian Response to Progressive Education," in *Essays on Canadian Education*, edited by Nick Kach, Kas Mazurek, Robert S. Patterson, and Ian deFaveri (Calgary: Detselig, 1986), 61-77; "The Implementation of Progressive Education in Canada, 1930-1945," in *Essays on Canadian Education*, edited by Nick Kach, Kas Mazurek, Robert S. Patterson, and Ian deFaveri (Calgary: Detselig, 1986), 79-96; Lynn Speer Lemisko and Kurt W. Clausen, "Connections, Contrarities, and Convolutions: Curriculum and Pedagogic Reform in Alberta and Ontario, 1930-1955," *Canadian Journal of Education* 29 (2006): 1097-126; and Patrice Milewski, "'I Paid No Attention to it': An Oral History of Curricular Change in the 1930s," *Historical Studies in Education* 24, no. 1 (Spring 2012): 112-129.
38 Amy von Heyking, "Implementing Progressive Education in Alberta's Schools," *Historical Studies in Education* 24, no. 1 (Spring 2012): 93-111.
39 See Jerome Bruner, *The Process of Education* (New York: Vintage, 1960).
40 Evelyn Moore and Edward E. Owen, *Teaching the Subjects in the Social Studies: A Handbook for Teachers* (Toronto: MacMillan Co. of Canada Ltd., 1956).
41 A.B. Hodgetts, *What Culture? What Heritage?: A Study of Civic Education in Canada* (Toronto: Ontario Institute for Studies in Education, 1968).
42 Hilda Taba, Mary C. Durkin, Jack R. Fraenkel, and Anthony H. McNaughton, *A Teacher's Handbook to Elementary Social Studies: An Inductive Approach*, 2nd ed. (Reading, MA: Addison-Wesley, 1971).
43 See Arthur L. Costa and Richard A. Loveall, "The Legacy of Hilda Taba," *Journal of Curriculum and Supervision* 18, no. 1 (Fall 2002): 56-62.
44 Ian Wright and David Hutchison, *Elementary Social Studies: A Practical Approach to Teaching and Learning*, 7th ed. (Scarborough, ON: Pearson Education Canada, 2010).
45 Susan E. Gibson, *Teaching Social Studies in Elementary Schools: A Social Constructivist Approach* (Toronto: Nelson Education, 2009), 91.
46 Roland Case and Penney Clark, eds., *The Anthology of Social Studies: Issues and Strategies for Secondary Teachers* (2008) and *The Anthology of Social Studies: Issues and Strategies for Elementary Teachers*, updated ed. (Vancouver: Pacific Educational Press, 2013).
47 See historicalthinking.ca/historical-thinking-concepts.
48 Mike Denos and Roland Case, *Teaching about Historical Thinking: A Professional Resource to Help Teach Six Interrelated Concepts Central to Students' Ability to Think Critically about History* (Vancouver: Critical Thinking Consortium, 2006).

49 Peter Seixas and Tom Morton, *The Big Six: Historical Thinking Concepts* (Toronto: Nelson, 2012).
50 Charles E. Phillips, *The Development of Education in Canada* (Toronto, W.J. Gage, 1957), 592.
51 J.H. Putman and G.M. Weir, *Survey of the School System* (Victoria, King's Printer, 1925), 174.
52 M.E. Lazerte, *Teacher Education in Canada* (Toronto: W.J. Gage, 1950), 44.
53 John Calam, ed., *Alex Lord's British Columbia: Recollections of a Rural School Inspector, 1915-36* (Vancouver: UBC Press, 1991), 174.
54 See Harry Smaller, "Teachers' Institutes: Instituting Proper Teaching," *Ontario History* 80, no. 4 (December 1988): 275-91 for a discussion of these points.
55 Patrice Milewski, "Teachers' Institutes in Late Nineteenth-Century Ontario," *Paedagogica Historica* 44, no. 5 (2008): 609.
56 Ibid., 619.
57 These were discontinued when Historica merged with the Dominion Institute in 2009.
58 Frank Arthur Jones, *The Preparation of Teachers in Ontario and the United States* (Ottawa: R.J. Taylor, Printer, 1916).
59 The Department of Education and the University of Alberta, "Joint Summer Session, 1936 and 1937," in Patterson, *Progressive Education*.
60 British Columbia Department of Education, *Summer School of Education Victoria July 5th to August 6th, 1937* (Victoria: Author, 1937), 7.
61 Quoted in Phillips, *Development of Education*, 597.
62 Ibid.
63 See Donalda J. Dickie, "Education via the Enterprise," *The School* 21, no. 9 (1940): 3-6 and "Democracy and the Enterprise," *The School* 31, no. 6 (1943): 464-9.
64 Amy von Heyking, *Creating Citizens: History and Identity in Alberta's Schools, 1905-1980* (Calgary: University of Calgary Press, 2006).
65 See Penney Clark, "The Historical Context of Social Studies in English Canada," in *Challenges and Prospects for Canadian Social Studies*, edited by Alan Sears and Ian Wright (Vancouver: Pacific Educational Press, 2004), 17-37. For *Canadian Social Studies* see http://www2.education.ualberta.ca/css/.
66 Calam, *Alex Lord's British Columbia*. School Inspector Alex Lord (later principal of the Vancouver Normal School) described his harrowing journeys to remote schools in his journals.
67 Interviewee #1504, "Quotes," in Patterson, *Progressive Education*.
68 Robert S. Patterson, "Voices from the Past: The Personal and Professional Struggle of Rural School Teachers," in *Schools in the West: Essays in Canadian Educational History* (Calgary: Detselig, 1986), 109.

69 See Gerry Friesen, "The Shape of Historical Thinking in a Canadian History Survey Course in University," in *New Possibilities for the Past: Shaping History Education in Canada*, edited by Penney Clark (Vancouver: UBC Press, 2011), 210-23.

70 Also see Victoria B. Fantozzi, "Divergent Purposes: A Case Study of a History Education Course Co-taught by a Historian and Social Studies Education Expert," *The History Teacher* 45, no. 2 (2012): 241-59.

71 Also, see Ruth Sandwell, "History Is a Verb: Teaching Historical Practice to Teacher Education Students" in *New Possibilities for the Past: Shaping History Education in Canada*, edited by Penney Clark (Vancouver: UBC Press, 2011), 224-42.

72 I would like to acknowledge the able and cheerful research assistance of University of British Columbia master's student, Susan Thompson.

4 The Poverty and Possibility of Historical Thinking: An Overview of Recent Research into History Teacher Education

SCOTT A. POLLOCK

This chapter discusses recent research on history and social studies teacher education and its effect on practice in Canada. Many of the studies summarized here are international, and indicate the extent to which Canadian scholars have been influenced by research conducted in the United Kingdom, the United States, and Australia in particular. While the focus is on studies examining instruction-enhancing practices, relevant research in social studies teacher education is included because history is taught within the context of social studies courses in many provinces in Canada.

An analysis of previous literature reviews highlights general shifts within history and social studies teacher education in the past twenty years. Recent research reflects growing interest among history teacher educators in historical thinking and the pitfalls and possibilities of enhancing student teachers' understanding of history as a discipline. While this research has led to some important discoveries regarding the nature of teachers' historical thinking, there is a pressing need for researchers to expand their focus if teacher education programs are to impact classroom teachers' ability to nurture students' historical thinking. In particular, there is a great need for collaborative work, including boundary projects conducted by historians and history teacher educators as outlined by Sears in this volume, if historical thinking is to transform history teacher education.

Previous Literature Reviews

In 1990 Banks and Parker wrote one of the first major literature reviews on social studies teacher education for the *Handbook of Research on*

Teacher Education.[1] The authors provided a systematic overview of social studies teacher education, concentrating on the structure and contents of the methods course, the characteristics of social studies teachers, and the underlying pedagogical goals of social studies educators. While Banks and Parker highlighted some interesting studies and pointed to general trends, such as the tendency of methods courses to focus upon general pedagogical issues rather than on those dealing specifically with the discipline of social studies, they were often forced to concede that the existing literature was too sparse or contradictory for them to draw definitive conclusions. The cause of this disappointing state of affairs is not addressed directly by Banks and Parker; however, their work seems to suggest that it could be explained by the existence of three conflicting conceptions of quality social studies teacher education: the cultural induction approach, the pedagogical effectiveness approach (i.e., a focus on effective teaching tactics), and the critical rationality approach (i.e., an emphasis on social critique and change).

Adler conducted the next major review of the social studies teacher education literature in 1991. This review aimed to provide an overview of the education of social studies teachers, including the curriculum of social studies methods courses, the textbooks used in methods courses, and the backgrounds of the student teachers. In this review, Adler noted a growing interest among researchers in the impact of field placements on student teachers, as well as an increasing amount of research on how the depth of teachers' subject or content knowledge affects their teaching. In the end Adler, like Banks and Parker, concluded by noting that "research on the teaching of social studies methods has been, on the whole, particularistic and unsystematic."[2] She lamented the lack of coherence within the field, and especially bemoaned the failure of researchers to build on one another's work. She was very critical of the research methodologies used in many studies, calling them "descriptive or quasi-experimental."[3] She argued that studies assessing the impact of a single teaching strategy used within a particular context are unlikely to provide insightful generalizations that may enhance teacher education more broadly.

Writing seventeen years later for the *Handbook of Research in Social Studies Education*, Adler pointed to some seismic shifts in the research landscape, but also highlighted the fact that the subfield of social science teacher education research could still be characterized as particularistic and unsystematic.[4] In terms of changes, Adler explained that the 1980s and 1990s saw a significant shift away from the deficit model of teacher education, which had focused on providing teachers with skills that were believed to be consistent with effective teaching. At the same time, there was a corresponding increase in research on teacher thinking, beliefs, and decision making. While the movement away from the deficit model was seen as positive and empowering for teachers, the research generated under this new paradigm was conflicting, small in scale, and limited in scope. In the end, Adler concluded her 2008 review on a rather pessimistic note, claiming that research into social studies teacher education was still characterized by a sense of "randomness" that made it "difficult to make generalizations about teacher beliefs, beyond the importance of acknowledging the beliefs they bring with them."[5]

Research in History Teacher Education

An analysis of research from 2005 to 2010 demonstrates that five major themes dominate research on social studies teacher education: teacher thinking and decision making; practical issues in the preparation of teachers, such as the use of effective instructional techniques; advocacy of critical social studies education; the use of technology in social studies teacher education; and facilitating the growth of student teachers' historical thinking. Researchers debate the extent to which teacher education programs can change teacher thinking and decision making. However, some studies support Sears' contention that it is challenging to change teachers' ways of thinking about the purpose and nature of history teaching. James found that despite the focus of their social studies methods course, student teachers failed to overcome "inherited discourses" about how to teach social studies. These discourses stressed protecting and sheltering children, thereby discouraging student teachers from teaching in ways that reveal the interpretive nature of historical knowledge.[6] Doppen, however, concluded that student teachers' coursework and field experiences in their teacher education programs could move them towards a belief in the value and efficacy of student-centred instruction in social studies.[7]

Canadian researchers of history education have focused considerable attention on teachers' disciplinary thinking, and particularly historical thinking. Historical thinking first began to blossom as an area of research in the United Kingdom over thirty years ago, and interest in this area has been accelerating within North America, Australia, and Europe for the past two decades. While there are many causes for growth in

Britain, the shift can be attributed in part to the work of scholars such as Phenix, who made strong philosophical cases for a disciplinary approach to education that emphasized "knowing how" over "knowing that."[8] These arguments were further buttressed by the growth of cognitive psychology. Jerome Bruner's work was influential in this regard, and his belief that students were best served by an inquiry-based education, with ideas and concepts at the core of each discipline, played an important role in the movement towards the disciplinary approach to history education.[9]

Capitalizing on this fertile environment, proponents of the disciplinary approach to the study of history in the United Kingdom founded the Schools History Project (SHP) in 1972. Its creation and the spread of SHP materials and syllabi to schools throughout the UK led to a proliferation of research as scholars attempted to understand and assess the impact of this approach on students.[10] While the research indicated that a disciplinary approach served students as well as or better than the traditional approach, the "new history" suffered setbacks in the United Kingdom, the United States, Canada, and elsewhere in the 1980s. While the reasons for this vary, a general political shift towards conservatism allowed some groups to push for a more traditional approach to history education in many regions.[11]

Supporters of the disciplinary approach to history began to make headway in the 1990s. In part, this was due not only to a changing political landscape, but to the continued shift away from a behaviourist approach to educational research. As the cognitive revolution in psychology continued to gain momentum, there was a sharp increase in the number of studies that attempted to explain teacher and student thinking from a more phenomenological perspective. In spite of the growing interest in phenomenological research, however, research into historical thinking in teacher education was still not an area of great interest. Thus, for example, the highly influential and still often-cited *The History Curriculum for Teachers* largely ignored teacher education, instead addressing questions such as: How do we justify the use of the disciplinary approach? What is known about students' historical thinking? What should a syllabus based on historical thinking concepts look like?[12] The underlying assumption seems to have been that if a strong case could be made for historical thinking, then teachers would be prepared to make the required shifts in their instruction.[13] This view was challenged, at first indirectly and later directly, in the work of Wineburg, McDiarmid, Seixas, and others.

Wineburg, who holds a PhD in psychological studies in education, has focused on historical cognition throughout his career. This interest led him to write a series of articles in the late 1980s and early 1990s about the impact of historical training on historical thinking and pedagogical decision making. Three of these papers raised significant questions about history teacher education, and thereby sparked increased interest in this issue. "Peering at History through Different Lenses" examined the pedagogical decision making of four novice social studies teachers who were teaching American history (only one of whom was a history specialist).[14] In this study, Wineburg found that the disciplinary background of the teachers significantly impacted their conception of history and the goals and conceptual frameworks that shaped their instruction. For example, the non-history specialists did not recognize that history is about interpretation and context, so their history lessons often consisted of a story to be recalled or recounted, one that occasionally included inaccuracies or misrepresentations. This recognition of the pedagogical impact of disciplinary frames of thinking raised, albeit indirectly, serious questions about teacher education programs, which tended to assume that student teachers already possessed a sufficient understanding of their subject and that teacher education programs should therefore focus on providing general pedagogical tools.

The problems inherent in this "add pedagogy and stir" approach to teacher education were also made evident in Wineburg and Wilson's "Models of Wisdom in the Teaching of History."[15] In this study, the two authors described the teaching of two expert pedagogues: Elizabeth Jensen and John Price. Both of these teachers were classroom veterans who possessed a deep understanding of the historical content they were required to teach. The teaching strategies that the researchers observed, however, could not have been more different. Jensen created a vibrant, student-centred classroom that was driven by debates and historical re-enactments. Price, on the other hand, took a teacher-centred approach dominated by lectures and Socratic discussions. Seeking to explain why two seasoned teachers with considerable historical knowledge and similar personalities would approach these lessons so differently, Wineburg and Wilson concluded that part of the answer lay in the teachers' beliefs about the purposes of teaching history. Their pedagogical reasoning was shaped by their understanding of the concepts embodied by the historical content, the nature of the discipline itself, and their students' needs and interests. Wineburg and Wilson highlighted the sophistication of these teachers' cognitive frames and the complexity of their pedagogical decision making and concluded that "both teachers possess rich and deep understandings of many things, understandings that manifest themselves in the ability to draw from a broad range of possibilities."[16] "Wrinkles in Time and Place" illustrated the impact of teachers' differing understandings and beliefs about the nature of the discipline, the history curriculum, and their pedagogical content knowledge on how they assessed students' work, implemented primary source analyses, and used textbooks in their history classrooms.[17]

Wineburg and Wilson's research has generated continuing interest in the impact of teacher beliefs on pedagogical decision making. For example, a recent study by van Hover and Yeager examined the pedagogical approach of a recent graduate of a teacher education program that emphasized teaching for historical thinking and historical inquiry. The beginning teacher, who had demonstrated a strong understanding of the knowledge and skills associated with such an approach, did not teach in this way in her secondary classroom. Like the teachers in Wilson and Wineburg's studies, rather than teaching in ways consistent with her training, she taught in a way that reflected her own beliefs in the purpose of history teaching: "to convey a sense of morals and values through historical stories so that she could shape her students' thinking and help them to grow into productive adult citizens/members of society."[18] Time and again, research studies confirm that transformative history teacher education will require more than simply teaching student teachers the tools of historical thinking.

The persistence of university students' cognitive frames was demonstrated by a study conducted by McDiarmid, who sought to determine the impact of a historiography seminar on undergraduate students' perceptions of history and history teaching. McDiarmid found that while the majority of the sixteen students moved away from their original, and naive, beliefs about history (e.g., that history was about "facts"), those same students continued to believe that history teachers should spend most of their time lecturing and teaching "facts." In short, while the students claimed the historiography course changed their conception of history, most held to old views about the teaching of history.[19]

McDiarmid's disappointing findings were mirrored by those of Seixas, who examined the impact of a teaching methods course specifically designed to induct student teachers into the historical thinking approach to history teaching. Seixas found that in spite of thorough instruction in the principal concepts, half of the students in his sample struggled, making poor pedagogical and historical judgments.[20] More recently, Fragnoli found that in her course, which directly addressed beliefs about the purpose of history instruction and modelled effective history instruction, student teachers remained anxious about their content knowledge and unconvinced of the efficacy of teaching for historical thinking.[21] Taken together, this research raised serious questions about the ability of teacher education programs, or at least the ability of a single course, to challenge student teachers' existing beliefs about (and practices of) history teaching.

More recent research has focused on three interrelated questions: How competent are student teachers in historical thinking? Can instruction in historical thinking overcome student teachers' prior conceptions of history and history teaching? If it can, will student teachers make effective use of this understanding? The answer to the first question seems to be that student teachers are poor historical thinkers, though this is attributed to their unfamiliarity and inexperience with this sort of disciplinary thinking, rather than a general lack of sophisticated reasoning.[22] The answers to the other questions are much less conclusive; however, there now seems to be a growing consensus that student teachers can overcome their preconceived notions if they are sufficiently open-minded, reflective, and in possession of alternative visions about the teaching of history and its purpose.[23] According to this research, the process of challenging their existing cognitive frames can be aided by direct discussion of the different orientations to the teaching of history (e.g., the storyteller, the scientific historian),[24] the development of meta-cognitive and reflective skills,[25] and a strong sense of the purpose of history teaching.[26] Research by McDiarmid and Vinten-Johansen has highlighted the importance of scaffolding in student teachers' attempts to apply their understanding of historical thinking in developing unit plans that could be completed by secondary school students.[27] Studies have also stressed the importance of factors outside of the teacher educator's control that tend to reinforce teacher-directed transmission of historical facts or stories. For example, research by Fehn and Koeppen found that student teachers' perceived need to cover curriculum and to control the classroom often undermined their belief in the efficacy of history teaching grounded in the extensive use of primary source material.[28] One of the student teachers in Meuwissen's study was blunt in his assessment of the utility of his methods course that emphasized historical thinking: "I felt like this was an indoctrination course based on one conceptualization of social studies teaching that isn't well supported in the schools."[29] Clearly in some cases the theory and practice gap in history teaching remains a chasm.

Taking Stock: The Poverty and Possibilities of History Teacher Education Research

Taken as a whole, the research into student teachers' historical thinking is both heartening and disappointing. While it is reassuring to see studies that confirm that it is possible to teach historical thinking to student teachers, the research seems to suffer from several methodological shortcomings that will need to be addressed if we are ever to gain any clear insights about effective history teacher education.

First, the existing research continues to be characterized by the particularism noted earlier by Adler: researchers examine the impact of a particular innovation, such as historical thinking, but very few studies build on the findings of earlier scholars. Second, there is a dearth of studies that measure change in student teachers' beliefs or understanding of historical thinking in a fine-grained fashion. While many researchers argue that specific learning experiences changed student teachers' general beliefs about history or history teaching, they do not assess student teachers' understanding of historical significance or empathy, for example, nor do they trace growth over time. In addition, little attention has been paid to how the identities of student teachers influence their historical thinking. This is a significant gap, especially given the growing interest of scholars on the impact of class, race, and gender on students' historical thinking.[30] Finally, most researchers have focused on changing the individual student teacher's historical thinking without adequate consideration of the challenge of effecting broader, institutional change in teacher education. Many studies have demonstrated that student teachers' teaching environments, their mentor teachers, and even the structure and expectations of teacher education programs generally can undermine students' belief in and ability to implement what is taught about effective pedagogy.[31] This makes a focus on individual thinking as the engine of instructional change a somewhat questionable approach.

There are many paths that researchers could take in order to fruitfully explore the possibilities of history teacher education. Scholars could undertake more nuanced assessments of student teachers' historical thinking by attending to their understanding of specific historical thinking concepts, such as significance, empathy, agency, and so on. They could also do large-scale research studies, since the research up to this time has been small-scale and qualitative in nature, not addressing what might be typical of student teachers' historical thinking, and what may be specific to the context of the study.

Rather than assessing the deficiencies of student teachers' historical thinking, researchers might simply identify student teachers' existing cognitive frames. As Sears points out in his chapter, we need to understand student teachers' beliefs and understandings about the nature and purpose of history teaching.[32] We need to "map the cognitive frames of beginning history teachers and take those into account in planning for teacher education." Existing studies have attempted to do this, but they are few in number, have tended to revisit the same themes rather than build on one another, and often categorize teacher beliefs so broadly that the analysis is not helpful.[33] Lévesque's chapter in this volume, on the other hand, demonstrates the value of assessing student teachers' historical consciousness and offers one example of how this might be done.

Researchers could examine, in more detail, if and how student teachers can apply their new disciplinary understandings of history in authentic classroom settings. Given the findings of McDiarmid and Vinten-Johansen, teacher educators must at a minimum provide student teachers with opportunities to embed historical thinking into teachable lessons and units.[34] Other case studies have also done this, but whether they provide insights applicable to a wide range of contexts and teacher education programs remains undetermined.[35]

Given the range of school contexts and teacher education programs across Canada, the task of improving history teacher education is likely to take many forms and include a mixture of systemic, institutional, and grass-roots changes.[36] Regardless of the context, however, a radical shift will require the collaboration of teachers, teacher educators, and historians – another engagement in the "boundary work" Sears advocates in his chapter. A few studies have identified the possibilities that emerge when a range of stakeholders collaborate to enhance history teacher education. Westhoff (a historian) and Polman (a teacher educator) worked with a high school teacher, a group of student teachers, and high school students on a historical inquiry that resulted in the creation of a website about their neighbourhood's history. This study demonstrated the impressive growth of student teachers' pedagogical content knowledge as they worked closely with the high school students in crafting guiding questions, identifying and interpreting primary sources, and presenting the story they created, all with the assistance of the historian, teacher educator, and high school teacher. Their participation in this community of practice demonstrated the complexity of making pedagogical judgments that enhance students' historical thinking while incorporating their prior knowledge and learning styles. As Westhoff and Polman conclude, student teachers' pedagogical content knowledge can be developed in courses, but they need "to practice it in authentic and supportive settings."[37] These supports must come from historians as well as teacher educators.

Historians teaching undergraduate history courses have begun to reflect on the important contribution they can make towards more authentic and intellectually rigorous history teaching in schools. History professors have acknowledged the benefits of teaching with an emphasis on historical thinking, despite the many pressures they face to concentrate on research at the expense of their teaching.[38] Indeed, scholars such as Belanger have attempted to make the historical method central to their undergraduate teaching and articulated their commitment "to think more carefully and critically about what good history teachers do at every level and how best to foster those skills in future history teachers."[39] Studies that have brought together historians and teacher educators, like von Heyking's in this volume, demonstrate what the educational community of practice can offer historians as undergraduate teachers, and how courses students take early in their university career can begin to challenge existing pedagogical frames. Increased contact between historians and teacher educators also benefits the educators, as improved teaching of historical thinking requires deep and thorough understandings of current historiography.

Boundary work also has the potential to bring teacher educators and classroom teachers closer together, and thereby enhance teachers' understanding of teaching for historical thinking. While there are many ways in which this could be done, one particularly interesting approach is the "professor in residence" model, which allows a professor of education to teach a K–12 class while being observed by student teachers. Burstein's experience with this model demonstrated its potential to combat many of the problems that student teachers typically encounter when they try to use the historical thinking approach.[40] For instance, the claim that historical thinking cannot be taught to K–12 students was undermined by direct experience, while the fear of trying to teach in this fashion was minimized by the student teachers' experience of team-teaching with the professor. Perhaps the presence and support of professors might help novice teachers as they progress through their stressful first years, a period during which many teachers give up their pedagogical beliefs and succumb to the status quo.

Conclusion

While the research interest in historical thinking has been a promising development for history teacher education, it is likely to have little impact if scholars working in this area do not move beyond their focus on individual student teachers' ability to think historically. While more research into student teachers' cognitive frames is warranted, this research needs to build on earlier work. It is also imperative that scholars interested in the promotion of historical thinking begin to consider the possibilities for reforming history teacher education more generally, and to consider the nature of reforms that may be required in the undergraduate teaching and the settings for practice teaching that student teachers experience. Moreover, Sears' insistence that we take the long view of teacher education and rethink the purpose and nature of professional development points to the need for research that leads to more effective professional learning for experienced teachers. One of the most significant findings of history education researchers over the past twenty years is that "history teachers draw upon techniques and understandings unique to the discipline, not upon an amorphous set of instructional tools."[41] Surely, this has implications for the nature of the professional development opportunities offered to teachers in the field, and not just for undergraduate teacher education programs. While it is a tremendous accomplishment to change a single student teacher's beliefs about history teaching, the ability of teacher educators to do so, and the likelihood that this change will persist in the classroom, will flourish with broader change within the history education community and sustained opportunities for professional learning throughout a teacher's career. Describing what this might look like is a challenge taken up by many of the authors who have contributed to this volume.

NOTES

1 James A. Banks and Walter C. Parker, "Social Studies Teacher Education," in *Handbook of Research on Teacher Education*, edited by W. Robert Houston (New York: Macmillan, 1990), 674-86.

2 Susan A. Adler, "The Education of Social Studies Teachers," in *Handbook of Research on Social Studies Teaching and Learning*, edited by James P. Shaver (New York: Macmillan, 1991), 211.

3 Ibid., 218.

4 Susan A. Adler, "The Education of Social Studies Teachers," in *Handbook of Research in Social Studies Education*, edited by Linda S. Levstik and Cynthia A. Tyson (New York: Routledge, 2008), 329-51.

5 Ibid., 346.

6 Jennifer H. James, "Teachers as Protectors: Making Sense of Preservice Teachers' Resistance to Interpretation in Elementary History Teaching," *Theory and Research in Social Education* 36, no. 3 (2008): 172-205.

7 Fran Doppen, "The Influence of a Teacher Preparation Program on Preservice Social Studies Teachers' Beliefs: A Case Study," *Journal of Social Studies Research* 31, no. 1 (2007): 54-64.

8 See, for example, Philip Phenix, "Key Concepts and the Crisis in Learning," *Teachers College Record* 58, no. 3 (1958): 137-43.

9 Jerome S. Bruner, *The Process of Education* (New York: Vintage Books, 1960).

10 Denis J. Shemilt, *History 13-16: Evaluation Study* (Edinburgh: Collins Education, 1980).

11 For a discussion of this in Canada, see Robert D. Gidney, *From Hope to Harris: The Reshaping of Ontario's Schools* (Toronto: University of Toronto Press, 1999); for the United Kingdom, see Robert Phillips, *History Teaching, Nationhood and the State: A Study in Educational Politics* (London: Cassell, 1998).

12 Christopher Portal, ed., *The History Curriculum for Teachers* (London: Falmer Press, 1987). See also A.K. Dickinson, Peter Lee, and Peter Rogers, eds., *Learning History* (London: Heinemann, 1984).

13 To some extent, at least in the UK, this assumption seemed to be valid. There, as a result of the adoption of a national history curriculum that was grounded in concepts of historical thinking, there were lively discussions among teachers as they struggled to understand and to teach historical thinking. For a discussion of this, see Christine Counsell, "Disciplinary Knowledge for All, the Secondary History Curriculum and History Teachers' Achievement," *The Curriculum Journal* 22, no. 2 (June 2011): 201-25.

14 Suzanne M. Wilson and Samuel S. Wineburg, "Peering at History Through Different Lenses: The Role of Disciplinary Perspectives in Teaching History," *Teachers College Record* 89, no. 4 (Summer 1988): 525-39.

15 Samuel S. Wineburg and Suzanne M. Wilson, "Models of Wisdom in the Teaching of History," *The History Teacher* 24, no. 4 (1991): 395-412.

16 Ibid., 411.

17 Suzanne M. Wilson and Samuel S. Wineburg, "Wrinkles in Time and Place: Using Performance Assessments to Understand the Knowledge of History Teachers," *American Educational Research Journal* 30, no. 4 (1993): 729-69.

18 Stephanie van Hover and Elizabeth Yeager, "'I Want to Use My Subject Matter to ...': The Role of Purpose in One U.S. Secondary History Teacher's Instructional Decision Making," *Canadian Journal of Education* 30, no. 3 (2007): 678.

19 G. William McDiarmid, "Understanding History for Teaching: A Study of the Historical Understanding of Prospective Teachers," in *Cognitive and Instructional Process in History and the Social Sciences*, edited by Mario Carretero and James F. Voss (Hillsdale, NJ: Lawrence Erlbaum Associates Publishers, 1994), 159-85.

20 Peter Seixas, "Student Teachers Thinking Historically," *Theory and Research in Social Education* 26, no. 2 (1998): 310-41.

21 Kristi Fragnoli, "Historical Inquiry in a Methods Classroom: Examining our Beliefs and Shedding our Old Ways," *The Social Studies* 96, no. 6 (2005): 247-51.

22 I. Barca, "Prospective Teachers' Ideas about Assessing Different Accounts," *International Journal of Historical Learning, Teaching and Research* 1, no. 2 (2001), http://centres.exeter.ac.uk/historyresource/journal2/barca.pdf; A. Virta, "Student Teachers' Conceptions of History," *International Journal of Historical Learning, Teaching and Research* 2, no. 1. (2001), http://centres.exeter.ac.uk/historyresource/journal3/finland.pdf; and E.A. Yeager and O.L Davis, "Classroom Teachers' Thinking about Historical Texts: An Exploratory Study," *Theory and Research in Social Education* 24, no. 2 (1996): 146-66.

23 For examples of studies that do not fit this trend, see Thomas Fallace, "Historiography and Teacher Education: Reflections on an Experimental Course," *History Teacher* 42, no. 2 (2009): 205-22; James, "Teachers as Protectors."

24 Timothy D. Slekar, "Case History of a Methods Course: Teaching and Learning History in a 'Rubber Room,'" *The Social Studies* 96, no. 6 (2005): 237-40.

25 Doppen, "The Influence of a Teacher Preparation Program."

26 Jill M. Gradwell, "Using Sources to Teach History for the Common Good: A Case Study of One Teacher's Purpose," *The Journal of Social Studies Research* 43, no. 1 (2010): 59-76.

27 G. Williamson McDiarmid and Peter Vinten-Johansen, "A Catwalk across the Great Divide: Redesigning the History Teaching Methods Course," in *Knowing, Teaching, and Learning History: National and International*

Perspectives, edited by Peter N. Stearns, Peter Seixas, and Sam Wineburg (New York: New York University Press, 2000), 156-77.

28 Bruce Fehn and Kim E. Koeppen, "Intensive Document-Based Instruction in a Social Studies Methods Course," *Theory and Research in Social Education* 26, no. 4 (1998): 461-84.

29 Quoted in Kevin W. Meuwissen, "Maybe Someday the Twain Shall Meet: Exploring Disconnections Between Methods Instruction and 'Life in the Classroom,'" *The Social Studies* 96, no. 6 (2005): 253-8.

30 See for example Terrie L. Epstein, "Sociological Approaches to Young People's Historical Understanding," *Social Education* 61, no. 1 (1997): 28-31; and Carla Peck, "'It's Not Like [I'm] Chinese and Canadian. I Am In Between': Ethnicity and Students' Conceptions of Historical Significance," *Theory and Research in Social Education* 38, no. 4 (2010): 574-617.

31 Anna Pendry, Chris Husbands, James Arthur, and Jon Davison, *History Teachers in the Making: Professional Learning* (Buckingham, UK: Open University Press, 1998); Kenneth M. Zeichner and B. Robert Tabachnick, "Are the Effects of University Teacher Education 'Washed Out' by School Experience?" *Journal of Teacher Education* 32, no. 3 (1981): 3-11; see also the studies by Meuwissen, "Maybe Someday the Twain Shall Meet," and Fehn and Koeppen, "Intensive Document-Based Instruction in a Social Studies Methods Course."

32 See also Fred A.J. Korthagen, "Situated Learning Theory and the Pedagogy of Teacher Education: Towards an Integrative View of Teacher Behavior and Teaching Learning," *Teaching and Teacher Education* 26, no. 1 (2010): 98-106.

33 Sears, this volume, p. 22. See for example D.S.G. Carter, "Knowledge Transmitter, Social Scientist or Reflective Thinking: Three Images of the Practitioner in Western Australia High Schools," *Theory and Research in Social Education* 18, no. 3 (1990): 274-317; Richard W. Evans, "Teacher Conceptions of History," *Theory and Research in Social Education* 17, no. 3 (1989): 210-40.

34 McDiarmid and Vinten-Johansen, "A Catwalk across the Great Divide."

35 See, for example, Robert Bain and Jeffrey Mirel, "Setting up Camp at the Great Instructional Divide: Educating Beginning History Teachers," *Journal of Teacher Education* 57, no. 3 (May/June 2006): 212-19.

36 For a discussion of the complexity of systemic reform in an American context, see Bruce A. VanSledright, *The Challenge of Rethinking History Education: On Practices, Theories, and Policy* (New York: Routledge, 2011).

37 Laura M. Westhoff and Joseph L. Polman, "Developing Preservice Teachers' Pedagogical Content Knowledge About Historical Thinking," *International Journal of Social Education* 22, no. 2 (Fall 2007/Winter 2008): 26.

38 See Ruth Sandwell in this volume; David Pace, "The Amateur in the Operating Room: History and the Scholarship of Teaching and Learning," *The American Historical Review* 109, no. 4 (October 2004): 1171-92; Elizabeth Belanger, "How Now? Historical Thinking, Reflective Teaching and the Next Generation of History Teachers," *Journal of American History* 97, no. 4 (March 2011): 1079-88.

39 Belanger, "How Now?," 1079.

40 Joyce H. Burstein, "Do As I Say and As I Do: Using the Professor-in-Residence Model in Teaching Social Studies Methods," *The Social Studies* 100, no. 3 (May/June 2009): 121-7.

41 Thomas Fallace and Johann N. Neem, "Historiographical Thinking: Towards a New Approach to Preparing History Teachers," *Theory and Research in Social Education* 33, no. 3 (2005): 331.

PART TWO

Nurturing Historical Thinking before Entering a Teacher Education Program

5 On Historians and Their Audiences: An Argument for Teaching (and Not Just Writing) History[1]

RUTH SANDWELL

Collectively, historians' work consists of constructing, deconstructing, and reconstructing a vast edifice of knowledge about the past, the generalizations and syntheses about which will vary according to the purposes of the historians and the audiences to whom they are directing any particular manifestation of their work. Notwithstanding the tendency of historians to identify their "real" historical work and their "real" audiences exclusively with their research and writing rather than with their teaching – particularly their undergraduate teaching – I am going to begin by arguing that historians "do" history as much in their teaching as they do in their scholarly research and publishing. For, notwithstanding important differences between the two, the history emerging out of the undergraduate classroom shares key, even essential elements with the history in scholarly journals. Drawing on recent research in the field of history education, I will go on to suggest that if history is something created and conveyed through undergraduate teaching as well as in original scholarly research and publications, the work of historians-as-undergraduate-teachers is arguably just as important, *or even more important* than the published versions of their original contributions to research. I will conclude by providing two reasons why this is a particularly good moment for professional historians to actively consider how, why, and in what direction they might change the way they teach the generalist and uninitiated audience that they encounter in their undergraduate classrooms.

History Is Taught as Well as Written

If history is a dialogue among people about the interpretation of meaningful evidence left over from the past, that dialogue occurs not only in historians' published articles and at scholarly conferences but also in their undergraduate teaching. Both scholarship and teaching require creative historical research, historical synthesis, and presentations of historical knowledge (in ways appropriate to the audience). Both scholarship and teaching also involve assessing other people's work and being assessed by them.

In spite of these similarities in kinds of activities, teaching is typically full of surprises for those historians or historians-in-training who encounter it from the professorial side for the first time; it is the differences between the two aspects of our work that are the most striking. While many historians embrace teaching, many (particularly in the early years of their work) also encounter it with a sense of frustration and even loss, often experiencing teaching as a dilution of what they identify as their *real* professional work – and an unwelcome distraction. "I had no idea the level of generalization that would be required," complained one of my colleagues early in her professorial career. "I had no idea I would have to teach so far out of my field," said another. "How could my students be so profoundly ignorant of everything in or about history?" said yet another. And, most pervasively, historians expressed this sentiment: "How can it *possibly* be taking up so much of my time?"

If historians perform the same actions in both undergraduate teaching and in scholarship, they perform them in very different ways.[2] This is because the audience for their historical knowledge is profoundly different in each case. The audiences' locations are different. Undergraduates today are usually present in real time in classrooms, and the medium of delivery is predominantly oral. Fellow scholars are seldom in the same room, though their written works might be read by the students. History conveyed through scholarship is typically heavily dependent on clearly identified primary sources, while history as taught in classrooms is likely to draw more on the work of other scholars, who may not even be identified by name, let alone by specific publication. Differences in the degree and kind of citation relate to the kinds of summaries and syntheses that historians are likely to use in their teaching, particularly in junior-level survey courses: these are almost always larger, broader, and more general than would be appropriate in scholarly publishing. We will return to this difference between specialist and generalist audience below.

Another notable feature that distinguishes historians' two audiences – students and peers – is the relationship that each has to the historian in terms of power and knowledge. Historians, in their scholarly role, engage more or less as equals in a dialogue among a community of learned professional specialists, and they engage most often and most intensively with those few scholars in the same sub-discipline or sub-sub-discipline as themselves. The historian-as-undergraduate teacher conversely engages as a knowledgeable expert in a dialogue with un-initiated learners. The formal procedures used by universities to assess undergraduate students, which differ from the conventions of peer re-view used to evaluate fellow scholars, contribute to the power relation-ship between historian and students. Part of the power differential comes from the imbalance in knowledge between expert and novice. Indeed, it has become a commonplace that professors cannot count on any subject knowledge in their undergraduate students, about any par-ticular topic, general trends, or about the nature of historical thinking that comprises part of the disciplinary knowledge of historians.

In addition to the differences in power, knowledge, and levels of generalization involved in historians' interactions with these different audiences, another notable distinction immediately impresses the un-dergraduate history professor who moves from writing a dissertation to delivering his or her first lecture to four hundred undergraduate students: the most salient difference is numbers. For the vast majority of historians, far more people are exposed to the history they convey through their teaching than through their writing.[3]

But the numerical importance of that audience for history does not end with the direct influence that undergraduate history professors have on their students. We know that a tiny minority of those in under-graduate history courses go on to further training and become academ-ic historians; others seek training in specific branches of public history, including archives, museums, or libraries. Studies have not yet deter-mined what proportion of students take undergraduate courses in Canada in the hope of becoming history and social studies teachers, but the informal polls that I carried out in all my undergraduate history courses in the late 1990s indicated that between 60 and 90 per cent of students in my history courses were at least thinking of applying to become history or social studies teachers. Regardless of what propor-tion of history undergraduate students end up teaching history and social studies, it is certainly the case that teacher education programs in Canada (and elsewhere) require prospective secondary history and so-cial studies teachers to have taken at least some undergraduate history courses. Teacher education programs in some provinces even require that prospective social studies teachers have taken a Canadian history survey course. Sometimes undergraduate history courses are the only professional training in history that history and social studies teachers receive. It is these history educators who go on to influence the historical thinking and knowing of thousands of students over the course of their careers. Professional academic historians' largest audience is, therefore, found in their teaching. And that audience is comprised overwhelmingly of generalists, not fellow academic specialists.

Given all this, it is surprising that historians have been so reluctant (with some important exceptions) to engage formally and as historians with the implications of what history *means* and what history is *for* with regard to their largest, nonspecialist, audience that they encounter in their undergraduate classrooms.[4] There are, I would argue, two pressing reasons why historians should engage in a dialogue about their numerically significant generalist audience at this time.

Why Talk about Historians as Teachers?: The Importance of History Education for the People in a Pluralist Democracy

First, undergraduate students are not only the most numerous recipients of the history that we do: this audience is important on other grounds. While historians mostly have stopped talking about the larger and more general purposes of the history they convey in their undergraduate classrooms (let alone what an understanding of history might do for the people of contemporary Canada), this has become a hot topic in other areas of society and academic research over the past few years.[5] Historians are well aware that academic history has changed significantly in the last generation or two: it is arguably more focused on differences within societies, and more comfortable with dissonance and fragmentation. Academic historians are more sensitive overall to imbalances of power, including those manifested in the unifying "grand narratives" favoured by earlier generations of historians, and now widely seen (unfavourably) as recapitulating authoritarian structures of knowledge.[6]

Historians may be surprised to learn, however, that international research in and discussions about history education in schools are now suggesting that it is precisely the ways that historians work – how they "do" history and the epistemological frameworks within which they practice – that are of particular value to schoolchildren and the general public alike. There has been considerable and escalating debate in recent years about the role and purpose of history education in public schools within democratic, pluralist societies.[7] Scholars in the field of education (whose work is summed up most eloquently, at least in North America, by Keith Barton and Linda Levstik in *Teaching History for the Common Good*) are arguing that history – and more particularly historical thinking and historical understanding – provides students (and the general public) with the best epistemological framework and analytical tools that they need to understand and navigate a complex social world. Historical thinking in all of its complexity provides the people with the broad humanistic knowledge vital to creating and critiquing valid truth claims within a pluralist participatory democracy.

Participants in the discussion within Canada have been careful to stress the widest possible definition of citizenship, one that explicitly eschews self-congratulatory forms of nationalism.[8] Leaving aside the fractious debates over whose history "counts" that followed the publication of Jack Granatstein's *Who Killed Canadian History?*, Canadian discussions have been distinguished by an emphasis on the promise that *historical thinking* – the disciplinary practices by which historians interpret evidence within meaningful narratives – holds for history education.[9] Historical understanding for the people, in other words, matters in ways that are deeply connected to historians' disciplinary practices.[10] As a result, history teaching in the high schools and even elementary schools in Canada is changing – it recognizes, celebrates, and tries to imitate what historians do in their research and writing. The generalist audience that historians encounter in their undergraduate classrooms, it turns out, may be the most important one that they encounter, not simply because more learn about history in the classroom than out of it, but because (according to proponents) historical thinking brings important advantages to citizens trying to make some sense of the complex, varied, and dynamic world in which we live, giving them the kind of understanding they need in order to effectively exercise their democratic voice. It is in the undergraduate classroom that most people experience their first, and often their only, experience with the historians who generate the historical thinking that may be of key importance in sustaining and nurturing a participatory democracy. Undergraduate classrooms, in short, provide the main conduit for moving disciplined historical understanding into the public realm. More accurately, they have the potential for doing so.

Let me give you two quick examples of the kind of historical thinking being talked about in relation to history teaching in secondary and elementary schools. In the 1980s, British history educator Peter Lee conducted interviews with hundreds of school children aged seven to fourteen in England as part of Project Chata "Concepts of History and Teaching Approaches." Students talked to him about what history was, what it meant, and how it was knowable. His task was to "map" changes in students' ideas about what history *is* between those ages. His focus was on the second-order disciplinary understandings of historians, such as using evidence, weighing significance, exploring cause and consequence, and continuity and change (as opposed to their understanding of first-order concepts, such as "fascism," "famine," or "genocide"). He investigated how students explained differing accounts of the same thing (the fall of the Roman Empire, the rise of industrialization, et cetera). Lee found a significant difference in the ways that children understood history. He posited a progression in students' ideas about history, or, more precisely, in students' ideas about historical accounts and their relation to the past, and he has presented these as levels of understanding.[11]

Progression in Students' Ideas about Accounts and Their Relation to the Past

(Aka Progression in Historical Understanding)

- The Past as Given:
  Stories are all about the same thing: the story is equivalent to something "out there."
- The Past as Inaccessible:
  We can't know – we weren't there. Nothing can be known.
  Differences in accounts result from the lack of direct access to the past.
- The Past as Determining Stories:
  Stories are fixed by the information available: there is a one-to-one correspondence.
  Differences in accounts result from gaps in information and mistakes.
- The Past as Reported in a More or Less Biased Way:
  Shift of focus from the *story* and *reports* to the *author* as an active contributor.
  Differences in accounts result from distortion (in the form of lies, bias, exaggeration, dogmatism); the problem is not just lack of information.
- The Past as Selected and Organized from a Viewpoint:
  Stories are written (perhaps necessarily) from a legitimate position held by the author.

Differences in accounts are a result of selection. Stories are not copies of the past.
- The Past as (Re-)Constructed in Answer to Questions in Accordance with Criteria
Shift of focus from the author's position and choice to the nature of accounts as such.
It is the nature of accounts to differ.[12]

Perhaps the most unusual aspect of Peter Lee's work is that he is not interested in ranking or rating students according to their place on this six-level chart. Instead, he has put much of his professional expertise over the past thirty years into developing ways of teaching students so that they can better learn the complex processes and forms of knowledge involved in thinking and knowing history better.

Peter Seixas, a history educator at the University of British Columbia, has taken up Peter Lee's work with second-order historical concepts in a Canada-wide history education project called The Historical Thinking Project. Seixas approached the "problem" of facts-driven, positivist, and boring history education in the schools by asking, "What constitutes an increase in historical understanding, and how can teachers assess it?" As he outlines in his article, "A Modest Proposal for Change in Canadian History Education," he is developing ways of teaching history that place historical thinking at the heart of teaching and learning history – although never, of course, abandoning the so-called "content" of history. He itemizes what it means to think historically, and is having considerable success in getting school boards and provincial ministries to change the structures and composition of history education to incorporate some of his proposals.

Why Talk about Historians-as-Teachers?: It Isn't Working

If the nonspecialist audience that historians encounter in their undergraduate classrooms just might be the most important audience they address in their careers, a second reason that historians should care about this audience is that recent research indicates a pervasive failure on the part of historians-as-teachers to convey what turns out to be the most important part of history education: a disciplinary understanding of what history *is* and what it *does*.

There have been no studies that I know of that document the practices of Canadian university history professors, or attempt to assess whether the "new" emphases – on more diverse history and on history-as-dialogue that characterize historical practice and, increasingly, history education in elementary and secondary schools – are making it into the undergraduate classroom.[13] If there are studies of this nature, historians in Canadian universities are not aware of them. There are some ideological issues involved. Teaching the more synthetic and general history that is generally assumed to be the important part of undergraduate education in Canada – whether organized by national boundaries and grand chronologies, by theme, or by issue – goes "against the grain" of the detailed and specific research and analysis that historians are trained to perform. And, in the early twenty-first century, when "fragmentation" and "dissonance" are the bywords of professionalism within the academy, the idea of imposing any synthetic narrative, particularly one rooted in such hegemonic structures as "nation" or "century," is anathema.[14] Many historians are simply uncomfortable with the kinds of simplistic syntheses they feel obliged to make as undergraduate teachers, as they do not identify these with the "real" history that they write.

If they are uncomfortable with the idea of broad generalizations, particularly at the level of the nation state, many historians are also hampered by a variety of structural factors within university education that are militating against teaching for understanding – historical or otherwise. The dramatic growth in average undergraduate class size and a perceived decline in students' basic historical knowledge can demoralize faculty; when the conditions conducive to meaningful teaching are being dissolved, it is not surprising that many professors take the path of least resistance and simply "cover the content." Pressured to provide such basic, general, and mass history education, historians may feel that they have neither the time nor the energy to explore with their students the disciplinary structures and methods of historical inquiry. Whatever the reasons, those elements that distinguish history from other kinds of knowledge and ways of knowing – the close analysis of primary documents in the context of a rich secondary literature – too often simply fall by the wayside in the huge classes and predetermined categories of analysis imposed on junior-level undergraduate courses, particularly on large survey courses. Compounding these problems is the fact that large general courses are often taught by junior faculty who can ill afford the kind of "bad professor" ratings that can easily fall on those historians who ask a little more of their students than the all-too-common "listen and regurgitate" model of undergraduate history education.

If attempts at teaching historical thinking seem to be limited, the overwhelming consensus from research over the past twenty years is that students do not have much familiarity with historical thinking. Most students simply do not have the knowledge or understanding to generate truth-based claims about complex social phenomena, past or present. Many are unfamiliar with the concept of evidence-based reasoning. Research over the past few years has documented a number of disturbing trends. Peter Lee's study of historical thinking among British elementary school students found that a significant number of four-teen-year-old students maintain that history is unknowable because "they weren't there and didn't see it" – though these numbers are improving, he hopes as a result of better history teaching. North American research about historical thinking suggests that my experience with much older undergraduate students is not atypical: a substantial proportion maintained that any particular history is not believable because somebody wrote it, and that somebody had a gender or race that prejudiced their interpretation, giving them a biased and therefore unreliable view of "what really happened."[15] Many expressed the belief that knowledge of history was possible only if appropriate surveys of enough people had been done; only then would it be possible to come up with the eyewitness accounts that in their mind constituted history.[16]

In his well-known study, "On the Reading of Historical Texts: Notes on the Breach Between School and Academy,"[17] Sam Wineburg described how high-achieving senior American students saw history as a fixed and authoritarian set of facts to be recounted. In his studies, only a few students at any level demonstrated any familiarity with the professional historians' concept that history is a careful, contested, and collective interpretive dialogue about evidence gathered around meaningful questions.[18] One particularly disturbing study revealed that undergraduate history majors moving through their four-year degrees had little awareness of history as a narrative constructed from evidence; confronted with professors' attempts to provide them with a nuanced and contested view of historical interpretations, many students assumed that the professor was simply confused about "what really happened."[19] Even when students have become acquainted with the skills and the resources that would allow them to participate in the process of history, in other words, they continue to understand history as a series of dead, inert, and generally inaccessible set of facts.[20] It is, unfortunately, quite possible for an undergraduate, even one majoring in history, to emerge from university, degree in hand, with little or no understanding that history is a dialogue constructed by people about evidence from the past. Students should not be held responsible for this. As Canadian historian Chad Gaffield famously generalized, if a basketball coach were to teach his sport the way that our professors teach history, it would not be until after the four years of an undergraduate degree had been completed, and graduate studies had begun, that the prospective player would finally be invited to try to get the ball in the net.[21]

It is particularly frustrating that outside the university, high school and elementary history education may be ready to make a move away from positivism and towards more nuanced interpretive frameworks for both practice and analysis. Just as teachers and school boards are embracing the importance of knowing how to think historically, undergraduate professors of history seem, on the face of it, to have abandoned their commitment to the larger purposes of history education. They miss opportunities to enhance historical understanding in their undergraduate classrooms, even though many of their students will, over the next few years, go on to teach in secondary and elementary school classrooms.

Undergraduate history professors in Canadian universities have not, it seems, succeeded in transmitting to their undergraduate students the kind of history they routinely practice in their scholarship. If the basic tenets of historical thinking and knowledge are not making it through to the general population, this is a problem. The solution to this problem, and the resolution of the tension between historians' work as scholars and as undergraduate teachers lies *not* in making the history we teach the same as the history we create as scholars. Instead, following the lead of Barton and Levstik, I would argue that the resolution lies in recognizing and addressing the purpose or purposes of history to a nonspecialist university audience, and to Canadian society in general. Somewhat paradoxically, I would argue that it is by paying *more* attention, not less, in undergraduate teaching to the *specific disciplinary knowledge of historians* that professors can best address the different purpose of undergraduate history. This is all the more important at this historical juncture, when, as we have seen, decreasing budgets and increasing student enrolments are putting more pressure on professors to teach for mass effect (aka "edutainment") rather than for increased understanding, and to teach in ways that confirm, rather than challenge, the shibboleths of popular history and mythmaking that all too often pass as historical knowledge within the population.

How historians go about initiating history undergraduates into disciplinary thinking should be a topic of lively discussion among professional historians. After all, there is a growing and potentially useful literature about how, exactly, historical thinking can be taught to learners. Should historians ensure that undergraduate students "do" history – examine primary documents in the context of secondary literature to build a meaningful narrative about a significant aspect of history or a past incident? Will they need more examples of how to do this, and if so, how will historians provide guidance in understanding the processes that historians have gone through in building their interpretations?

Conclusions

There is compelling evidence that what undergraduate history professors are teaching in the undergraduate classes is potentially of great importance to our society. Arguably, historians as undergraduate teachers are in the best position – best in terms of their disciplinary knowledge, their relative freedom to teach what and how they want, and their strategic position as the primary educators of future history teachers and educators – to convey the kinds of historical understanding that scholars are suggesting "the people" need in a pluralist democracy. Historians as undergraduate teachers need to find ways to strengthen the disciplinary knowledge they communicate through their undergraduate classes. I believe that citizens have a human right to be taught how to think critically about their society, and a political right within our democratic system to learn to think critically about the nation state and other areas of their lives in which they exercise some political control. Too many students emerging from undergraduate classrooms have a view of history so simplified and generalized that the distinct disciplinary strengths of history are in danger of disappearing altogether; along with them disappear the reasons for teaching history to a general audience. The next generation of historians – who, like today's historians, will be teachers and not just writers – need to change that.

NOTES

1 This chapter is the keynote address delivered to the "Where the Archives Ends: A Graduate Student Conference on History and Its Uses," the McGill-Queen's University History Graduate Student Conference, Queen's University, Kingston, 11 March 2011. An earlier, abbreviated

version was published as "Synthesis and Fragmentation: The Case of Historians as Undergraduate Teachers," *Active History*, April 2011, http://activehistory.ca/papers/rsandwell/, accessed 16 March 2014.

2 Shirley H. Engle, "Late Night Thoughts About the New Social Studies," *Social Education* 50, no. 1 (1986): 21, cited in Alan Sears, this volume. On this theme, see also Scott Pollock, this volume; Ruth Sandwell, "History Is a Verb: Teaching Historical Practice to Teacher Education Students," in *New Possibilities for the Past: Shaping History Education in Canada*, edited by Penney Clark (Vancouver: UBC Press, 2011), 224-42; Chad Gaffield, "The Blossoming of Canadian Historical Research: Implications for Policy and Content," in *To the Past: History Education, Public Memory and Citizenship Education in Canada*, edited by Ruth Sandwell (Toronto, University of Toronto Press: 2006), 88-102; Ruth Sandwell, "School History vs. the Historians," *International Journal of Social Education* 30, no. 1 (Spring 2005), 9-17; Peter Seixas, "Parallel Crises: History and the Social Studies Curriculum in the USA," *Journal of Curriculum Studies* 25 (1993): 235–50; and Peter Seixas "The Community of Inquiry as a Basis for Knowledge and Learning: The Case of History," *American Educational Research Journal* 30, no. 2 (1993): 305-24.

3 A few years ago, I contacted every history department in universities across Canada asking for enrolment data relating to one history course only, the survey in Canadian history. I learned that more than 8,000 students per year take this course, in its various forms.

4 For a recent overview of historians' sense that they are retreating from both public history and discussions of history-as-taught, see Ruth Sandwell, "'We Were Allowed To Disagree, Because We Couldn't Agree on Anything': Seventeen Voices in the Canadian Debates Over History Education," in *History Wars and the Classroom: Global Perspectives*, edited by Tony Taylor and Robert Guyver (Charlotte, NC, Information Age Publishing, 2012), 51-76; Stéphane Lévesque, *Thinking Historically: Educating Students for the Twenty-First Century* (Toronto: University of Toronto Press, 2008), especially Chapter 1. There are a number of important exceptions to this, including Desmond Morton, "Canadian History Teaching in Canada: What's the Big Deal?" in *To the Past: History Education, Public Memory and Citizenship in Canada*, edited by Ruth Sandwell (Toronto: University of Toronto Press, 2006), 23-31.

5 There is a large and growing literature on the research into the role, potential and real, of history education for the citizenry of liberal democracies. For a review of these, see Keith C. Barton and Linda S. Levstik, *Teaching History for the Common Good* (New Jersey and London: Lawrence Erlbaum

Associates, 2004). For a discussion of the Canadian literature on the subject, see Ken Osborne, "Teaching History in Schools: A Canadian Debate," *Journal of Curriculum Studies* 35, no. 5 (2003): 585-626.

6 For a discussion of Canadian historians' perceptions of this transformation, see Sandwell, "We Were Allowed to Disagree."

7 See Seixas, "Parallel Crises" and Barton and Levstik, *Teaching History for the Common Good*. Lévesque, *Thinking Historically*, provides a particularly good summary of the literature relating to this point in his introduction.

8 Osborne, "Teaching History in Schools: A Canadian Debate," and Ken Osborne, "To the Past: Why We Need to Teach and Study History," in *To the Past*, edited by Ruth Sandwell, 103-31.

9 Peter Seixas' work in establishing procedural historical thinking as important components of history education at the elementary and secondary level across Canada is the best example of the success of this trend. For an overview of his success, see Peter Seixas, "A Modest Proposal for Change in Canadian History," *Teaching History* 137 (December 2009): 26-30; Sandwell, "We Were Allowed To Disagree."

10 The literature on this topic, national and international, is extensive. For samples of the Canadian discussions, see Sandwell, ed., *To The Past* and Penney Clark, ed., *New Possibilities for the Past: Shaping History Education in Canada* (Vancouver: UBC Press, 2011). Notable exceptions include Desmond Morton, Margaret Conrad, and Gerald Friesen.

11 Peter Lee, "Understanding History" in *Theorizing Historical Consciousness*, edited by Peter Seixas (Toronto: University of Toronto Press, 2004), 154; Peter Lee, "Putting Principles into Practice: Understanding History" in *How Students Learn: History in the Classroom*, edited by M. Suzanne Donovan and John D. Bransford (Washington: The National Academies Press, 2005), 31-77, http://www.nap.edu/openbook/0309089484/html/31.html.

12 Ibid.

13 Tim Stanley looks at a much-used undergraduate history textbook to argue that many of the old assumptions remain. Timothy J. Stanley, "Whose Public? Whose Memory?: Racisms, Grand Narratives and Canadian History" in *To the Past*, edited by Ruth Sandwell, 32-49.

14 For a fuller discussion of this, see G. Williamson McDiarmid and Peter Vinten-Johansen, "A Catwalk across the Great Divide: Redesigning the History Teaching Methods Course," in *Knowing, Teaching, and Learning History: National and International Perspectives*, edited by Peter N. Stearns, Peter Seixas, and Sam Wineburg (New York: New York University Press, 2000), 156-77. For a contrary argument in favour of synthesis and "big

history," see Alan MacEachern, "A Little Essay on Big: Towards a History of Canada's Size," in *Big Country, Big Issues: Canada's Environment, Culture, and History*, a special issue of *Perspectives* 2011 no. 4 (Munich: Rachel Carson Center, 2011), 6-15, http://www.environmentandsociety.org/sites/default/files/2011_4_big_country.pdf, accessed 16 March 2014.

15 Ruth Sandwell, "Reading Beyond Bias: Teaching Historical Practice to Secondary School Students," *McGill Journal of Education*, 38, no. 1 (Winter 2003): 168-86.

16 Peter Lee, "Putting Principles into Practice: Understanding History" in *How Students Learn: History in the Classroom*, and Peter Lee and R. Ashby, "Progression in Historical Understanding in Students Ages 7-14," in *Knowing, Teaching, and Learning History: National and International Perspectives*, edited by Peter Stearns, Peter Seixas, and Sam Wineburg (New York: New York University Press, 2000), 199-222.

17 Sam Wineburg, "On the Reading of Historical Texts: Notes on the Breach Between School and Academy," *American Educational Research Journal* 28, no. 3 (Fall 1991): 495-519.

18 There is a large literature on these studies, summarized nicely in Barton and Levstik, *Teaching History for the Common Good*, and in the Canadian context by Osborne, "To the Past."

19 Isabel Barca, "Prospective Teachers' Ideas about Assessing Different Accounts," *International Journal of Historical Learning, Teaching and Research*, 1, no. 2 (2001), http://centres.exeter.ac.uk/historyresource/journal2/barca.pdf. See also Veronica Boix-Mansilla, "Historical Understanding: Beyond the Past and into the Present," in Stearns, Seixas, and Wineburg, eds., *Knowing, Teaching, and Learning History: National and International Perspectives*.

20 After critically examining historical documents, however, he discovered "one remarkable and unexpected problem ... After three days of this [critical inquiry] activity, the teacher pulled students together to discuss their conclusions ... Each student had an opinion, and they were eager to share. *But none of the opinions had any relationship to the evidence that they had just spent three days evaluating.* Students did not use the evidence to reach conclusions; they were just making up what they thought must have happened." Keith C. Barton, "'I Just Kinda Know': Elementary Students' Ideas about Historical Evidence," *Theory and Research in Social Education*, 25, no. 4 (1997): 415.

21 Chad Gaffield, "Towards the Coach in the History Classroom," *Canadian Issues Thèmes Canadiens* (October/November 2001): 12-14.

6 Canadian History for Teachers: Integrating Content and Pedagogy in Teacher Education

AMY VON HEYKING

Canadian teacher educators, like their international colleagues, have grappled with the complex question of how best to transform history teaching in schools. Curriculum reforms across Canada, grounded in recent research in history teaching, urge a shift away from the transmission of historical information towards the cultivation of historical ways of thinking. These reforms reflect the belief that "history is the most sophisticated way we currently have of knowing about and organizing the past, and that it attempts to meet certain criteria."[1] They require that history teaching facilitate students' ability to reason in the discipline, understand its core concepts, and apply the discipline's criteria in crafting historical questions and assessing the validity of accounts. As Alan Sears indicates, this means that teacher educators will need to reshape powerful cognitive frames and foster new identities[2] so that teachers see themselves as "practitioners of the discipline"[3] and not simply as conduits of historical information.

Researchers have long asserted that an approach to history teaching in schools that emphasizes disciplinary knowledge cannot be implemented simply by requiring social studies student teachers to take more undergraduate history courses.[4] Ruth Sandwell explains that this is largely because those undergraduate courses cannot be relied upon to foster historical thinking or encourage students take up historical questions in critical, active, or interactive ways.[5] As Seixas and Webber demonstrate in this volume, there are considerable challenges associated with fostering a sophisticated understanding of history, particularly within the context of the curriculum and instruction course(s) required of social studies majors in faculties of education.[6] Following Shulman's notion of *pedagogical content knowledge*, and the results of

Wineburg and Wilson's research, history education researchers argue that "history teachers draw upon techniques and understandings unique to the discipline, not upon an amorphous set of instructional tools."[7] The opportunities to enhance student teachers' pedagogical content knowledge, however, are often undermined by structures basic to many teacher education programs that typically see arts or science faculties delivering the "content" of the students' subject major, and the education faculties providing the courses in "pedagogy." This compartmentalization of duties related to history teacher education often means that student teachers are not directly confronted with or forced to reconsider their beliefs about the purpose of history instruction in schools, and the implications of those beliefs on their teaching practice. Student teachers simply do not have multiple or sustained opportunities to develop a robust understanding of relevant historical information, the ways in which historians acquire and structure that information, and how they can make the subject meaningful for K–12 students.

This study drew on recent research on the effectiveness of courses that specifically attend to the development of pedagogical content knowledge. It assumes that the most appropriate contexts in which to develop student teachers' pedagogical content knowledge in history are *history* courses that address all the relevant facets of this knowledge: the facts and concepts of the discipline, the structure and epistemology of the discipline, the preconceptions that children bring to the discipline, and the elements that children find most difficult. According to Fallace, the purpose of such a course "is not to turn preservice teachers into historians, but rather to convey a more accurate view of the epistemological value of history, and to provide tools for more meaningful, authentic instruction."[8] Studies by McDiarmid and Vinten-Johnson, and by Fallace, demonstrate that courses designed and implemented collaboratively by education and history professors can become deeply transformative experiences for student teachers;[9] however, as Fallace argues, "preservice and inservice teachers need the opportunity and the intellectual support to allow the difficult connection between content and pedagogy to develop. Professors from both sides on campus are needed to make this happen."[10]

This project represents my first attempt to work closely with a colleague on the *other side of the campus* to create a course that bridges the content and pedagogy divide. It sought to assess student teachers' cognitive frames regarding history as a discipline and the purpose and nature of history teaching. It also attempted to gauge the effectiveness of addressing pedagogical content knowledge within the context of an undergraduate Canadian history course. Many interesting observations emerged. The course certainly challenged participants' beliefs about the purpose and nature of history as a discipline. The participants demonstrated growth as historical thinkers. At the conclusion of the course, they expressed the belief that the purpose of history pedagogy was to enhance disciplinary thinking, but struggled to design a task that would do so effectively. The course, however, provided me (the researcher and an education professor) and the instructor (a history professor) with a crucial and authentic opportunity to model effective pedagogy, and the student teachers with an experience of developing learning activities that brought to light the complex connection between content and pedagogy. It demonstrated the need for multiple and sustained efforts to build student teachers' understanding and ability to teach for historical thinking.

Goals of the Study

The course featured in this study was a survey of the major events of Canadian history since Confederation. The instructor, a tenured professor in the faculty of arts and science, brought a strong emphasis on historical thinking to her teaching. She required critical analysis of conflicting historical accounts, integrated frequent work with primary sources, and emphasized the importance of understanding the perspectives of historical actors. The instructor and I worked together to plan the course, select appropriate readings, and design assignments that would enhance the opportunities for students to understand the pedagogical implications of emphasizing historical thinking. In this course, which we referred to as "Canadian History for Teachers," we wanted students to receive instruction on epistemological and pedagogical issues as they learned the specific historical content in the course.

As the education researcher, I designed the study that accompanied the course. The study aimed to:

- determine university students' beliefs about the nature and purpose of history instruction at the university, and within the K–12 school system;
- assess the nature and extent of university students' content knowledge and pedagogical content knowledge in history;

- ascertain the impact of a history course designed to integrate epistemological and pedagogical knowledge into the content of post-Confederation Canadian history on students' disciplinary understanding and their beliefs about history teaching and learning.

The history professor was the assigned instructor for the course. While I assisted in the planning of the course, my role was generally restricted to that of researcher. When the instructor was absent I taught two classes, both related to assigned readings on historical thinking and history teaching and learning.[11] I helped design the learning activity in one class, which required that students compare and contrast accounts of the Riel Rebellions (using a set of assigned questions) drawn from seven different school textbooks dating from 1897 to 2009. Course requirements included a review of a scholarly article in history[12] and a final assignment in which the students could either write an analytical essay about one primary source or create a learning activity for a high school classroom using three related primary sources. The final examination was created by the instructor, and included essay questions that required students to address elements of historical thinking such as significance, evidence, and perspective.

Data Collection

There were forty-four students enrolled in History 2720 ("Canada Since 1867"), twenty of whom intended to enter the faculty of education and become classroom teachers. Two students were already in the faculty of education.[13] Thirty-two students participated in the study. The participants completed open-ended questionnaires at the beginning and end of the course. They were asked about the purpose of history instruction at the university and K–12 level and the nature of historians' work. Students also were observed as they engaged in learning activities. Copies of participants' coursework (assignments, examinations) were collected as data. As their final assignment, twelve of the participants chose to select three primary sources and complete a set of learning activities. Seven students participated in one-hour interviews upon completion of the course. This allowed us to explore the impact of the course on their beliefs and understandings regarding the nature of historical inquiry and of history teaching in more depth and detail. What follows is an analysis of data drawn from the questionnaires, assignments, and follow-up interviews with participants.

Understanding History and Historical Thinking

At the outset of the course, in response to the open-ended question-naire, half of the participants (the names of all have been changed) defined history as the study of the past, or as an explanation or inter-pretation of past events. Jennifer, for example, said that, "History is putting these past events in context so one can better understand why such events took place." About one-third of the participants suggested that history implies some selection of past events based on significance. Susan wrote that history "includes events which have impacted a group of people," while Barbara described history as "bigger world or nation changing events." It was interesting that ten participants struggled to distinguish between the concepts of "the past" and "history," arguing that the past includes personal history while history is national, or that the past is more recent and history more remote. Many participants stated that history consists of a grand narrative that defines Canadian identity. For example, Bob insisted, "our history needs to bring us to-gether as a nation." Barbara stated that "I do think it is important for Canadians to learn the closest possible version of the truth. The best way of [sic] Canadians to be proud of their history is to be knowledge-able, meaning we all need to have a similar understanding as to what really happened."

One-third of the participants, at the outset of the study, demonstrated an understanding of the nature of history that was consistent with the third (out of six) stage of Lee and Ashby's scheme of progression in students' ideas about accounts.[14] Like many of the young children in Lee and Ashby's studies, these participants saw a direct correspon-dence between the past and history, seeing accounts as "fixed by the information available."[15] Participants like Danielle described history as "a record of the past." Jerri asserted that "all Canadians should be in-formed of the same information which should be the whole truth." The other two-thirds of participants revealed understandings more in line with Lee and Ashby's fourth stage, acknowledging the interpretive na-ture of history, but attributing this ambiguity to the bias of authors rather than as stemming from a valid viewpoint or the nature of the historical questions asked. Susan argued that Canada's history "will always be told by people who will always have unique opinions and prejudice." Many of these participants pointed specifically to regional variations in "Canada's story," like Catherine who insisted that "differ-ent regions of Canada have different events that shape them."

By the end of the course, most participants had progressed in their understanding of historical accounts, acknowledging the role of the historian in shaping the story of the past. Some, like Rebecca, stayed in a stage-four relativism with regard to historical interpretation: "After our first discussion on Louis Riel I was shocked to realize that I had 'swallowed' historical knowledge without questioning prior to this class. It was really helpful to look at various primary and secondary sources on specific subjects to see the different ways Canada is, and was presented. This knowledge will help me to properly question things such as textbooks and take the information 'with a grain of salt.'" Cory also seemed to demonstrate scepticism rather than articulating an understanding of history as a well-supported argument about the past: "I had never questioned texts before and generally assumed well it's a textbook. It has to be true and accurate. I feel I was naïve and now have a more realistic view of how historians work."

Others, like Victor, were able to identify the skills historians might use in analysing primary sources: "I learned that history is more than just looking at a source and taking for granted that it is true and factual. Backgrounds need to be checked and sources verified." Teri explained: "Historians ask questions about what happened in the past to find out and analyze more information. They keep an open mind to the information they find … they also look at the sources of other historians to determine if these sources are appropriate." Jennifer wrote that the course "taught me to look at sources and decide whether they are valuable and reliable." These participants clearly drew on the criteria the course instructor had stressed in class activities that involved analysing primary sources and in the assigned article review, for which they had been asked to evaluate the value and reliability of the historians' sources. Virtually all the participants in their final questionnaire identified questioning and analysing sources, or the more general development of critical thinking skills, as the most important lessons they had learned about historians' work.

Most participants agreed with Anna, who in describing the work of historians wrote, "a historian is not a passive researcher of the past, but an active participant in reconstructing events that have gone by." Danielle, who had earlier insisted that history was "more about the facts of an event," at the conclusion of the course recognized that historians' thinking skills "allow us to understand why we are learning what we are and why it occurred, not just the facts that we don't know for sure are true, exact, or in full detail." In her final assignment, she analysed Prime Minister John Diefenbaker's 20 February 1959 speech to the House of Commons about terminating the development of the Avro Arrow aircraft. She attended to the historical context of the speech and identified the range of historical questions it raised about Canada's relationship to the United States and the impact of the Cold War on Canada. In other words, she moved away from understanding history as the "facts of the past" towards understanding that historians use evidence to make arguments about the past. Bill's experience of interrogating primary sources throughout the course left him with the understanding "that sources can contain pertinent information on a range of topics beyond what the actual source is presenting/talking about." By the end of the course, therefore, most participants articulated understandings of history more aligned with Lee and Ashby's highest level of progression: "the past as (re-)constructed in answer to questions in accordance with criteria."[16]

Virtually all participants acknowledged that the course played a role in increasing their understanding and appreciation of the interpretive nature of the discipline. Barbara said, "I think the most important thing I learned is that history changes. I learned that as time progresses, our understanding and perspective of history changes." The lesson using the different textbook accounts of Riel clearly had an impact, as many participants mentioned this activity as helping them understand the evolution of historical interpretations. Bill wrote: "The most important thing I have learned is that Canada's interpretation of history (all history) changes over time. Canadian history viewed Riel as a savage and [he] slowly develops into a hero."

Many participants identified the importance of perspective to the work of historians, both in terms of understanding the perspective of historical actors, and in acknowledging how our own perspective shapes historical inquiry. Susan said, "Historical thinking requires historians to place themselves in the shoes of individuals who lived historical events and attempt to understand them, how they felt and why they felt that way," and that "historians must be able to examine historical documents critically without being critical of opinions held at the time under examination." Jodi wrote that the course demonstrated "how historians have to look at multiple perspectives to grasp why certain actors/groups thought/felt/acted the way they did. This class also really demonstrated the importance of recognizing modern perspective and how it differs from the way people thought in the past." In the follow-up interviews at the conclusion of the course, participants stressed the impact of learning activities in which they had struggled to articulate, make sense of, and occasionally defend perspectives they had not previously considered: those of the FLQ during the October Crisis, supporters of Japanese internment, or women who rejected female suffrage. They acknowledged the challenges of, but also the importance of, stepping outside their contemporary world view in making sense of people's actions and attitudes in the past.

What accounts for this shift in participants' understanding of the purpose and nature of history as a discipline? The instructor's pedagogical approach consistently integrated historical thinking as she focused on a survey of events in Canada's past. When she lectured, she often made reference to varying historical interpretations of events or ideas (and the reasons for those interpretations); she made clear connections between past events and current political, economic, and social issues; and she provided illustrations of the beliefs and values of historical actors in order to stress the importance of appropriate historical empathy. About every fourth class was set aside for an interactive learning activity that usually involved analysing primary documents, interpreting scholarly articles that offered conflicting accounts of the same events, or working more directly with elements of what she called "the historian's craft." These were the learning activities to which participants often made reference in their questionnaires and interviews when they identified memorable experiences or explained why their thinking about history and historical thinking had changed.

But if the participants' understandings changed, to what extent did their assignments and examinations actually demonstrate growth in their historical thinking? The first course assignment required students to select a scholarly article written by a historian from a list provided by the instructor. The students were required to analyse the author's argument and assess the primary sources used to support the argument. Many participants were able to summarize the author's argument; however, they struggled to assess the sources, often failing to distinguish between the secondary sources that authors cited to provide the historiographical context for their arguments, and the primary sources that the authors used as evidence to support their claims.

As the course progressed, participants became more familiar with the nature of primary source analysis and had numerous opportunities to practice analysing sources in class, often examining multiple sources that reflected diverse or even conflicting perspectives on specific historical events. These experiences helped participants like Danielle realize:

In using multiple primary sources you play to their strengths and weaknesses giving the best research. By using them together you can assure that you don't have a lack of information or facts, and you will have that many more differing perspectives and views. You have more than one way to check the facts that you are reading and observing and you may able to tell what parts of the event were lacking or left out. Used together the primary sources would give a well-rounded encounter of the event better than a single primary source could.

In her final examination, Rebecca was able to refer to specific documents she had reviewed as the class explored the Conscription Crisis to explain that "by examining the different viewpoints historians can see why the topic was debated so heatedly and can portray the arguments in a valid and fair way." While these participants understood that historians need to examine a range of primary sources that reflect diverse views on a historical issue, they continued to read the sources primarily for the information they could provide, assuming that somehow combining all the information would lead to a valid conclusion.

Other participants were able to move beyond reading the primary sources for information and to interrogate the sources. In his final examination, Addison explained, "When using primary sources it is possible to gain valuable insight into people's perspectives and attitudes. However the goals of the source must be kept in mind when looking for facts. Using these sources in conjunction with others will provide the most reliable base from which to gain the most reliable evidence." His final course assignment included an analysis of an editorial cartoon that was published in the *Vancouver Sun* in 1981. He addressed the source's purpose and intended audience. He also considered to what extent the cartoonist's view might have been consistent with public opinion in British Columbia on the Trudeau government's fiscal policy in the early 1980s. He clearly demonstrated the ability to make appropriate inferences from a primary source.

Anna, too, asked questions about the purpose and audience of her primary source, a 1908 report by W.L. Mackenzie King written while he was deputy minister of labour justifying the exclusion of South Asian immigrants to Canada. Her nuanced analysis questioned "the forthrightness of the report," arguing "King's need to balance Canada's rights as a sovereign nation with her duties as a colony of England places him in a delicate bargaining position that is made more complex by the fact that India is also a colony of Britain." James analysed CBC radio shows from 1942 that described women's contributions to the Royal Canadian Air Force Women's Division. He asked, "But why were these radio shows created? Was it to inform Canadians on the events that were taking place, or to gather recruits for the long war ahead?" He identified how the nature of the arguments made, the personal testimonies, and even the background music were tactics designed to win recruits. Of the thirty-two participants, twenty-five clearly grew in the ability to think like historians as they interrogated their sources, demonstrating skills Sam Wineburg compares to those of prosecuting attorneys: "They did not merely listen to testimony but actively drew it out by putting documents side by side, locating discrepancies, and questioning sources and delving into their conscious and unconscious motives."[17]

Most participants showed an impressive ability to understand and articulate historical perspectives, and all the participants who were interviewed commented that the instructor's consistent emphasis on "perspectives that seemed odd to us" was one of the most engaging elements of the course. One participant said in her interview: "Why would women *not* want the vote? Now I get it." Anna, in her final examination, insisted that the decision to intern Japanese Canadians during World War II "could have made sense at the time." Pointing to "connections and loyalties continuing to exist between Japanese Canadians and their homeland, the incomplete surveillance of the RCMP, and the uncertainty of the times," she concluded that "maybe this issue was not as cut and dry as it seems today." One of the optional final examination questions asked: "If you were going to write a textbook about post-Confederation Canada, what content would you include? What themes would you emphasize? Why?" In his answer, Bill insisted that he would include sources that reflected differing perspectives on every theme he included in the text in order to enhance students' critical thinking skills. One of his examples was: "What did the Government think of the October Crisis? The military? Human rights organizations? Quebecers? Natives? People throughout Canada?" It is significant that in addition to acknowledging the importance of perspective in history he was able to identify potential, relevant voices to include in his collection. In his final examination, James identified specific qualities that would determine or change people's perspectives on historical events: the power they have in society, their loyalties or sense of identity, and the discovery of new information about an event or issue. Participants clearly benefited from the instructor's multiple efforts to engage them with diverse and varying perspectives from the past.

Most impressive were the students who used their historical understanding to consider the ethical dimension of history and make connections to issues that continue to face Canadians, particularly since the instructor rarely made these connections explicit in her lectures. In her final assignment, Rebecca analysed primary sources related to women's suffrage and the Persons Case, and in the learning activity she designed, she asked students to identify what the documents revealed about the creators' views of women's nature and proper role. She then asked them to consider: "What are some ways that society is still gendered?" In her final examination, Barbara argued that racism was at the root of the decision to intern Japanese Canadians, but she went on to say that "the racist perspectives we look back on are still common perspectives in contemporary Canadian society." She called profiling in airport security a prime example of the ways Canadians still make assumptions about people based on race. Though these were not responses common to the majority of students, they demonstrate these participants' efforts to connect an understanding of past events and beliefs to contemporary issues: an example of the contribution historical thinking can make to informed and thoughtful democratic citizenship.

Understanding History Teaching

Was the course equally as successful in enhancing participants' pedagogical knowledge? At the beginning of the course, when asked about the purpose of history instruction, one-third of participants stressed the importance of a national historical narrative that would foster Canadian identity and sense of pride in the country. John wrote, "It is vitally important that Canadians learn the same story of Canada's past … it plays a major role in national unity … Another reason is that when learning history there should only be one story, there should not be a favoured version but rather one totally neutral, objective one." Even participants who acknowledged the importance of fostering critical thinking skills within university history courses did not see that as important or possible within secondary school history classes. Danielle stated: "I think history teaching in university is about the facts as in K–12 schools but it also about understanding reasoning, interpreting, and thinking past just the general facts. There is more about opinion and perspective, not just a one-sided factual story. I also think history in university goes into further depth with the facts than that which you can go in K–12 schools."

When asked at the conclusion of the course, only two participants remained convinced that students in K–12 classrooms could not and should not engage in the same kind of historical thinking that they had just experienced in the course. Linda explained that if such thinking were demanded of students, it could only be "a very limited extent, because K–12 is about acquiring basic knowledge, not about questioning methods." All the other participants now felt differently, such as Miranda, who commented: "Students in K–12 can learn how historians do history from the beginning. Students should learn how historians know certain things; they need to know why they should think a certain way, and knowing how historians arrive at their answers could determine how they will think. This should be taught through critical thinking techniques right from K–12." Brennan agreed, saying, "Looking at more than one side, questioning sources, all types of things could and should be done. Even at a young age I feel this can be true. One problem is it can be time consuming, so for to what extent? As much that can be fit in." James insisted that "historical thinking should be taught. This will help develop critical thinking and an inquisitive attitude."

What accounts for this shift in beliefs about the importance of teaching disciplinary thinking within the context of secondary school history? It is certainly possible that participants felt compelled to express a positive assessment of children's potential to think historically since I led the class through assigned reading that made this argument.[18] When we talked about the reading, I provided teaching suggestions and examples of children's work that demonstrated an ability to determine the significance of historical events, analyse primary sources, and engage in authentic, perspective-taking exercises. Participants who were interviewed, however, attributed the transformation in their thinking to the teaching style of the course instructor. They called the course a "great illustration of how to help students think critically." They felt the course was very engaging because of the emphasis on disciplinary thinking and believed that this approach "would be much more interesting for kids."

The course seemed to enhance participants' appreciation for a hands-on approach to history teaching, but could they apply their new disciplinary understanding to their design of classroom activities for students? First I must acknowledge the generosity of the course instructor in agreeing to include what we called "a pedagogical option" in the final assignment for the course, giving participants the opportunity to design a learning activity for high school students using three primary sources. The instructor and I had numerous discussions about this assignment, including a difficult one when the instructor revealed that she felt the participants who chose to complete learning activities were choosing "the easy option." Her views were entirely consistent with those that Belanger argued are common of most historians: "Developing lesson plans and other curriculum materials becomes something 'less' ... a demonstration of pedagogical technique rather than as a way to show understanding of historical thinking skills."[19] The instructor was concerned that the draft I had written of the assignment requirements was too detailed and directive. I felt that the participants had had very limited instruction on pedagogical issues related to history teaching and would require significant assistance in order to make appropriate pedagogical judgments in their lesson planning. Moreover, because the assignment not only required that they demonstrate historical thinking in their analysis of the sources, but that they apply that thinking in crafting authentic, appropriate teaching activities, I felt the pedagogical option was in fact more intellectually rigorous.

In the end, the assignment requirements were to "conduct your own research to find three primary sources on the same topic. Your 2000-word analysis must include a brief description of each primary source, and a set of questions or a learning activity using those sources that could be used in a classroom setting." Participants were directed to review the four functions of using primary sources in classrooms as outlined by Keith Barton[20] and then answer the question: "Which of those four goals is addressed in your questions/activity, and how does your questions/activity engage students in meaningful and appropriate historical thinking?" They were not required to select specific topics or to identify relevant outcomes from the Alberta Program of Studies in Social Studies. They could craft their activity around any Canadian history topic of interest to them.

The twelve participants who chose this option applied the source analysis skills that they had practised in the course with varying levels of success. Six participants selected sources related to Canada's experience in World War II; two focused on Canadian soldiers in World War I; two chose documents related to Aboriginal residential schools; one addressed women's suffrage; and one worked with documents related to the National Energy Policy of the early 1980s.

Three of the participants had difficulties in selecting sources that were thematically related or could be used to focus on a coherent historical question. Tanya chose a letter written by a Canadian soldier during World War II, a poem written by a soldier about Dieppe, and a photograph of Ottawa high school students sorting mail in November 1943. Not only did she fail to articulate the issue or question that these three disparate sources addressed, her learning activity required students to write a letter or diary entry describing their current lives to place in a time capsule, an activity with a remote connection to the sources at best. Barbara likewise selected a father's 1943 letter to his son serving with Canadian forces in Italy, an excerpt from a memoir written by a Canadian veteran about his experiences during the post-war occupation of Germany, and a photograph of a Canadian soldier during World War II. While these participants chose sources from the same general time period or associated with a broad topic, the fact that there was no single, coherent historical question that they addressed made designing an authentic learning activity problematic.

Even though some had difficulty selecting appropriate sources, participants were generally successful in analysing their primary sources and providing adequate historical context. They drew information from the sources, but most also addressed why and for whom the source was created, identified what position the source seemed to take on an issue, and compared and contrasted the perspectives reflected in the sources. These were the kinds of questions the course instructor had often included in their primary source analysis exercises. Brennan, for example, noted that the CBC television clip about residential schools he selected was intended to give its audience, Canadian viewers in the 1950s, a positive impression of the purpose and impact of these schools. He paired this clip with a radio interview with residential school survivors. Bob compared and contrasted a Canadian War Records Office report on the Battle of Vimy Ridge with an account written by a British journalist, noting "the advantage of this is that seeing two different perspectives on the battle from two separate countries provides a good comparison."

Some participants, however, struggled with crafting authentic and meaningful learning activities using the documents. Tanya designed a task that required students to work at stations examining the letter, poem, and photo from World War II: "while at each station, each student would have to answer the five Ws." Addison, too, focused his activity around drawing information about the National Energy Policy from the sources, rather than interrogating the sources. However, students in his activity were to use the information they gathered to brainstorm inquiry questions in order to further explore the purpose and impact of the NEP. This was certainly an appropriate strategy to motivate historical inquiry, which is one of the purposes for using primary sources in classrooms that Barton outlines. Others succeeded in crafting questions that would help high school students interrogate the sources. Riley, for example, asked students to read Mackenzie King's address to Canadians on 5 September 1939 and consider: "What was Mackenzie King's tone in this document and why is it that way? Why would it be important to state that Canada is acting as a free nation?"

The participants focused their learning activities around the elements of historical thinking that the instructor had stressed in the class, particularly historical perspective. Unfortunately, in their attempts to encourage students' emotional connection to or appreciation of the historical event or phenomenon, they often asked students to engage in activities that would actually encourage presentism and undermine the cultivation of appropriate historical empathy. For example, in Brennan's lesson he asked students to examine a photograph of residential school students: "Examining a photograph of a residential school class the students are asked to place themselves in the spots one of the students in the photograph [sic]. Using their list of characteristics and experiences which make up who they are, they are to imagine what it would be like to be forced into a school like the residential schools." Catherine asked students to examine a World War I soldier's letter home and a photograph of a trench at the front from the perspective of someone with a relative fighting overseas: "The students will need to write back to their brother/father/cousin at the frontlines voicing their appreciation and why they are appreciative." Riley asked students to respond to a newspaper article written by a retired military officer in 1940 because "Canadians are a proud people and this is displayed here. The article can be used as a way to show the patriotism of Canadians in wanting to have a bigger role in the war." The participants might easily have been redirected towards strategies and questions that would help high school students recognize and take more authentic historical perspectives, but the course instructor and I agreed that I would not provide any assistance to the participants who chose this assignment.

Some participants successfully asked students to analyse the sources and engage in perspective-taking exercises. Significantly, the most successful participant completing this assignment was actually in the final year of a five-year combined bachelor of arts/bachelor of education degree program. Jodi had already completed the required social studies curriculum and instruction courses in the faculty of education and two rounds of student teaching before enrolling in this Canadian history course. This was her last semester of coursework before completing the final student teaching internship required by the program. Her final assignment reflected a fundamentally different way of engaging high school students in historical thinking than the other participants. Her use of primary sources was authentic, and her questions and activities reflected a deep understanding of curricular outcomes and the nature of high school classrooms and students.

Jodi selected three sources related to residential schooling: a photograph of residential schoolchildren in southern Alberta in 1900; a video clip celebrating the opportunities available to Aboriginal children in residential schools that aired on CBC television in 1955; and a radio interview with residential school survivors recorded by CBC radio in 1993. She drew on her student teaching experiences to acknowledge that high school students would have preconceptions and misconceptions about this topic, so she structured her learning activity to give students the chance first to examine the photograph and make observations that would reveal their prior understandings. The teacher would be provided with a valuable opportunity to address misconceptions and to direct further study by helping students to craft powerful questions. She asked students to consider the purpose and audience of the CBC television clip, explaining that "rather that stating the piece is simply inaccurate, students need to look at perspective and consider what the piece is trying to accomplish, and to whom it is speaking." Concluding with the radio interview provided students with a contrasting perspective; students were made aware of the legacy of the abuse that many Aboriginal children suffered. As Jodi stressed, "only when the sources are combined and contrasted can we begin to fit the perspectives together to create a more complete picture of residential schooling."

Most impressive was Jodi's follow-up activity: "Having answered so many questions about why residential schools were established, and what some of the consequences were and why, we cannot leave our learning at 1993." Jodi went on to describe a concluding activity in which students would research how the issue has been addressed by governments, or examine organizations that have been established to assist residential school survivors. By putting a controversial historical topic into contemporary social and political context, Jodi thoughtfully attended to the role of historical thinking within the context of the high school social studies program, and met her own goal for history instruction: "students are shown that understanding history has an essential role in changing the world of today." By any measure, Jodi showed impressive disciplinary knowledge and crafted meaningful, authentic opportunities for her students to develop as historical thinkers. She brought many complex understandings together to demonstrate her pedagogical content knowledge.

Conclusion

Examining all the data, I initially came to the same conclusion that Belanger did after her first experience teaching her "American History for Educators" course: "Clearly, teaching students how to think historically did not necessarily teach them how to teach historical thinking."[21] Upon reflection, however, I concluded that the course had enhanced participants' historical thinking, engaged them in an active and interactive study of Canadian history, and encouraged them to examine their own beliefs about the nature and purpose of history teaching. The fact that participants struggled in creating learning activities that would facilitate growth in high school students' historical thinking indicates the difficulty and complexity of the task. In the same way that we could not expect children to be sophisticated historical thinkers after their first exposure to history, it would have been unreasonable to expect all participants to demonstrate sophisticated pedagogical content knowledge after this single history course.

The "Canadian History for Teachers" course did not perfect – but it certainly enhanced – participants' content knowledge of post-Confederation Canadian history and their epistemological understandings of history as a discipline. Their coursework reflected the consistent attention the instructor had given to principles of historical thinking, specifically analysing primary source evidence, examining historical perspective, and attending to multiple narratives about Canada's past. The course was a powerful trigger for raising questions and confronting issues related to teaching that the participants had not previously considered, particularly the purpose of history instruction and the opportunities history provides for enhancing students' critical thinking. The participants clearly benefited from the opportunity to consider the cognitive and pedagogical implications of the subject matter they were learning.

While six of twelve participants crafted acceptable history learning activities, it is significant that the participant with the most education courses seemed best able to bridge the content and pedagogy divide and to use her new historiographical and epistemological knowledge to craft meaningful history learning opportunities. McDiarmid also found in his study that the student in his historiography seminar who had already completed education courses was the only one to consider not just how he might teach history, but how he might best help his students learn history.[22] In other words, this student, like Jodi, more effectively bridged the content/pedagogy divide because he could realistically anticipate having to teach this content in the future. This purposeful anticipation of teaching meant that Jodi could create questions and craft activities that drew on her emerging teacher knowledge of the nature of high school learners and the structure of an effective lesson. She drew on her subject matter knowledge and gave an authentic demonstration of pedagogical content knowledge. As well, she was able to ground her teaching activity in a clear curricular mandate.

Other participants who had completed an "Introduction to Teaching" course required of students prior to entering the faculty of education were able to articulate a clear pedagogical purpose in their topic selection for the learning activity and to identify a learning outcome that they hoped their students would meet. Their stated purposes, however, were generally naive or they were actually antithetical to the goal of enhancing historical thinking, such as being commemorative. Catherine, for example, in her follow-up interview explained that she created a teaching activity about the experience of Canadian soldiers in World War I, because she "wanted students to appreciate the sacrifices these men made for them. We need to give students a chance to celebrate these men outside of Remembrance Day." On the other hand, Rebecca spoke to the significance of women's suffrage and the insights it could provide for current discussions about and challenges to human rights. Like Jodi, she sought to help high school students appreciate the relevance of the past in shaping and challenging contemporary beliefs and values.

All the participants who were in or who planned to apply to the BEd program (half the students in the course) valued the epistemological and pedagogical insights they gained through the course. In follow-up interviews, participants commented that the instructor's discussion of her teaching philosophy and her explanations for why she chose particular teaching strategies encouraged them to think about how they would teach the material, even as they were learning about events in Canada's past: "I found myself thinking, how would I teach this?" They described their final assignment (to create learning activities) as being much more interesting and relevant than the essays they were typically required to write in history courses.

These findings affirm Belanger's assertion that history professors must take their role in history teacher education seriously. She argues:

> By not providing sufficient opportunities for our students to produce non-traditional historical scholarship, we run the risk of conveying to our future teachers the idea that historians do not truly value teaching and do not see it as an intellectually rigorous activity, one that requires the same level of discipline and understanding as original scholarship.[23]

It follows that if history professors provide opportunities for student teachers to develop lesson plans or teaching materials, professors acknowledge the complexity and importance of teaching. By making clear their own efforts to "do history" in their teaching, they empower student teachers to acknowledge the rigour and depth of disciplinary knowledge that is required to teach effectively. The opportunity to create teaching materials, and specific opportunities for pedagogical reasoning, must occur many times if history teacher education is truly going to be a transformative experience for our student teachers. Howard Gardner asserts that disciplinary thinking can develop if teachers challenge the misconceptions students have about the content and method of the discipline; provide rich opportunities for students to "do the discipline"; and provide many strategies for approaching the discipline in ways that attend to multiple learning styles.[24] "Canadian History for Teachers" began this process but also proved that the effort must be sustained and creative.

These findings suggest that if we are going to provide multiple opportunities for student teachers to develop their pedagogical content knowledge, the typical pattern of teacher education programs may be problematic. Most are after-degree programs – ones that direct students to complete curriculum and instruction (i.e., pedagogy) courses after their "content" courses. A better history teacher program may be one that is more interdisciplinary, fostering close collaboration among colleagues in education faculties and history departments. Students would complete courses in curriculum and instruction earlier in their programs, and return to their history courses with the opportunity to grapple with issues of pedagogy. Naturally, this would require professors from both sides of the campus to collaborate on course content and delivery, but, as this small study demonstrates, this is certainly possible.

NOTES

1 Peter Lee, "From National Canon to Historical Literacy," in *Beyond the Canon: History for the Twenty-First Century*, edited by Maria Grever and Siep Stuurman (New York: Palgrave Macmillan, 2007), 50.

2 Alan Sears, "Moving from the Periphery to the Core: The Possibilities for Professional Learning Communities in History Teacher Education," this volume, p. 12.

3 Ibid., p. 13.

4 See for example, G. Williamson McDiarmid, "Understanding History for Teaching: A Study of the Historical Understanding of Prospective Teachers," in *Cognitive and Instructional Processes in History and the Social Sciences*, edited by Mario Carretero and James F. Voss (Hillsdale, NJ: Lawrence Erlbaum Associates, 1994), 159-85.

5 See Ruth Sandwell, "On Historians and Their Audiences: An Argument for Teaching (and Not Just Writing) History," this volume.

6 Peter Seixas, "Student Teachers Thinking Historically," *Theory and Research in Social Education* 26, no. 3 (1998): 310-41.

7 Thomas Fallace and Johann N. Neem, "Historiographical Thinking: Towards a New Approach to Preparing History Teachers," *Theory and Research in Social Education* 33, no. 3 (2005): 331.

8 Thomas D. Fallace, "Historiography and Teacher Education: Reflections on an Experimental Course," *The History Teacher* 42, no. 2 (2009): 217.

9 G. Williamson McDiarmid and Peter Vinten-Johansen, "A Catwalk across the Great Divide: Redesigning the History Teaching Methods Course," in *Knowing, Teaching, and Learning History: National and International Perspectives*, edited by Peter N. Stearns, Peter Seixas, and Sam Wineburg (New York: New York University Press, 2000), 156-77; Fallace, "Historiography and Teacher Education," 205-22.

10 Fallace, "Historiography and Teacher Education," 217-18.

11 The assigned readings were Peter Seixas and Carla Peck, "Teaching Historical Thinking," in *Challenges and Prospects for Canadian Social Studies*, edited by Alan Sears and Ian Wright (Vancouver: Pacific Educational Press, 2004), 109-17; and Robert B. Bain, "Into the Breach: Using Research and Theory to Shape History Instruction," in *Knowing, Teaching, and Learning History*, edited by Peter N. Stearns, Peter Seixas, and Sam Wineburg (New York: New York University Press, 2000), 331-52.

12 For this article review assignment, the students selected a scholarly history article from a list provided by the instructor. One of the articles was my own, "Fostering a Provincial Identity: Two Eras in Alberta Schooling,"

Canadian Journal of Education 29, no. 4 (2006): 1127-56. Because we were attempting to model the synergistic relationship between doing history and teaching history, the instructor decided that it was important for the students in the course to realize that the education researcher in their midst was also a historian of education.

13 Students at our university can complete a two-year BEd after an approved undergraduate degree, or complete a combined degrees program (BA/BEd) in five years.

14 Peter Lee and Rosalyn Ashby, "Progression in Historical Understanding among Students Ages 7-14," in *Knowing, Teaching, and Learning History*, edited by Peter N. Stearns, Peter Seixas, and Sam Wineburg (New York: New York University Press, 2000), 199-222.

15 Ibid., 212.

16 Ibid.

17 Sam Wineburg, *Historical Thinking and Other Unnatural Acts* (Philadelphia: Temple University Press, 2001), 77.

18 Peter Seixas and Carla Peck, "Teaching Historical Thinking," in *Challenges and Prospects for Canadian Social Studies*, edited by Alan Sears and Ian Wright (Vancouver: Pacific Educational Press, 2004), 109-17.

19 Elizabeth Belanger, "How Now? Historical Thinking, Reflective Teaching, and the Next Generation of History Teachers," *The Journal of American History* 97, no. 4 (2011): 1080.

20 See Keith C. Barton, "Primary Sources in History: Breaking Through the Myths," *Phi Delta Kappan* 86, no. 10 (2005): 745-53.

21 Belanger, "How Now? Historical Thinking, Reflective Teaching, and the Next Generation of History Teachers," 1083.

22 McDiarmid, "Understanding History for Teaching," 177-8.

23 Belanger, "How Now? Historical Thinking, Reflective Teaching, and the Next Generation of History Teachers," 1080.

24 Howard Gardner, *Changing Minds* (Boston: Harvard Business School Press, 2006), 139-40.

PART THREE

History and Social Studies Teacher Education Programs in Canada

7 What Is the Use of the Past for Future Teachers? A Snapshot of Francophone Student Teachers in Ontario and Québec Universities

STÉPHANE LÉVESQUE

What role does the past play in the lives of history student teachers? Do they see teachers as reliable sources of information about the past? How does history help define their teaching practice? Student teachers face a critical task. Throughout their history education programs, they are encouraged by their professors to nurture a professional learning community and develop as practitioners of the discipline. At the same time, they eagerly venture into the practice of the classroom where issues of acculturation, conformity, discipline, and efficiency often put them on an outbound trajectory, as if the domains of history and schooling were two mutually exclusive communities. Barton and Levstik note that this often means that "what we do as teacher educators has little influence on their [teachers'] classroom practice."[1] Other studies have confirmed the limited impact of pre-service education on teachers' beliefs and practice teaching.[2]

There are many reasons for this puzzling state of affairs. A major principle emerging from this collection is that people's ideas about history shape their future understanding and use of the past. As Sears (this volume) observes, "a clear lesson from the cognitive revolution is that teachers come to the teaching of history with preconceived and powerful ideas of what the discipline is and how it should be taught, and any approaches advocated in pre-service methods courses or in-service educational opportunities will be filtered through those frames."[3]

Another related principle supported by ample research is that knowing history is more complex and challenging than mastering discrete historical bits.[4] Disciplinary content and habits of minds are deeply counterintuitive.[5] They require generous doses of methodical learning and regulated practice. In order for teachers to partake in a professional learning community, they must be exposed to and engaged in the process of doing history. "Engaging teachers in communities of practice that actually do history," Sears contends, "has the greatest potential to break down the resistances of long-standing cognitive frames and develop the kind of complex disciplinary understanding necessary for fostering historical thinking."[6] Universities, and faculties of education in particular, are supposed to educate students in the arcana of the disciplines, to introduce them to what historians do and how they think about the past. But do they? To what extent is teacher education succeeding in introducing future generation of teachers to historians' ways of thinking?

This is where the concept of "historical consciousness" helps connect these two principles. First discussed in German literature some forty years ago, the concept is now common in the fields of history and collective memory. However, as Laville observes, historical consciousness "is hard to pin down. It is even less clear what role it might play in relation to the teaching of history."[7] For the purpose of this study, historical consciousness can be defined as a mode of *temporal experience*, *historical interpretation*, and *life orientation*. For Rüsen, temporal experience entails the ability to search and look at past relics, while historical interpretation and orientation provide the abilities to bridge time (past, present, and future) and utilize interpretations for personal life decisions – what he calls a "meaning-creating activity" of the mind.[8] The function of history, from the perspective of historical consciousness, is to act as a primary mode of orientation in present life situations in reference to a usable past.[9] History becomes a temporal frame, a sort of intimate mirror "into which the present peers in order to learn something about its future."[10] It is this notion of historical consciousness that helps us to understand the experience and context in which learners operate when they look at and make use the past (and its residua) in their own lives. Just as historians explore and construct historical narratives based on accepted theories and forms of representations, non-historians' own ideas about history inform their representations and understanding of the past. If one wishes to know how teachers conceive of the discipline, it becomes imperative to venture into their minds and explore their prior knowledge and ideas about history and the profession.

This exploratory study on student teachers and historical consciousness is grounded in this theoretical framework. For over a decade, international scholars in the United States, Australia, and Western Europe have been investigating the collective memories and historical consciousness of youth and adults.[11] They have provided the public and the scholarly community with a more robust understanding of how people "use and think about the past."[12] The impacts of these studies are diverse and broad reaching. Here in Canada, they have led to significant research initiatives, including Charland's comparative study on history, identity, and citizenship among French Canadian students in Montréal and Toronto and Létourneau's on Québec history and youth.[13] It is perhaps the recent pan-Canadian survey led by Létourneau and his team, *Canadians and Their Pasts*, that provides the most comprehensive review of people's understanding and use of history. Using a detailed questionnaire with a representative sample of nearly 3,000 adult Canadians across the country and in both official languages, *Canadians and Their Pasts* offers powerful evidence that "no matter what its source, the extent of the public's engagement with the past in Canada and elsewhere is remarkable, suggesting that historical consciousness is alive and well."[14] As comprehensive as it is, *Canadians and Their Pasts* presents no specific data on prospective teachers. One is thus left to extrapolate from the findings to this particular educational population. In 1998, Seixas already had noticed this gap in the research literature and alerted his colleagues to the importance of studying "student teachers thinking historically."[15]

Building on the national examination *Canadians and Their Pasts*, this small-scale study looks at the ideas that some francophone student teachers had about history and education as they were completing their teacher education degrees in the provinces of Ontario and Québec during the academic year 2009–10.[16] Inspired by the wide-ranging questionnaire of Létourneau et al., this study investigates various aspects of historical consciousness, which is defined by use of the past, understanding and use of sources, significance of the past, and conception of history education. Voluntary participants (n = 79) enrolled in teacher education programs (history didactics) from three Canadian universities (one in Ontario, two in Québec) completed a ten-page (sixty-question), multiple-choice questionnaire on their understanding and use of history. The questionnaire was presented to all BEd history students in their history didactics courses during the 2009 fall session.[17] Of the total number of student teachers present in class, 79 participants (47 in Ontario, 32 in Québec) returned the completed questionnaire. More specifically, 57 per cent were female and 43 per cent male. The great majority of participants (79 per cent) were born between 1980 and 1990. Of the total, 50 per cent were born in Québec, 37 per cent in

Ontario, 4 per cent in other provinces, and 8 per cent in foreign countries. More specifically, 33 per cent considered themselves "Québécois," 14 per cent "Franco-Ontarian," 14 per cent "Canadian," and 11 per cent "French Canadian" (see Figure 7.1 for results by subgroup).[18] In terms of education, 81 per cent had an undergraduate degree and 15 per cent a master's degree. Of the total, 63 per cent had taken ten or more history courses at the university level (see Figure 7.2).[19] As might be expected, the limited number of participants in the study and the unbalanced number of respondents per institution make it difficult to generalize from the findings. Adapting a large-scale measuring instrument to this small student population is a significant challenge. A section of the conclusion addresses this point.

Findings

Uses of the Past

Contrary to popular belief – but consistent with Canadian and international findings – student teachers from this study have extensive engagement with the past. In many instances, the intensity of their activities is greater than the Canadian average. In response to the questions dealing with what they have done in the last twelve months, 100 per cent indicated that they had watched historical movies, 98 per cent had looked at old photographs, 97 per cent had used the Internet for historical purposes, 93 per cent had read history books (excluding university textbooks), and 92 per cent had visited museums (see Figure 7.3). The least popular activities were working on a movie or photo album/personal journal (42 per cent said no), saving important objects (28 per cent said no), and working on a family tree (77 per cent said no). Significantly fewer student teachers engaged in the last two activities compared to the respondents in the study *Canadians and Their Pasts* (74 per cent in that study indicated they had preserved objects, and 57 per cent had worked on family history).

When looking at the level of intensity, 72 per cent used the Internet ten times or more for historical purposes, 62 per cent read more than three historical novels and 46 per cent visited more than three museums in the last twelve months (see Figure 7.4). Age could be an important factor in explaining these results. As the majority of student participants are in their twenties, they spend more time doing activities

Figure 7.1: Ethnic origins (in percentage by subgroup)

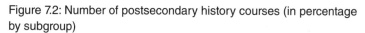

Figure 7.2: Number of postsecondary history courses (in percentage by subgroup)

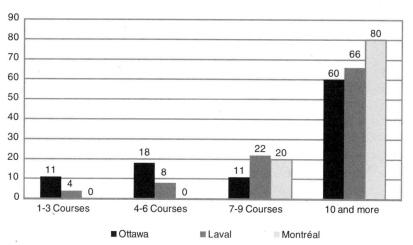

Figure 7.3: Uses of the past (activities done in the last twelve months in percentage)

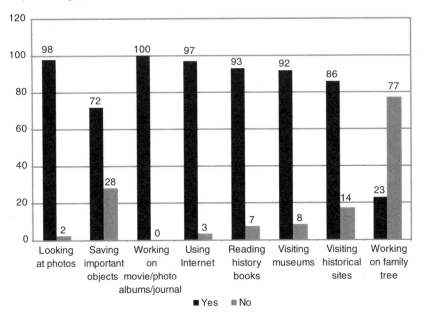

Figure 7.4: Frequency for uses of the past (in percentage per category)

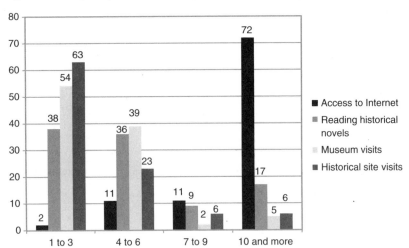

in line with youth culture (watching movies and surfing the Internet) and have fewer opportunities to gather and preserve the past. This is a significant level of historical engagement.

Participating in activities dealing with the past affects people's sense of connection to history. Other studies have documented this "presence of the past" in the consciousness of citizens. Canadian and US findings clearly show that what matters most to people is the personal and intimate past.[20] Respondents feel most connected to history when they encounter it in family stories, social gatherings, and celebrations. It is also this intimate past that appears to be most significant to people in daily life situations. Two-thirds of those in the *Canadians and Their Pasts* survey, for example, indicated that the history of their family was the past that was most important to them; however, less than half (44 per cent) rated Canada's past as being very important.[21] Results from the student teachers are more balanced (see Figure 7.5). If 81 per cent claim to be "very interested" in history in general, the difference in scores between the family past (53 per cent were "very interested" in their family history) and collective past (52 per cent were "very interested" in their province's history) is insignificant. Respondents feel almost equally interested in the history of their family and the histories of their province or country. There is only a slight difference between interest in provincial history (52 per cent) and Canadian history (46 per cent). This variation is most perceptible in the Laval subgroup, which rated provincial history first in terms of the history they were most interested in (64 per cent), family history second (55 per cent), and Canadian history third (46 per cent). This is to say, then, that participants in this study do not mainly feel connected to history through intimate encounters. While these are very important to them, the collective past of their community, whether "community" is understood in provincial or national terms, is also central to their sense of historical significance. In a way, this finding supports the previous results on the uses of the past (Figure 7.3). Student participants were least likely to engage in activities that pertained to personal and intimate history, such as working on a family tree, preserving objects, or creating family albums.

Understanding of Sources

The second section of our survey looked at participants' understanding of the sources of historical information. The trustworthiness of sources is important to consider because it helps us understand how people

Figure 7.5: Interest in various types of history (in percentage by option)

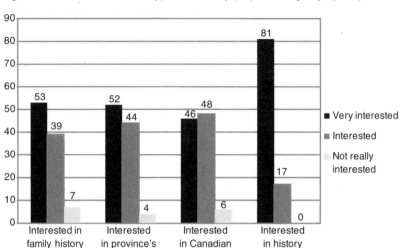

value or locate authority to convey truth in history. The Canadian and US surveys both discovered that the historical sources people trust most are museums and their artefacts, followed by history books and personal/family stories. Teachers, on the contrary, are considered a very reliable source by only 30 per cent of Canadian respondents. Despite its accessibility, the Internet is perceived by citizens as one of the least reliable historical sources (8 per cent of respondents rated it as "very reliable").

What do student teachers think about the trustworthiness of sources, including teachers? Results (see Figure 7.6) indicate, unsurprisingly, that the most reliable source for them is "historians" (48 per cent responded "very reliable") followed by "historical museums" (46 per cent responded "very reliable") and "historical sites" (38 per cent responded "very reliable"). Similarly to the general population, the Internet was considered very reliable by only a minority (4 per cent) of participants, although many (46 per cent) indicated that they thought reliability depended on the websites. Interestingly, student teachers rated "teachers" as less trustworthy (10 per cent responded "very reliable") than history textbooks (23 per cent responded "very reliable"), but indicated in greater proportion (64 per cent) that history teachers were generally reliable sources about the past. No significant discrepancy was found between the three subgroups on this aspect of

Figure 7.6: Trustworthiness of sources about the past (in percentage)

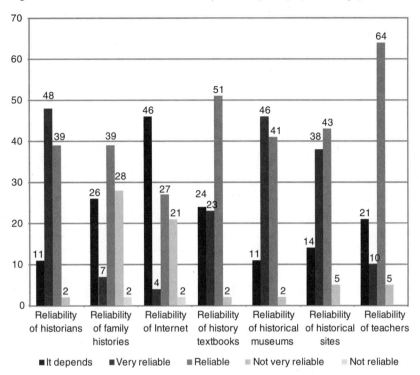

historical consciousness. Equally interesting, it is the family stories category that received the highest score (28 per cent) for being "not very reliable" sources of information. Again, this represents a significant departure from both the Canadian and US surveys, but it shows consistency with previous findings on the use and significance of the intimate past. Student teachers do not think family accounts are very trustworthy ways of knowing about the past. On the contrary, they see official realms of history (museums, historical sites, and historians) as more reliable sources to consult.

Perceptions of History Education

The last aspect of our study looked at school history and education. More specifically, participants had to answer questions pertaining to the rationale and goals of history, the importance of various fields of history, the merit of teaching methods and value of instructional resources, and their confidence as a teacher. On the question regarding rationale for history in school, participants offered mixed responses, but there was only a 7 per cent difference between the first and fourth options (see Figure 7.7).

A total of 26 per cent indicated "identity formation" as the rationale for including history in school. This was followed closely by "citizenship education" (22 per cent), "moral and critical thinking" (21 per cent), and "historical thinking" (19 per cent). Only "multicultural education" received a significantly lower score (10 per cent) from participants. Differences emerged between subgroups. The two Québec populations ranked "citizenship education" much higher than did the overall average (34 per cent for Laval and 42 per cent for Montréal) but placed "multicultural education" significantly below the average (7 per cent for Laval and 1 per cent for Montréal). This finding seems to be a direct effect of the new Québec curriculum, which places great emphasis on the twin concepts of "history and citizenship education." In Ontario, on the contrary, participants' focus on "historical thinking," "moral and critical education," and "multicultural education" is slightly higher than the average (23 per cent, 22 per cent, and 14 per cent respectively).

Participants also rated the core competencies that they believe school history should develop in the students. Competencies, in the field of didactics, are *savoir-faire* needed to perform a given task in a competent manner. Three dominant competencies emerge as being the most significant to participants in the findings (see Figure 7.8). They are, in order of significance, understanding the present (36 per cent); comprehending key events and actors (*histoire événementielle*, 28 per cent); and doing historical inquiry (27 per cent). Despite the extensive inroads that on-line simulations, games, and historical films have made in popular culture, only 1 per cent of participants felt it is important to use these in teaching history in schools. Understanding factual knowledge about the past is also a relatively unimportant goal for student teachers. In all three subgroups, student teachers overwhelmingly considered "understanding the present" to be the most important competency to develop in students.

When asked what particular aspects of the past should be taught in school history (see Figure 7.9), 39 per cent indicated that they believe social history is the most important field, followed by political history (24 per cent) and contemporary history (21 per cent). Surprisingly, comparative and global history (13 per cent) and military history (1 per

Figure 7.7: Rationale for history in Canadian schools (in percentage)

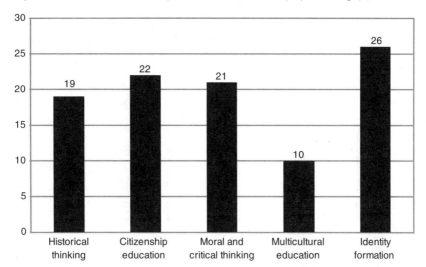

cent) received significantly lower scores. Some differences appear between subgroups, with Laval participants placing political history first (32 per cent) and Montréal participants placing comparative and global history third (with 21 per cent).

Student teachers navigate between two worlds: the scholastic world of teacher education and the practical world of the classroom. They learn about theory and practice at the university and hopefully apply these during their practicum experiences in school. In this context, what teaching strategies do they think are most relevant to school history? What resources best support their approaches? According to the findings (see Figure 7.10), the two dominant strategies are the lecture (26 per cent) and research project (25 per cent). These are followed by group activities (19 per cent), cable TV/film education (15 per cent), and computer simulations and games (9 per cent).

When asked to choose the most relevant teaching resources (see Figure 7.11), participants selected primary source archives (28 per cent), followed by textbooks (19 per cent), movies (19 per cent), and museums (15 per cent). Surprisingly, the Internet, computer simulations and games, and the media received less than 10 per cent each, making them relatively unpopular teaching resources for participants.

Figure 7.8: Historical competencies to develop in school history (in percentage)

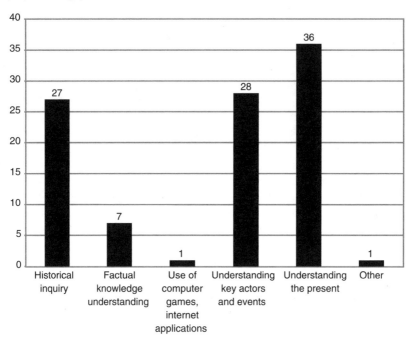

While the three most preferred school teaching approaches are the same for the Ottawa and Montréal subgroups, the selection order is different for Laval participants. For them, the lecture is still the most popular teaching strategy (30 per cent), following by group work (25 per cent), cable TV/film education (20 per cent), and research projects (16 per cent). In terms of resources (see Figure 7.11), again, the first two results are similar for Ottawa and Montréal but different for Laval. Instead of choosing archives followed by textbooks, participants in the Laval subgroup ranked historical movies first (33 per cent) followed by textbooks (28 per cent). Archives came in third, with 18 per cent of responses. It is the Ottawa subgroup that placed the highest focus on archival records (36 per cent), followed closely by Montréal at 28 per cent.

Figure 7.9: Fields of study in school history (in percentage)

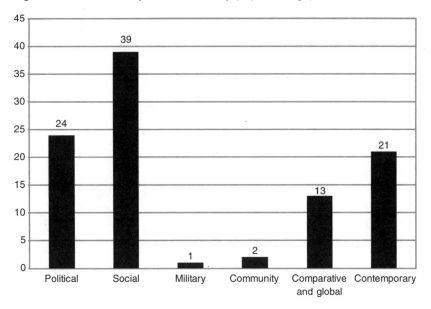

Figure 7.10: Preferred teaching strategies in school history (in percentage)

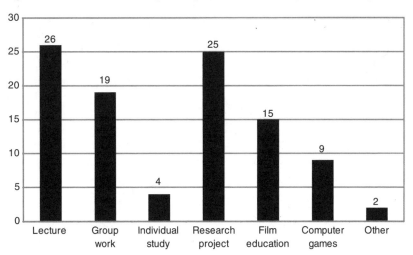

Figure 7.11: Most pertinent teaching resources (in percentage)

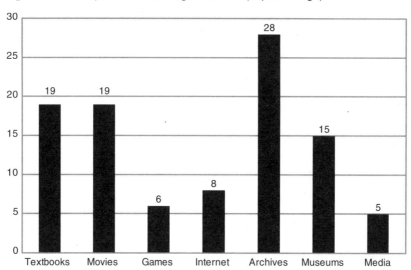

The last questions of our survey asked student teachers to rate their self-confidence in teaching school history (see Figure 7.13). Very few participants (16 per cent) indicated that they have a "very thorough" knowledge of history, in response to the question, "How would you qualify your disciplinary knowledge?" (see Figure 7.12). The great majority (66 per cent) believed that they have a "thorough" knowledge of the discipline, with a minority (18 per cent) declaring that they have a "not very thorough" understanding. It is the participants from Ottawa who indicated in higher number a "not very thorough" knowledge of history (24 per cent), while the Laval subgroup had the lowest percentage (9 per cent) of responses that fell into this category. Results from Figure 7.12 are correlated with those in Figure 7.2, showing that student teachers who have taken many history courses are more likely to declare that they have a thorough knowledge of history

Finally, in answer to the question, "What is your level of confidence in teaching history to students?" (see Figure 7.13), 62 per cent of participants reported having confidence in their ability. Almost equal numbers either felt "very confident" (17 per cent) or "not very confident" (19 per cent). Only 2 per cent indicated that they were "not confident" in teaching history. As in the previous table, variations emerge between

Figure 7.12: Knowledge of history (in percentage by subgroup)

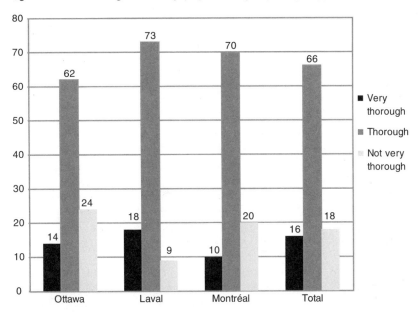

subgroups. This time, however, it is the Ottawa participants who feel the most confident (26 per cent) and the Laval ones the least confident (5 per cent) in teaching history to students. These results suggest that there is no clear correlation between students' self-reported knowledge of history and their level of confidence in teaching history. Other studies have documented the fundamental differences between "content knowledge" and "pedagogical content knowledge."[22] Mere disciplinary expertise, as Shulman found, "is likely to be as useful pedagogically as content-free skill."[23] To be both competent and confident, history teachers must perform a didactic transposition of the subject for pedagogical purposes. Disciplinary knowledge is a necessary but insufficient condition for successful practice teaching.

Discussion and Conclusion

What can we conclude from this study on student teachers and historical consciousness? It is perhaps useful to remind the reader that the exploratory nature of the study makes it difficult to generalize

Figure 7.13: Level of confidence in teaching history to students (in percentage by subgroup)

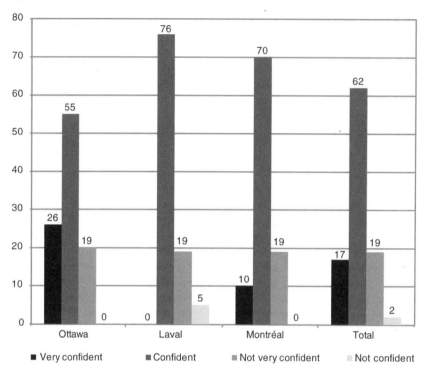

these findings to the prospective teacher population, even in French Canadian universities. Only replicating the methods used in *Canadians and Their Pasts* would allow for this. Also, the fact that teacher education programs vary considerably between provinces renders comparative analysis problematic at this point. The survey should be conducted either as an entrance instrument when students start their programs or as an exit assessment at the end of their BEd degree when all candidates have completed their course requirements and have engaged in practice teaching. This would help us compare how participants in each subgroup respond to the questionnaire. For example, the fact that some students in this survey had practicum experience prior to completing the questionnaire might have affected their responses, notably with regard to their level of confidence in teaching school history. Similarly, the multiple-choice questionnaire did not allow students to explain their ideas. Answers such as "identify formation" are too short and vague to capture what respondents had in mind. Is it personal or collective identity? Canadian and/or Québec? Only a series of follow-up (and open-ended) questions would allow students to unpack their selection. Still, it is possible to offer some tentative conclusions and suggestions for further research initiatives in teacher education.

The first striking element from this study is the range and intensity of students' engagement with the past. Long before they enter teacher education, prospective teachers have developed powerful ideas about history and education. These ideas are by no means restricted to formal education; they include a variety of "cultural tools" available to them in the wider society. Whether it is a movie, the Internet, a book, or a museum, participants make extensive use of these cultural artefacts in their daily life. From the findings, history is clearly a temporal frame for orienting students' actions and structuring their sense of personal and professional identity. Unlike the participants in *Canadians and Their Pasts*, however, student teachers do not primarily relate to history through the intimate past. Family history is important to them, but not at the expense of the collective past of their province and country. In fact, student teachers' ways of using the past are very different compared to the activities described by Canadian and international surveys. Few students gather and preserve family objects, write journals, or work on genealogies. Rather, they eagerly consume various historical goods available to them on the Web, in bookstores, or in local theatres. The study of Létourneau et al. suggests that the family is the lens through which Canadians engage the past. There is no clear indication from this study that student teachers have the same mode of orientation. Their historical consciousness does not function primarily in response to intimate interests that they deeply value and trust. This is particularly evident in the way participants judged the reliability of sources about the past. Formal realms of history, such as museums and historians, are the most trustworthy sources in their view. Family stories and even members of the teaching profession, on the contrary, are not seen as "very reliable," suggesting a significant awareness of these sources' limitations.

Despite the diversity of activities in which student teachers were involved, there is a remarkable consensus among the participants from the selected Québec and Ontario universities. Both in their ideas and uses of the past, these francophone students from Ottawa, Montréal and Québec City share many characteristics. In spite of some variations in scores, they engage in similar activities about the past and value the same kinds of sources and histories. Participants in this study had more in common with each other than did the diverse Canadian population surveyed by *Canadians and Their Pasts* or other international studies. This suggests that historical consciousness could be age and educationally related. Student teachers overwhelmingly came from the same age cohort (born between 1980–90) and had similar linguistic and educational backgrounds, in terms of university degrees and number of history courses. It is thus possible that their educational environment and their teaching trajectories (if not vocation) are key determinants in distinguishing these professionals from the rest of Canadian society with regard to their representations of the past.

As a matter of fact, a key element that makes the participants of this study unique, and therefore unrepresentative of the wider Canadian population surveyed, is their transitional status as "student teacher." Unlike common citizens, who use the past in more personal and intuitive ways, prospective teachers have already initiated, some more effectively than others, a transposition of their mental representations of the past into the domain of professional education. This is particularly evident in the section of the questionnaire dealing with practice teaching. The great majority of participants conceive of the discipline beyond what Rüsen calls "lebenspraxis," that is, the uses of history for practical life.[24] It is true that many ranked "understanding the present" as the main goal of history in school. But a closer look at their idea of a usable past reveals some clear reference to notions of "historical thinking," "critical thinking," and "citizenship education." Prospective teachers, from this perspective, seem to have a more critical consciousness than most people, at least in the way they represent history in its scholastic form.[25] They know that some sources are more trustworthy than others, and they know that intimacy and familiarity with the past does not guarantee reliability. They also accept that historical study plays different functions in social life, not primarily (or exclusively) a temporal orientation *à la mode du jour* for self-interest.

But this conceptualization also appears to be informed by pedagogical traditions and curricular practices. Findings suggest significant differences in how participants conceive their role and their identity as history teachers. On the questions pertaining to teaching strategies and resources, student teachers' responses vary considerably. In Ottawa, for example, the use of historical inquiry and research projects are the dominant approaches to school history, but in Laval the majority of participants continue to favour lectures with some group work. The same divergence is reported in the use of teaching resources. Ontario students placed much higher value on primary source archives (36 per cent of total) than their Laval counterparts (18 per cent). The fact that participants were at different stages of their education degree, some in Québec having practicum experience, could affect these results. Still, Charland came to the same conclusion in his comparative study of history students and teachers. He found that 60 per cent of high school students in Québec were taught through lectures, compared to only 37 per cent in Ontario.[26] His follow-up interviews with teachers led in the same direction. Charland suggests that the professional culture and the curricular requirements help explain these pedagogical preferences. In Québec, he observes, high school history teachers must meet the requirements of a compressed and loaded curriculum that surveys a broader historical period than the Ontario high school system, which is spread over three years (Grades 7, 8, and 10). As such, teachers often feel pressured to "cover" the program of study through a method that they perceive to be efficient – the traditional lecture. Practical imperatives, in this view, take precedence over sound pedagogical considerations. Prospective teachers in transitional status who have ventured into the classroom prior to the survey might be tempted to welcome the wisdom of common practice, the one already familiar to them.

Perhaps more influential is the examination set by the Ministry of Education, Leisure and Sports of Quebec that many consider a state instrument intended to control teachers' planning and content delivery. Québec students cannot graduate from high school unless they successfully complete the Canadian and Québec history exit test. Studies in the United States have confirmed that standardized testing impacts the teaching culture. It tends to "reduce teaching to low levels of intellectual engagement and teachers to implementers of externally designed curricula and pre-packaged materials intended to help them teach to the test."[27] Incoming teachers, inexperienced and often under probationary contract, could be significantly affected by state examination. This is to say that teacher education programs do not operate in a vacuum. Student teachers can be encouraged to nurture a community of practices in the field and to be introduced to innovative pedagogical approaches with engaging learning resources during their professional education. But these are unlikely to be internalized by beginning teachers if they run against the cultural practices already in place in the school system. Other studies have documented this disconnect and suggest that coherent programs, well-coordinated with the faculty and the school system, "seem to be able to graduate individuals who show beliefs similar to those of their faculty."[28] This lack of coherence may well explain why all participants in this study eagerly use the Internet in their everyday business but surprisingly find the Web or technology to be largely irrelevant in the context of the classroom. This is a twenty-first century paradox. Is it possible that digital natives, born and raised with technology, operate on fundamentally different modes when they open the doors of the school?

Clearly, student teachers are in a difficult position. As teacher educators, we often see them as potential agents of change. We introduce them to novel ideas and research-informed practices. We also encourage them to reflect on the prior knowledge and "folk theories" that they bring to school and unconsciously perpetuate in class. In the words of Sears, "if a central function of history teaching is to teach the disciplinary processes of history, which are at the heart of work in historical thinking, then a key role for teacher education should be to set teachers on an inbound trajectory, to nurture them as practitioners of the discipline themselves."[29] To some extent, this preliminary study indicates that these history student teachers are well positioned to implement practices that nurture disciplinary reasoning in their classrooms. Yet, teacher education is short-lived, a compressed drive-through program in many jurisdictions in Canada. Prospective teachers take many courses for their degree but only gain a limited exposure to history didactics. As an example of this, VanSledright calculated that student teachers literally spend 95 per cent of their schooling time learning to teach history through observing in elementary and high school classrooms.[30] The result is that most of teachers' history education takes place outside the academy in more "natural settings."

In these circumstances, it becomes imperative in teacher education to create overlapping "boundary practices" so that prospective teachers establish new connections across the disciplinary and educational communities of practices. They must understand and be exposed to both the nature of history and pedagogy during and after their history and education degree programs. Compared to the Canadian average, participants in the study are relatively active agents of historical consciousness on numerous fronts: their academic background, engagement, and reflection. The challenge for them is to use their personal and professional identities as "history educators" productively within the classroom in order to confront established assumptions about schooling and the passive role of students in history education. One first step in this direction is to map out the historical consciousness of student teachers; we need to acquire a better understanding of their *temporal experience,* their *historical interpretation,* and their *life orientation.* Surveys – such as the one adapted from this exploratory study and now available online in both official languages (www.surveymonkey.com/s/historiprof) – can serve as a blueprint for collective reflection on how to operationalize the notions of historical thinking and consciousness within the broad context of education.[31] With such reflection, it becomes possible to envisage the instruments and strategies needed to recruit suitable candidates, adapt our programs of study in history and education, and develop successful models of cross-boundary communities of practices.

NOTES

1 Keith Barton and Linda Levstik, *Teaching History for the Common Good* (Mahwah, NJ: Lawrence Erlbaum Associates, 2004), 255.
2 See Maria Teressa Tatto, "The Influence of Teacher Education on Teachers' Beliefs About Purposes of Education, Roles, and Practice," *Journal of Teacher Education* 49, no. 1 (1998): 66-77; James Raths, "Teachers' Beliefs and Teaching Beliefs," *Early Childhood Research and Practice* 3, no. 1 (2001): 385-91; and Neils Brouwer and Fred Korthagen, "Can Teacher Education Make a Difference?" *American Educational Research Journal* 42, no. 1 (2005): 153-224.
3 Alan Sears, "Moving from the Periphery to the Core: The Possibilities for Professional Learning Communities in History Teacher Education," this volume, p. 16.
4 See Peter Stearns, Peter Seixas, and Sam Wineburg, eds., *Knowing, Teaching, and Learning History: National and International Perspectives* (New York: New York University Press, 2000); Bruce VanSledright, *In Search of America's Past: Learning to Read History in Elementary Schools* (New York: Teachers College Press, 2002); and Stéphane Lévesque, *Thinking Historically: Educating Students for the Twenty-First Century* (Toronto: University of Toronto Press, 2008).
5 Sam Wineburg, *Historical Thinking and Other Unnatural Acts: Charting the Future of Teaching the Past* (Philadelphia: Temple University Press, 2001);

and Howard Gardner, *The Development and Education of the Mind: The Selected Works of Howard Gardner* (New York: Routledge, 2006), 131-68.

6 Sears, "Moving from the Periphery to the Core," p. 18.

7 Christian Laville, "Historical Consciousness and History Education: What to Expect from the First for the Second," in *Theorizing Historical Consciousness*, edited by Peter Seixas (Toronto: University of Toronto Press, 2006), 167.

8 Jörn Rüsen, "Historical Consciousness: Narrative Structure, Moral Function and Ontogenetic Development," in Seixas, *Theorizing Historical Consciousness*, 69.

9 Rüsen, "Historical Consciousness," 70.

10 Ibid., 67.

11 See, for instance, Magne Angvik and Bodo von Borries, eds., *Youth and History: A Comparative European Survey on Historical Consciousness and Political Attitudes among Adolescents* (Hamburg: Körber-Stiftung, 1997); Roy Rosenzweig and David Thelen, *The Presence of the Past: Popular Uses of History in American Life* (New York: Columbia University Press, 1998); Paula Hamilton and Paul Ashton, "Australians and the Past," *Australian Cultural History* 23 (2003): 1-216; Nicole Tutiaux-Guillon, "La conscience historique des jeunes: Deux enquêtes," *Historiens et géographes*, 396 (November 2006): 255-7; and the most recent publication for Australia from Paul Ashton and Paula Hamilton, *History at the Crossroads: Australians and the Past* (Sydney: Halstead Press, 2010).

12 Roy Rosenzweig, "How Americans Use and Think about the Past: Implications from a National Survey for the Teaching of History," in *Knowing, Teaching, and Learning History: National and International Perspectives*, edited by Peter Stearns, Peter Seixas, and Sam Wineburg (New York: New York University Press, 2000), 262-83.

13 Jean-Pierre Charland, *Les élèves, l'histoire et la citoyenneté: Enquête auprès d'élèves des régions de Montréal et de Toronto* (Québec: Presses de l'Université Laval, 2003). See also Jocelyn Létourneau, "Young People's Assimilation of a Collective Historical Memory: A Case Study of Quebeckers of French-Canadian Heritage," in *Theorizing Historical Consciousness*, 109–28.

14 Margaret Conrad, Jocelyn Létourneau, and David Northrup, "Canadians and Their Pasts: An Exploration in Historical Consciousness," *Public Historian* 31, no. 1 (2009): 33. For more details on the project and latest publications visit www.canadiansandtheirpasts.ca.

15 Peter Seixas, "Student Teachers Thinking Historically," *Theory and Research in Social Education* 26, no. 1 (1998): 310-41.

16 Given the regional nature of education in Canada, provinces and universities have established their own programs of school history and of teacher
education. In Ottawa (Ontario), teacher education is offered as a post-
graduate degree extending over two semesters (September to April).
Students enter the BEd program with various disciplinary backgrounds
and select subject areas (known as "teachables") according to their studies.
In Québec, teacher education is offered as an integrated, four-year program during which student teachers must take both courses in education
and in their respective disciplines. As a result, participants in this study
were at different stages of their teacher education. That being said, all of
them were enrolled in history didactics courses and some had spent time
in the classroom during their school practicums.

17 A noted above, students in this study were not necessarily at the same
stage of their BEd programs. The participants from Ottawa were in the
first semester of the BEd, while the ones from Laval and Montréal were at
various stages of their degrees, depending on their course selections and
school subjects (teachables). No specific data was recorded on their practice teaching experience, but considering the organization of the teacher
education programs in the two provinces, only some participants from
Québec might have had practicum experience prior to completing the
questionnaire.

18 Given the diversity of collective identities in the Canadian context, the
question dealing with ethnic identity was left open in the questionnaire.
Results presented here are thus self-descriptions emerging from the findings. Some categories (e.g., French Canadian and Franco-Ontarian) are not
necessarily mutually exclusive but highlight the diverse and even contested nature of Canadian identities as reported by participants.

19 For matters of presentation clarity and practical comparison between subgroups, results in the study are presented in percentage of total responses.

20 Rosenzweig and Thelen, *The Presence of the Past*; Conrad, Létourneau, and
Northrup, "Canadians and Their Pasts," 15-34.

21 Conrad, Létourneau, and Northrup, "Canadians and Their Pasts," 29-30.

22 See Lee Shulman, "Knowledge and Teaching: Foundations of a New
Reform," *Harvard Educational Review* 57 (1987): 1-22; Susan Adler, "The
Education of Social Studies Teachers," in *Handbook of Research in Social
Studies Education*, edited by Linda Levstik and Cynthia Tyson (New York:
Routledge, 2008), 329-51; Keith Barton and Linda Levstik, "Why Don't
More History Teachers Engage Students in Interpretation?" *Social
Education*, 67 (2003): 358-61; Peter Seixas, "Beyond Content and Pedagogy:
In Search of a Way to Talk about History Education," *Journal of Curriculum*

Studies 31, no. 3 (1999): 317-37. In French scholarship, the matter is discussed under "relation didactique" and presented in various writings, including Henri Moniot, *Didactique de l'histoire* (Paris: Nathan, 1993); Mostafa Hassani Idrissi, *Pensée historienne et apprentissage de l'histoire* (Paris: L'Harmattan, 2005); and Robert Martineau, *Fondements et pratiques de l'enseignement de l'histoire à l'école: traité de didactique* (Québec: Presses de l'Université du Québec, 2010).

23 Lee Shulman, "Those Who Understand: Knowledge Growth in Teaching," *Educational Researcher* 15, no. 2 (1986): 8.

24 Jörn Rüsen, *Rekonstruktion der Vergangenheit* (Gottingen: Vandenhoeck and Ruprecht, 1986). Here I am relying on the ideas from Peter Lee, "'Walking backwards into tomorrow': Historical Consciousness and Understanding History," *International Journal of Historical Learning, Teaching and Research* 4, no. 1 (2004), available at http://www.heirnet.org/IJHLTR/journal7/lee.pdf.

25 Rüsen, "Historical Consciousness," 74.

26 Charland, *Les élèves, l'histoire et la citoyenneté. Enquête auprès d'élèves des régions de Montréal et de Toronto*, 99.

27 Avner Segall, "Teachers' Perceptions of the Impact of State-Mandated Standardized Testing: The Michigan Educational Assessment Program (MEAP) as a Case Study of Consequences," *Theory and Research in Social Education* 31, no. 3 (2003): 287-325. See also S.G. Grant and Cinthia Salinas, "Assessment and Accountability in the Social Studies," in *Handbook of Research in Social Studies Education*, edited by Linda Levstik and Cynthia Tyson (New York: Routledge, 2008), 219-36.

28 Tatto, "The Influence of Teacher Education on Teachers' Beliefs About Purposes of Education," 76.

29 Sears, "Moving from the Periphery to the Core."

30 Bruce VanSledright, *The Challenges of Rethinking History Education: On Practices, Theories, and Policy* (New York: Routledge, 2010), 172.

31 For the latest results on the pan-Canadian survey, see Stéphane Lévesque, "L'histoire, 'essentielle à la compréhension du Canada d'aujourd'hui': Sondage pancanadien auprès des futurs enseignants d'histoire," in *De nouvelles voies pour la recherche et la pratique en Histoire, Géographie et Éducation à la citoyenneté*, edited by Marc-André Ethier and Eric Mottet (Brussels: De Boeck, 2014), chap. 8.

8 Through the Looking Glass: An Overview of the Theoretical Foundations of Quebec's History Curriculum

CATHERINE DUQUETTE

In his chapter "Moving from the Periphery to the Core: The Possibilities for Professional Learning Communities in History Teacher Education," Alan Sears notes that student teachers have:

> ... little or no actual experience with the processes they will be teaching and, therefore, probably aren't very good at them themselves; as well, in my view much more importantly, the candidates have a strong cognitive frame that history teaching essentially involves the passing on of historical information and not the fostering of historical thinking.[1]

This situation holds true in Quebec, as elsewhere in Canada. Many student teachers experience a discrepancy between the history they have been taught at university and the history they are asked to teach at the elementary and high school levels. Because of this, when the Ministry of Education, Leisure and Sports of Quebec (MELS) decided to completely reform the history curriculum in the late 1990s by emphasizing the learning of historical thinking, many teachers found themselves at a loss as to how to implement this new program.[2] Among the questions that arose from this situation, the most important one, in our opinion, concerned the nature of historical thinking. What intellectual skills are associated with historical thinking, and how can teachers foster the development of these skills? It would be wrong to assume that teachers were left alone to find answers to their questions. On the contrary, they were bombarded with a multitude of suggestions from the MELS, from pan-Canadian projects such as The Historical Thinking Project, and from francophone researchers in didactics of history. This situation may have led to greater confusion rather than greater understanding. Does the MELS view historical thinking in the same way as The Historical Thinking Project?[3] Are there significant differences in their theoretical understandings of the concept? If so, is it still possible to encourage student teachers and teachers to use pedagogical material that has not been specifically developed for the Quebec history curriculum? Conversely, could the unique aspects of the Quebec curriculum improve how history is taught across the country? This chapter will try to address these questions, first by establishing the theoretical foundations of historical thinking as understood by the Quebec curriculum, and second by illustrating how this model might influence the university instruction that student teachers receive.

The Structure of Quebec's History and Citizenship Education Curriculum

Before moving further in our discussion, it is necessary to illustrate the structure and theoretical foundations of Quebec's new history and citizenship education curriculum. The theoretical foundations of this curriculum can be found in the report submitted by the *Groupe de travail pour l'enseignement de l'histoire*, also known as the *Lacoursière Report* (from the name of the leader of the project, Quebec historian Jacques Lacoursière).[4] Among the recommendations in the report, it is suggested that history, as a school subject, must not be limited to memorizing facts but should, on the contrary, promote students' ability to:

> sort out current affairs, to understand the present, to make their own opinion, to exercise their analytical and critical abilities, etc. In short, [school history should be] a formation that allows one to understand a complex society as ours and to behave within it in an autonomous and thoughtful fashion.[5]

These recommendations were generally accepted by the MELS, which then noted in the curriculum that the purpose of history at school is

> not to make students memorize a simplified, student-friendly version of the academic knowledge produced and constructed by historians, nor to ensure that they acquire factual learning of an encyclopedic nature, but rather to enable them to develop competencies that will help them understand social phenomena of the present in light of the past.[6]

Going beyond factual knowledge and developing a critical understanding of history can therefore be considered the *mot d'ordre* of this new curriculum. It also underlines that history is the discipline that allows students to understand the present by studying the past. Students are invited to question the past using a series of intellectual skills specific to the discipline of history; in other words, they must learn how to think historically. The MELS is not the first governmental body that proposed a history curriculum based on historical thinking. The United States, for example, was already noting in 1996 in its *National Standards for History* that "true historical understanding requires students to engage in historical thinking."[7] Therefore, Quebec is not a pioneer in basing its curriculum on historical thinking; rather, it can be argued that the province is following a trend already well in place elsewhere.

However, the intellectual skills – also named competencies – associated with learning how to think historically are in some ways unique to the province. Quebec's curriculum recommends that history should be taught through the development of two specific competencies.[8] These competencies involve learning how to examine social phenomena from a historical perspective, and secondly, how to interpret social phenomena using the historical method.

According to the MELS, the first competency enables students to understand the past from a historical perspective. In other words, it allows students to:

> consider the past of social phenomena and to see them as in terms of duration by looking for elements of continuity and change. They also learn to look at the context in which they emerge and to ask questions about the beliefs, attitudes and values of contemporaries and witnesses of the period. To take into account the complexity of a given phenomenon and, at the same time, see it as a whole, they examine its various aspects, as well as their interaction. They realize that the historical perspective precludes hasty conclusions.[9]

The second competency involves developing a research method that allows students to answer the questions brought forth by the first competency. In order to help teachers identify the steps associated with the historical method, the MELS proposed a set of specific operations illustrated in Figure 8.1.[10]

According to the curriculum, through developing both competencies, students will gain the ability to engage in historical thinking. In

Figure 8.1: The historical method of research as viewed by the MELS

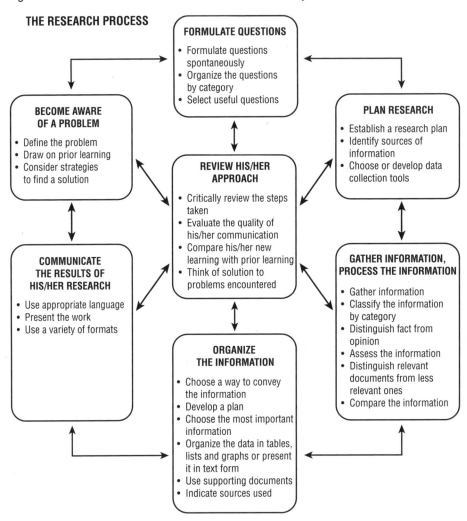

THE RESEARCH PROCESS

FORMULATE QUESTIONS
- Formulate questions spontaneously
- Organize the questions by category
- Select useful questions

BECOME AWARE OF A PROBLEM
- Define the problem
- Draw on prior learning
- Consider strategies to find a solution

PLAN RESEARCH
- Establish a research plan
- Identify sources of information
- Choose or develop data collection tools

REVIEW HIS/HER APPROACH
- Critically review the steps taken
- Evaluate the quality of his/her communication
- Compare his/her new learning with prior learning
- Think of solution to problems encountered

COMMUNICATE THE RESULTS OF HIS/HER RESEARCH
- Use appropriate language
- Present the work
- Use a variety of formats

GATHER INFORMATION, PROCESS THE INFORMATION
- Gather information
- Classify the information by category
- Distinguish fact from opinion
- Assess the information
- Distinguish relevant documents from less relevant ones
- Compare the information

ORGANIZE THE INFORMATION
- Choose a way to convey the information
- Develop a plan
- Choose the most important information
- Organize the data in tables, lists and graphs or present it in text form
- Use supporting documents
- Indicate sources used

practice, however, teachers and student teachers found this curriculum difficult to implement in the classroom. One of the issues was lack of guidelines on how to assess both competencies.[11] In response, in fall 2010 the MELS released a new document that detailed the expected learning progression and included a more specific list of the intellectual skills students should gain through the study of history.[12] This document states that by the end of their fourth year of high school (Grade 10), students should be able to:

- examine social phenomena of the present and of the past;
- situate social phenomena in time and space;
- establish facts;
- characterize a specific social phenomenon;
- establish comparison;
- determine causes and consequences;
- identify elements of continuity and change;
- associate different facts with one another;
- establish links of causality; and
- characterize the evolution of a society.

When taken as a whole, the curriculum presents a view of historical thinking as being composed of two main concepts: a historical perspective that includes most of the intellectual skills found in the 2010 learning progression document, and a historical method that refers directly to the research method associated with the second competency. Figure 8.2 proposes a synthesis of MELS's definition of historical thinking.

This overview of the Quebec history curriculum points to how historical thinking is its key component. Looking at how the concept of historical thinking is presented, one wonders at the choices made by the MELS. Why is historical thinking divided in two specific competencies? On what basis is the ministry selecting each intellectual operation and then dividing them into two competencies? In other words, on which theoretical frameworks is the current curriculum established and why?

Theoretical Foundations of Historical Thinking Emerging from Francophone Research

Historical thinking is a well-known concept in both French and English academia. For now, we will centre our attention on the theories found in the French literature. More precisely, we will compare the three models of historical thinking that dominate the literature to see how they might have influenced how historical thinking was represented in the curriculum. The first model discussed will be Robert Martineau's,[13]

Figure 8.2: Synthesis of historical thinking as understood by the Quebec curriculum

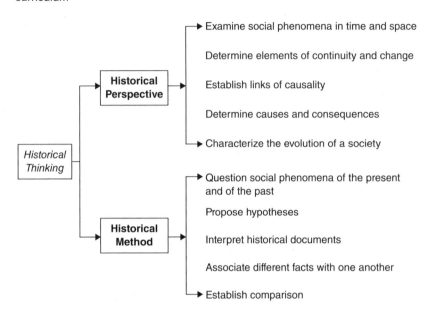

then Christian Laville's model,[14] and finally, Alain Dalongeville's model[15] (which shares similar elements with the model of Mostafa Hassani Idrissi).[16] This review will allow us to explore how each model might have influenced the conceptualization of historical thinking in Quebec's history curriculum.

Martineau's Model

Robert Martineau proposes dividing historical thinking into three different dimensions, which are then subdivided into several concepts, as follows:

- **An Attitude for History, that includes**
  an understanding of historical knowledge;
  a historical consciousness;
  a conception of history as a scientific discipline;
  a critical mind;

an understanding of historical thinking's role in the production of
history; and

an understanding of the social value attached to history and the
value of learning historical thinking.

- **The Language of History,** that includes facts, concepts, and
theories.
- **A Historical Method,** that includes the ability to problematize; the
ability to rationalize a problem; and the ability to explain a problem.

Laville's Model

The division proposed by Martineau can be traced back, in part, to the
theories found in Christian Laville's work. According to Laville, historical thinking can be divided into two different skills that must be
used together to make sense of the past:

- **historical perspective**, or, taking an interrogative attitude towards
the past and the present; and
- **historical reasoning**, which includes:
  getting familiar with a problem;
  formulating the problem into a question;
  making a hypothesis;
  verifying the hypothesis with the help of the available data; and
  making a conclusion (either rejecting or confirming the
  hypothesis).

Dalongeville and Hassani Idrissi's Model

On the other side of the Atlantic, Hassani Idrissi and Dalongeville
propose an understanding of historical thinking centred on problem
solving. The elements that compose the "problem solving method" of
historical thinking are as follows:

- getting familiar with an historical problem;
- making a hypothesis;
- checking the hypothesis; and
- coming to a conclusion that brings forth a new historical problem.

When compared, the three models share some similarities. Martineau,
Laville, Hassani Idriss, and Dalongeville all agree on pursuing histori-

cal thinking with a "hypothetico-deductive" approach. This approach invites students to form a hypothesis and to check its validity, after interpreting the available evidence (a critical step). Some authors, such as Dalongeville and Hassani Idrissi, seem ready to reduce the process of historical thinking to this single method. However, this opinion is not shared by all; in particular, Laville insists on the importance of jointly developing both a historical perspective and a historical method in order to interpret the past. For Laville, only after mastering both elements does historical thinking become truly a form of thinking. This view is shared by Martineau, who specifies that:

> What distinguishes historical thinking from other ways of thinking are not its procedures, strongly influenced by a historical method shared by all social sciences, nor the concepts used, since a large number are not specific to the discipline, but a "historical attitude," meaning the behaviour that it conditions [our translation].[17]

Teaching a form of historical thinking exclusively based on learning a method is, for Martineau and Laville, equal to ignoring the operations that are specific to the discipline of history. Reducing historical thinking to the operations associated with historical perspective ignores the fact that students also require tools to complete a critical and methodical study of the past.

Let's now compare these three models with the MELS model of historical thinking. In order to do so, we will use the synthesis presented in Figure 8.2 and compare its elements with the ones found in the models suggested by Martineau, Laville, and Dalongeville and Indrissi. The goal is to establish the origins of MELS's understanding of historical thinking.

As demonstrated in Figure 8.3, the division of historical thinking into historical perspective (first competency) and historical method (second competency) in the Quebec curriculum can be tied to the models of Laville and Martineau. Moreover, the five-step method proposed in the curriculum is similar to the method proposed by Laville and Dalongeville and Hassani Idrissi. One could argue that for the curriculum, therefore, that historical thinking is viewed as a form of problem solving. Students are prompted to answer present-day questions through studying the past.

While it seems clear that the three models discussed here have in some way influenced the curriculum, some choices made by the MELS

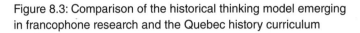

Figure 8.3: Comparison of the historical thinking model emerging
in francophone research and the Quebec history curriculum

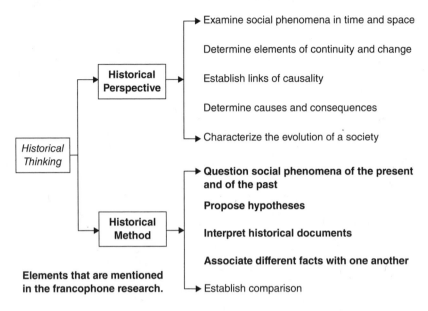

cannot be linked to francophone research. This is particularly the case
with the skills associated with a historical perspective. Indeed, Laville's
model is rather vague in regards to historical perspective, as the author
does not mention specific intellectual operations that allow one to take
a historical perspective. Martineau lists skills that are vastly different
than the ones promoted in the Quebec curriculum. Why does the MELS
believe that taking a historical perspective requires skills such as establishing continuity and change or cultivating historical empathy? Other
models of historical thinking might be able to answer this question.

Theoretical Foundations of Historical Thinking Emerging
from The Historical Thinking Project

In order to better understand the theoretical framework of the curriculum's key concept, we will look at another model of historical thinking, broadening our scope of research to include theories found in the
English literature. Because of its importance and popularity among

education ministries across Canada,[18] the model proposed by Peter Seixas in The Historical Thinking Project will be the focus of this section.[19] Seixas proposes that to think historically, students must master six second-order concepts, which are:

- historical significance;
- historical perspective (historical empathy);
- causes and consequences;
- continuity and change;
- interpretation of primary source evidence; and
- ethical dimension of history. [20]

According to The Historical Thinking Project, the concept of historical significance leads students to question the larger meanings of the events studied in class. In Quebec, for example, students might ask why the battle of the Plains of Abraham holds such significance for the francophone society. Next, the concepts of continuity and change, as well as causes and consequences, allow students to find their bearing in time with key ideas such as periodization, synchrony, anteriority and posteriority. Historical empathy, also named historical perspective in Seixas' research, helps students to understand the culture, customs, and ideologies of past societies.[21] Students must not simply put themselves "in the shoes" of someone who lived in the past; instead, they must understand that present society is vastly different than past societies.[22] It would not be possible to develop these second-order concepts if students were not first taught how to interpret historical evidence, both textual and iconographical. Seixas proposes that the final second-order concept would involve applying an ethical dimension to the past. As stated in the project web page, the process of crafting meaningful history cannot be parted from making ethical judgments. These judgments allow students to use what they have learned from the past to confront today's issues. Returning to the historical thinking model found in the Quebec curriculum, it is possible to connect a number of Seixas' second-order concepts to the model, as shown in Figure 8.4.

Comparing the MELS model with Seixas' ideas suggests that most second-order concepts are related to taking a historical perspective. Although Seixas' second-order concepts and the curriculum's core operations are similar, the curriculum's organization – into two different competencies – displays an emphasis on problem solving that is not necessarily found in The Historical Thinking Project. Indeed, in his

Figure 8.4: Comparison of the model proposed by The Historical Thinking Project and the model found in the Quebec curriculum

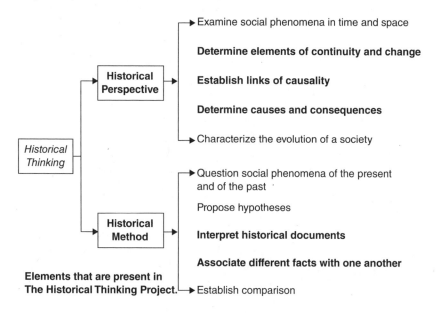

model, Seixas does not emphasize a specific research method, since each second-order concept brings forth a set of questions that frame the learning of history. Moreover, two concepts, namely historical significance and the ethical dimension of history, are not found within the curriculum. Although historical perspective includes continuity and change, historical empathy, and causes and consequences, the ethical dimension of the past is absent. This might be explained by the fact that – contrary to the other second-order concepts – this type of judgment does not produce a historical "reflex," to use Martineau's term.[23] In other words, ethical judgment seems to be based on values rather than on critical thinking. It seems that for the MELS, historical thinking is a form of critical thinking, as it prompts students to develop a nuanced and evidence-based understanding of the past. The MELS would appear to prefer assigning a different intellectual operation to historical perspective, namely the characterization of the past.[24] For example, students will learn about life in New France by exploring the political, social, and economic aspects of that society. As a result, they come to understand the past's complexity. It is perhaps because of its desire to promote a critical understanding of the past that the MELS chose not to include an ethical dimension in its model of historical thinking.

Historical Thinking in the Quebec Curriculum: A Mixed Model

The quest to find the theoretical foundation of historical thinking as expressed in Quebec's history curriculum has proven to be a difficult one. Our review finds that the MELS seems to have been inspired by a multitude of models, rather than a single one as is usually the case. We could argue that the MELS promotes a mixed model that was influenced by both French and English academia. For example, the new francophone history curriculum in Ontario is primarily based on Seixas' understanding of historical thinking.[25] Maybe Seixas' model is not fully taken into account in the Quebec curriculum because the curriculum preceded the full establishment of The Historical Thinking Project. Francophone research in the field of didactics also accounts for some of the model's characteristics. Indeed, Laville had been arguing for a historical thinking-based curriculum since the end of the 1970s.[26]

Nevertheless, one thing remains clear: the MELS's curriculum exhibits a unique understanding of historical thinking. This situation creates challenges and concerns for teachers and student teachers. For example, should student teachers and teachers use pedagogical material that was not specifically created for the Quebec curriculum? Does this understanding of historical thinking reflect politics in Quebec and if so, should student teachers and teachers be aware of this? Does this model provide sufficient guidance for class implementation and evaluation? In other words, what are the consequences of these ministerial choices on the formation of student teachers and the daily lives of teachers?

Challenges of Teaching Historical Thinking in Regards to the Quebec Curriculum

Teachers and student teachers in Quebec must work with a unique understanding of historical thinking. How does this affect how history is taught on a day-to-day basis? Does the model's complexity promote a more passive teaching of the discipline or, on the contrary, "move teachers towards the core of historical practice and help historians become better teachers?"[27] What overall changes in teaching can we expect from the new Quebec history curriculum? Although this question requires a long-term empirical study to be fully answered, it is still possible to identify the areas in which we can expect change. Among them is the teacher education programs offered at universities. How do student teachers react to this unique understanding of historical education? This section of the paper will look briefly at the challenges that the competency-based history curriculum presents for student teachers. After describing Quebec's education programs, this section will discuss three different challenges: the discrepancy between the history taught at university and the history taught in high schools, the universality of the tools used to teach historical thinking, and the difficulty of evaluating historical thinking.[28] A better understanding of these challenges will allow us to identify how the competency-based curriculum might or might not help bring student teachers from the periphery to the core.

Student Teachers and the Learning of Historical Thinking

Before continuing, a few words must be said on the coursework required to obtain a bachelor of education (BEd) in Quebec. Like some other provinces, students in Quebec can enter a BEd program without previously completing a bachelor of arts degree. Student teachers instead complete a four-year program that includes classes in the fields of history, geography, and pedagogy. Student teachers need to take a set number of credits in both in pedagogy and in their teaching discipline. For example, the program at the Université du Québec à Chicoutimi[29] requires that they take fifty-seven credits in pedagogy divided into sixteen mandatory courses plus one optional course. In their teaching discipline (history and geography), they need sixty-three credits divided into eighteen mandatory courses plus three optional courses. They also complete four fieldwork assignments that enable them to gain first-hand experience in the classroom. At the end of their studies, student teachers receive both a BEd diploma from the university and a teaching certificate from the province of Quebec. During their time at university, student teachers take up to three methods or didactics classes. It is in these classes that student teachers encounter the demands of the curriculum and its understanding of historical thinking. Therefore, it is in the methods class that student teachers realize the challenges involved in teaching historical thinking.

History at University versus History Taught in High School

Our review of the competency-based curriculum has shown that the MELS wishes high school students to become active in learning history, focusing less on memorizing facts and more on learning the different intellectual skills associated with historical thinking. However, as Sears indicates in his chapter, student teachers have very little experience in historical thinking, because most, but not all, history classes received at the undergraduate level focus on learning a specific narrative. This situation can prove difficult for student teachers. They are asked to help their students develop intellectual skills that the new teachers might not even have heard of before encountering the history curriculum.[30] The discrepancy between how student teachers learn about history and how they are asked to teach it causes various reactions. In our own methods class, there seems to be two kinds of reactions. First, some student teachers feel somewhat relieved that their aspirations to teach in more active fashion are encouraged by the curriculum. Second, other student teachers are less enthusiastic because they imagine teaching a history class should involve an all-knowing teacher delivering a fact-based narrative.[31] Whatever their initial opinion, all student teachers find that understanding and implementing the new curriculum to be a challenge, as they have few (or no) examples, either in high school or at university, of how to teach a history class based on historical thinking.

The Universality of Pedagogical Material

Because they have not always experienced historical thinking in their own schooling, student teachers often turn to the available pedagogical material to help them achieve the goals of the curriculum. The popularity of the website *Récit de l'univers social*, which was specifically created for teaching the Quebec history curriculum, is a proof of the need for some form of aid. Moreover, student teachers must deal with the MELS's unique understanding of historical thinking. This renders the use of pedagogical materials (such as the one developed by The Historical Thinking Project) difficult, since these materials do not always take into account the specificities of the Quebec curriculum. As previously explained, the mixed model of historical thinking favoured by the MELS emphasizes problem-based learning that is not necessarily associated with Seixas' second-order concepts. Although one could argue that it is still feasible to adapt The Historical Thinking Project's pedagogical material, one should keep in mind that student teachers often lack the experience and sometimes even the understanding to do so. This particular situation makes it even more crucial that student teachers have "the opportunity to do some history themselves and grapple directly with making sense of evidence and other elements of historical thinking."[32] Student teachers must go to the archives, interpret evidence, and debate ideas; in other words, they must learn to do history if we wish them to develop enough experience to fully comprehend the demands of the Quebec curriculum. Once student teachers have gained a better sense of the epistemology behind historical thinking, they will be able to adapt the available pedagogical material to their specific needs.

Evaluation and Historical Thinking

One of the questions most often heard among student teachers – and teachers – concerns the evaluation of historical thinking. Since historical thinking consists of a set of skills that are developed over time, how can both teachers and student teachers chart with precision the evolution of historical thinking in their students? Little is known at the moment of this progression, and yet this topic is of key importance if we wish to promote historical thinking in the classrooms. Indeed, what level of historical thought can be expected of a Grade 10 student? How can we engage student teachers to teach history using an approach based on historical thinking if we do not provide them with an evaluation method? Moreover, do all intellectual skills associated with historical thinking present the same level of difficulty for all students? In other words, is it more difficult for students to learn historical empathy than to identify causes and consequences? Neither the Quebec history curriculum nor the study of its theoretical foundation provides answers to these questions. Studies such as The Historical Thinking Project, to our knowledge, are only beginning to inform teachers with information on these crucial questions. The MELS has tried to deal with this problem recently by providing teachers with a progression of learning document.[33] Unfortunately, this document mostly refers to factual knowledge and not to the evaluation of historical thinking. In his article, Sears points out the importance of transforming history education through focusing on the teaching of historical thinking. However, if we wish for student teachers and teachers to modify their methods – some radically so – it seems important to provide them with the means of evaluating their students in a fair and precise manner. It might be that until we have a clearer understanding of how historical thinking develops in students and have means of evaluating this progression that the move from "periphery to the core" advocated by Sears will be difficult to achieve.

Conclusion

A review of the theoretical foundations of the Quebec history curriculum enables us to realize not only the plurality of meanings associated with the concept of historical thinking but also the challenges connected with its teaching. It also suggests that much work must still be done if we wish to promote, as Sears does, a teaching of history based on interpretation rather than on memorization. Indeed, although the MELS has taken an important step in developing a history curriculum based on historical thinking, the curriculum is but one element in the equation. A fundamental understanding of historical thinking seems essential for student teachers who need this information to comprehend the many demands of the curriculum and implement a more active form of learning in their own future history classrooms. This seems to be even more crucial for student teachers in Quebec, as the curriculum reflects a unique understanding of the concept of historical thinking. Because of this, student teachers depend on historians, didacticians, and history teachers to work together to help them attain a clearer comprehension of historical thinking that they will, in turn, pass on to their own students.

NOTES

1 Alan Sears, "Moving from the Periphery to the Core: The Possibilities for Professional Learning Communities in History Teacher Education," this volume, p. 12.
2 Ministère de l'Éducation, du Sport et des Loisirs du Québec (MELS), *L'école, tout un programme, programme de formation au premier cycle du secondaire,* Chapter 7 (Québec, 2003): 337-68.
3 Previously called *The Benchmarks of Historical Thinking.*
4 Groupe de travail sur l'enseignement de l'histoire, *Se souvenir et devenir. Rapport du groupe de travail sur l'enseignement de l'histoire* (Québec: Ministère de l'Éducation, Mai, 1996): 1-80.

5 Ibid.,12.
6 MELS, 337
7 *National Standards for History*, available online at http://www.nchs.ucla
   .edu/Standards/, accessed 18 March 2014.
8 A third competency can also be identified in the Quebec history curriculum. Its goal is to promote the development of citizenship education. The
   curriculum thus states that students should construct his or her consciousness of citizenship through the study of history. Citizenship education
   plays such an important part in the new history curriculum that the MELS
   changed the title of the course to History and Citizenship Education.
   According to the curriculum, first and second competencies are used to
   build the third competency. In order words, students must think historically in order to construct their understanding of citizenship. Although citizenship education is an important part of the current curriculum, we feel
   that analysing it would exceed the scope of this article, for our focus is
   strictly on the development of historical thinking, which can be linked to
   the two first competencies.
9 MELS, 302.
10 Ibid., 324.
11 Michel D. Laurier, "Évaluer des competences: pas si simple," *Formation et
   Profession* (April 2005): 14-17.
12 On the matter of evaluation of competencies in history, the reader can consult the manifest prepared by the Association québécoise des enseignant(e)
   s en Univers Social (AQEUS), available online at http://aqeus.recitus
   .qc.ca/spip.php?article196, accessed 5 November 2011.
13 Robert Martineau, *L'histoire à l'école, matière à penser...* (Montréal:
   L'Harmattan, 1999).
14 Christian Laville, "Enseigner de l'histoire qui soit vraiment de l'histoire,"
   Mélanges René Van Santbergen. No. spécial des *Cahiers de Clio* (Brussels,
   1984), 171-7.
15 Alain Dalongeville, *L'image du barbare dans l'enseignement de l'histoire* (Paris:
   L'Harmattan, 2001).
16 Mostafa Hassani Idrissi, *Pensée historienne et apprentissage de l'histoire*
   (Paris: L'Harmattan, 2005).
17 Martineau, 146.
18 Indeed, the new francophone Ontario history curriculum, among others,
   are based on the model proposed by The Historical Thinking project.
   The curriculum is available online at: http://www.edu.gov.on.ca/fre/
   curriculum/secondary/canworld910curr2013.pdf, accessed 28 March
   2014.

19   Although this section will focus on the model proposed by Peter Seixas, the reader should note that other authors promote similar models such as Stéphane Lévesque in his book, *Thinking Historically: Educating Students for the Twenty-First Century* and Roland Case and Mark Denos in their book, *Teaching to Think Historically*.

20   Peter Seixas, "Conceptualizing the Growth of Historical Understanding," in *The Handbook of Education and Human Development*, edited by David R. Olson and Nancy Torrance (Oxford: Blackwell, 1996), 765-83.

21   One should not associate historical empathy with a form of sympathy for past society. Historical empathy is a process that allows one to take into account the customs and contexts of past society needed to understand people's actions, while sympathy is mostly a pejorative and paternalistic vision of the past. There is no critical understanding of the past in sympathy, which is solely a judgment based on current values.

22   The Historical Thinking Project, online at http://historybenchmarks.ca/, accessed 18 March 2014.

23   Martineau, 146.

24   MELS, 345.

25   The curriculum is found online at http://www.edu.gov.on.ca/fre/curriculum/secondary/canworld910curr2013.pdf, accessed 28 March 2014.

26   Christian Laville, "Place et rôle de l'enseignement de l'histoire, principalement dans l'enseignement secondaire, pour la formation de l'homme du XXᵉ siècle," *Bulletin de la SPHQ*, 17, no. 2 (April 30, 1979): 5.

27   Sears, this volume.

28   A fourth challenge can be added to our list. It involves the telling of a narrative to foster in students a form of social identity. Closely linked to politics, this subject has, in past years, been a source of debate among historians and didacticians. However popular, we will not address this question in this text for two reasons. First, until recently, this debate was not oriented toward teacher education programs, but instead, the debate focused mostly on the narrative chosen by the MELS for its curriculum. Even today, the debate does not question whether or not student teachers should master a form of historical thinking. Second, the complexity of the debate would bring us far from the intended subject of this article. For a review of this debate, see the special 2007 edition of *Bulletin d'histoire politique* on the "Débât sur le programme d'enseignement de l'histoire du Québec."

29   Université du Québec à Chicoutimi (UQAC), département d'éducation, online at http://programmes.uqac.ca/7665.

30 Marc-André Éthier and David Lefrançois, in collaboration with Sabrina Moisan, "Trois recherches exploratoires sur la pensée historique et la citoyenneté à l'école et à l'université," *Histoire, musée et education à la citoyennté* (2010), 286.

31 The results of a study conducted by Éthier et Lefrançois in 2007–8 seem to concur with our own observations, as the authors found that half of the students teachers were favourable to the competency-based curriculum, while the other half were less in favour. For further information, see Éthier et al., 267-88.

32 Sears, this volume.

33 Available online at http://www1.mels.gouv.qc.ca/progression-Secondaire/, accessed 18 March 2014.

9 Troubling Compromises: Historical Thinking in a One-Year Secondary Teacher Education Program

PETER SEIXAS AND GRAEME WEBBER

History and social studies educators in Canada generally accept the idea that student teachers should emerge from their pre-service programs with an understanding of history as an active, knowledge-generating process rather than a passive absorption of stories about the past – however well told or well written by others.[1] This idea is now a fundamental part of the Canadian history education discussion.[2] Nevertheless, teacher education programs – like school curricula – are battlegrounds for competitions over time and resources. History has to carve its place in multidisciplinary social studies.[3] And the social studies methods courses too often find themselves in competition (not intrinsically, but institutionally) with developmental psychology, assessment, literacy, diversity, social justice, and the other areas into which teacher knowledge – and faculties of education – have been conceptualized and segmented. Moreover, no matter how well designed the on-campus portion of a teacher education program, unless it is well coordinated with the practicum, the gap between university and school is often too wide for student teachers to bridge without institutional support.

This paper provides a double case study, perhaps "double action research," from the perspectives of a teacher education instructor (Peter) and a student teacher (Graeme), as we negotiated the demands of the same overcrowded and time-starved program from two different positions. We aim to provide pictures of what is possible, despite the challenges and competing demands, when an experienced professor and a well-prepared student teacher focus on historical thinking. We then extrapolate from this double narrative to consider what kinds of reforms might lead to stronger outcomes for more student teachers in this program and other settings.

The study is set within the context of a one-year, postsecondary bachelor of education program that is currently implementing a multiyear reform planning process. Most students begin the program in September and finish in the first weeks of the following August, with classes interspersed with a two-week practicum in the fall and a thirteen-week practicum beginning in February. The reformed program will make "inquiry" and social justice issues more central, but there has been minimal attention to strengthening the disciplinary orientations that this chapter and volume address.

Research on History and Social Studies Methods Courses

A quick glance through the last two decades' reviews of research reveals a paucity of interest in subject- or discipline-specific teacher education research.[4] In the 1990 *Handbook of Research on Teacher Education* (the first of its kind), there is a 173-page section on "Teacher Education in the Curricular Areas," thirteen pages of which are devoted to social studies.[5] Of the studies discussed, there are only six dedicated to the investigation of social studies methods courses. The review focuses instead on such issues as the selection, previous education, and beliefs and pedagogical orientations of social studies teachers. In the second edition of the *Handbook*, there is no section on subject area methods courses at all.[6]

More targeted, for our purposes, is the 2005 review of research on the impact of social studies methods courses by Clift and Brady.[7] They note the paucity of research on social studies methods courses in three earlier literature reviews. Clift and Brady examine eleven studies with strikingly similar approaches: all of them used qualitative methods with small numbers of participants, often in a single semester, focusing on "changes in pre-service teachers' beliefs or abilities to engage in practices recommended by the teacher education program."[8] Many of the studies were conducted by a researcher who was also the instructor, and none of the studies followed student teachers beyond the practicum into their teaching careers. Largely conforming to this methodological pattern, McDiarmid and Vinten-Johansen, a teacher educator and a historian who taught pre-service teachers together, propose a solution to the division between historians and history educators:

collaborative delivery of history education.[9] They apologize for lacking the "systematically collected and analyzed data needed to determine whether the[ir] anecdotal evidence [from students] is anything more than self-serving."[10]

Two other studies, both conducted by one of the coauthors of this chapter, follow the same pattern: qualitative case studies involving a few student teachers enrolled in a course taught by the researcher. In "Student Teachers Thinking Historically," Seixas analyses the lesson plans that student teachers developed to help their students interrogate primary sources. Two of the student teachers' lesson plans were successful, and two were unsuccessful. Seixas' method includes both textual analysis of the lesson plans and interviews with the four student teachers.[11] Methodologically different from the Clift and Brady findings, and closer to the current study, is Seixas' "History, Memory and Learning to Teach," for which he enlisted two student teachers as coauthors. The study explores how radically divergent family memories were incorporated into the collaborative on-campus planning and in-school teaching of a unit on World War II for Grade 11.[12]

Segall further shook up the researcher/researched role.[13] As a doctoral student who recently had graduated from a social studies teacher education program, he wrote a dissertation on the methods course (taught by Seixas) in the program he had just completed, using critical theory to analyse the experiences and ideas of six students. He found an overwhelming concern with "the discourse of organization and planning," an orientation that he dismissed as inhibiting a more thoughtful program for future teachers. We will return to this later.

Our Paths to the Social Studies Methods Course

Peter

My major in history at the small, competitive Swarthmore College outside of Philadelphia was a default position: I didn't know what else to do. History was one piece of an education in the liberal arts. As graduation approached in 1969, like most of my classmates I was thinking more about the politics, ethics, and history of the war in Vietnam than about a career. In spite of having taken no education courses, I entered social studies teaching in a tough North Philadelphia school, and received a draft deferment for doing so. After one year of trial by fire, I escaped to British Columbia.

Two decades later, in 1990, I started teaching at the University of British Columbia. I brought to the job twelve years of experience (not counting my Philadelphia initiation) teaching high school in Vancouver, as well as a PhD in history from UCLA. From the beginning of my post-secondary career, I hoped to bring insights from both of these sources to my work in the faculty of education.

In my first year at UBC, there were three courses available for those who were preparing to teach social studies: an introduction to social studies methods course required of all students; an introduction to history methods course, which enrolled those with undergraduate history majors; and an introduction to geography methods course for those with backgrounds in geography. Fresh from teaching in British Columbia schools, I argued that all graduates of the program would be teaching both geography and history in British Columbia's integrated social studies courses, and I spearheaded a revision of the specialized courses into one required social studies methods course.

During the two decades since that revision, I have taught that course in most years, alongside three other sections taught by other instructors, with twenty to thirty-five students in each. The faculty of education must meet a quota in the number of students enrolled, but it is faced with frequent shortfalls in math and science applications. Social studies is an admissions area that takes up the enrolment slack, regardless of the demand for new social studies teachers in the schools. The three or four instructors (a mix of graduate students, sessional instructors, and tenure-track professors) work closely together, coordinating syllabi and assignments. With new resources and research literature, my growing teaching experience, and, most importantly, the input and ideas of colleagues, graduate teaching assistants, and sessional instructors, the course gradually evolved into its current form.

Graeme

My journey to becoming a social studies teacher has been a gradual one. In Grade 4, I recall writing, to the amazement of my teacher, "When I grow up, I want to be a social studies teacher!" To be sure, the seed was planted at an early age. Throughout high school, it was always in the back of my mind that, in the end, I wanted to become a social studies teacher. However, dreams of a career as a professional soccer player came to the forefront of my consciousness; thus, my aspirations of teaching were forgotten by the time I entered university.

Having been admitted to Cornell University to play on the varsity soccer team, I signed up for a couple of American history courses in my first semester (because English and Psychology 101 were both full!) and rediscovered my passion for history. Whether it was the academic environment or the bloodshed that occurred in the American Civil War that inspired me, I fell in love (again) with history and began to pursue my aspirations of becoming a social studies teacher in earnest. During my undergrad program, I studied concepts that would reemerge in my teacher education program, such as the critical study of primary sources and the importance of authorship in historical texts.

After transferring to Queen's University and completing my BA, I worked for a year in the ESL industry before entering the bachelor of education program at UBC. Though I enjoyed my time working with students all around the world, I wanted to teach a topic that I was truly passionate about. This brings us to the social studies methods course where I met Peter.

Challenges in the Course and Program

Peter

The teacher education program at UBC is overcrowded. Faculty members admit that overlapping courses, duplication of assignments, insufficient time outside classes, and lack of overall coordination place extraordinary demands on students during the first term. Too often, the intensity does not necessarily signal either intellectual rigour or practical educational impact.

Within the program, the methods course is where most students learn how to put lessons together, framing them around big, important questions; how to connect lesson objectives with classroom activities that might achieve those objectives; and how to design assessments to measure student achievement. In the methods course, they practise building a sequence of lessons that aim to develop students' understanding of a subject over a couple of weeks and culminate in an activity that demonstrates that understanding: in other words, they build a unit of study. They learn, further, to balance variety and coherence in their units. Stated in this way, the course might sound like a generic course in curriculum and instruction that is not tied to a particular school subject area. But the generic takes shape and makes sense in relation to the school subject of social studies. While all of this is eminently "practical" in terms of preparing to teach, it is also very intellectually demanding. There are no easy formulae for achieving relevance, coherence, logistical manageability, and disciplinary integrity in course planning.

The subject of social studies has a long and troubled history of trying to define itself. It has been conceptualized as citizenship education, as the analysis of contemporary problems, and as a mix of multiple social science disciplines. All of the questions raised by these approaches could be dealt with through a broad, expansive *history* curriculum that incorporates geography and the social sciences. But teachers, students, and the teaching licensure agencies might balk at a "history education methods" course being at the core of a program to train teachers in a jurisdiction where the school subject is defined as "social studies." And so the course is called "social studies methods."

Students arrive at the beginning of the social studies teacher education course with varying backgrounds, strengths, and weaknesses. Of the twenty-five students in my section in 2010, fifteen had majors in history, and the remaining were scattered among physical education, geography, career education, and home economics. Many, including some of the history majors, had sketchy knowledge about large chunks of Canadian history, world history, historical methods, and even contemporary events. While it would have been helpful for most of the students to have taken a history methods course that focused much more on how to teach the substantive issues of Canadian history (e.g., the evolution of French-English relations) or world history (e.g., revolution, empire, and nationalism), it would be difficult to justify such a course as "social studies methods" without providing a similar geography (if not economics and political science) survey. So, we do none of this. Where it surfaces in the course, historical subject matter is incidental, unsystematic, parenthetical, and canonical (Riel, Japanese internment, World War I, the Great Depression, et cetera).

Graeme

Coming into the teacher education program, I had grand hopes of creating a vibrant classroom that was exciting, collaborative and stimulating. I wanted to get students interested in and excited about history – and to promote critical thinking as much as possible. In short, I wanted to change the world, but what new teacher does not? I viewed the teacher education program as the vehicle to get in the schools and accomplish these goals.

Within the teacher education program, Peter's social studies methods course was the one place where students' subject specializations really emerged. Most of the other classes cover topics such as exceptionalities, social justice, and principles of teaching, because students are from a variety of disciplines. The social studies methods course was a welcome dose of practical instruction – for instance, how to plan and implement a lesson – amid courses with other kinds of foci. It was nice to move away from discussions of political correctness and toward questions such as, "How do we actually teach this stuff?"

The major challenges that I faced in the social studies methods course all involved the creation of lesson plans and their implementation. Through these struggles came two specific questions, which most new teachers probably grapple with. The first question – "Why is this taking so long?" – came after I had spent eight hours working on my first ninety-minute lesson plan. Surely not all lessons would take so long to create! The second question – "What role should the textbook play in my teaching?" – was prompted by the first lesson that I taught in the two-week October practicum (halfway into the fall term). It consisted of students being given a question to answer from the textbook, students answering the question, and then the class sharing what they had come up with. This lesson was not an enjoyable one to teach! Through the social studies methods course and the Benchmarks of Historical Thinking Project, my two questions were tackled.

A Design for Historical Thinking in the Social Studies Methods Course

Peter

The 419-page, large-format *Anthology of Social Studies* provides core readings for the course.[14] Its thirty-four chapters contain far more material than could be digested in a term. For a multiauthored anthology of this size, the volume is far more coherent than a naive browser might expect. Roland Case was author or coauthor of more than a third (thirteen) of the chapters, and exercised a firm editorial hand over the rest. The pieces fit smoothly together as an exposition of (and implementation guide for) Case's well-developed and widely disseminated conception of critical thinking for the social studies classroom. However, the second edition of the anthology highlights history education far more than the first edition, reflecting the advances that have been made in conceptualizing historical thinking for teaching. The opening chapter is now Ken Osborne's "The Teaching of History and Democratic Citizenship," and eight other articles focus specifically on history education, far outnumbering the "one-off" chapters on peace, Aboriginal, multicultural, and law-related education. Geography is allotted two chapters. The course syllabus includes fifteen of the chapters, five of which are specifically related to history, including those by Ruth Sandwell (on using primary sources), Ken Osborne (as mentioned above), and Penney Clark (on using visual sources). Other assigned chapters deal with Case's conception of critical thinking, or planning and assessment more generally, and those chapters are not focused on any particular discipline.

Course readings in history education outside of the *Anthology of Social Studies* explore ideas that could be approached from a nondisciplinary frame, but which are given far more traction through disciplinary treatment. In "'They Thought the World Was Flat?': Applying the Principles of *How People Learn* in Teaching High School History," Robert Bain shows how he transforms topics and objectives into large problems-to-be-solved, in order to construct a thoroughly *inquiry-based* course, driven by questions and dilemmas.[15] The problem at the centrepiece of his course is also at the core of the discipline of history: the relationship between the past itself and accounts of the past. In other words, how do we know what we know? The problematizing of historical accounts was a theme that ran throughout Bain's course. The second part of the article explores some *history-specific cognitive tools* that students can use to tackle this problem.

In the course, we approach the use of textbooks through insights provided by Sam Wineburg in "On the Reading of Historical Texts."[16] Wineburg's seminal study demonstrates the "breach" between how historians and high school students read the same historical sources. The students read texts for information and rarely consider problems of authorship, genre, and context. The historians first contextualize sources, thinking about the authors and their positions, interests, backgrounds, credentials, and purposes for writing what they wrote. Wineburg observes that the students – who are top performers in their courses – are trained through high school textbooks to read in exactly the way he observes in his exercise. Citing Crismore, Wineburg observes that textbook authors write with voiceless authority, "providing little indication that interpretation had anything to do with the words on the page."[17] Wineburg's article prompts a discussion, in the methods course, of the uses and pitfalls of textbooks. Further, it leads to critiquing Paul Neufeld's chapter in the *Anthology of Social Studies*.[18] Neufeld's focus is exclusively on developing students' reading comprehension in social studies, which comes at the expense of helping students to pay attention to context and authorship.

The history education articles by Bain and Wineburg set the key themes of the course: how to frame big inquiry questions, and how to use textbooks and other sources, respectively. Similarly, the first assignment asks students to construct a lesson plan around the analysis of one or more primary source documents. While there is room for a student to design a media studies or geography lesson (and some do), the preparation for the assignment most often leads students to centre their lesson plan on the historical interpretation of photographs, artefacts, or short written sources. We spend a class analysing photographs from Canadian history – from late nineteenth-century western settlement and from the Depression era – as well as analysing some short written pieces. Other than learning how to structure a lesson (objectives, activities, resources, assessment – all coherently tied to one another), the focus is on developing a sequence of questions that help student teachers lead their students through a close examination of textual and contextual detail, in order to arrive at inferences about what can be learned from the documents.[19]

Thus, by the time student teachers arrive in week seven (of eleven) – to the section of the course entitled "What is Historical Thinking?" – they have, in fact, done a lot of thinking about historical thinking. In this section, they read Peter Seixas' "Purposes for Teaching Canadian History," and they are formally introduced to the six historical thinking concepts that provide the framework for The Historical Thinking Project.[20] However, the exploration of these six concepts is limited to a few short, in-class exercises at this moment in the course. The week is typically overcrowded. It coincides with students' return from their introductory two-week practicum, and that must be digested. As well, the culminating unit plan assignment, which is to be completed in a series of well-articulated steps over the next four weeks, has to be introduced.

By the end of week seven, historical thinking optimally has become part of the vocabulary of the course. It surfaces again when we consider the uses of film in the screening of "The Ballad of Crowfoot"; when we discuss assessment; and when students analyse questions (both multiple-choice and document-based essay questions) from the Begbie Canadian History Contest.[21] The assembly and writing of the unit plans dominate the final weeks. In 2010, as usual, the vast majority of students (twenty-two of twenty-five students) chose history topics, reflecting the curricula that they were planning to teach during the long (January–April) practicum. The exceptions were one student who compared world religions (with a historical component), and two students who focused on global sustainability.

The Experience of Historical Thinking in the Social Studies Methods Course

Graeme

The theme of historical thinking took a while to develop within the context of the course, as there was a decent amount of time devoted to introducing the subject of social studies, becoming familiar with the BC curriculum, and taking a couple of preliminary stabs at lesson planning. Historical thinking was a topic that some students had an easy time getting their heads around, while some struggled to see how this concept fit in with the course. A few classmates were always complaining about the stress that was put on historical thinking: "I'm a P.E. teacher, why should I care about how we view history?" Others were clearly unfamiliar with the study of history: "Where am I supposed to find a primary source?" While there was griping, there was also a general acceptance of the importance of teaching critical thinking and critical reading of history.

Students used the six historical thinking concepts of The Historical Thinking Project to the extent that they found them useful. Almost everyone had a different opinion of the concepts: some students saw them as useless, irrelevant, and unhelpful in terms of engaging with history. Others felt that certain aspects of the concepts could be useful, but that the concepts were oversimplified and the list was not exhaustive. Still others felt that the concepts should be used during every lesson, as much as possible. This leads to the question: what did *I* think of them?

My view of the concepts probably fell for the most part into the latter category, but that is not to say that good historical teaching can *only* occur if the historical thinking concepts are used. A master teacher is a master teacher: if you are good at what you do, it does not matter what framework you use. I viewed them as a means to an end. If the end is the curriculum, then you can engage with the subject matter critically in many different ways. For me, using the historical thinking concepts helped me to cover the curriculum and to ensure that critical thinking was an integral part of all my lessons. The concepts require a certain level of higher-order thinking; using them guarantees that students will do more than memorize facts. In addition, the concepts helped me to tackle my two main questions: "Why is this taking so long?" and "What role should the textbook play in my teaching?"

I found the historical thinking concepts to be a great time-saving tool, as I would scaffold my lesson plans around them. For example, putting the concept of "evidence" at the centre of the lesson made my job easier. Instead of having to create questions about how to critically examine a primary source, I would use the evidence template, select a primary source, and then the main body of the lesson would be taken care of.

My question about how to use the textbook in my teaching was also solved using the historical thinking concepts. I would frame a section of a textbook with a historical thinking concept, and build the lesson from there. For example, I wanted to do a lesson about inventions during the Renaissance, and I needed to decide how to focus it. Using the concept of "cause and consequence," I had the students study an invention from the Renaissance and then think about how these inventions manifested themselves later in history, including their present-day forms.

For a beginning teacher, The Historical Thinking Project made it much easier to access history as a subject to be taught. Not only did it embed critical thinking into the curriculum, it served as an effective time-saving device and a way for me to unpack how to use the textbook.

A First Taste of Historical Thinking for Grades 8 and 9

Graeme

Going into my practicum, I tried to structure my units and lesson plans around historical thinking concepts. Over the course of the first two units I taught (one Grade 8, the other Grade 9), I was able to use all six concepts from The Historical Thinking Project. Obviously, some lessons went better than others – as you would expect from any beginning teacher. Overall, though, my initial experiences with teaching historical thinking were quite positive. The concept of "continuity and change" was particularly adaptable, and I used it with both grade levels, in a unit on the Renaissance with Grade 8 students, and in a unit on Canadian First Nations with Grade 9 students. I centred both of these lessons on analysing the present day compared with a historical period and illustrating the ways things have changed and stayed the same.

For the unit about First Nations peoples for Grade 9, I structured the lesson around the question, "What are the most significant ways that Plains culture has changed and stayed the same since the pre-contact era?" I started the lesson with a discussion of what it must have been like for First Nations people when Europeans tried to take away all of their land and their homes, leaving them with very little. As a class, we then reviewed the section in the textbook titled "The People of the Plains," taking note of how they operated as a community, what sorts of traditions they had, and how they migrated seasonally and hunted the buffalo. The lesson asked students to compare the textbook's description of the Plains people with how these same people were portrayed in a modern documentary about life on a Cree reserve. After watching this documentary, a couple of things particularly struck the students. One was the way that the Cree living on the reserve were a close community that relied on each other for nearly everything – something that had been highlighted in the textbook as well. The other was how the Cree were now quite immobile; they stayed isolated on the reserve, and people who move away are an exception. At the end of the lesson, the class debated what was more significant: that the Cree remained a close-knit community or that they had lost much of their ancestors' freedom of movement.

In the Grade 8 unit on the Renaissance, the lesson focused on the question, "What are the biggest differences between marriage and family life during the Renaissance and the present?" The students were immediately excited when they learned that we were going to deal with the topic of marriage. (At least, the girls became excited; the boys became sheepish!) The lesson began with a discussion of student's views on marriage: whether they ever wanted to get married, whether they wanted to have children, and whether men or women generally have more power in a relationship. As a class, we then analysed a chart comparing marriage in the Renaissance with marriage in the present day. We looked at such categories as: average age difference between brides and grooms; average age difference between mothers and fathers; average age of first marriage; and average family size. I asked the class questions about what the statistics in these categories could tell us about what life was like during the Renaissance and how life had changed. Students concluded, among other things, that during the Renaissance men had more power; that modern people have much more choice in whom they marry; and that during the Renaissance it was not very fun to be a woman. To conclude the lesson, students were put into groups and asked to create two thirty-second skits comparing how a married couple would have interacted during the Renaissance and how they might interact in the present day.

I received minimal support in my efforts to incorporate historical thinking into my planning after I left Peter's class and entered my practicum. Though my faculty adviser and sponsor teachers gave advice on how to improve my practice, they focused on aspects other than my use of historical thinking. They made suggestions for classroom management, questioning techniques, and construction of test questions, but not for the overall direction of my unit plans or the history-based activities. If teacher education programs are trying to produce social studies teachers who have a firm grasp on certain skills, there must be opportunities to cultivate these skills outside of the social studies methods courses. As it stands, I studied the importance of historical thinking during two social studies courses but nowhere else during or after my practicum.

Gaps, Opportunities, Recommendations

In 2010, Peter managed to squeeze historical thinking into the social studies methods course, which was itself squeezed into an overcrowded fall term, with no systematic coordination with other courses on "Principles of Teaching," "Assessment," or "Adolescent Development." It was left to the student teachers themselves to make connections – or not. After he was finished with Peter's course, Graeme went off to the practicum, and found that working with the historical thinking concepts to which he had been briefly exposed gave form and purpose to his lessons. His rationale was twofold: he had found that the concepts helped students to think more critically and deeply *and* that the concepts helped him to plan and manage more efficiently. Notwithstanding Segall's concerns, there was no dichotomy for this beginning teacher between good planning and teaching historical thinking. Indeed, though we cannot prove it through this small research exercise, it seems likely that those who plan and organize poorly would also provide students with fewer opportunities for engaged historical thinking.

Preparation for teaching history as an active knowledge-generating process is enormously complex and demanding. Our dialogue points towards at least two directions for improvement; neither of them is particularly difficult to articulate, but both of them would be difficult to achieve.

The first tactic for improvement that emerges from our dialogue concerns the pre-program preparation, selection, and admission of student teachers. As Alan Sears writes in this volume, there is no substitute, in terms of gaining experience, for *doing* the discipline that one is preparing to teach. Learning history, then, should be thought of as an apprenticeship in the contextualization and interpretation of evidence, the weighing of multiple causal factors, the evidence-based imagining of real lives very different from our own, and the judicious assessment of the ethical demands that the past places on the present. One must have mastered these practices in order to teach them, but helping student teachers to achieve this mastery is too tall an order for the teacher education program itself. Only student teachers who are *already* proficient in historical thinking are ready to learn the complex and demanding task of shaping experiences for the young novices who will enter *their* classrooms.

Both Graeme and Peter noted the diverse disciplinary backgrounds of the students in their class, only three-fifths of whom were history majors. And, as Ruth Sandwell suggests in her chapter, many history majors complete undergraduate programs without having paid systematic attention to historiographical methods or gained a common vocabulary for discussing how the discipline works. Ironically, establishing rigorous, well-articulated requirements for entering history student teachers might contribute to reforms all the way across the campus in the history department's undergraduate program.

Second, it will always be difficult to make disciplinary practices and ways of knowing foundational components of teaching and learning when they are considered peripheral to the teacher education program. The effectiveness of any coursework is diluted (if not diminished altogether) if the orientations, concepts, and vocabulary taught on campus are not sustained through collaboration among the triad of on-campus instructors, faculty advisers, and school advisers. Simultaneous and coordinated programs for in-service professional development would help to develop a common vocabulary and shared understandings of the nature and needs of the school subject of history among all those who have a hand in training new teachers.

In this intellectual environment, history student teachers might thrive: lessons learned in university classrooms would not wither when the student teachers arrive in the schools.

The discourse around teacher education reform, both at the University of British Columbia and beyond, is strikingly thin on the question of teaching disciplinary ways of thinking. And while scientific thinking and mathematical thinking are relatively well established and understood within and beyond education circles, what it means to *think historically* is only now becoming part of the conversation. The relative paucity of research on the social studies methods courses – where historical thinking has its small window of opportunity – has important implications for the advancement of the field. Grossman and Schoenfeld posit that the central place for pedagogical content knowledge is in the training of teachers, but without studies that examine how pedagogical content knowledge is actually taught and under what circumstances student teachers can bring these understandings to the classroom, history educators will continue to fly by the seat of their pants.[22]

NOTES

1 Alan Sears starts from this point in "Moving from the Periphery to the Core: The Possibilities for Professional Learning Communities in History Teacher Education," this volume.

2 Peter Seixas, "A Modest Proposal for Change in Canadian History Education," *International Review of History Education* 6 (2010): 11-26.

3 Peter Seixas, "A Discipline Adrift in an 'Integrated' Curriculum: History in British Columbia Schools," *Canadian Journal of Education* 19, no. 1 (1994): 99-107.

4 Scott Pollock's chapter in this volume provides a more thorough review of this research literature, but bears a similar complaint.

5 James A. Banks and Walter C. Parker, "Social Studies Teacher Education," in *Handbook of Research on Teacher Education*, edited by W. Robert Houston (New York: Macmillan, 1990), 674-86.

6 J. Sikula, T. Better, and E. Guyton, eds., *Handbook of Research on Teacher Education*, 2nd ed. (New York: Simon and Schuster Macmillan, 1996).

7 Renee T. Clift and Patricia Brady, "Research on Methods Courses and Field Experiences," in *Studying Teacher Education: The Report of the AERA*

Panel on Research and Teacher Education, edited by Marilyn Cochran-Smith and Kenneth M. Zeichner (Mahwah NJ: Lawrence Erlbaum Associates, 2005), 309-424.

8   Ibid., 322.

9   G. Williamson McDiarmid and Peter Vinten-Johansen, "A Catwalk across the Great Divide: Redesigning the History Teaching Methods Course," in *Knowing, Teaching, and Learning History*, edited by Peter N. Stearns, Peter Seixas, and Sam Wineburg (New York: New York University Press, 2000), 156-77.

10 Ibid., 176.

11 Peter Seixas, "Student Teachers Thinking Historically," *Theory and Research in Social Education* 26, no. 3 (1998): 310-41.

12 Peter Seixas, Daniel Fromowitz, and Petra Hill, "History, Memory and Learning to Teach," in *Understanding History: Recent Research in History Education*, vol. 4 of *International Review of History Education*, edited by Rosalyn Ashby, Peter Gordon, and Peter Lee (London: RoutledgeFalmer, 2005), 116-34.

13 Avner Segall, *Disturbing Practice: Reading Teacher Education as Text* (New York: Peter Lang, 2002).

14 Roland Case and Penney Clark, eds., *The Anthology of Social Studies: Issues and Strategies for Secondary Teachers*, vol. 2 (Vancouver: Pacific Educational Press, 2008).

15 Robert B. Bain, "'They Thought the World Was Flat?': Applying the Principles of *How People Learn* in Teaching High School History," in *How Students Learn: History, Mathematics, and Science in the Classroom*, edited by John Bransford and Suzanne Donovan (Washington: The National Academies Press, 2005), 179–213.

16 Samuel S. Wineburg, "On the Reading of Historical Texts: Notes on the Breach between School and Academy," *American Educational Research Journal* 28, no. 3 (1991): 495-519.

17 Ibid., 512.

18 Paul Neufeld, "Reading Comprehension in Social Studies," in *The Anthology of Social Studies: Issues and Strategies for Secondary Teachers*, edited by Roland Case and Penney Clark (Vancouver: Pacific Educational Press, 2008), 161-9.

19 Seixas, "Student Teachers Thinking Historically."

20 Peter Seixas, "The Purposes of Teaching Canadian History," *Canadian Social Studies* 36, no. 2 (2002). For more information about The Historical Thinking Project, see http://historicalthinking.ca, accessed 18 March 2014.

21 The film can be seen at the National Film Board of Canada website at
    http://www.nfb.ca/film/ballad_of_crowfoot/; for information about the
    Begbie History Contest materials, see http://www.begbiecontestsociety
    .org/.
22 Pamela Grossman and Alan Schoenfeld, "Teaching Subject Matter," in
    *Preparing Teachers for a Changing World: What Teachers Should Learn and Be
    Able To Do*, edited by Linda Darling-Hammond and John Bransford (San
    Francisco: Jossey-Bass, 2005), 201-31.

10 Engaging Teacher Education through Rewriting That History We Have Already Learned

KENT DEN HEYER

How might we use historical perspective, or, more accurately, multiple historical perspectives to address a number of issues facing teacher education in general and·history education more specifically? These issues include teacher education's limited influence on future classrooms dominated by expectations for coverage and control practices, the depoliticized manner in which we currently take up the "historical" in teacher education, and the regnant form of knowledge as a thing valuable only to the extent it can be exchanged for preferred material and symbolic positioning within the vulture capitalist machinations increasingly dominating school-university spaces.[1]

While these are related issues, I primarily focus here on the latter curricular concern for regnant forms of knowledge and knowing and how that concern illustrates the inadequacy of exploring teacher identity as a professional affiliation. I hope to point to directions beyond this inadequacy by drawing on curriculum theory and by offering an expanded conception of historical perspective that can be used to engage student teachers in their creation of multiple Canadian history narratives.

There are two distinguishable ways to think about historical perspective, one related to the past and the other related to the present. I will discuss these in greater detail later. Each constitutes an important component of historical thinking. The second sense of historical perspective, however, receives inadequate attention. Alan Sears' contribution to this volume speaks to a need to attend to historical perspectives in the present as much as those located in the past.

While Sears makes many excellent points, to begin I highlight only two: the importance of attending to students' prior knowledge or "cognitive frames," and Sears' call for history educators to work as brokers who cross boundaries. Sears wants history educators to assist their students to move on an "inward trajectory" towards the "community of practice" populated at the core by those with competencies in historical thinking. Sears also notes that "core" competencies can change as new definitions or concepts find a place within the community of practice. Engaging seriously with these points necessitates that we use historical perspective as a frame for our present beliefs about schooling, learning, and indeed, history itself.

Context

What we mean by historical perspective and how we adopt it in our teacher education classrooms is an especially relevant topic in Alberta in light of a recently implemented provincial K–12 social studies program. The new program asks that teachers help K–12 students use content to inquire into two central themes: citizenship and identity. Its most noteworthy feature, however, is its call for teachers to address citizenship and identity through the "multiple perspectives" of Aboriginal and francophone communities in regards to different interpretations of Canada's past and contemporary issues such as globalization. Unnamed in the program is another historical perspective discussed further below, from and about which almost all content is drawn for the provincial high school standardized test – a particular English Canadian perspective.

Many practicing teachers and student teachers are stressed about this new K–12 social studies program. Their stress centres on what constitutes a perspective and is mostly articulated in regards to Aboriginal perspectives. These are understandable anxieties. Aboriginal perspectives are for many a foreign territory despite the availability of an immense number of resources from which one could learn. One veteran teacher interviewed for a study by David Scott makes this point directly:

> I don't know what the Aboriginal perspectives [are]. I can't represent them. The only time I can talk about Aboriginal perspectives is when I talk about conditions in their communities and residential school experience. Here I can say Aboriginal people have been badly treated. But I cannot say what the Aboriginal perspective is on mining and logging.[2]

In this richly detailed study with five practicing secondary teachers, which examined how the teachers understood and enacted "multiple perspectives" in their classrooms, Scott concludes:

There was a marked resistance to providing room for Aboriginal and Francophone perspectives and a general absence of engagements with these perspectives in the classroom. This can be partially attributed to their belief that [these perspectives] are only relevant in relation to a historical event or issue involving these groups.[3]

However we may define perspective, this study reveals that for these teachers, "alternative" perspectives only matter in relation to "special" topics or to the events when the teachers believe these particular groups were either directly involved or negatively impacted.

Dwayne T. Donald has also done extensive work related to Aboriginal perspectives with teachers in Alberta preparing for the recent program implementation. He identifies a "cultural disqualification" argument used by many teachers to justify their nonengagement with Aboriginal perspectives. He notes, "the pedagogical logic implied is that teachers are only allowed to teach about their own cultures – a logic that the field of education has never upheld."[4] For example, it is quite likely these same teachers would not feel disqualified – nor would they be expected to exempt themselves from – teaching about the impoverished eighteenth-century Gaelic-speaking Scots and their immigration to present-day Manitoba and farther west.

As they relate to "multiple perspectives," these findings indicate that we are not dealing here merely with a lack of information or a deficiency in the skills of historical thinking as presently defined. Issues related, for example, to Aboriginal Alberta elicit difficult emotions, reflecting a colonial legacy and ongoing land disputes (including disputes over land from which immense oil, gas, and mineral wealth is currently being extracted). These are dark holes for many of our mainstream practicing teachers and our student teachers that continue to fester as symbolic and material divisions at the heart of the Canadian nationalist project. While such divisions can be read from multiple perspectives, we can understand why many practicing and student teachers avoid doing so as they positively identify with the ideals represented in this nationalist project rather than its dissonance.

The operative identity here is not professional. Rather, the operative identity is one wrapped up in a nationalist project-historical perspective that provides easy "marks" for those who claim that some perspectives are "special interest" or "revisionist" – claims that become privileged as commonsensical by their repetition in textbooks and media. Thus, perhaps one object of attention for history teacher educators should be the nature of historical identifications themselves, the emotional/psychodynamic hold they have on us when we enter the classroom, and the way these identifications impact what we feel more or less comfortable to talk about.

Framing Stances

In addition to how we learn to identify with some but not other perspectives and stories as part of "our" history, history teacher education would benefit from attending to another kind of relationship to knowledge and knowing. Sears points to the work of Gardner and Barton and Levstik among others to highlight findings that young people enter our classrooms with pre-established understandings about history. Likewise, student teachers have "a strong cognitive frame that history teaching essentially involves the passing on of historical information and not the fostering of historical thinking."[5] In accordance with their apprenticeship of observation, many student teachers will also seek to embody an inherited teacher script as one who explains (rather than explores) and provides answers (rather than questions). It is crucial to note, as in the context described above, that this script exists outside the purview of current debates over what constitutes the doing of history. Student teachers are likely to be passive consumers of knowledge itself regardless of the subject concerned.

Segall and Gaudelli reflect on their teaching of social studies student teachers. About those experiences, they note that "what most often took place was a 'performance of learning' rather than learning: there was learning that did not get implicated and students who did not implicate themselves or their practicum environments in that learning."[6] They offer an explanation to account for this situation: students come to their courses habituated as consumers of theory and practice rather than as generators of such. In other words, Segall and Gaudelli conclude that their students prefer to engage theory, readings, and their own learning in a "readerly" rather than a "writerly" manner.[7]

In a readerly approach to learning texts, the knowledge that counts is assumed to reside in the text itself, and the reader-student's task is to extract and re-present their knowing in accordance with schooled expectations. In contrast, a writerly approach to texts calls upon readers to create multiple and often-tentative meanings with reference to the context of their lives. It is in the "con" and "dis" of junctures between the text and context that meaning and value in this view are created: "In this sense, the writerly text asks that the reader 'write' while reading."[8] In contrast to the readerly desire that Segall and Gaudelli note that their students have to extract the presumed prespecified knowledge, in a writerly approach meanings emerge when something is lost – the habit of learned relationships to the texts of our learning lives (as taken up most profoundly in curriculum theory) and a presumption about certainty as to what we can claim to know (both a curricular and history education contribution to learning).

In identifying this pressing need for writerly engagements with knowledge and knowing, we cross a border between history education as a concern for disciplinary competency and curriculum theory. As for Sears' assertion that brokering is needed between history educators, teachers, and historians, I think it equally necessary for a brokering between history education and curriculum theory: that area of inquiry that studies the formation of education subjects and the educated subjectivities we as teachers presume to teach and to what end(s). I turn now to suggest a useful distinction in curriculum theory that could inform teacher education work in history and social studies.

Brokers and Boundaries

A distinction between *curriculum-as-thing* (the delivery of a body of facts, skills, and attitudes to the student body) and *curriculum-as-encounter* (the ways in which our shared sense making is itself a historical legacy that requires explicit study) reflects two differing interpretations of *curriculum* in the curriculum studies literature that informs teacher education.

Questions about curriculum as a "thing" centre on how best to convey the body of content that students should acquire, what techniques assist in this acquisition, and what assessments best measure acquisition. This interpretation of curriculum "focuses on success or failure in the production of intended understandings or cognitions. Hence ... the tendency [is] to see education as a matter of production, rather than formation."[9] For Tony Whitson, an interpretation of curriculum as a program organized to produce intended consequences can be neither adequately enacted in classrooms nor studied as an object of scholarly attention without a consideration of "the larger curriculum of [students' and teachers'] lives beyond the school."[10] Several other scholars exemplify scholarship from this broader curricular – "curriculum-as-encounter" – orientation.[11]

Reviewing their York University teacher education program, Britzman et al. find that differing practices in teacher education reflect different questions: "The central question that orients much of our [current] work as teacher educators is: How do we teach (other) people to teach?"[12] This question, they argue, guides teacher education as an "instrumentalist practice" where "classrooms are essentially places to practice techniques without regard to the complexities of the student's life."[13] Avoiding such complexities marginalizes the vital questions we might ask about "what racial, sexual, class, and gendered inequalities do to techniques, students, and teachers."[14] Each of these dimensions of human subjectivity-identification profoundly shape people and, therefore, shape what future teachers likely are (and are not) comfortable to address in their classrooms.

There are two parts to the argument that taking up the idea of curriculum as encounter would benefit history and social studies teacher education. First, it is necessary for all involved to learn from knowledge already possessed. Second, it is vital to learn from those questions, issues, or alternative perspectives (i.e., "difficult" rather than confirmatory "lovely knowledge") that potentially put at risk what we can claim to know about schools, teaching, and learning, including the teaching and learning that occurs in teacher education.

As "thing," curriculum produces particular "readerly" relationships, in which students take up a distanced stance of removed acquisition. As one of my education students in class described her award-winning success as a high school student, "Look, I just wanted to know what I needed to know, I didn't want to have to think about it." In contrast, as "encounter," curriculum seeks to normalize a different kind of relationship, in which students are implicated in a writerly manner with the texts of their learning lives. As the same student stated moments later in frustration, when pushed to explain what her "success" might say about learning to teach in schools: "Yes, but if we have students think all day, when will we get anything done?" What approaches to historical core competencies that we are presently considering could possibly address the "prior beliefs" referenced here? None.

This curricular distinction between thing and encounter helps us to engage powerful and pre-existing relationships to text (i.e., schooling, what counts as knowledge and appropriate claims about knowing) that history, from a disciplinary point of view, cannot raise, let alone address in teacher education. That is why we have two very different enterprises: history as a scholarly report of something having to do primarily with the past, and history/social studies education as scholarly teaching having to do primarily with the present and the (hoped-for) future. Of course, this distinction is not so simple. As we see further below, even history as scholarly report is intimately tied to present historical perspectives, and contemporary education is, sadly, tied to those perspectives that should be past.[15]

The relevance of this distinction between thing and encounter lies in a) acknowledging the powerful relationship students already have with institutionalized knowledge and knowing; and b) affirming that there is much to be learned about teaching from a reexamination of these relationships along with their inherited and specific content. Let me provide a brief example in regards to this last point about content.

As Daniel Francis describes, many if not most non-Aboriginal Canadians arrive in our classrooms with inherited knowledge about Aboriginal peoples besides knowledge that hinders an engagement with multiple perspectives.[16] This knowledge most often concerns an "imaginary Indian" that Donald argues needs to be confronted:

> Canadians [need to] realize that their formal education and socialization has, both subtly and overtly, presented them with a theory of Indigenousness that has shaped and conditioned their ability to respond to Aboriginal presence and participation encountered in their daily lives.[17]

Taking Donald's point seriously (as a curriculum-as-encounter) requires broadening our notion of what constitutes curriculum and what history and social studies teacher education needs to address. To do this, we require ideas, concepts, and activities that may unsettle and complicate, or confirm and inspire, deeply held intellectual beliefs and emotional investments related to: (a) what we have learned about ourselves and "others"; (b) those from whom we have learned; (c) learning theory as a general topic; (d) learning theory as it relates to becoming a teacher; and (e) learning to teach history and social studies in institutions.

Harnessing the potential of these curricular questions necessitates a new guiding question. Rather than asking how we can teach (other) people to teach core competencies or procedures, I propose that we ask: "What can we learn about teaching and history from re-reading in a 'writerly' manner what and how we have been taught?" Such a question creates richer potential for a "Christopherian encounter," or what I have explored elsewhere as an "event," as students learn about teaching by re-writing what they already know but have likely not had opportunity to adequately re-cognize. How is it, for example, that regardless of geography, so many mainstream Canadians have this "imaginary Indian" free-floating outside historical context as a thought-virus that even the highly "educated" pass on to the newly arrived?[18] What chance do mainstream Canadians have to learn from "multiple perspectives" in teacher education if this widely distributed imagery is not first reconsidered?

This guiding question takes seriously the processes of considering prior knowledge and "framing stances" towards knowing – exactly the encounter that needs to happen within teacher education. It also extends identifications beyond a rather narrow notion of induction into a shifting professional designation. Identity here is a learned formation – a schooled subjectivity – that both emerges from and contributes to unstable identifications with particular classed, gendered, sexualized, and racialized affiliations. Following Lisa Farley, and as explored in greater depth in my final section, this is the work required to become "a *historical* subject: defined as a capacity to tolerate – and narrate – the disillusionment of encountering the otherness that history both references and provokes on the inside."[19]

Having identified what I hold to be a key curricular distinction– a call for recognizing what can be gained in teacher education through distinguishing curriculum as a thing from curriculum as an encounter, and through distinguishing training from an education, in which subjectivity is the key text – let me recross the border to more familiar territory to identify several other key concepts that should be included at the centre of history education.

Historical Perspective(s)

The field of history education confines issues of perspective to the past: students should try to understand the contexts in which those in the past operated in order to come to a reasoned judgment about their intentions and actions. This requires that we "take on" a person's (or people's) perspective. In this way, perspective-taking has been linked to empathy – an understanding of the situations or psychological states in which historical others operated.[20] For Peter Seixas, "taking historical perspective means understanding the social, cultural, intellectual, and emotional settings that shaped people's lives and actions in the past."[21]

Keith Barton and Linda Levstik prefer the term "perspective recognition," writing that "perspective accords well with intuitive notions about the complex elements of individual viewpoints."[22] "Multiple perspectives" therefore involves the study of contextual influences on different beliefs, values, or political opinions in the past: for example, the need for students to consider the contrasting opinions about slavery held by those living during the US antebellum south.

Building on Seixas' work, Mike Denos and Roland Case note that historical perspective-taking involves "understanding the prevailing norms of the time more than ... adopting a particular person's point of view." Denos and Case also state that "presentism is the antithesis of historical perspective: Presentism is the imposition of a contemporary perspective when interpreting events in the past."[23] In regards to the historical concept of "significance," however, they also write, "What will be judged to be significant may vary depending upon an individual's or group's perspective."[24] So, there are some tight lines to negotiate here.

On the one hand, I should learn to hold my present perspective at bay in order to sufficiently understand conditions affecting the perspectives of historical others. On the other, it is precisely my present perspective (or, more accurately, the perspective of the group with which I identify) that determines what I will recognize as significant about the past in and about particular cases. With this double handedness, we arrive at two distinct but mutually necessary interpretations of the history with which teacher educators should be concerned.

History is of course about the past. Educators like those cited above focus on past events to develop skills or historical competencies. Equally, however, history is also about what one or another group decides is significant about the past for us all to learn in public school – significant because you do not make it to a teacher education program without having sufficiently re-presented that perspective to "make the grade" on standardized tests. History is not only about the past, therefore. Rather, it is just as much about a selection of those aspects of the past that serve or agree with some group's present perspective. It is this second meaning of history that I argue requires greater attention than it has received to date.

Grand Narratives: Curriculum as Encounter

An English Canadian grand narrative (what most of my student teachers assume to be one and the same as the past) dominates the school story of English Canada. As explored in more detail elsewhere, this is an exclusionary narrative that shapes textbooks into chapters (e.g., "the settling of the west," implying a lack of settlement prior to European arrival) and shapes the temporal organization of teaching in university history departments across the country (e.g., pre- and post-Confederation university courses).[25] Summarizing research on the topic, I note the following characteristics of grand narratives:

- They offer people simple and easily digestible plot lines that belie both the complexity of the past and its uncertain emergence into a present.
- They form an interpretive template that, along with repetitive over-generalizations of we/them or ours/theirs, absorbs more specific narratives. This template diminishes the complexity of the historical processes involved in community formation and identification. Left unexamined, "we" become easily ensnarled in "mistaken identities" through "a series of references or canonical figures that sometimes narrowly coincides with what Canada or Quebec was or actually is."[26]
- They are stories in which "women, Aboriginal people, and immigrants are secondary characters in young people's story of Quebec" and elsewhere, as research shows.[27]

Teacher educators can safely assume that many of their mainstream students have inherited grand narratives as a basic framework for understanding both the past and their present identifications (e.g., Americans, Canadians). Otherwise, they would have been unlikely to make the grade and have the opportunity to take a university class. As one of my student teachers writes:

[F]rom kindergarten to graduation, we are constantly bombarded (and completely unaware) of the grand narrative. We learn how white men *civilized* the aboriginals, settled North America and created *Canada*.

Given the preponderance of grand narratives reported in the scholarship across provincial and national populations, I find it curious, to say the least, that we have no examples in the teacher education/history education literature of how to engage these stories as an educative opportunity.[28] On the other hand, it is not surprising, given that so many teacher educators and their mainstream students understand curriculum as a "thing" rather than as an "encounter." This, I argue, needs to change. To aid such change, I now explicate in more detail what I mean by historical perspective and illustrate its efficacy for teacher education in history and social studies.

Historical Perspective and Narratives

As Shemilt observes, narratives are "interpretations whose epistemological status differs from the facts incorporated into them."[29] Facts, such as people, dates, and events, and knowledge of geography constitute one level of historical knowledge, while "emplotments" that link these data into stories are another:

> The meaning of stories is given in their emplotment. By emplotment, a sequence of events is "configured" ("grasped together") [such that] any given set of real events can be emplotted in a number of ways, can bear the weight of being told as any number of different kinds of stories.[30]

The work of William Cronon highlights both this distinct epistemological status and the role current-day "historical perspectives" play in "emplotting" facts into historical narratives.[31]

Cronon examines the books of two US historians, both published in 1979. These historians "dealt with virtually the same subject" and "had researched many of the same documents, and agreed on most of their facts, and yet their conclusions could hardly have been more different."[32] Using their words, Cronon argues that every scholarly narrative constitutes a value-laden creation:

> In the final analysis, the story of the Dust Bowl was the story of people, people with ability and talent, people with resourcefulness, fortitude, and courage … They were builders of tomorrow … Because of those determined people … the nation today enjoys a better standard of living.[33]
>
> The Dust Bowl was the darkest moment in the twentieth-century life of the southern plains … The Dust Bowl was the inevitable outcome of a culture that deliberately, self-consciously, set itself the task of dominating and exploiting the land for all it was worth.[34]

How did two well-regarded historians dealing with the same archival sources and facts come to such different conclusions?

While these narratives concern the same agreed-upon set of facts, the facts are read through divergent historical perspectives that give rise to two entirely different "stories."[35] What happened, or what is reasonable to believe about the facts of the matter and their sources, is not the primary lesson that we can take from these historians. Rather, the facts are always emplotted or strung together like a story-threaded necklace woven out of present concerns, in Cronon's estimation: "In both cases the shape of the landscape conformed to the human narratives that were set within it and so became the terrain on which their different politics contested each other."[36]

These historical findings speak as much to or from present concerns as speaking from the past itself or from the evidence by which we interpret the past. Thus, investigating with student teachers the role of historical perspectives in emplotting events into the grand and "(un)usual narratives" is to aid both their historical competence and the clarity of their own subjective commitments as future teachers.[37] To this end, several important conceptual resources require emphasis.

The first is *narrative trajectory*, which refers to the linkage of present issues to antecedent events and plausible future outcomes. In interpreting an issue of concern, a trajectory is an identifiable politicized value commitment that weaves together past events, a present issue of concern, and a lesson for the present-future into a single story as illustrated by Cronon's example above.

These commitments that shape historical facts into different stories both emerge from and contribute to differing *historical perspectives*. We need to distinguish a *historical perspective* from a *historical point of view*. I use the term "historical point of view" to refer to the application of human cognition to an *event* – considering different points of view on what is reasonable to believe might have happened. By contrast, a historical perspective refers to the application of human cognition to a *narrative* – considering what a single event *means* or signifies in relation to other events in order to evaluate "what is going on?"

In a value-laden reading, we might identify a historical perspective theoretically (e.g., neoliberal, Marxism, feminism); as emerging from a position of concern having to do with ethnicity, gender, or class; or as stemming from any other position (or combination of positions) from or for which someone utilizes an identifiable analytical framework. Whatever the case, a historical perspective is a contemporary political lens that endows events with meaning and significance by linking several or more events together to create a narrative trajectory. Note the difference in emphasis between point of view and perspective.

The goal of aiding students' critical thinking about a historical point of view – as we see with the emphasis on primary sources – concerns what happened, hoping that the skills learned will somehow help students understand what is presently going on where they live as citizens.[38] The question of what is going on, however, requires that students be able to recognize how events are emplotted by historical perspectives to create meaning and significance (for example, in their textbooks). Thus, locating history education's object (e.g., an event and related primary sources) and subject (e.g., historical procedures or problems) as primarily having to do with the past is highly inadequate if schools are to be places where democratic lives and judgments begin. After all, and as Cronon's study details, historical judgments about what happened are intimately tied to an often-tacit assertion about what is going on and about what we need to be concerned. By not attending to historical perspective as a present frame, we as history educators are profoundly ahistorical.

Based on these distinctions between historical trajectory, perspective, and point of view, student teachers were required to complete a "digital multiple historical narrative assignment" as part of their social studies methods course. This project asked student teachers to research and produce at least two digitally rendered narratives (totalling eight minutes of video or less) to convey different interpretations of Canadian history. In groups of two or three, student teachers researched differing historical perspectives of their choice and employed these perspectives to create their narratives. I required that each narrative tie together a minimum of three events and share at least one event in common with the other narrative(s). That is, student teachers conveyed one narrative using at least three events and then returned to one event of their choice to begin telling another narrative from a second historical perspective (they could if they wished also use the same three events in the two different narratives). The assignment had one significant limit: students could not re-present a grand narrative.

While the videos were produced in groups of two or three, each student teacher was required to hand in an individual reflection paper addressing several questions:

1 What intellectual challenges in the process of representing multiple narratives did you encounter?
2 What troubled you about this assignment?
3 What aspects of this project would you use in your classroom and what would you change?

These papers were collected electronically and merged into one searchable PDF file for analysis.[39] The headings that follow and insights from

Figure 10.1: An example of intersecting narrative trajectories.

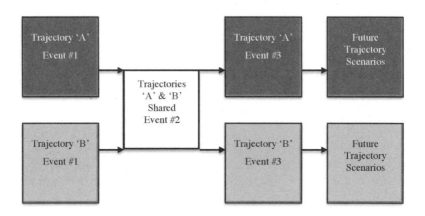

student teachers' papers articulate exactly the kinds of prior knowledge and identifications that history educators need to address when
organizing their curriculum as an encounter.

Confronting a Grand Narrative

At the most obvious level, the assignment disrupts student teachers'
identification with the veiled nature of the grand narrative: veiled in
both its ubiquitous presence that requires no name (as evident in the
absence of such a named perspective in the new provincial program of
studies), and, simultaneously, its deafening presence that frustrates
the consideration of alternative historical perspectives and narrations.
M, for example, expresses discomfort in encountering a previously un-
recognized gulf between an inherited historical perspective and the
"truth" of the past: "What we have been exposed to all our lives," he
wrote, "is somebody's spin on certain events and it kind of depressed
me to wonder what reality really is, and to think how brainwashed I
probably am." P's reflection paper sums up the most commonly identified challenge groups encounter during this assignment: "We found
it difficult to fully circumvent the clutches in terms of both perspectives and assumptions of an all-encompassing, intrinsically colonial
and intensely reductionist grand narrative." These students confront
the absent presence operating behind official historical accounts. They

recognize a powerful and (purportedly) perspective-less mythos central to the nation-state project.

In a related point, some students also write about confronting other disturbing and inherited cultural tools in their historical sense making. B's reflection on his group's video offers a particularly poignant example. In their first rendered narrative, they offer the historical perspective of Anglo-North American economic, political, and religious agents as enforcers of an alleged natural law of racial hierarchy still at work in Canada today. Sharing the "event" of church-run residential schools, their second narrative is a feminist exploration of gendered power relationships in the home and church in Canada and explores women's struggle to access sites of formal power.[40] B struggles in his reflection paper with what he already knew but did not adequately recognize:

> During the process of creating the video, I wrote out the narrations that I wanted to use during the bulk of the video. The first was to come from a supremacist perspective. The challenge that arose intellectually was the realization that it was easy to write; frankly, too easy ... This is a bit startling. It feels like there is a genuine racist somewhere in me that is being suppressed. That is not something that I want to believe. Conversely, for the second narrative, I found writing the script from a feminist perspective to be frustrating, in some ways, daunting ... I could easily replicate the "angry feminist" voice, that wasn't the problem. There simply was a tension for me in that my internal reaction to feminism was not what my rational brain knows. I have to pose the question to myself: Why is it easier for me to become a racial supremacist than a feminist?

During our debriefing in class of what was learned during the assignment, B voluntarily shared this insight and the necessity of his question. I encouraged B to move beyond feelings of guilt. Rather, we considered the question of why some historical perspectives and not others are readily available as sense-making tools for student teachers' historical understandings and their emerging commitments as teachers who will likely work with students who have comparable orientations in their future classrooms.

In addition to having students explore the ways in which their historical sensibilities have been shaped by the anglophone Canadian grand narrative, the individual reflection papers resulted in several other notable insights into the challenges presented by multiple historical perspectives.

Representation of Others More Difficult Than Assumed

Students struggle with how best to locate and articulate marginalized narratives in ways that do not reproduce the reductionist portrayals they learn to associate with the grand narrative. In this sense, students' digital narratives revealed a desire to empathize with other people/perspectives while working to ensure that their representations were accessible to their colleagues. K, for example, states, "My group was up way to [sic] late arguing over whether we should use an image of an Inuit man on ice hunting with a spear. How stereotypical is that! But we have so little time [to tell this story]."

Appeals to Truth and Reality

Frustrated with this tension of representation, some student teachers call on "realist" notions of history and identity: they expressed a belief that a "full" or "truthful" understanding of "what really happened" is possible independent of interpretation/historical perspective/emplotment. F writes that "it was hard to put yourself in the shoes of a different perspective. This is because no matter how much I learn and research, I will never *gain a full understanding* of what it is like to be a minority in Canada" (emphasis added). Employing what Donald names above as a "cultural disqualification" argument, T again states that membership in an "other" group is required to correctly represent their perspective: "The idea that I can accurately represent a varied and marginalized perspective is problematic as I am not a true representative of the perspective we chose to use." T suggests that a "real life encounter with someone invested and intimately connected with a different perspective may have brought about a completely different emplotment of the narrative" than those constructed by herself and her peers from their own group's perspective.

Cracked Identities

K ties together many of the tensions student teachers experience in trying to assemble their research and produce the video component. K struggles with expectations that she provide a voice for other groups. Of the Inuit and the Quebecois, she writes, "these are huge groups of people of all economic, social and political backgrounds, with varying beliefs. To lump them in a group and give their collective perspective seems to diminish their individual complexities." She sums up her exploration of representation, construction of historical narratives, and the difficulty of teaching a marginalized perspective:

> I feel that might be the point of the assignment, to grapple with the difficulty of giving another perspective. All groups of people are complex and have complexities that cannot easily be captured and portrayed in a small video presentation. This relates to the fact that in our classrooms time is limited and the "other" perspective we may offer may be a very limited or small reflection on that group.

While reading the past through alternative historical perspectives is indeed difficult, some students now recognize the need for multiple perspectives to approximate historical-contemporary complexities: "The idea," according to J, "of capturing only the most important aspects of a situation based on a single group's perspective seemed almost impossible; realistically I am not doing the event any kind of justice."

Indicative of how the assignment revealed that historical work is emotionally demanding, D writes:

> The freedom of the assignment, and the subjectivity of different people's perceptions of historical events, worried me that we were somehow doing this assignment wrong. As a student who received content all of my life, I questioned our capability to provide a different perspective on historical events. This teaching approach makes me uncomfortable because I feel it requires a finer grasp on historical content than I feel I have right now. This approach requires supplemental research and deep thinking. Applying my knowledge of history to historical thinking and multiple perspectives has been one of the hardest things I have been asked to do at this university.

I am less sure than D is that more historical content is needed to engage with "multiple perspectives," such as in this assignment. For example, C's reflection best depicts the emotional and difficult thought process involved in opening up to marginalized historical perspectives:

> What troubled me during this assignment was my lack of empathy towards any narrative but the grand narrative before this project began. I am going to have to go into a classroom and teach social studies to a group of students who have received the grand narrative their whole lives as well.

Our class, and this project in particular, was the only time that I have seen the grand narrative challenged. Now I have to go into my future career and try and stop this narrative from being passed on without anyone ever questioning it. This project definitely puts the student into a role that they are not use to [and] creates anxiety and this is disturbing because of the nervousness I experienced while questioning the grand narrative during this project.[41]

As this insight suggests, we need something more than a focus on historical knowledge, competencies, or prior cognitive frames as presently defined. Orientations found in curriculum theory help negotiate these emotional-knowledge-knowing tensions that result when students confront and reread in a writerly manner those institutionally privileged stories they have taken to be their own. In short, curriculum theory broadens the texts that should be in play when learning to teach.

Not surprisingly, and despite their own powerful experiences with the assignment, students are sceptical about – and, perhaps, emotionally unprepared to take up – its practicality for their imminent and high-stakes practicums as a hopeful beginning to their careers. The anglophone Canadian grand narrative dominates for the duration of schooling the subjectivities shaped therein, and this "relates to the fact that in our classrooms time is limited and the 'other' perspective we may offer may be [...] very limited." Indeed, it is difficult "to modify a structure of understanding that is so dominant and persuasive"[42] or, I add, to reread in a writerly manner a learned relationship to institutionalized knowledge and knowing.

Conclusion

Student teachers who present Canadian history through multiple historical perspectives experience many of the tensions inherent in learning to teach. They struggle to avoid culturally reductive or stereotypical images of otherness. They seek to tame historical complexity for ease of communication, and they have a somewhat fraught encounter with how to make sense of history, and historically informed identifications, given the slippery nature of historical identity/perspectives/emplotments.

To reread a grand narrative creates the opportunity for teacher candidates to interrogate its sources and the historical perspective from which it springs. Doing so opens familiar frames of historical understanding to question and analysis. This opening, that becomes available from the curriculum-as-encounter orientation that I suggest, is the precondition necessary to make historical procedures or concepts potentially relevant. If students do not pay attention to the need to organize curriculum around the goal of creating the possibility for "Christopherian" moments (or, more powerfully, "truth-events"), students will likely continue to underestimate the importance of historical concepts as a helpful heuristic to develop what Farley describes as "a capacity to tolerate – and narrate – the disillusionment of encountering the otherness that history both references and provokes on the inside."[43]

Faced with encountering their own "otherness" in relation to the historical perspective dominating their schooling, many students call upon a realist notion of history: they assert that it is possible to fully and accurately apprehend the past once all the facts are taken into account. Students extend this realist assumption to the perspectives of groups with which they do not identify either in historical or contemporary terms. I read this as an attempt to restabilize after their identity with a particular historical perspective as mainstream Canadians was disrupted. They previously were prepared to teach *the* story as the truth of the past; now, they recognize the dissonance at the heart of historical work in general (e.g., between the past and what we can reasonably claim about it) and the historical identifications/perspective/emplotment they learned in schools to think of as their own.

Note the common character of a realist understanding of history and of a "readerly" engagement with the texts of our learning lives. In both cases, what is to be learned proceeds on the assumption that there are answers to extract rather than meanings to create. The creativity and commitments that shape scholarly work recede into the background of more pressing concerns for performing teacher scripts. This is why "coverage and control" pedagogy dominates both public social studies classrooms and teacher education: we put so little on the table that requires writerly engagement. Not surprisingly, therefore, teacher education lacks influence in future classrooms.

So often there is nothing really at stake in the enterprise of teacher education. Few, for example, would say they are against critical thinking or that, as future teachers, we shouldn't help youth become better historical thinkers: "Just tell me what it is I need to know." Perhaps our students are excited in our teacher education classrooms, for example, to work with primary documents (which I fully support and do). This, however, has little implication for status quo coverage and control practices, because the practices and the cultural norms related to knowledge and knowing are themselves inadequately explored. Shift focus to the ways these historically curious practices shape our own subjective identifications and commitments, and something vital and humanizing becomes implicatively present. This, however, requires that teacher educators do what they ask of their students and reread in a writerly manner what and how they have been taught about what "counts" in –and as – history education.

NOTES

1 K.C. Barton and Linda S. Levstik, *Teaching History for the Common Good* (Mahwah, NJ: Lawrence Erlbaum Associates, 2004); Lisa Cary, "The Refusals of Citizenship: Normalizing Practices in Social Educational Discourses," *Theory and Research in Social Education*, 29, no. 3 (2001): 405-30; Kent den Heyer, "History as a Disciplined Ethic of Truths," in *New Possibilities for the Past: Shaping History Education in Canada*, edited by Penney Clark (Vancouver: UBC Press, 2011), 154-72; M.A. Peters, *Knowledge Economy, Development, and the Future of Higher Education* (Rotterdam: Sense Publishing, 2007); Thomas Popkiwitz, "Knowledge, Power, and Curriculum: Revisiting a TRSE Argument," *Theory and Research in Social Education*, 26, no. 1 (1998): 83-101; Avner Segall, "Critical History: Implications for History/Social Studies Education," *Theory and Research in Social Education* 27, no. 3 (1999): 358-74; Avner Segall, "What's the Purpose of Teaching a Discipline Anyway? The Case of History," in *Social Studies – The Next Generation*, edited by Avner Segall, Elizabeth Heilman, and Cleo Cherryholmes (New York: Peter Lang, 2006), 125-39; and David G. Smith, "The Specific Challenges of Globalization for Teaching and Vice Versa," *Alberta Journal of Educational Research* 46, no. 1 (2000): 7-25.
2 David Scott, "Teaching Multiple Perspectives: New Possibilities for History Education" (paper presented at the Annual Meeting of the American Educational Research Association, New Orleans, Louisiana, April 2011), 10.
3 Ibid., 1.
4 Dwayne T. Donald, "The Curricular Problem of Indigenous: Colonial Frontier Logics, Teacher Resistances, and the Acknowledgement of Ethical Space," in *Beyond "Presentism": Reimagining the Historical, Personal, and Social Places of Curriculum*, edited by James Nahachewsky and Ingrid Johnston (Rotterdam: Sense Publishing, 2009), 32.

5 Alan Sears, "Moving from the Periphery to the Core: The Possibilities for Professional Learning Communities in History Teacher Education," this volume, p. 12.
6 Avner Segall and William Gaudelli, "Reflecting Socially on Social Issues in a Social Studies Methods Course," *Teaching Education* 18, no. 1 (2007): 72.
7 Ibid., 79. This is a distinction made by Barthes. See Roland Barthes, *S/Z*, trans. R. Miller (New York: Hill & Wang, 1974).
8 Dennis Sumara and Rebecca Luce-Kapler, "Action Research as a Writerly Text: Locating Co-Labouring in Collaboration," *Educational Action Research* 1, no. 3 (1993): 390.
9 Tony Whitson, "Decomposing Curriculum, vs. Curriculum-as-Text," *Journal of Curriculum and Pedagogy* 5, no. 1 (2008): 132.
10 Ibid.
11 Deborah Britzman, *Practice Makes Practice: A Critical Study of Learning to Teach*, 2nd ed. (Albany, NY: State University of New York Press, 2003); Deborah Britzman, Donald Dippo, Dennis Searle, and Alice Pitt, "Toward an Academic Framework for Thinking about Teacher Education," *Teaching Education* 9, no. 1 (1997): 15–26; Terrence R. Carson, "Closing the Gap between Research and Practice: Conversation as a Mode of Curriculum Research," *Phenomenology and Pedagogy* 4, no. 2 (1986): 73–85; Terrence R. Carson, "The Time of Learning: A Dilemma for Teacher Education's Response to Diversity" (paper presented at the CATE Invitational Conference on Research in Teacher Education, Winnipeg, Manitoba, November 2007).
12 Britzman et al., "Toward an Academic Framework," 15.
13 Ibid.,16.
14 Ibid.
15 den Heyer, "History as a Disciplined Ethic of Truths."
16 Daniel Francis, *The Imaginary Indian: The Image of the Indian in Canadian Culture* (Vancouver: Arsenal Pulp Press, 1992).
17 Donald, "The Curricular Problem," 38
18 den Heyer, "History as a Disciplined Ethic of Truths."
19 Lisa Farley, "Radical Hope: Or, the Problem of Uncertainty in History Education," *Curriculum Inquiry* 39, no. 4 (2009), 538.
20 Peter Lee, "History Teaching and the Philosophy of History," *History and Theory* 22, no. 4 (1983): 19-49.
21 See The Historical Thinking Project at http://historicalthinking.ca.
22 Barton and Levstik, *Teaching History*, 207.
23 Mike Denos and Roland Case, *Teaching About Historical Thinking* (Vancouver: Critical Thinking Consortium, 2006), 46-7.

24 Ibid., 10.
25 den Heyer, "History as a Disciplined Ethics of Truths"; Kent den Heyer and Laurence Abbott, "Reverberating Echoes: Challenging Teacher Candidates to Tell Entwined Narrations of Canadian History," *Curriculum Inquiry* 41, no. 5 (2011): 605-30.
26 Jocelyn Létourneau, "Remembering Our Past: An Examination of the Historical Memory of Young Québécois," in *To the Past: History Education, Public Memory and Citizenship in Canada,* edited by Ruth Sandwell (Toronto: University of Toronto Press, 2006), 79
27 Létourneau, "Remembering Our Past," 74; Penney Clark, "A Nice Little Wife to Make Things Pleasant: Portrayals of Women in Social Studies Textbooks," *McGill Journal of Education* 40, no. 2 (2005): 241-65; and Bruce VanSledright, "Narratives of Nation-State, Historical Knowledge, and School History Education," *Review of Research in Education* 32, no. 1 (2008): 109-46.
28 S.G. Grant, *History Lessons: Teaching, Learning, and Testing in US High School Classrooms* (Mahwah, NJ: Laurence Erlbaum Associates, 2003); Peter Seixas, "Review of Research in Social Studies," in *Handbook of Research on Teaching,* edited by Veronica Richardson (Washington, DC: American Educational Research Association, 2001), 545-65; and S.W. Wilson, "Research on History Teaching," in *Handbook of Research on Teaching,* edited by Veronica Richardson (Washington, DC: American Educational Research Association, 2001), 527-44.
29 Dennis Shemilt, "The Caliph's Coin: The Currency of Narrative Frameworks in History Teaching," in *Knowing, Teaching, and Learning History: National and International Perspectives,* edited by Peter N. Stearns, Peter Seixas, and Sam Wineburg (New York: New York University Press, 2000), 87.
30 Hayden White, *The Content of the Form: Narrative Discourse and Historical Representation* (Baltimore, MD: Johns Hopkins University Press, 1987), 173, 44.
31 William Cronon, "A Place for Stories: Nature, History, and Narrative," *The Journal of American History* 78, no. 4 (1992): 1347-76.
32 Ibid., 1347
33 Bonnifield, as quoted in Cronon, "A Place for Stories," 1348.
34 Worster, as quoted in Cronon, "A Place for Stories," 1348.
35 Ibid., 1348.
36 Ibid., 1362.
37 Jennifer Tupper and Michael Cappello, "Teaching Treaties as (Un)usual Narratives: Disrupting the Curricular Commonsense," *Curriculum Inquiry* 38, no. 5 (2008): 559-78.

38 den Heyer, "History as a Disciplined Ethic of Truths."
39 Students were guaranteed anonymity, and therefore are referred to only by capital letter.
40 It is worth noting that most students also grappled with what actually distinguishes an "event" from a "process," or a "trend" from a series of happenings with both similar and dissimilar qualities.
41 Recent arrivals to Canada may not be inculcated into a grand narrative. Nonetheless, engaging the dominant grand narrative would help them interpret the logic of contemporary Canada's dominant political, economic, and social groups.
42 Létourneau, "Remembering Our Past," 83.
43 Farley, "Radical Hope," 538.

11 "Walking the Talk": Modelling the Pedagogy We Profess in History and Social Studies Methodology Courses

ROLAND CASE AND GENIE MACLEOD

What you do speaks so loudly I cannot hear what you say.
— R.B. Dierenfield (1959)

David Livingstone is reported to have said that teaching by example is not the best way – it is the only way. Robert Blume wrote, "Teachers teach as they are taught, and not as they are taught to teach."[1] This advice must be taken seriously if methodology instructors hope to affect how their students teach when they eventually reach their own classrooms. Unfortunately, scant attention has been paid to the role of university-based methodology instructors in the widely reported inadequate state of history and social studies teaching in Canadian elementary and secondary schools.[2] Surprisingly, relatively few studies document how teacher educators teach, or gauge how the structure of teacher education programs impacts the practice of student teachers.[3] As Wideen et al. observed, most studies of teacher education focus on the roles and responsibilities of student teachers in their own learning rather than on those of teacher educators.[4]

Recently, a seasoned teacher explained to me[5] that, years earlier, he had resented having to return to the university to complete two methodology courses in his areas of specialization after he had completed his extended practicum. For him, completing these courses on how to teach in his subject areas was a pointless exercise. Thankfully, not all student teachers are as disparaging of their methodology courses as this teacher was. However, my impression – acquired over twenty years of teaching in faculties of education and working with 17,000 practicing teachers – is that many teachers feel that while they learned a few notable lessons from various courses, the teacher education program offered little else of lasting value to their own practice. We do not conclude from this that what instructors offer to student teachers lacks merit. In fact, we hold quite the opposite view: much of what is presented has great value. Our point is that not enough of these important lessons are getting through to students and staying with them in their own teaching.

Studies in the United States suggest that we can make a difference in teacher education. When comparing beginning teachers accepted into the profession with very little preparation to those who completed a teacher education program, Linda Darling-Hammond and others concluded that "teachers' effectiveness appears strongly related to the preparation they have received for teaching."[6] Further, studies such as those by Swennen, Lunenberg, and Korthagen found that teacher educators were more likely to demonstrate what they call "congruent teaching," or teaching in the way they would want their student teachers to teach, if they are supported by professional development workshops that address strategies for congruent teaching.[7]

The received view is that university instructors "do it right" and that beginning teachers are socialized into less desirable practices by the regressive influences of traditional teachers and the oppressive realities of day-to-day teaching.[8] Yet, many university instructors are as likely as public classroom teachers to "cover the curriculum"; "to tell rather than to teach"; to espouse critical thinking, but to assess for recall; and to recommend but not follow through on such noble practices as differentiated instruction, assessment for learning, and teaching for understanding. A handful of studies warn of the dangers of "transmissive" teaching within teacher education (and within education in general), and advocate a modelling approach consistent with the strategies we will outline here.[9]

Our contention is that teacher educators are likely to succeed in both preparing student teachers for their own classroom teaching and providing meaningful lessons that stick with them if teacher educators do more to "walk the talk" regarding the pedagogical practices we espouse.

Why "Walking the Talk" Matters

Before discussing specific areas in which methodology instructors may fail to "walk the talk," let us suggest in general terms how incongruent teaching – the gap between teaching rhetoric and actual practice – in university classes influences student teachers.

Lack of Skill Development

The most obvious gap between rhetoric and practice in methodology courses is that student teachers do not have an opportunity to learn first-hand about the teaching methods we want them to use in their own classrooms. While "demonstration" lessons on particular strategies are useful, they do not develop student teachers' skill in using these methods as thoroughly as if these strategies were mirrored in the day-to-day teaching. For those who might only have talked about differentiated instruction, the challenge is to create a course that is differentiated for our students' abilities, interests and needs. Doubtless, the conditions operating within the public school system will inevitably expunge some of the ideas promoted in university methodology courses, but it is worth speculating whether student teachers would be better able to resist these negative pressures if they had extensive first-hand experience with the methods in their own learning. I recall one student teacher's comment at the end of a methodology course where I had tried especially hard to "walk the talk": the student noted that throughout his program he had heard about the methods that I had used in our course, but only after they were embedded in my course did he actually feel confident in his ability to use them in his own teaching.

Lack of Understanding

I remember listening in disbelief as a social studies methodology instructor proudly recounted, as evidence of his support for the work of The Critical Thinking Consortium, how he devoted two entire classes to discussing the elements of our critical thinking model. Not only is it unlikely that his students would have developed any skill in using our ideas in their own teaching, it is doubtful they would even understand our approach. The very premise of our approach is that meaningful *understanding* of subject matter is unlikely unless students are involved in thinking rigorously with and about the ideas. The importance of thoughtful engagement with ideas as a method of learning has been known in Canadian educational circles for over 160 years. In his classic study of teaching practices in Canadian public schools, Egerton Ryerson noted:

If the mind of the child when learning, remains merely passive, merely receiving knowledge as a vessel receives water which is poured into it, little good can be expected to accrue. It is as if food were introduced into the stomach which there is no room to digest or assimilate, and which will therefore be rejected from the system, or [sit] like a useless and oppressive load upon its energies.[10]

The limitations of merely presenting ideas to student teachers became obvious to me when I changed the way I taught an article on the various purposes of social studies education.[11] Previously, I had assigned the article as background reading, and in class provided examples to explain the various concepts and invited student discussion. Only when I assigned an activity – in which a matrix of competing purposes were physically mapped in the classroom and students had to take up a position in the room according to their valuing of the goals – did I realize that the students hadn't understood what they read nor what I had "taught." It became apparent during the process of trying to identify and defend their views that students were actually seeing for the first time the implications of each purpose. The activity, which I had thought would be a way of *applying* their understanding of the various conceptions, was instead a way of *engendering* students' understanding of the purposes.

This point is made more forcefully by Wesch, who reminds us that teaching is not a necessary condition for learning and who urges university professors to worry less about *teaching* subject matter – explaining, illustrating, and answering questions – and focus more on the quality of the *learning* experiences we provide for students.[12] In other words, engaging students in richly structured learning activities involving the ideas and practices we want to encourage may be more valuable than enriching our content delivery techniques.

Lack of Commitment to Pedagogical Practices

It seems unrealistic to assume that merely espousing the virtues of various teaching practices will be sufficient to cultivate positive student teacher attitudes towards them. As Dierenfield observed fifty years ago: "Students in education classes will tend to receive what they hear with a large 'pinch of salt' unless the professor applies what he 'professes' to his own instruction."[13] There are direct parallels between the research on instilling civic values in students and the process of developing appreciation for pedagogical values associated with inquiry learning in our student teachers. In her meta-analysis of studies on the effects of civic instruction, Torney-Purta found that program content – what teachers "taught" – was less influential in nurturing positive student attitudes than was the extent to which teachers modelled the desired values in their daily teaching.[14]

Lessons from the study of civic education practices suggest that the bigger the gap between teacher-espoused rhetoric about civic life (e.g., presumed innocence until proven guilty) and actual classroom practice (e.g., determining student culpability based on scant facts with no presumption of innocence), the more cynical students became about society.[15] In a similar vein, I have often heard student teachers complain that faculty of education instructors expect them to engage their students in a rich menu of learning tasks but that these instructors often lecture or conduct whole group discussions for most of the class time. This failure to model best practice is reflected cynically in the familiar adage: those who can't do, teach; and those who can't teach, teach teachers. One possible explanation for failing to "walk the talk" is a lack of class time to implement this approach in teacher education courses. In response, it might be asked what the point is of using existing methods if they have modest effect on student teachers' practices. Furthermore, the time required may not be as extensive as some might fear. For example, Swennen et al. reported that after just one day of congruent teaching-oriented workshops, all the teacher educators in the study demonstrated congruent teaching techniques in their subsequent lessons.[16]

Having talked in general terms about the importance of walking the talk, we now consider the consequences of incongruent practices in three areas:

- assimilation of content;
- assessment for learning; and
- self-regulated independent thinking.

But let us clarify our approach. We are not providing empirical evidence of the incidence or frequency of instructor behaviour in methodology classes. Rather, we are suggesting that *when* these incongruent practices occur, they are likely to undermine student teacher efficacy. If none of the inconsistencies we discuss are commonplace, then our arguments are obviously moot, but we believe that incongruent teaching is relatively widespread. Further, we suspect that even those who have tried conscientiously to "walk the talk" may be surprised to learn of the importance of taking even more steps along this path, and the opportunities that can result.

Assimilation of Content

Exposing students to ideas is not the same as fostering student assimilation of ideas. The latter refers to students coming to understand and, to some extent, internalize ideas (if not necessarily to adopt them). To the extent that we "cover" content – introduce ideas to students without allowing time or creating opportunities to engage critically with the ideas – we are not promoting assimilation. Earlier, we suggested that understanding (and even recalling of information) is unlikely unless students have worked through or engaged in some meaningful way with the subject matter they are expected to learn. While we believe few would dispute the importance of supporting students in assimilating the content of our methodology classes, we wonder if all of our practices uphold this principle.

Assigned Responsibility for Student Assimilation of Ideas

Regrettably, we may often communicate to our student teachers that it is primarily their job, not ours, to make the connection between their learning and our teaching. Many teacher educators may feel that it is sufficient to assign relevant readings, cover the key research, and review the main approaches and practices. However, this view is problematic for educators who believe in constructivist learning – that is, meaningful learning that occurs when learners make sense of and assess new ideas though the lenses of their existing beliefs and experiences. Although a teacher can't make a student assimilate the subject matter (nor, for that matter, can a teacher make a student recall the information), it is an open question whether or not teachers should take extra steps to ensure that it is likely that most students will understand. As was suggested earlier, we shouldn't believe that our responsibilities as educators rest entirely in the realm of our "teaching" – especially when learning within a constructivist paradigm requires more active student engagement. Otherwise, we may be in danger of embodying the contradiction reflected in the familiar adage about the surgeon who announces that the operation was a success but the patient died. We are not implying that educators are responsible for ensuring that every student "learns" what is taught; rather, our point is that educators are remiss when they acknowledge that many students will not fully grasp the material unless they are supported in assimilating the ideas, but then neglect to provide consistent opportunities for students to do so.

The consequences of delegating primary responsibility for sense-making to our students are three-pronged: (1) many student teachers will not actually be able to make sense of the desired content; (2) they will have a limited repertoire of easily embedded strategies to employ when helping their own students assimilate the content; and (3) perhaps worst of all, they may be encouraged to believe that they can follow our lead and assign primary responsibility for sense making to their elementary and secondary students.

Dubious Efforts to Support Assimilation of Ideas

Even if we recognize a co-responsibility with our students to ensure that they make sense of what is presented, we may not be doing enough on this front if the hands-on activities we use to support students' assimilation of content are inconsistent or misplaced.

Our efforts are inconsistent if we do not provide a learning activity for every (main) aspect of the content that we want our students to understand. But one might ask, "How could we possibly construct opportunities for our students to think about and digest everything we want to teach in our courses?" The answer to this question, of course, is that we cannot possibly do this for every topic. But the question remains whether we are better served by simply providing opportunities where we can or by reconsidering how much we attempt to teach so that we teach a few topics well, rather than many topics superficially. Belanger, reflecting on two years of designing the curriculum for American History for Educators, observes,

> At the conclusion of the first semester of History 105, it was clear that narrowing the content of the course and giving students opportunities to work with primary sources had made them more aware of what historians do. In their reflections about what they had learned, students often noted the differences between their high school history classes and History 105.[17]

The choice we face in this respect is identical to the one student teachers face in trying to cover the prescribed curriculum. The problem, to paraphrase a school principal commenting on the tendency to add more and more topics to the curricula, is this: the thicker the curriculum, the less room there is for thinking.[18] Many of us may have admonished our students with Howard Garner's axiom, "coverage is the enemy of understanding,"[19] but have inconsistently adhered to this precept in our own teaching.

Educators' efforts to promote student teachers' assimilation of the content may be misplaced if the activities do not actually help students digest the ideas in meaningful ways. Let us illustrate the limitations of two commonly used activities: student presentations of assigned readings and teaching ideas, and student creation of lesson and unit plans.

- Involving students teachers in presenting research findings or in teaching ideas to their colleagues may support assimilation of ideas for those students who actually prepare the presentations, but for the rest of the class the experience is often little more than receiving information that may or may not be clearly presented. These presentations are meaningful for the rest of the class only if they involve opportunities for the audience to use the ideas, perhaps by deciding for themselves how particular situations might be addressed using various theories or teaching approaches.
- One of the most common activities intended to support student teachers in assimilating content involves asking them to create lesson or unit plans that incorporate the ideas addressed in the course. These assignments may not be as effective in developing understanding as they seem once we acknowledge a difference between "applying" an idea (seeing the implications in a particular context) and "digesting" the idea (understanding what the idea means). We assume that asking students to apply principles or approaches in a lesson or unit plan requires them to make sense of these practices; otherwise, how could student teachers competently infuse them into their plans? Unfortunately, the reality is that many students make either a well-intentioned but misguided effort or, worse yet, they take a perfunctory stab at applying the ideas without adequately understanding them. We are aware of how many teacher educators dread grading these lesson and unit plans, and we have a theory about why this is such a disheartening experience: while reading student teachers' "applications" of the ideas in their plans, we come to the realization that far too many students didn't "get it."

To avoid potential confusion, assignments in lesson planning are necessary. Our point is that they may not be very effective in engendering understanding of the ideas we are teaching, because they presuppose that the understanding is already developed. We may encourage greater assimilation by providing, as a first step, examples of successful and unsuccessful lesson plans that use the featured ideas and by inviting our students to distinguish between them and to explain their reasoning.

Assessment for Learning

Assessment for learning is an approach that suggests that students must have opportunities to practice what they are learning, receive timely constructive feedback on their progress, and, once they have reached their peak learning, be held accountable for the achievement. An analogy often used to illustrate these principles is the training of sprinters for a race: running coaches provide many opportunities for their protégés to improve performance without penalty in preparation for the final race that will determine their ranking.

One might think that assessments for learning practices, while embedded within student teachers' practicum experiences, are impossible in methodology courses. However, we wonder whether the reasons for an inability to "walk the talk" wouldn't also apply to our student teachers in their own classrooms. For those of us who want to do more, we discuss two practices that help to embed assessment for learning in our courses: providing multiple opportunities for feedback and building student ownership for assessment.

Multiple Opportunities for Feedback

I was surprised when I first learned of my graduate students' resistance to the number of thesis rewrites I expected of them. I understood why only after learning how few of them at any point in their schooling had been asked to undertake significant revisions. Certainly, they had not been asked to rewrite an assignment multiple times. It seems common in education to assign one-shot tasks and then move on to another topic. Assessment for learning requires that we provide opportunities to revisit core ideas in various ways, with appropriate feedback in each case before assigning a grade. Giving feedback is time-consuming; hence, it can only happen in conjunction with a robust program of student self- and peer-assessment. With such a program in place, opportunities proliferate for providing meaningful feedback.[20] These opportunities are made possible when it is expected that students will pre-assess their draft lesson plans, article summaries, and short assignments; that they will share them with other students who are held accountable for providing quality, constructive advice; and that they will revise their work prior to submission to the instructor. This may mean that assignments meant to help students understand key ideas are reviewed collectively but are not submitted for grading, and that only later lesson plans are evaluated for evidence that students both understand the key ideas and are able to apply them effectively in a particular context. However, as many of us have come to realize, peer- and self-assessment, which are crucial to providing students with multiple opportunities for feedback, are ineffectual if not counterproductive unless students assume ownership for assessing their learning.

Student Ownership for Assessing Their Learning

I have long been troubled by how many students apparently fail to recognize that marks must be earned. Rather, it seems many students view teachers as dispensers of arbitrary marks. With this mentality, assessment becomes a kind of holiday gift exchange: students present the teacher with a product and hope the teacher reciprocates by "giving" them good marks. If students are lucky and the teacher is in a favourable mood, they get a good mark. If the teacher doesn't like how students chose to do the assignment, they get a lousy grade.

To counter this prevalent view, I began to explore ways of communicating the criteria for assessment, but I continued to "own" the evaluation process – I was simply being more explicit about what the rules were. Gradually, I learned to share responsibility for assessment with my students by negotiating criteria, by articulating the standards jointly with the class, and eventually by involving students in peer- and self-evaluation. Students were expected to self- and peer-assess the major assignments using detailed rubrics that I had carefully developed. The class had reviewed these rubrics and modified them as necessary. It was difficult initially to get students to use the descriptors as the basis for their assessments. Either the students hadn't really internalized these criteria or they ignored them, preferring to assign themselves the rating that they hoped to get. This situation improved after much practice and with the addition of a rubric in which I evaluated students on their ability to self- and peer-assess in a criteria-based, fair-minded manner. The result – as those who have been able to get their students to effectively use a rubric can attest – was a significant shift away from the teacher as the sole arbiter of standards towards the teacher and students sharing the responsibility for assessment. Several scholarly studies also have found that a collaborative approach to assessment results in a richer learning experience for student teachers and teacher educators.[21]

After several years of trial and error, I recall a student commenting that in previous university courses he would regularly ask what he had to do to get an "A." If he thought the instructor's requirements were too onerous, he would ask what was needed for a "B." In these classes, the standards were external to the student. Fortunately, the student felt differently about my course. Because he had participated in setting meaningful criteria and standards, he didn't feel that these were simply my priorities, and he didn't have to worry about or guess what mark I would give him because the assessment rubrics were there for him to apply. He saw my job as corroborating his assessments; I was no longer the arbitrary dispenser of marks. At the end of the course, he remarked that for the first time in his university career he hadn't done the bare minimum in order to get an acceptable grade. Instead, he had wanted to do his best – the marks weren't a factor, because he knew they would follow. He knew what his work was worth because he had been a full participant in the evaluation.

Self-Regulated Independent Thinking

If you are at all like me, you cringe in the early days of a methodology course when beginning student teachers take out their notebooks, ready to copy verbatim our wise prescriptions on how to teach. Despite our insistence that there are no recipes for teaching and that student teachers must think things through for themselves, I wonder how many student teachers harbour the suspicion that we are simply hiding the truths of teaching from them because we want them to discover the truths for themselves – or that we don't actually know the answers. Perhaps many of us abandon our resolve in the face of relentless questions about the right way to teach and begin recommending our favourite strategies as the approach that our students should follow.

It is imperative that student teachers understand that becoming a teacher – or, for that matter, learning anything important and difficult – requires careful contemplation of the ideas and rigorous attention to the implications of these ideas for our beliefs and actions. The consequences of not learning this lesson are alarming: student teachers will be inadequately prepared for teaching and inclined throughout their careers to look at professional development as a prescription instead of a source of ideas. Perhaps most alarming, they are more likely to perpetuate a "transmissive" approach to learning, and to perceive their job as being akin to how they had perceived the role of their former teachers: to tell students what they need to know.

Promoting Independent Mindedness

Over the last ten years, I have asked many hundreds of student teachers whether they believe that thinking for oneself is an important goal in university. Typically, 60–75 per cent of students indicate that it is important. I then ask these students to recall writing essays: how many of them worried as much or more about having the answer that the professor preferred as they worried about figuring out what they really believed? When I re-ask my initial question about the importance of independent thinking versus replicating the professor's view, a clear majority of students revise their answer. They acknowledge having been reluctant to deviate from the professor's views where marks were concerned.

My informal surveys of education students about the conflicted nature of independent mindedness are consistent with research of undergraduate and graduate students outside of education. As Wolcott explains, accounting students commonly "view coursework as game in which it is their job to figure out what the professor wants and then to stack up evidence to support that position."[22]

My most successful experiences in getting student teachers to think for themselves began when I indicated early on in my courses that there were two kinds of questions that students could ask of teachers: "Tell me what to do and say," and "Help me advance my own thinking and actions." I would explain that for the first weeks of my class, students were allowed to ask either kind of question, but that after that time, I would respond only to "help me advance my thinking" questions. I offered examples of the "tell me" kind of questions, and I inquired what these sample questions might look like if they were reframed as questions that would assist students in advancing their own thinking rather than simply telling them what to do. We practised reframing questions, and students began to attempt "help me advance my thinking" questions. My stock response was, "Well, what do you think?" followed by, "Why do you think that?" Depending on the answer, I might prompt further thinking by proposing a hypothetical situation that embodied their suggestions, but pretty clearly would result in a less than optimal outcome. My consistent refusal to provide an answer before students showed that they had thoroughly considered the issue helped students to realize that they could actually work out their own thoughtful answers and rarely needed me to affirm them. Having their questions persistently thrown back at them meant that they developed a much deeper understanding of (and ability to use) the ideas than I had seen with my previous students.

Teaching to Think Critically

A recent reviewer of a social studies methodology anthology that I co-edited suggested that we do more to promote critical thinking when we provide explicit critiques of various social and educational practices. The review raised for me the question of how many instructors distinguish between teaching students how to think critically and teaching students to be critical. This distinction became clear to me several years ago when I was invited to join a panel with University of British Columbia law professor Joel Bakan, creator of the award-winning documentary *Corporations*. He believed that we were pursuing the same goal of encouraging our students to think critically, whereas I suggested that we had two very different agendas. In my view, his aim was to teach students to be critical of corporations, and my interest was in getting students to think critically *about* corporations. Unlike him, I wasn't prejudging what students' conclusions should be about corporations. My interest was to ensure that they looked rigorously at the key evidence (favourable and unfavourable) from various perspectives before making up their own minds. I explained that I encouraged my students to disagree with any view I expressed, promising bonus marks for students who were able, in an assignment, to support a position counter to the view that I had espoused.

The implications for the classroom of blurring the distinction between teaching "to think" and teaching "what to think" are evident in Moisan's very recent study of twenty history teachers in Quebec. She hypothesized that because of their experiences in teacher education (among other factors), teachers saw history as the transmission of a common culture or a received opinion on an issue – not as an opportunity to invite students to think critically about their own interpretations. As she explains, "when they spoke of interpretation, teachers were not referring to those that students could make for themselves by working with sources, but the teacher's implicit view of the course of history."[23] If we don't consistently require students to reach their own responsible conclusions, and support them in that effort even if they disagree with the professor, we shouldn't be surprised when our student teachers do not treat their students any differently.

No doubt other of our teaching practices may be at odds with the pedagogical principles that we espouse. But we believe that we have provided ample food for thought about three main conclusions that we hope you will consider:

1 commonly used pedagogy in history and social studies methodology courses is often inconsistent with the theory and practice its purports to teach;
2 it is possible to teach methodology courses in a manner that more closely models the pedagogy espoused in these courses; and
3 "walking the talk" is not only necessary – it is more likely to successfully prepare students to teach in desired ways in their own classrooms.

NOTES

1 Robert Blume, "Humanizing Teacher Education," *The Phi Delta Kappan* 52, no. 7 (1971), 412.
2 Ken Osborne, "The Teaching of History and Democratic Citizenship," in *The Anthology of Social Studies: Issues and Strategies for Secondary Teachers,* edited by Roland Case and Penney Clark (Vancouver: Pacific Educational Press, 2008), 3-14; Roland Case, "Beyond Inert Facts," in *The Anthology of Social Studies: Issues and Strategies for Elementary Teachers,* edited by Roland Case and Penney Clark (Vancouver: Pacific Educational Press, 2008), 33-47.
3 John Loughran and Amanda Berry, "Modelling by Teacher Educators," *Teaching Teachers* 21, no. 2 (2005): 193-203; Anja Swennen, Mieke Lunenberg, and Fred Korthagen, "Preach What You Teach! Teacher Educators and Congruent Teaching," *Teachers and Teaching: Theory and Practice* 14, no. 5-6 (2008): 531-42; Marvin Wideen, Jolie Mayer-Smith, and Barbara Moon, "A Critical Analysis of the Research on Learning to Teach: Making the Case for an Ecological Perspective on Inquiry," *Review of Educational Research* 68, no. 2 (1998): 130-78; and Miriam Ben-Peretz, Sara Kleeman, Rivka

Reichenberg, and Sarah Shimoni, "Educators of Educators: Their Goals, Perceptions and Practices," *Professional Development in Education* 36, no. 1-2 (2010): 111-29.

4 Wideen, Mayer-Smith, and Moon, "A Critical Analysis of the Research on Learning to Teach."

5 All references in the article to one of the authors in the first person pertain to the senior author, Roland Case.

6 Linda Darling-Hammond, Deborah Holtzman, Su Jin Gatlin, and Julian Vasquez Heilig, "Does Teacher Preparation Matter? Evidence About Teacher Certification, Teach for America, and Teacher Effectiveness," *Education Policy Analysis Archives* 13, no. 42 (2005): 2.

7 Swennen, Lunenberg, and Korthagen, "Preach What You Teach!"

8 Ken Osborne, *Canadian History in the Schools* (Toronto: Historica Foundation, 2004), 22-7. Available online at https://www.historicacanada .ca/?page=.index.

9 Loughran and Berry, "Modelling by Teacher Educators"; Amanda Berry, *Tensions in Teaching about Teaching: Understanding Practice as a Teacher Educator* (Dordrecht: Springer, 2007); Mieke Lunenberg, Fred Korthagen, and Anja Swennen, "The Teacher Educator as a Role Model," *Teaching and Teacher Education* 23, no.5 (2007): 586-601; Swennen, Lunenberg and Korthagen, "Preach What You Teach!"; Elizabeth Belanger, "How Now? Historical Thinking, Reflective Teaching, and the Next Generation of History Teachers," *The Journal of American History* 97, no. 4 (2011): 1079-88; Ellen Swartz, "Casing the Self: A Study of Pedagogy and Critical Thinking," *Teacher Development* 8, no. 1 (2004): 45-65; Wideen, Mayer-Smith, and Moon, "A Critical Analysis of the Research on Learning to Teach."

10 Egerton Ryerson, *Report on a System of Public Education for Upper Canada* (Montreal: Lovell and Gibson, 1847), 56-7.

11 Penney Clark and Roland Case, "Four Purposes of Citizenship Education," in *The Anthology of Social Studies: Issues and Strategies for Elementary Teachers*, edited by Roland Case and Penney Clark (Vancouver: Pacific Educational Press, 2008), 18-29.

12 Michael Wesch, "Anti-teaching: Confronting the Crisis of Significance," *Education Canada* 48, no. 2 (2008): 4-7.

13 Robert Dierenfield, "Let's Practice What We Teach," *Journal of Teacher Education* 10 (1959): 207.

14 Judith Torney-Purta, "Psychological Perspectives on Enhancing Civic Education through the Education of Teachers," *Journal of Teacher Education* 34, no. 6 (1983): 30-4.

15 Daniel Duke, "Looking at Schools as a Rule-Governed Organization," *Journal of Research and Development in Education* 11, no. 4 (1978): 116-26.

16 Swennen, Lunenberg, and Korthagen, "Preach What You Teach!"

17 Belanger, "How Now? Historical Thinking, Reflective Teaching, and the Next Generation of History Teachers," 1082.

18 Cited in Vera Goodman, *Simply Too Much Homework* (Calgary, AB: Readings Wings, 2007), 17.

19 Cited in Fabrizio Antonelli, *From Applied to Applause* (Toronto: Ontario Secondary School Teachers' Federation, 2004), 42.

20 Belanger, "How Now? Historical Thinking, Reflective Teaching, and the Next Generation of History Teachers"; Loughran and Berry, "Modelling by Teacher Educators."

21 Clare Kosnik, "The Effects of an Inquiry-Oriented Teacher-Education Program on a Faculty Member: Some Critical Incidents and My Journey," *Reflective Practice* 2, no. 1 (2001): 65-80; Swartz, "Casing the Self: a Study of Pedagogy and Critical Thinking"; Belanger, "How Now? Historical Thinking, Reflective Teaching, and the Next Generation of History Teachers"; and Loughran and Berry, "Modelling by Teacher Educators."

22 Susan Wolcott, "Student Assumptions about Knowledge and Critical Thinking in the Accounting Classroom," (paper presented at the Southwest Regional Meeting of the American Accounting Association, 1997), 10.

23 Sabrina Moisan, "Historical Thinking in Quebec History Education," *THEN/HiER E-bulletin*, 19, no. 3 (2011): 3.

12 Teaching Student Teachers to Use Primary Sources When Teaching History

LINDSAY GIBSON

Define the Problem

Throughout the past century, one of the recurring themes for reformers in history education has been the importance of using primary sources to teach history.[1] In the last four decades, a growing body of research in educational psychology and history education has focused on theories, practices, and strategies for using primary sources effectively to teach history.[2] By 2005 it could be stated that belief in the importance of using primary sources for teaching history had achieved a degree of ortho-doxy among history and social studies educators.[3] Reproductions of millions of primary sources have become widely available online for free, or at minimal cost, on "a scale, hitherto unimaginable."[4] Maps, photographs, oral histories, official documents, magazines, newspa-pers, artwork, personal documents, and other items are readily avail-able in textbooks, tests, source packages, and online archives. Despite the widespread availability and near consensus about the importance of using primary sources to teach history, research suggests that the "po-tential of primary sources is not being fully realized in Canadian history and social studies classrooms."[5]

But why aren't primary sources being used more effectively in Canadian classrooms? As Sears, summarizing extensive research, ar-gues in this volume, students spend years in history class reading about history, historical processes, and even great historians, but never actu-ally doing any history. They haven't had to think historically because they have been passive consumers of the end products of others' his-torical thinking.[6] Sears argues that this has two serious implications for preparing student teachers to be able to teach historical thinking:

student teachers often have little experience working with the processes they will be teaching, and as a result they are often at the beginning
of their understanding of historical thinking; and student teachers often have a strong cognitive frame that teaching history essentially involves the passing on of historical information and not the fostering of
historical thinking. Sears is not suggesting that teaching student teachers to think historically is an insurmountable task. Sears is, however,
arguing that the kind of understanding student teachers need to move
from the periphery to the core of their profession may be more difficult
to cultivate than originally expected because, as he notes, quoting
Gardner, "disciplinary content and disciplinary habits of mind may be
deeply counterintuitive," or because, as Wineburg suggests, historical
thinking is an "unnatural act."[7] If teachers are to use sources of historical evidence more effectively, they require "pedagogical content
knowledge," which includes a deep and accurate understanding of
how historical knowledge is constructed, how knowledge is represented to students, how to build on or challenge students' prior knowledge,
and how to help students analyse sources.[8]

Research suggests that teachers need opportunities to examine the
pedagogical and cognitive implications of the subject matter if they are
to develop activities, lessons, and courses that help students develop
meaningful knowledge.[9] Fallace believes that the possibility of prospective teachers developing pedagogical content knowledge from
their knowledge of both historiography and pedagogy is an ambitious,
but achievable, goal that requires intellectual support and opportunities to adapt theory into practice.[10] Simply put, teachers learn how to
use historical evidence in their teaching by "doing it" – by developing
lessons and activities that focus on the use of historical evidence. If
Sears is right about history teachers working on the margins of the discipline and seeing themselves as passive recipients of history, then the
way to change this is to help them to change their minds about what the
discipline is, and also to develop a new sense of who they are and what
their role is in relation to the discipline.

To do this, teacher education should aim to set teachers on an inbound trajectory, to nurture them as practitioners of the discipline using
"boundary practices" between two related and overlapping communities of practice: history and education. Although there is a growing literature on the historical thinking of students, student teachers, and
teachers, there has been relatively little examination of student teachers
learning to construct historical thinking exercises for their students.[11] In

this chapter, I describe a "boundary project" that I assigned to a cohort of student teachers in a social studies methods class in the fall semester of 2010 that asked them to create "sets" of primary and secondary sources focused on an important historical topic in the British Columbia curriculum.[12] My purpose is to discuss the benefits and limitations of using this assignment with student teachers in order to assess how well this assignment was able to improve their ability to use primary sources in their teaching effectively.

What Was the Strategy/Activity?

My purposes in asking student teachers to create sets of primary and secondary sources included focusing them on an important historical topic in the BC curriculum, while teaching them how to identify, select, and use evidence to teach history more effectively. In this way, I hoped also to improve their understanding of history and historical evidence; to introduce them to aspects of historical thinking; to improve their understanding of Chinese Canadian history; and to help them build the necessary understanding to complete other document-based lessons and activities in the course.

I used this assignment in a required secondary social studies methodology class entitled "Social Studies Curriculum and Instruction" (also known as EDCP 332) that I was teaching in fall 2010 at the University of British Columbia. The class met for two hours, three times per week for thirteen weeks, except for a two-week orientation practicum that ran during weeks six to eight. This assignment was one of five required assignments for the course. It was introduced in the fourth week of classes and due at the end of the sixth week.

Student teachers were asked to choose one of fifteen topics for the assignment, all of which focused on Chinese Canadian history (e.g., working conditions while building the CPR, Chinese Canadian involvement in World War II, the 1907 Anti-Asian Riot in Vancouver). I decided to limit the topics to Chinese Canadian history so that students could share information and resources, and because I was familiar with many of the print and online resources available as part of a project I was working on. Students would have preferred to choose a topic that they would be more likely to teach in their practicum, a preference that I will accommodate in the future.

For each set of sources, student teachers were asked to carefully select seven to ten primary sources that met certain criteria. Sources needed to:

a) represent the perspectives of different stakeholders in the event or issue;
b) be suitable for their intended audience; and
c) provide sufficient and relevant evidence for students to answer the proposed question.

Analysing multiple primary sources engages students in inquiry-based, active learning and reminds them that they cannot depend on any single source for reliable knowledge.[13] Inspired by research that suggests that history teachers, in order to teach effectively, should focus on crafting open-ended and meaningful questions,[14] I also required that each set of sources point towards an overall question that:

a) had the potential to engage students;
b) required students to make a judgment;
c) addressed an important historical idea, event, issue, or question in the curriculum; and
d) was historically significant.

Research has clearly articulated the need for both prior knowledge and scaffolding activities if primary documents are to promote historical understanding.[15] Student teachers were therefore also asked to include several excerpted paragraphs from secondary sources such as a textbook, historian's account, or encyclopedia to help students understand the important contextual information about the issue or event being discussed in the primary sources. For each primary and secondary source included in their sets, student teachers were asked to provide a bit of contextual and bibliographic information about the source – such as the title, when it was created, who created it, and what it is – so that the students in the classroom would have enough background to understand the source. Whenever possible, student teachers were also encouraged to include original copies of primary sources to captivate students' interest and to humanize historical actors. Furthermore, student teachers were asked to anticipate words in the primary sources that students might find obscure or difficult to understand, and provide in-text definitions to clarify their meaning.[16] Student teachers were given an "exemplar" set of sources that they could consult to help them understand the expectations for the finished assignment.

In total, we spent seven hours of class time over two weeks doing different activities designed to help student teachers successfully complete the assignment. Student teachers were presented with a background information sheet on the basics of historical evidence (primary and secondary sources, traces and accounts), a PowerPoint presentation of reasons for using historical evidence to teach history, and an activity that assessed their understanding of historical evidence. In other activities, student teachers were invited to compare a primary and secondary source on the same topic to illustrate the benefits and limitations of using both kinds of sources for teaching history.

Another activity presented a sample set of primary and secondary sources and asked student teachers to develop criteria for determining whether a primary source and sets of sources were appropriate for classroom use. In a subsequent activity, student teachers were instructed to examine the exemplar set of sources provided and to use the criteria to determine whether each of the sources in the set was appropriate. Another class focused on helping student teachers create their own set of sources; in this class, student teachers engaged in activities and learned strategies for developing an overall question, selecting potential sources, supplying contextual information for each source, and creating a background sheet. Student teachers were also given a list of web resources and online databases for locating primary and secondary sources on Chinese Canadian history.

In the last class before submitting their completed sets, student teachers exchanged their sets with a partner and used the assessment rubric to determine the overall quality of each other's set. This activity provided student teachers with valuable feedback about their set, and allowed them to make any necessary revisions before the assignment was due in the following class. Two of the seven hours of class were spent engaged with the Wallace B. Chung and Madeline H. Chung Collection housed in the UBC Library, where UBC history professor Henry Yu spoke about Chinese Canadian history, and archivist Sarah Romkey gave us a tour of the Chinese Canadian collection and explained how to use the online database to search for potential sources.

How Successful Was the Activity?

My purpose in this essay is to reflect on how well the assignment was able to help student teachers design a classroom activity that effectively uses historical evidence. In order to determine this, I created a rubric that focused on the important criteria for assessing effective use of historical evidence. A successful assignment would include the following:

- an overall question for the set of sources that engages students, requires students to make judgments, addresses an important curriculum outcome, and is historically significant;
- a background information sheet that outlines the important contextual information required to answer the question;
- seven to ten appropriate and relevant primary sources that are varied in format, type, and perspectives presented;
- important contextual information about the origin, creator, and type of each source; and
- appropriate in-text definitions and clarification for words in the primary sources that are obscure, difficult to understand, or have different historical meanings today than in the past.

After using these criteria to assess student teachers' submitted sets of sources – as well as analysing lesson plans, observing in-class activities, and taking note of e-mails and conversations with student teachers before and after the assignment was completed – I offer the following evaluations of their successes and failures in designing a classroom activity that effectively uses historical evidence.

Researchers have suggested that creating effective topic questions that guide the investigation of historical evidence is difficult for student teachers because they have little practice transforming their knowledge into learning opportunities for students and often struggle to find the "right words" for their questions.[17] Although most of the students constructed adequate questions for their sets of sources, some questions had significant flaws. Several student teachers constructed questions that were simply too large (e.g., "Determine to what extent the present-day government is responsible for injustices of the past"), or that asked for opinions rather than evidence-based judgments (e.g., "What is your opinion of the relationship between Chinese and European peoples in British Columbia around the turn of the 20th century?"). Others combined two or three different questions into one incomprehensible question (e.g., "What do these sources suggest about the formal response to the riots? Consider the damage that was caused by the riots and the attitudes that seem to be conveyed through the textual sources. How appropriate was the way that the media and the government responded to the riot?").

Student teachers also had difficulty selecting primary sources that provided relevant evidence for the question being asked. For example, one student teacher focused on the question of whether the government response to the 1907 Anti-Asian Riot was appropriate, but selected primary sources that focused on the destruction and results of the riot rather than on the government response. The lack of relevant evidence available to answer a few of the questions led some student teachers to an important insight about the limitations of primary evidence. Some came up with the time-tested solution that historians rely on: they found that it was easier to modify the question to fit the sources than it was to find primary sources to fit a particular question.

Many of the student teachers also struggled to provide the scaffolding that their students would inevitably need to analyse the evidence. Although my work with student teachers on this assignment emphasized (and required) that teachers adapt primary sources as needed,[18] many student teachers failed to make their document sets pedagogically appropriate for students. In-text definitions often were not provided for words, phrases, or ideas that would be difficult for students to understand. Several student teachers included large passages of text rather than excerpting one or two of the most important paragraphs. Clearly, it is difficult for student teachers to make sources appropriate for those whose reading comprehension abilities are unknown to them.[19]

The difficulty that student teachers had in providing adequate scaffolding went deeper. Given the amount of writing that student teachers have done by the time they enter teacher education, I assumed that they would easily be able to construct paragraphs of pertinent background information for their sets of sources, or at the very least identify relevant sections of reliable secondary sources and insert them into the background section. I was surprised to discover that this was one of the most poorly done sections of the completed assignments. Some of the background paragraphs were too general and didn't focus on the topic at hand, while others provided too much information and either answered the question for the students or privileged one potential answer over others.

I attribute the student teachers' difficulties in creating background materials and in understanding the scaffolding that their students would need to analyse primary documents to three possible explanations: the student teachers struggled to anticipate what information was needed to provide students with historical context (which was similar to the difficulty they had in adapting primary sources for students); the student teachers underestimated the difficulty of writing factual, neutrally worded background sheets; or the student teachers did not have a deep enough understanding of their historical topic to provide a detailed, accurate, and concise summary. These possibilities support McDiarmid and Vinten-Johansen's finding that many student teachers were shocked when they discovered that they would need to continue researching and learning about historical topics in order to teach them well.[20]

One of the major limitations in how I prepared students to success-fully complete this assignment was that I did not provide student teachers with enough strategies, activities, or tools to help them teach their students how to analyse and interpret the evidence in-cluded in their sets of sources. What became clear to me is that if we expect student teachers to design activities that invite students to analyse and interpret a variety of primary sources, student teachers will need to be taught strategies, tools, and activities that help them understand how to use the primary sources effectively. This might include activities for contextualizing and corroborating evidence, or determining source reliability.

Conclusion

Despite the difficulties that student teachers faced when developing sets of sources, there are several reasons to believe that supporting stu-dent teachers in learning to identify and select sets of sources for teach-ing history is worthwhile. All of the students were able to adequately complete their sets of sources despite a relative dearth of primary sources in Chinese Canadian history, which suggests that the assign-ment is manageable for student teachers and teachers alike. Although several of the student teachers complained about the difficulty of creat-ing sets of primary sources, almost all of them felt that this assignment prepared them to teach history more effectively. In reflective e-mails, several student teachers expressed the opinion that the assignment helped them to build the necessary skills for selecting appropriate primary sources for teaching history. The process of framing a critical question, identifying appropriate primary sources, making sources pedagogically appropriate for their students, and writing background paragraphs helped to improve the student teachers' ability to design evidence-based activities. Despite recognizing these benefits, student teachers complained that this kind of task was too time-consuming to be completed on a regular basis. Despite reassuring them that they are not expected to develop a set of sources for each lesson or historical topic they address, I sensed that this factor alone was one of the most significant impediments preventing student and experienced teachers from regularly using sets of primary sources in their teaching.

The challenges that student teachers faced in this assignment were also important in helping them understand the complexity of designing evidence-based activities. Every student teacher had to make some revisions to their assignments before they were accepted. Although some student teachers resented having to revise an assignment that they believed was already "done," I felt that it was important for them to realize that activities utilizing primary sources require constant cycles of trial, revision, and reflection before they can be considered complete. Similarly, the difficulty that the student teachers faced when creating sets of sources further reinforced the idea that teaching history is intellectually demanding, a reality that some of the teachers may have underestimated when they began teacher education. As Alan Sears suggests in this volume, the majority of history teachers may simply not be ready or willing to take on the combination of intellectual rigour and good pedagogical practice needed to move a history teacher from the periphery to the core of their profession.

If we as teacher educators are serious about expecting student teachers to use historical evidence when teaching history, we must be realistic about addressing the factors that prevent this from occurring. This assignment provided some important suggestions for improving the preparation of student teachers to use historical evidence when teaching history. In order for student teachers to be convinced of the value of using multiple sources of evidence to teach history, they must be presented with activities that help them understand the benefits and limitations of using evidence. If teachers believe that teaching history using historical evidence is not an appropriate fit with the curriculum or their method of teaching, they will abandon it.

Student teachers also require instruction about the nature of historical evidence and the discipline of history. It would be a mistake to assume that student teachers' previous experience with history in high school or university provides them with enough understanding of the discipline of history. Any program that attempts to teach pre-service teachers to use multiple sources of evidence when teaching history requires activities and resources that improve their understanding of historical evidence and its importance in the construction of historical knowledge.

NOTES

1 Peter Seixas, "Student Teachers Thinking Historically," *Theory and Research in Social Education* 26, no. 3 (1998): 310-41; and Ken Osborne, "Fred Morrow Fling and the Source Method of Teaching History," *Theory and Research in Social Education* 31, no. 4 (2003): 466-501.

2 Samuel S. Wineburg, "On the Reading of Historical Texts: Notes on the Breach between the School and the Academy," *American Educational Research Journal* 28, no. 3 (1991): 495-519; Ruth W. Sandwell, "Reading Beyond Bias: Using Historical Documents in the Secondary Classroom," *McGill Journal of Education* 38, no. 1 (2003): 168-86; and K.C. Barton, "'I Just Kinda Know': Elementary Students' Ideas about Historical Evidence," *Theory and Research in Social Education* 25, no. 4 (1997): 407-30.

3 K.C. Barton, "Primary Sources in History: Breaking through the Myths," *Phi Delta Kappan* 86, no. 10 (2005): 745-53; and Ruth W. Sandwell, "History Is a Verb: Teaching Historical Practice to Teacher Education Students," in *New Possibilities for the Past: Shaping History Education in Canada*, edited by Penney Clark (Vancouver: UBC Press, 2011), 224-42.

4 Ibid., 229.

5 Ibid.

6 There has been a substantial research literature written on this. See, for example, G. McDiarmid and P. Vinten-Johansen, "A Catwalk across the Great Divide: Redesigning the History Teaching Methods Course," in *Knowing, Teaching, and Learning History: National and International Perspectives*, edited by Peter Stearns, Peter Seixas, and Samuel S. Wineburg (New York: New York University Press, 2000), 156-77; Ruth W. Sandwell, "School History Versus the Historians," *International Journal of Social Education* 20, no. 1 (2005): 9-17; C. Bohan and O.L. Davis, "Historical Constructions: How Social Studies Teachers' Historical Thinking is Reflected in Their Writing of History," *Theory and Research in Social Education* 26, no. 2 (1998): 173-97; E. Yeager and O.L. Davis, "Classroom Teachers' Thinking about Historical Texts: An Exploratory Study," *Theory and Research in Social Education* 24, no. 2 (1996): 146-66; Ruth W. Sandwell, "The Internal Divide: Historians and their Teaching," in *Bridging Theory and Practice in Teacher Education*, edited by Mordechai Gordon and T.V.

O'Brien (The Netherlands: Sense Publishers, 2007), 17-30; Thomas Fallace and Johann N. Neem, "Historiographical Thinking: Towards a New Approach," *Theory and Research in Social Education* 33, no. 3 (2005): 329-46; and Bruce A. VanSledright, "What Does It Mean to Think Historically ... And How Do You Teach It?" *Social Education* 68, no. 3 (2004): 230-33.

7   Sears, this volume, p. 17; Gardner, *Changing Minds*, 138; Samuel S. Wineburg, "Historical Thinking and Other Unnatural Acts (Why Study History)," *Phi Delta Kappan* 80, no. 7 (1999): 488-501; Samuel S. Wineburg, *Historical Thinking and Other Unnatural Acts: Charting the Future of Teaching the Past* (Philadelphia: Temple University Press, 2001), 272; Wineburg, "On the Reading of Historical Texts," 495-519; Thomas D. Fallace, "Once More Unto the Breach: Trying to Get Preservice Teachers to Link Historiographical Knowledge to Pedagogy," *Theory and Research in Social Education* 35, no. 3 (2007): 427-46; and K.C. Barton and L.S. Levstik, *Teaching History for the Common Good* (Mahwah, NJ: Lawrence Erlbaum Associates, 2004), 288.

8   K.C. Barton and L.S. Levstik, "Why Don't More History Teachers Engage Students in Interpretation?" *Social Education* 67, no. 6 (2003): 358-61; and Thomas D. Fallace, "Historiography and Teacher Education: Reflections on an Experimental Course," *The History Teacher* 42, no. 2 (2009): 205-22.

9   G. McDiarmid, "Understanding History for Teaching: A Study of the Historical Understanding of Prospective Teachers," in *Cognitive and Instructional Processes in History and the Social Sciences*, edited by M. Carretero and F. J. Voss (Hillsdale, N.J.: Lawrence Erlbaum Associates, 1994), 159-85.

10   Fallace, "Historiography and Teacher Education: Reflections on an Experimental Course," 205-22.

11   Seixas, "Student Teachers Thinking Historically," 310-41.

12   This assignment grew out of a project that I had been working on with The Critical Thinking Consortium (TC2) in the summer of 2010 that aimed to create an online repertory of carefully selected primary and secondary sources so that teachers don't have to search for appropriate sources every time they want to use them.

13   Barton, "Primary Sources in History: Breaking through the Myths," 745-53.

14   Ibid.; Fallace and Neem, "Historiographical Thinking: Towards a New Approach," 329-46; Peter Seixas, "Beyond 'Content' and 'Pedagogy': In Search of a Way to Talk about History Education," *Journal of Curriculum Studies* 31, no. 3 (1999): 317-37.

15   Peter Seixas, "The Community of Inquiry as a Basis for Knowledge and Learning: The Case of History," *American Educational Research Journal* 30,

no. 2 (1993): 305-24; Seixas, "Student Teachers Thinking Historically," 310-41.

16 Samuel S. Wineburg and Daisy Martin, "Tampering with History: Adapting Primary Sources for Struggling Readers," *Social Education* 73, no. 5 (2009): 212-16.

17 McDiarmid and Vinten-Johansen, "A Catwalk across the Great Divide: Redesigning the History Teaching Methods Course," 156-77; and Seixas, "Student Teachers Thinking Historically," 310-41.

18 Wineburg and Martin, "Tampering with History: Adapting Primary Sources for Struggling Readers," 212-16; and Seixas, "Student Teachers Thinking Historically," 310-41.

19 Seixas, "Student Teachers Thinking Historically," 310-41.

20 McDiarmid and Vinten-Johansen, "A Catwalk across the Great Divide: Redesigning the History Teaching Methods Course," 156-77.

13 Learning to Learn in New Brunswick Teacher Preparation: Historical Research as a Vehicle for Cultivating Historical Thinking in the Context of Social Studies Education

THEODORE CHRISTOU

This chapter describes an experiment in history teacher education that took place within the broader educational context of social studies teacher preparation at the University of New Brunswick. The experiment was premised on the supposition that a robust understanding of the relationship between historical thinking and both the teaching and learning of history demands discussion about, and immersion in, authentic historical research, and that this an appropriate social studies approach. As Alan Sears suggests in this collection, student teachers must *do* history in order to challenge the dominant world view that identifies history teaching with a mechanistic transmission of knowledge defined simplistically as dates, important figures, and disconnected trivia. Unfortunately, student teachers typically lack experience with and understanding of authentic historical processes – both of which they need, Sears argues, in order to move from the periphery to the core of their profession. Further, if said student teachers' cognitive frames are identified exclusively with what Sears calls the "mechanistic" means, and if the meanings, processes, and purposes of history education are to be challenged, we must anticipate frustration. Border crossing is not always easy, particularly when travelling on an "inbound trajectory" towards the core – an "active" realm of historical engagement – requires that we scrutinize our cognitive frames. These frames are the very things that we use to examine, interpret, and speak about our practice. We struggle to critically examine our cognitive frames, or world views, because these are the very lenses that enable us *to* examine the world. It is, perhaps, for this reason that historical thinking seems counterintuitive.

The Problem

Learning to Learn about Teaching Social Studies and Science is a required course for all student teachers in the elementary stream of the bachelor of education program at the University of New Brunswick. The course differs from other compulsory components of the student teachers' program of study in that it concentrates on disciplinary structure as opposed to methods, and it treats two general subject areas – social studies and science – as opposed to one. There were thus two tensions inherent in how the course was structured. First, my concern for teaching disciplinary thinking had to be framed within the context of a course that treated two subjects. Second, social studies is a subject that is necessarily interdisciplinary – weaving together history, geography, politics, and other fields – and my interest in cultivating historical thinking privileged one particular field.

The course was developed during a dramatic reorganization of teacher education at the university, when a two-year curriculum was transformed into an eleven-month program. The reasons, both pedagogical and expedient, for the development of this course explain its long and somewhat complicated title. In condensing the program from two years of study to one, cross-curricular thinking relieved congestion in the very full schedule of courses. If student teachers were to have opportunities to pursue elective courses in areas of their needs and interests, there needed to be fewer mandatory courses; each of the subject areas in the curriculum, however, had to be represented in courses. After taking Learning to Learn, which in some respects could be seen as introducing and framing both social studies and science, student teachers could pursue further learning in an elective course concentrating on either of the two.

Previously, the instructors treated science and social studies distinctly; each discipline was allotted one class (two hours) per week. This chapter concentrates solely on one aspect of the course: history education within the context of social studies. Elementary-stream student teachers enrolled in the course needed it to graduate, yet in general, they had minimal expertise with disciplinary studies in either science or social studies. For this last reason, the course was intended to approach these subjects as disciplines, which would permit a more robust understanding of what these fields actually are, as well as how they relate to other subjects. The direction pursued in the course was premised on an argument articulated by Veronica Boix Mansilla and Howard Gardner in the following terms: "Students need more than a large information base to understand their ever-changing world. They need to master disciplinary thinking."[1]

The Course Curriculum

While history is taught within the broader context of social studies classes in New Brunswick's elementary and middle schools, this course was designed to examine the subjects social studies and science at the expense of teaching methods rooted in curriculum standards. Consequently, from an instructional design perspective, the course is problematic; in addition to supporting the conceptually lofty aim of learning to learn about teaching, the usual concern remains about making the course useful and meaningful within the context of the particular curriculum that students would be teaching and interpreting.

With twenty-two classes in the teaching term (two two-hour meetings a week for eleven weeks), would it be possible to fully explore two distinct subject areas and relate these to teaching and learning in elementary classrooms? Only half of the teaching days – eleven in total – concentrated on the social studies. Two of these were assigned for field trips to local historical sites and museums, while one involved a guest speaker on the subject of historical thinking. Eight days were devoted to seminars on social studies, which, as a collection of disciplines and approaches, encompass a broad range of subjects. Using the subject categories outlined by Roland Case and Penney Clark in the course textbook, *The Anthology of Social Studies: Issues and Strategies for Elementary Teachers*,[2] these seminars examined content knowledge; critical thinking; information gathering and reporting; social and personal values; individual and collective action; instructional planning; learning resources; and student assessment as aspects of social studies education.

Developing a Strategy and Activity

In spite of these limiting factors, I decided to cultivate historical thinking through an environment of authentic research in history. This approach, as others have argued throughout this collection of essays and elsewhere,[3] is already shaping the discourse of history and social studies teachers across the country. To paraphrase Alan Sears once more, the course's intent was to give an opportunity for student teachers to actively make history rather than to passively receive it. We had the ulterior motive of inviting students to rethink the purposes, means, and ends of history education, as well as their relationship to the discipline. From hypothesis, to data collection, to peer review, and to publication, the course would engage student teachers as a scholarly community in a study of the world around them. And it was, indeed, during one particularly excited discussion with my colleague and partner in social studies education, Alan Sears, that we struck upon the research theme for the course: a history of science education in New Brunswick.

In groups of two or three, the student teachers conducted research on one decade of the province's educational history, concentrating on the teaching and learning of science. Our goal was that this research frame would tie together the two subjects under examination in the course and make a significant contribution to our understanding of New Brunswick's educational past. The completed project would, we hoped, be published online. Once a week, following social studies seminars grounded in readings from the course textbook, students would engage in a discussion period in order to share resources as well as stories of progress, success, and frustration with the research. Rather than discussing or debating the meanings and aims of cultivating historical thinking in elementary education, therefore, we sought to operationalize historical thinking as a class project. This chapter explores how we used research as a vehicle for exploring historical thinking in the context of this interdisciplinary education course.

The course syllabus, upon final revision, began with the following course description:

> In this course, we will explore the notion of teaching and learning a discipline through the study of teaching social studies and science.
>
> There are three interwoven concerns here, which we will frame as questions to explore in the course. Firstly: *What are social studies and science?* Secondly: *What do we do when we learn about these disciplines?* Thirdly: *How can we most effectively teach social studies and science in elementary school classrooms?*
>
> As we consider these questions, we will engage both individually and collectively with a series of readings, videos, field trips, discussions, debates, writing tasks, research queries, and presentations. A principle aim

here is to combine thinking about social studies and science as disciplines, doing representative work, and planning to teach these subjects in ways that develop critical habits of mind.

Having collected all the university's resources on New Brunswick's educational history, I asked my students to form small groups, to make a hypothesis about the province's educational history, and then to attempt to falsify this hypothesis through research. The falsification aim emerged spontaneously during the second class while discussing Karl Popper, and it was meant to integrate social studies as a field of research with science. Double-blind peer review of each project was undertaken for two weeks prior to the deadline for final submissions. Each student teacher was assigned two email addresses to which they sent their projects at a particular time and day. Each, further, received two projects, which they had one week to review using the rubric created for this project in the course. Constructive feedback was to ensure that each project would be of publishable quality. Vital to both disciplines of social studies and science is the scholarly community that works to read, review, and share ideas.

Following the peer review of each project, students had ten days to revise their work before submission. In the spirit of authenticity, I aimed to publish and disseminate their work to the public. Because the cost of publishing and distributing hard copies of the work was prohibitive, and because spaces made available by the university such as Blackboard were not open to the public, I developed a webpage for the publication of my students' research. At http://www.theodorechristou.ca, student teachers, educators, and researchers, as well as the general public, can read the research projects.

Evaluating the Process

In sum, the published work consists of a set of texts on the history of education in New Brunswick over the twentieth century. In regards to the explicit aim to pursue authenticity in the course, the student teachers' work has made an important contribution to our knowledge of the province's pedagogical past, particularly concerning social studies and science. Further, student teachers have reported that when asked – both in job interviews and in discussions with associate teachers in the schools – what their approach to social studies will be in the classroom, each of the student teachers draw on the online resource in order to explain that history is more than mere content or process.

Student journals submitted to me on completion of the course recorded the students' weekly reflections on the disciplines of social studies and science. Without fail, the students describe the importance of *doing* history, not memorizing it. These journals convey a conviction that educators must not rely strictly upon textbooks in order to teach history. Reflecting the arguments of the Progressivist school of educators in the early twentieth century, student teachers referred to textbook learning and examination as "passive" learning.

As the student teachers dug deeper into the resources, their initial fears about doing research in a subject that was foreign to them gave way to frustrations regarding what sources to use, what ideas were relevant, how to discuss ethical questions sensitively, and how much context should be included in the discussion in order to best support their claims. These frustrations were the subject of discussions in class, and they were documented in journal entries such as the one below:

> Throughout the research for our project I discovered several interesting characteristics of history. One of these characteristics was the difficulty in developing our scope. In the early part of our research we found many books and began sorting through the accumulated information to determine what we needed and what was either not relevant to our research or what was duplicated within our materials. Following the initial difficulty in developing our focus, the research process began. This brought forth an array of questions, answers, intrigue and further research. At points though, this was difficult and frustrating, as questions emerged from our initial research that remained unanswered. For example, when attempting to find information specifically about the history of New Brunswick we were unsuccessful … Reflecting on the project as a whole, we discovered invaluable information and insight into the methods of research and development of a project and further knowledge on sources of information, which will be effective tools in our future teaching.

Both personal reflection and public discussion were thus used as means of working through student frustrations during the project. The former I could not address until the course ended and the journals were submitted; however, the latter required immediate attention. Initial discussions began as questions directed to me and required me to reiterate the course's intentions and the place of research in the course. As the course continued, discussions relating to the aims of the course dissipated, and questions about the actual research, sources, and archives were increasingly directed towards the peer group. I explained to my students on several occasions that I was, somewhat paradoxically, elated that they were experiencing such frustrations. As teacher educators, we must expect that student teachers will be frustrated by our efforts to challenge the cognitive frames with which we approach history education. We should encourage student teachers to understand such frustration as evidence of deeper learning.

Conclusion

In hindsight, my most serious concern is the disconnect that student teachers felt between the ways that they had learned history and the way that they now intended to teach it. They worried that teachers, parents, or administration might see the purposes of history within social studies education differently and challenge their approach. They were sceptical about their ability to challenge other people's cognitive frames. They spoke of the system of schooling in the province as if it had a cognitive frame of its own, which bore a "passive" outlook and aim for history education. In a difficult job market that had led many of my students to go abroad to teach, it is easy to understand why many student teachers hesitate to challenge the status quo.

To what extent will the student teachers seek to operationalize historical thinking in their own teaching? Teacher educators from all subjects are concerned that disciplinary knowledge is deepened in the course of study and that the experiences evoked through teacher education are powerful enough to transform future teaching and learning. Encountering new ways of thinking about history education is positive, but the sense that one must conform to the system in order to gain acceptance can be overwhelming. There are some indications that this course succeeded in combating such conformity. The first is underlined by student teachers' comments to me – noted above – that they were able to use the published projects from our course to talk to administrators and veteran teachers about history as process. Student teachers expressed that the way they conceived of history and its purposes had shifted to a degree. Seventy-five per cent of student journals, collected at the end of the course, note that history is something that we learn by doing, not by memorizing. Forty per cent of students mentioned ways that they would try to involve their students in authentic history projects, such as partnering with local archives or using family history to explore social history. Fifteen per cent of students commented on exemplary teachers they had worked or studied with, who had engaged their classes with projects that changed the ways that learners understood, and found their place within, history.

This course not only nurtured historical thinking by allowing student teachers to actively participate in the delights and difficulties of historical research, but it also gave student teachers the opportunity to build a scholarly community in the course of their teacher education programs. As Alan Sears has argued, active engagement in "boundary work" of this kind has great potential for ensuring ongoing professional development through linking student teachers to the world of historical thinking and history education outside the classroom. Having constructed a project that remains in the public domain – a resource that serves a public purpose – this teaching experiment supports an ongoing relationship with professional educators and parents. The published resources on the history of education in New Brunswick facilitate and enable future discussion about historical process within social studies education. The student teachers in my class worked as a tightly knit scholarly community rather than as individuals. As a result, they will see each other as valuable resources going forward and look for such communities in their practice.

Moving from the periphery to the core takes time, and it also requires networks to support the inward trajectory. Helping student teachers to find ways to transform their practice and to integrate historical thinking into social studies classrooms outside of my own requires that I rethink my commitment to student learning so that it extends longitudinally and qualitatively. This will entail greater involvement with professional development opportunities in the local district and province, particularly sustainable structures such as professional learning communities in schools.

NOTES

1 Veronica B. Mansilla and Howard Gardner, "Disciplining the Mind," *Educational Leadership*, 65, no. 5 (2008): 14.
2 Roland Case and Penney Clark, eds., *The Anthology of Social Studies: Issues and Strategies for Elementary Teachers* (Vancouver: Pacific Educational Press, 2008).

3 Peter J. Lee and Alaric K. Dickinson, eds., *History Teaching and Historical Understanding* (London: Heinemann Educational Books, 1979); Sam Wineburg, *Historical Thinking and Other Unnatural Acts: Charting the Future of Teaching the Past* (Philadelphia: Temple University Press, 2001); Peter Seixas, ed., *Theorizing Historical Consciousness* (Toronto: University of Toronto Press, 2006); Penney Clark, ed., *New Possibilities for the Past: Shaping History Education in Canada* (Vancouver: UBC Press, 2011); Stéphane Lévesque, *Thinking Historically: Educating Students for the Twenty-First Century* (Toronto: University of Toronto Press, 2008); and Linda Levstik and Keith C. Barton, *Doing History: Investigating with Children in Elementary and Middle Schools*, 4th ed. (New York: Routledge, 2011).

14 When in Doubt, Ask: Student Teacher Insights into Research and Practice

JOHN JC MYERS

Defining the Problem

Student teachers who are hoping to teach history in the secondary school system in Ontario enter professional teacher education programs with a minimum of subject knowledge guaranteed by admission standards. They emerge as newly qualified teachers who are expected to have developed a broad range of teaching skills and habits of mind. These include a desire to find out about the students and the school in which they will teach, a solid grasp of instructional methods, knowledge of the factors influencing how they will teach, and the habit of reflecting on their actions and on those of their students.

However, as educational psychologist Lee Shulman, who has studied teaching along with other professions for decades, has argued, teaching is one of the most difficult of professions to do well. In the address he delivered when he received his honorary degree at the University of Toronto in 2007, he pointed out the complexities of teaching by comparing the fields of teaching and medicine. He noted that teachers have classrooms of twenty-five to thirty-five students. In comparison, doctors treat only a single patient at a time. Even when working with a reading group of six to eight students, teachers are assessing and facilitating the learning of decoding skills, comprehension, performance, and engagement of those students while simultaneously observing the actions of the other two dozen students in the room. "The only time a physician could possibly encounter a situation of comparable complexity," Shulman pointed out, "would be in the emergency room of a hospital during or after a natural disaster."[1] Classroom teaching, he concluded, "is perhaps the most complex, most challenging, and most demanding, subtle, nuanced, and frightening activity that our species has ever invented."[2]

Most teachers would agree. No initial teacher education program, regardless of its quality, can adequately prepare teachers for all they need to know, and history teachers are no exception. A rich research literature has powerfully underscored the point that the complexity of the craft requires ongoing teacher learning.[3] As Alan Sears argues in this volume, the problem for prospective history teachers is particularly acute for two reasons: first, students generally have had little exposure to historical thinking or "doing history" by the time they enter student teacher programs, and hence "have little or no actual experience" with the processes that they will be teaching. Even more serious, Sears argues, is the fact that "candidates have a strong cognitive frame that history teaching essentially involves the passing on of historical information." Sears argues that the solution to these problems must include developing communities of practice among various kinds of history educators, including historians. These communities, by means of the "boundary work" that they encourage, will allow history teachers to make the huge transition from being on the periphery of the profession to being at its core: to remake their identity as teachers of *historical thinking* and not historical facts. This has to happen *over the duration* of their careers, and history teachers, as well, must ensure that *student teachers* are "inducted" to similar kinds of "cross-boundary teams to both facilitate their own rethinking of what it means to teach history and lay the groundwork for future collaboration."[4] This chapter supports this contention: if these solutions are ignored, too many history teachers will continue to operate in the periphery of the discipline with little understanding of what history is and how it works.

This chapter suggests that if student teachers are going to begin the transformations in identity and practice that Sears argues are necessary to change history teaching, they may need some prompting and guidance in their teacher education programs before they will be convinced of the need for change. But many students interpret quite differently the disjuncture that Sears identifies between the "core" practices (newly identified as "historical thinking" and emerging most visibly from the universities) and the typical Canadian history classroom, where teachers are on the "periphery" of the history teaching profession. Anecdotal evidence (from my teacher education classrooms and those of my colleagues) suggests that many student teachers observe this disjuncture and dismiss it as the difference between the theories propounded by so-called experts and the realities of teaching high school history in Canada.[5] This chapter, therefore, argues that student history teachers need a new way of approaching the familiar theory-versus-practice divide if they are to meet the challenge of remaking history education in Canada. I present here one simple but effective strategy that instructors can use in their classrooms to "induce" prospective history teachers into wider communities of practice and also into the realization that theoretically-informed research can help them understand how and why *change is needed* within the history education system.

The Strategy

Here is an effective strategy that I have used in my teacher education history classrooms. After their practicum, students were invited to make explicit links between the research on history teaching and learning that they had studied in their teacher education classrooms and their own practice during the practicum. I begin here by describing the strategy, and the key role that active reflection played in enabling students to *describe* their recent classroom experiences. Then, I *explain* the research/practice divide that the strategy revealed. The chapter presents some of the findings from this exercise, demonstrating its effectiveness in this history methods course.

Why Reflection?

What have researchers said about the importance of reflection in teacher education? *Preparing Teachers for a Changing World: What Teachers Should Learn and Be Able to Do*, argues that reflection helps teachers draw inferences from work in the classroom as a guide for further action and helps them to move rapidly through the trial and error phase of early teaching to quality self-assessment and self-adjustment through metacognitive thinking. It allows them to explore their deeply held, yet largely tacit, assumptions about teaching and learning in order to test their true efficacy. It allows them to refine and adapt their teaching to the maximum benefit of the learner and to make the necessary connections among policy, research, and practice, often mentoring with colleagues both informally and through more formal professional learning communities.[6]

The Need for Reflection in the Teaching and Learning of History

In the area of history education, there are some discipline-specific complexities that students become aware of by reflecting on their practice. These include, most significantly, the tension between teaching history as a fixed fact-filled narrative (a kind of history typically identified with school teachers) and teaching historical thinking, which includes a deeper understanding of second-order concepts such as causation and the skills needed to analyse and evaluate evidence (a kind of history typically identified with university teacher education programs and the larger academic research world). This is manifested in the classroom: teachers feel pressured to rely on textbooks to meet ministry goals and expectations, both real and perceived (which emphasize "history as fact" or "history as a noun"), but there is also an impetus to teach "history as a verb" through the study of primary sources.[7] Another manifestation of this disjuncture can be seen in the media. The public fixates on test scores and students' lack of historical "facts," as opposed to emphasizing historical understanding as student teachers are taught to do in the classroom. Finally, student teachers also experience confusion and misunderstanding while implementing too many ideas; in all phases of teacher development, from pre-service to in-service, history educators simply try to do too much![8]

My course generally follows the following schedule, and I work to include elements of reflection in all phases. Classes in September and October introduce the course, and cover unit and lesson planning, an overview of the Ontario curriculum, and assessment terms. In November, students have their first four-week practicum period and apply what they have learned to teaching real kids in real classrooms. In December, January, and February, we refine and expand from our initial coursework students' understanding of teaching and learning. The second practicum comes in March, and April is the time for synthesis using the assignment below.

The Assignment

Students were asked to complete this reflection assignment after the second practicum. I had explained the criteria and standards for the students' responses in the initial course outline and had demonstrated various elements in the classroom and in practicum work. Students were presented with insights and were asked to provide their reflections, first in writing during class time, and then in a group discussion with the class immediately afterwards.

The first set of insights (about teaching) comes from Darling-Hammond and Bransford (editors), *Preparing Teachers for a Changing World*.[9] Darling-Hammond and Bransford state that good teachers share two kinds of expertise:

1 *Routine expertise* refers to possessing a core set of competencies that they apply throughout their lives with increasing efficacy. These include course, unit, and lesson design, assessment planning and practice, and a repertoire of teaching strategies that becomes more refined and skillfully used with experience. In a history classroom these include working with primary sources; using questions to promote historical thinking; establishing classroom routines; and managing the variety of resources available for the study of a topic: from guest speakers to textbooks to the Internet.
2 *Adaptive expertise* goes beyond initial core competencies to expand both the breadth and depth of one's expertise, even though in the short term efficiency may be reduced. There is no magic formula. Even if there were a magic formula, it would not be enough to tell you how to gain adaptive expertise since much of what works is contextual. Teachers do not come from cookie cutters! This competency not only involves a degree of improvisation but may over time result in changes to one's routine expertise.

Darling-Hammond and Bransford go on to point out that new teachers need to learn that being a teacher is different from being a student. This need often becomes apparent when new teachers want to be the students' friend. Thinking like a teacher, they argue, does not mean that you will "do" like a teacher when you are in the middle of a class. Thus, teachers need to develop sound habits of mind in order to handle the complexities of classroom life.

At this stage of their careers, many teachers referred to general aspects of teaching such as class management. For purposes of this volume, I offer samples relating more specifically to history teaching. All names are fictitious, but the comments are verbatim. Shannon reflected, "One difference in my second practicum was my ability to ask higher order thinking questions. Using my checklist I made sure that in every lesson that involved a question-answer sequence I would have three to five such questions: all related to the lesson and unit expectations." Next is Clive's account, one (among many) documenting the importance of being flexible, taking advantage of teachable moments, and reacting positively to unpredictable events:

> Adaptive expertise is extremely important, especially in the context of a history classroom. Quite often during my history practicum, my students would catch me completely off guard with the things that they found so very interesting. For example, we were discussing politics during the [D]epression in my Grade 10 history classroom, and I could hardly believe the response that I got from my students. They were enthusiastic, asking questions, and even making their own predictions for the upcoming election this year. Originally I had planned on more or less skimming over the political stuff, as I had assumed that my chatty 16 year-old students would find this boring anyway. Turns out I could not have been more wrong! As teachers, it is crucial that we are able to take advantage of these "teachable moments" and to adapt our lessons accordingly. You just never know what might strike a chord with your students.

A number of students commented on the important transition that new teachers need to make from being a successful high school and university student to teaching students who struggle and who may not strive to become history teachers or professional historians. This might require unlearning habits developed in high school and university. For example, Claire noted: "Before the practicum I was under the impression that lengthy lectures were necessary for the students to become knowledgeable on the topic being discussed. This is how I was taught. Now that I am back from practicum … the lecture I had planned is too long. I know that I will lose the students' attention …" Odile had a particularly thoughtful reflection on the importance of classroom experience in dealing with the vast range of behaviours and issues that teachers need to respond to:

> How does one prepare for students using derogatory terms toward each other in class, an un-enrolled student walking into the classroom from the hallway to shout curses at a student or you (the teacher), or a student disputing the accuracy of historical facts being presented because he/she was

taught differently in their home country? Pardon the cliché, but there is no substitute for experience. Only through the unsophisticated strategy of trial and error can a teacher effectively understand and successfully deal with the breadth of issues that will undoubtedly arise over the course of a school year.

I drew the second set of insights from decades of research about how students learn in the classroom, and presented them after the second practicum as outlined below:

1   Students come to the classroom with preconceptions about how the world works. If their initial understanding is not engaged, they may fail to grasp the new concepts and information, or they may learn them for purposes of a test but revert to their preconceptions outside of the classroom.
2   To develop competence in an area of inquiry, students must (a) have a deep foundation of factual knowledge; (b) understand facts and ideas in a conceptual framework; and (c) organize knowledge in ways that facilitate retrieval and application.
3   A "metacognitive" approach to instruction can help students take control of their own learning by defining learning goals and monitoring their progress in achieving them.[10]

There were more history-related responses to these insights, as would be expected. A number of students drew the following important lesson from this synthesis of insights into how we learn: we need to link new learning to what learners already believe. Stephen's reflection was particularly insightful:

The idea that students do come into the classroom with preconceptions about how the world works, is a very true and important idea that teachers need to be aware of. I believe that it is important for teachers to try and get a good idea of where the students are coming from before teaching them what they have to know to ensure that students actually internalize what is taught rather than understand it at a very artificial level for the exam. During my first practicum when I taught the WW2 unit my AT [associate teacher] warned me of exactly this before I was to plan my lesson on Japanese Internment. My AT informed me that since most of the students in the class were Chinese they may not sympathize with what happened to Japanese Canadians in internment and that I should work harder to find a way to make that connection so they do understand the severity of the situation.

Bruce also noted the importance of locating students in the past by making strong links between past and present: "I began my unit on the Depression by examining economic realities for people caught up in the current recession. We examined articles and photos in the newspaper about people looking for work and food banks to show the connection between then and now." Commenting on how knowledge does not equal understanding, and that the latter comes from linking facts and ideas to larger conceptual frameworks, Omar reflected on his experience as follows:

For my practicum I had a two-part activity dealing with the Winnipeg General Strike. The first part of the activity was a discussion of the Winnipeg General Strike looking at what happened, who was involved and what the major issues were. With the second part the students had a chance to apply what they learned. They did this by engaging in a combination of role-playing and debating. It allowed the students to really engage with the material that they learned the day before. In the town meeting the students had to take on a particular role and air their concerns. There were seven different roles that they could play so it was not just a matter of workers taking on employers. It was a home community of people with different interest … the students get a much better idea of what is going on.

The third set of reflections explores how, by carefully scaffolding student learning, we can identify our goals and monitor our progress towards achieving them. Ghadah reflected on the importance of scaffolding as follows:

When I taught Grade 12 history through film, my Associate Teacher wanted the class to read a specific article on the Rwandan genocide, and it was a twenty five-page academic journal article. It is important to expose students in the university stream to this kind of material, especially in Grade 12, but they must be given explicit strategies for handling it, or it will be overwhelming and frustrating, rather than a valuable learning opportunity. When I taught the article, I showed students a literacy strategy called marking the text, where students use different coloured highlighters to mark things they read that they already knew, things that surprised them and things that provoked questions. Looking for these specific things helped students focus their reading, which is important in such a large piece. Showing my students an explicit tactic, and explaining why it works, puts another learning tool in their toolkits. The metacognitive piece comes in when we not only teach students strategies, but how and when to use them. The next time my history through film students are faced with large complicated piece of text, I hope they look into their toolkit (metacognition!) and pick a strategy that will help them learn effectively, whether it is marking the text or another equally valid strategy that will work for them.

Kimberly used the strategy "ticket out the door" or "3-2-1" to have students reflect on what they had done and what they had learned in their class. In this way, "the student is asked to think about which methods they preferred when learning the material and consider the best way they learn." Kimberly noted this strategy's potential to increase the teacher's knowledge of what teaching techniques are important, for "this also allows the teacher to 'talk' to each student and get to know their learning processes better in order to tailor lessons to suit the ongoing needs of the classroom."

Conclusion

The exercise described above allows students to confront some of the disparities between the *historical thinking* emphasized in the research-based teacher education classrooms and their experiences – most often in places that Sears would describe as being on the periphery of history education – in high school history classrooms. The reflection assignments, therefore, not only allow students to explore some of the many challenges in making the discipline intelligible, meaningful, and memorable to the young. They also forcefully illustrate the need for drawing on multiple communities of support – including researchers and experienced teachers – when learning how to teach history well.

The reflections offered here are samples. The assignments described in this chapter can be done in any teacher education program. Future questions include:

• What is the balance between discipline-specific and generalized reflections?

• Does this balance change throughout a teacher's career?

My task as a teacher educator is to help foster this habit in students so that it has a permanent place in their toolkit for teaching and learning.

NOTES

1 L.S. Shulman, *The Wisdom of Practice: Essays on Teaching, Learning, and Learning to Teach* (San Francisco: Jossey-Bass, 2004), 258.
2 Ibid., 504.
3 J. Hattie, *Visible Learning: A Synthesis of Over 800 Meta-analyses Relating to Achievement* (New York: Routledge, 2009); A.L. Costa and B. Kallick, *Assessment Strategies for Self-Directed Learning* (Thousand Oaks, CA: Corwin, 2004); L.M. Earl, *Assessment as Learning* (Thousand Oaks, CA: Corwin, 2003); and G. Wiggins, *Educative Assessment* (San Francisco: Jossey-Bass, 1998).
4 Sears, this volume, p. 22.
5 Keith Barton and Linda Levstik explore student teachers' failure to internalize the lessons learned in teachers college in their *Teaching History for the Common Good*, and come to the conclusion that professional identity for history teachers extends only to their ability to "control the class" and "cover the curriculum" – hence Sears' call to "make new" the identity of student history teachers. Keith C. Barton and Linda S. Levstik, *Teaching History for the Common Good* (New Jersey and London: Lawrence Erlbaum Associates, 2004).
6 Karen Hammerness, Linda Darling-Hammond, and John Bransford, "How Teachers Learn and Develop," in *Preparing Teachers for a Changing World: What Teachers Should Learn and Be Able to Do*, edited by Linda Darling-Hammond and John Bransford (San Francisco: Jossey-Bass, 2005), 358-89.
7 Ruth Sandwell, "History Is a Verb: Teaching Historical Practice to Teacher Education Students" in *New Possibilities for the Past: Shaping History Education in Canada*, edited by Penney Clark (Vancouver: UBC Press, 2011), 224-42.
8 Clare Kosnik and C. Beck, *Teaching in a Nutshell: Navigating Your Teacher Education Program as a Student Teacher* (Routledge: New York, 2011); and D.B. Reeves, *Transforming Professional Development into Student Results* (Alexandria, VA: Association for Supervision and Curriculum Development, 2010).

9 Linda Darling-Hammond and John Bransford, eds., *Preparing Teachers for a Changing World: What Teachers Should Learn and Be Able to Do* (San Francisco: Wiley, 2005).

10 M.S. Donovan and J.D. Bransford, "Introduction," in *How Students Learn: History, Mathematics, and Science in the Classroom*, edited by M.S. Donovan and J.D. Bransford (Washington, DC: The National Academies, 2005), 1-2.

PART IV

Boundary Work:
Sustaining Communities of Practice

15 Can Teacher Education Programs Learn Something from Teacher Professional Development Initiatives?

CARLA L. PECK

"Do you mean to tell me that what is written in the history textbook isn't what really happened?"

My answer to this question, which was asked by an experienced teacher during a week-long summer institute focused on teaching historical thinking, was short and succinct: *"Yes."* A murmur started to creep around the crowded lecture theatre and I could tell that, at least for some in the room, the idea that historical narratives like those in history textbooks are constructions (involving the use of evidence to make decisions about historical significance, analyse continuity and change, or understand historical perspectives) was something new. If history isn't what is found in textbooks, what is it? This moment clarified for me the importance of addressing what Alan Sears contends is a fundamental flaw in teacher education programs: that is, that most student teachers "have a strong cognitive frame that history teaching essentially involves the passing on of historical information and not the fostering of historical thinking."[1]

When students graduate from a teacher education program, they are "beginning teachers." This term has a double meaning. The first meaning implies that these recent graduates are about to embark on their teaching career. The second meaning of the term is that new graduates are novice teachers who require support and mentorship in order to develop into knowledgeable and confident members of the teaching profession. Even the most outstanding student teacher needs this kind of support when he or she begins teaching, for no teacher education program can provide *all* of the knowledge, skills, tools, or habits of mind that teachers require when they begin their career. In addition, research on pedagogy, on how students learn, and on the various disciplines taught in schools is constantly emerging, which means that the knowledge, skills, tools, or habits of mind that teachers require will continue to change. This means, of course, that it is not only beginning teachers who require support, but experienced teachers as well. As this volume suggests, ongoing teacher professional development has a role to play in supporting not only beginning teachers' entry into the teaching profession, but also experienced teachers who seek opportunities for professional growth throughout their teaching careers. In this chapter, I will review some of the research on professional development in history education and will present findings from longitudinal research that investigated the effects of a two-year professional development project on teaching historical thinking with K–12 teachers in Alberta. I conclude with some suggestions about what teacher education programs might learn from teacher professional development initiatives.

Professional Development in History Education

Scholars researching professional development (PD) programs for classroom teachers have raised several criticisms of continuing teacher education, particularly in regard to its impact on teachers as well as its influence on students and classroom life. Some outright dismiss PD programs as "woefully inadequate."[2] Several studies support the claim that there are considerable deficits in PD, especially where teachers were concerned. For example, one large-scale quantitative study found that fewer than 50 per cent of teachers characterized their PD experiences as useful,[3] while another found that social studies teachers, compared to their peers in different subject areas, were the second least likely to agree that PD is effective.[4]

In terms of PD programs focused on teaching history specifically, research is spotty and limited in its conclusions[5] and is almost nonexistent in Canada. Debates continue about what (and how much) teachers require in order to teach history effectively, with a range of suggestions permeating the literature: more (or better) disciplinary, pedagogical, and curricular knowledge; clarification of epistemological beliefs about the purpose of teaching history; and better understanding of source work, to name a few.[6] Some research on PD in history education has found that teachers' beliefs about the discipline of history influence not only how they teach it,[7] but also determine how they fit new epistemological or historiographical insights into their practice.[8] VanSledright, Maggioni, and Reddy identified three of the most common epistemic positions among the secondary school teachers in their study: the *copier* (the past happened and history chronicles it), the *subjectivist* (history is whatever the knower decides it is – all opinions are valid or right), and the *criticalist* (balances the copier or objective and the subjectivist orientations to the past).[9] These conceptual views are typically resistant to change without sustained PD. For example, one follow-up study with classroom teachers found that seven of the twenty-one participants "continued to exhibit a relatively generic and instrumental view of teaching for historical thinking" despite having participated in PD that challenged these views.[10]

Several studies emphasize the importance of using primary sources in the history classroom.[11] One teacher reported that as a result of history PD, she had "started to use primary documents to cover what's in the curriculum, not as part of an historical investigation."[12] Many researchers have found that simply introducing primary sources into history lessons does not change the method of history instruction. As Sandwell notes, "research has confirmed that simply providing students with access and opportunities to work with primary documents is not enough to promote their effective use."[13] There is a risk that without continuing PD, teachers will employ primary sources as gimmicks in an otherwise lecture-driven course or use them as the arbiter of dispute when asking interpretive questions.[14] In other words, primary sources can provide interesting visuals or be offered as "proof," but if students are not repeatedly and effectively taught how to work with them, they will not learn how to use them in historical investigations. Barton's curious finding that even after being taught how to engage with primary sources, students made up answers without relying on the sources they'd just analysed exemplifies this point.[15]

With continuing PD, some teachers were able to assimilate new approaches to history teaching, such as cultural encounters or cross-curricular connections, into their exiting pedagogies.[16] After following teachers throughout a three-year intensive history PD program, Sawyer and Laguardia identified six major new learnings, including: the importance of historical content in teaching history; the value of an aesthetic/imaginative history curriculum; the dynamic nature of history curriculum; the political and transformative nature of history curriculum; the cultural nature of history curriculum; and the intersection of history

252 Carla L. Peck

curriculum and students' lives.[17] Sawyer and Laguardia's findings make a sound case that deep learning can occur when PD is sustained over many years.

Context

In 2005, the province of Alberta began a five-year, staggered implementation of a newly revised K–12 social studies program of studies.[18] In April of that year, the provincial government announced $26 million in funding "for curriculum and teacher professional development," of which $12.8 million was dedicated to textbooks and other resources and $6 million was targeted for professional development.[19] In the new Alberta social studies program, historical thinking is included as one of six "dimensions of thinking" and is only briefly described before being broken down into specific grade-level skills students are expected to master.

Social studies curricula in Canada have begun to attend to "dimensions of thinking," with historical thinking taking on a prominent role as curricula are revised. However, in many social studies curricula, historical thinking is not clearly articulated, or it is broken down into a discrete set of skills. For example, in the revised Alberta Education *Program of Studies for Social Studies (K–12)*, historical thinking is defined as follows:

> Historical thinking is a process whereby students are challenged to re-think assumptions about the past and to reimagine both the present and the future. It helps students become well-informed citizens who approach issues with an inquiring mind and exercise sound judgment when presented with new information or a perspective different from their own. Historical thinking skills involve the sequencing of events, the analysis of patterns and the placement of events in context to assist in the construction of meaning and understanding, and can be applied to a variety of media, such as oral traditions, print, electronic text, art and music.[20]

This articulation of "historical thinking," while ambitious in terms of its connection to citizenship, remains inadequate in terms of providing teachers sufficient direction for how to develop students' capacity to "think historically." In addition, it characterizes historical thinking as a set of skills that includes sequencing, analysing patterns, and contextualization. These become more advanced in each grade (e.g., by the end of kindergarten, students should be able to "differentiate between events and activities that occurred recently and long ago,"[21] and by the end of Grade 6, students should be able to "use primary sources to interpret historical events and issues"[22]) but the document does not guide teachers in how to achieve these curricular outcomes with their students. Curriculum documents do not usually include instructional advice, making the case for professional development that much stronger, particularly when new or revised curricula are vastly different from previous versions. This was the case in Alberta, where the new social studies curricula required different ways of teaching historical thinking.

While historical thinking involves these and other processes, academic work on historical thinking (sometimes called historical understanding) conceptualizes historical thinking in a much broader sense. In essence, history can be divided into two types of concepts.[23] First-order, or substantive, concepts are the content of history lessons: concepts such as "revolution," "Confederation of Canada in 1867," or "the Chinese Head Tax." Second-order or procedural concepts are the "ideas that provide our understanding of history as a discipline or form of knowledge … they shape the way we go about doing history."[24] Examples include "continuity and change" or "cause and consequence." Second-order concepts differ from substantive, first-order concepts in that the latter make up the content of our history lessons, whereas the former provide a *framework* for investigating the past.[25]

The Professional Development Project

From August 2008 to June 2010, in partnership with two professional development consortia in Alberta,[26] I launched a PD project focused on teaching teachers how to use a framework for historical thinking in two major urban centres in Alberta. Nineteen teachers from "Northcity"[27] began the project in August 2008, and nine (five new, four returning) participated in the second year. Thirteen teachers from "Southcity" began the project in October 2008, and eleven (eight new, three returning) teachers participated in the second year. The two groups of teachers spent five PD days (each) over the course of the school year learning about historical thinking concepts (HTCs) and collaborating on the development of lesson plans, assessment tasks, and rubrics based on the HTCs and the new Alberta social studies curricula. In the first year, the primary focus was on *historical significance, continuity and change*, and *evidence.* In the second year of the project, the primary focus was on developing teachers' understandings of *evidence, historical perspective-taking, ethical judgments in history,* and *cause and consequence.* The teachers piloted their tasks with their students and selected examples of student work that met various levels of expectations across the grade levels.

Methodology

Data were collected over the two years of the project and included anonymous teacher questionnaires administered at the end of each year, teacher reflections, teacher work products (lesson plans and support materials), and samples of student work from the teachers who participated in the PD project. In addition, four teachers agreed to individual interviews and classroom observations, which were conducted six to twelve months after the project ended. It is important to note that it is difficult for me, as the PD facilitator and later the one interviewing and observing the teachers, to distance myself from the project. Throughout the interviews, I encouraged the teachers to be honest with their feedback and comments, but it's quite possible that they felt they could not be as candid as they might be with someone more detached from the project.

In this chapter, I draw on all of the questionnaire data and on the classroom observations, teacher and student work products, and interview data from two teachers. These two teachers were chosen because they participated in one year of the professional development project, worked collaboratively in the same school, and taught the same grades and topics. These teachers are not representative of the entire group of teachers who participated in the PD project, nor can their experiences be generalized beyond their own context. However, their perceptions can shed light on aspects of professional development that may affect teachers' teaching – and students' learning – of history.

Participants

At the time of the study, Janis had more than twenty years' experience teaching at the middle school level and was starting to consider retirement. Janis has a four-year bachelor of education degree and teaches Grade 7 social studies at a large charter school in southern Alberta. Janis participated in the first year of the historical thinking professional development project and encouraged her colleague, Xavier, to enrol in the project in its second year.

Xavier is Janis's colleague and also teaches Grade 7 social studies. He has been teaching for ten years – five abroad and five in Canada. He has a bachelor of arts degree with a major in history, and a two-year bachelor of education degree. Xavier and Janis regularly collaborate on social studies unit plans and assessments, and they have been supportive of each other's efforts to incorporate the historical thinking concepts (as articulated during the PD they attended) into their teaching. They meet regularly to discuss and plan new units, and to revisit ones they've previously taught. To date, they have developed extensive unit plans (that they both teach) that focus on historical significance, evidence, and the ethical dimension of history.

During the three days that I observed in their classrooms, Janis and Xavier were beginning a unit on Confederation, which had "historical significance" as its core historical thinking concept. Students were tasked with using three criteria for gauging historical significance (the event had deep consequences; it affected a lot of people; and it affected people over a long period of time) to decide upon the eight most significant events leading to Confederation (or, when Canada became a country). Students were given sixteen picture cards that included a date, a title, an image, and a short caption describing the event and had to work in small groups to narrow the sixteen events down to eight. The requirements for the students' final products included a visual timeline of the eight events that their group selected, as well as individual essays explaining the historical significance of one event of the student's choosing.

Findings

Teachers' Pedagogical Content Knowledge

Pedagogical content knowledge[28] is knowledge that teachers employ to explain the central ideas of a discipline to students. In this case, the pedagogical content knowledge at the heart of this professional development project and research is "historical thinking," and in particular, the concepts at the core of The Historical Thinking Project. In the beginning of the project's first year, most teachers (11-Northcity, 7-Southcity), when choosing from a list of statements, described their knowledge of the HTCs as ranging from "completely zero" to "I knew about some

HTCs, but I didn't really know how to have my students engage in them." Only five Northcity teachers and four Southcity teachers felt that they held more knowledge at the beginning of the project, and only one of these teachers felt that he/she "was well versed in historical inquiry even before this project started."

In the beginning of the project's second year, most (8) of the teachers who completed the survey described their knowledge of the HTCs as ranging from "completely zero" to "I would describe my knowledge about historical thinking prior to beginning this project as tacit and spotty." The three returning teachers felt that they had more knowledge than this at the beginning of the project, and one of these teachers felt that he/she "was well versed in historical inquiry even before this project started" (See Table 15.1).

By the *end* of the first year of the project, only one Northcity teacher and no Southcity teachers described their knowledge of the HTCs as ranging from "completely zero" to "I knew about some HTCs, but I didn't really know how to have my students engage in them." Instead, the majority of teachers in both regions described how their knowledge and understanding of the HTCs had grown, with two teachers from each region (four in total) feeling that they were "well versed in historical inquiry now that the project is over." By the end of the second year, the majority of teachers in both regions described significant growth in their knowledge and understanding of the HTCs (See Table 15.2).

Both Janis and Xavier expressed having grown in their understanding of "historical thinking" (HT) compared to before they engaged in the PD project. Janis's description focused more on the interpretive aspect of HT, whereas Xavier's description was related to the qualitative nature (depth) of the thinking required of students. Janis reflected:

> I guess I use the phrase "are you thinking like an historian"? Are you looking at the different viewpoints? It's not just reading the textbook and taking it at its word. I had an explorer project and I had students showing me two different websites saying two different things and I said, ok, how are you going to decide which one to believe? … ok, how are you going to decide? And I think that's what's important for these kids, so that they become good consumers … So I think thinking like an historian means we have to look at all the viewpoints, and look at their biases … the students start to see both sides of an issue … So I think that's what historical thinking is about – looking at all the viewpoints of the different people and asking questions about it.

Table 15.1 Knowledge of HTCs at Beginning of Project

	Year 1	Year 2
Completely zero!	2	0
I only knew how "historical thinking" is defined in the Program of Studies.	9	3
I knew that "history" is a construction, but I did not know how historians went about their work.	1	1
I would describe my knowledge about historical thinking prior to beginning this project as tacit and spotty.	1	4
I knew about some historical thinking concepts (like chronology and significance), but I didn't really know how to have my students engage with them.	5	2
I knew about some historical thinking concepts (like chronology and significance), and I have been having my students engage with them even before this project started.	5	0
I had been introduced to the 6 historical thinking concepts but hadn't yet integrated them into my planning or teaching.	2	0
I had been introduced to the 6 historical thinking concepts and had started to experiment with them.	1	0
I feel like I was well versed in historical inquiry even before this project started.	1	1
TOTAL	27	11

Janis's ideas about historical thinking were apparent when I observed her teaching. In her introduction to the Confederation project that focused on the concept of historical significance, Janis said, "Yesterday, you came up with some really good facts about the Deportation of the Acadians. But facts will be forgotten in a few days. We need to think like an historian. Now, we can't study everything that happened from now (Deportation) to Confederation. We need to make choices. Deciding on historical significance is how we can make these choices." Janis then introduced three criteria for deciding the historical significance of an event, criteria she learned during the PD project (deep consequences; for many people; over a long period of time), and asked students to think about the Deportation of the Acadians using these criteria. One by one, she modelled how to apply each criterion to assess whether or not the event should be considered historically significant, and she challenged the students to draw on the background information they had learned the day before to justify their decisions and support their

Table 15.2 Knowledge of HTCs at End of Project

	Year 1	Year 2
Completely zero!	0	0
I only know how "historical thinking" is defined in the Program of Studies.	0	0
I know that "history" is a construction, but I still do not know how historians go about their work.	0	0
I would describe my knowledge about historical thinking at the end of this project as tacit and spotty.	0	0
I know about some historical thinking concepts (like chronology and significance), but I don't really know how to have my students engage with them.	1	0
I know about some historical thinking concepts (like chronology and significance), and I have been having my students engage with them.	7	2
I haven't yet integrated some or all of the 6 historical thinking concepts into my planning or teaching.	5	0
I have integrated some or all of the 6 historical thinking concepts into my planning or teaching.	10	8
I feel like I am well versed in historical inquiry now that the project is over.	4	1
TOTAL	27	11

answers. Janis's approach to teaching historical thinking reflects her understanding of it; that is, she teaches students to take an analytical approach, weighing information against criteria and providing evidence to support their positions.

Xavier relied heavily on the six historical thinking concepts (HTC) when explaining his understanding of historical thinking: "I've described it to my colleagues as a deeper level of thinking about history. I mean, obviously there are the [historical thinking] concepts, and once you go through each concept, it's a deeper level of thinking that's not above the children's heads."

During my observations, Xavier's stance that historical thinking is not beyond the capabilities of his students came through clearly in his teaching of the Confederation unit plan. He regularly engaged his students in thoughtful discussions about the meaning of each criterion for significance, and challenged students to consider whether all three criteria must be satisfied before an event can be "declared" historically significant. The students seemed ready for this challenge. One student said, "It depends on which event you are talking about." Another student said, "The three criteria work together to determine an event's significance." When asked if it were okay to change their minds about an event's significance, the students agreed that ideas might change after more research.

Students – even young ones – are capable of engaging in historical thinking activities; this has been well documented in the research literature.[29] A key to success, it seems, is that teachers do not underestimate the capabilities of their students. In addition, scaffolded learning experiences such as those provided by Janis and Xavier go a long way towards helping students engage in meaningful historical inquiry.

Barriers

On the questionnaire, teachers described several barriers to their work on the project, with "time to devote to the project" being the most significant. Even with five professional development days (approximately forty hours) devoted to the project over the course of a school year, time was still a significant factor in teachers' ability to develop their lesson plans and implement their work. Other barriers were:

- difficulty understanding the historical thinking concepts;
- lack of support from school/district personnel;
- technology issues;
- timing of workshop meeting days;
- lack of availability of materials;
- number of workshop meeting days; and
- difficulty finding ways to integrate historical thinking concepts into curriculum.

Janis and Xavier agreed that time was the most significant barrier to integrating the HTCs into their teaching. However, they noted that this was not a new dilemma; lack of time has always been a teacher's worst enemy.

Increased Confidence: Teachers and Students

Xavier and Janis reported that their confidence in teaching and assessing historical thinking grew as a result of the extended PD project. Several factors contributed to Xavier's growing sense of confidence, including the opportunities to dialogue with the PD facilitator (me), to try out his ideas in the classroom in-between the PD sessions, and to have discussions with other teachers who were also trying out these ideas. The biggest confidence enhancer to date has been his students' responses to his new approach to teaching history:

> It [the PD project] was the greatest confidence booster of my career thus far. What I mean by that is, because the concepts were proving to be so successful in the classroom in gaining interest, in momentum with students, all of a sudden my own confidence as a teacher, I feel went through the roof. Now, you could think conversely, what if you never had success? Well, I've never not [sic] had success with the historical concepts. So it's brought so much out of students that it ends up bringing out the confidence in me to keep going with them (HTC) and that's why I feel like it continuously gives me momentum.

Janis's increased confidence came in regards to planning and assessment. She reported a stronger sense of direction in her unit and lesson plans, as well as a clearer sense of how to assess students' historical thinking:

> I now identify an HTC at the very beginning of a unit of study, I model it with them, give them a chance to work on it in small groups, and then give them a chance to work on it individually. Previously it was basically, read the textbook, take some notes on it and then do a project. I think it's the projects that are really different – it was really hard to plan them because I didn't have a focus, I didn't have a starting point. I didn't say, "ok my students need to look at this from this viewpoint ... " It's definitely given me a way to think about what I really want students to understand. And I think it's led me to a better assessment at the end ... because I work my way through to ... "Are you thinking for historical significance? Did you tell me the three things (criteria)?"

Like Xavier, Janis's increased confidence emerged because she perceived a qualitative improvement in students' capacity to think historically:

> Before students just read a textbook and tried to memorize facts. Once they actually have to start to thinking about it, they start to remember it and they start to question things, and I think they start to see connections as we go from event to event ... The HT approach forces students to think because the answers aren't in the textbook.

At the end of my three-day observation in her classroom, Janis offered the following analogy to explain the effect of the HTCs on students' learning of history:

> You know when you go to the eye doctor and they have the lenses on you, and they ask you, "Which is clearer, number 1 or number 2?" Well, you can see through the number 1 lens just fine, but then the doctor clicks over the number 2 lens and suddenly everything becomes clearer. That's what the HTCs do for students. They make history click. They make history clearer for students.

A somewhat surprising finding emerged from the interviews and was confirmed in my classroom observations: both Xavier and Janis reported that students who may not be the strongest academically, or who are shy or quiet, seem to blossom in the classroom when the HT approach is used:

> Students that wouldn't raise their hands earlier in the class to the whole group are willing to share with their small group why they think something is important. So this is giving them the confidence to express their opinion ... The ones that struggle on a written test can do well on these assignments where they have to think ... When it comes to being able to talk about things, they are doing amazing things. (Janis)
>
> For me, it's that shy kid who thinks social studies is not only boring, but they also don't want to speak up because they are shy. For me, success is that the concepts bring out deeper thinking in them and their ability to express it because they want to express it ... now we're talking about significance, about perspective, about ethics, about documents that are really quite interesting because they are so historical and they want to talk about them because they find them interesting. For me success is that they find Canadian history interesting again. (Xavier)

The teachers' confidence not only increased – so did the teachers' perceptions of the confidence level of some students in their classes.

During my observations in both teachers' classrooms, I noted a high degree of engagement on the part of the students and was impressed with the twelve- and thirteen-year-olds' use of the criteria for historical significance in their conversations with their peers. Students were debating which events were the most historically significant and some seemed willing to reevaluate their arguments based on new evidence. In their written work, they focused less on producing narrative accounts of each event and more on developing arguments for why an event was historically significant and thus deserving of a place on the group's timeline. One students' written justification of the historical significance of the Great Migration illustrates this point:

> Without a doubt, the Great Migration (1815–1850) was the most significant event that led to Canadian Confederation. For one, it provided immigrants with jobs and homes, and a chance to escape challenges they were facing in their own countries. It had a vast impact on Canadian culture, giving it its unique, diverse population. Lastly, it led to the development of new towns, cities and businesses, which brought Canada one step closer to becoming a country. The occurrence of the Great Migration made Canada what it is today.

Concluding Comments

In this chapter, I summarized the scant literature on teachers' professional development in history education, as well as provided an overview of teachers' perceptions of how long-term professional development impacted their history teaching. Although these findings cannot be generalized to a larger group, they suggest that a well-structured, long-term professional development project can be highly effective, at least for these teachers, in increasing teachers' understanding of historical thinking and their capacity and confidence in teaching history, and that these effects can last beyond the professional development experience. As Sears argues, changing teacher practice can be challenging because it involves making fundamental changes in teachers' beliefs about what history is and how it should be taught. Such change is possible, though, as the experiences of Janis and Xavier demonstrate. Crucial factors in these teachers' success include the teachers' continued collaboration and support of each other's efforts, as well as their commitment to professional growth. Importantly, Janis and Xavier sometimes experienced the success of the long-term PD program in different ways; for example, Janis found increased confidence in planning and assessment, while for Xavier, increased confidence came as a result of his students' success. This is interesting to note. Because Janis and Xavier experienced virtually the same PD (although in different years) and because they have a tremendously collaborative working relationship, it would be easy to assume that their experiences and perceptions of the PD were very similar. This would be a mistake. Individual experiences of shared PD programs merit investigation and can shed important light on the different ways in which teachers experience and implement the ideas and strategies learned.

In teacher education programs, elementary-track students take between three to six credits of social studies pedagogy courses, but it should be noted that these are not courses that focus exclusively on teaching history. Students who wish to become secondary social studies teachers may take more courses (between six and twelve credits) focused on social studies pedagogy, but again, these courses may not (depending on the institution) focus exclusively on teaching history. Given the prominent place of history within social studies,[30] it seems imperative that teacher education programs find ways, at the very least, to introduce teacher candidates to the concept of "historical thinking," including some pedagogical approaches for engaging students in critical historical inquiry. Perhaps more importantly, beginning teachers should leave their teacher education programs not only with a solid foundation upon which they can begin their teaching careers, but also with an understanding that there is still much to learn.

For the teachers who participated in the first year of the project, it was not until the end of the year that they began to feel even somewhat knowledgeable about the historical thinking concept they were working with. Therefore, they required significant time to develop their lesson plans. Those teachers who participated in both years of the project reported, in the second year, a deeper understanding of the historical thinking concepts. For all but one teacher, the framework of historical thinking as articulated in The Historical Thinking Project was completely new; hence, learning about and incorporating the historical thinking concepts into their practice required a fundamental shift in their understanding of history and how to teach it. It is crucial that teachers have time to develop their own understanding of the historical thinking concepts if they are going to embed historical thinking into their teaching. Yet, even with forty hours of professional development (each year) dedicated to this one project, some still struggled to understand the concepts and find ways to integrate them into their teaching. The importance of providing teachers – beginning or otherwise – with opportunities for long-term professional development cannot be overstated. Again, I agree with Sears, who argues for a "lifespan" view of teacher education.[31]

If PD is to lead to transformative thinking and teaching, PD developers need to (1) take into account teachers' prior knowledge, experiences, and needs; (2) clarify and collaboratively decide upon purpose(s) of PD; (3) build PD communities; (4) provide for long-term PD in diverse environments (face-to-face, school-based, online); and (5) create PD activities that are active, that produce cognitive dissonance, and that encourage reflection. In addition, it is important to remember that a teacher's PD needs may be specific to the stage of his or her career – research seems to suggest that beginning teachers require more PD. However, even teachers at the middle and end of their careers require PD, but their needs will be very different from those of beginning teachers. These factors need to be taken into account when designing PD for teachers.

Although there are many factors that may contribute to teachers reporting negative experiences in professional development programs, it is perhaps more productive to discuss what makes PD work, according to the literature. Effective PD programs account for teachers' understandings of the purposes of PD, their competencies and capacities as professionals, and the differing needs of teachers based on experience. Whatever the purpose, PD facilitators and participants must develop a shared understanding of the goal(s) or purpose(s) of a particular session for it to be effective. Having a collective goal for PD directly affects both the content and delivery of sessions or workshops.[32] In order to ensure shared goals, PD should be driven by local needs and collaboratively planned, rather than being a set of prepackaged requirements that teachers are obligated to meet.[33] Collaborating with teachers on the goals and content of PD means recognizing them as professionals who are responsible for, and can make choices about, their own professional growth and learning.[34]

Faculties of education provide special opportunities for community collaboration. While some teachers are confronted with too many contradictory expectations when dealing with both university and public school cultures,[35] the academy nonetheless has much to offer PD programming. As mentioned earlier, teachers are often expected to just sit and listen during PD workshops, which is the pedagogical model that future teachers in faculties of education are taught to avoid.[36] Collaborative work between pedagogical scholars and PD developers and facilitators would likely ameliorate this unsatisfactory status quo. Partnerships between subject area specialists and PD designers could also serve as a vehicle for ensuring that new research is being communicated to, and implemented by, practicing teachers. Feedback from PD participants could also be used to make strategic decisions about what to include in teacher education curricula,[37] as well as make new areas for research visible.

NOTES

1 Alan Sears, "Moving from the Periphery to the Core: The Possibilities for Professional Learning Communities in History Teacher Education," this volume, p. 12.

2 Hilda Borko, "Professional Development and Teacher Learning: Mapping the Terrain," *Educational Researcher* 33, no. 8 (2004): 3.

3 Linda Darling-Hammond, Ruth Chung Wei, Alethea Andree, Nikole Richardson, and Stelios Orphanos, *Professional Learning in the Learning Profession: A Status Report on Teacher Development in the United States and Abroad* (Stanford: National Staff Development Council and The School Redesign Network at Stanford University, 2009).

4 Bruce Torff and Katherine Byrnes, "Differences across Academic Subjects in Teachers' Attitudes about Professional Development," *The Educational Reform* 75, no. 1 (2011): 26-36.

5 Stephanie van Hover, "The Professional Development of Social Studies Teachers," in *Handbook of Research in Social Studies Education*, edited by Linda S. Levstik and Cynthia A. Tyson (New York: Routledge, 2008), 352-72.

6 Keith C. Barton and Linda S. Levstik, *Teaching History for the Common Good* (Mahwah, NJ: Lawrence Erlbaum, 2004); Suzanne M. Donovan and John D. Bransford, eds., *How Students Learn: History in the Classroom* (Washington, DC: The National Academies Press, 2005); Peter Seixas, ed., *Theorizing Historical Consciousness* (Toronto: University of Toronto Press, 2004); Bruce VanSledright, "Fifth Graders Investigating History in the Classroom: Results from a Researcher-Practitioner Design Experiment," *Elementary School Journal* 103, no. 2 (Nov 2002): 131-60; and Samuel S. Wineburg, *Historical Thinking and Other Unnatural Acts: Charting the Future of Teaching the Past* (Philadelphia: Temple University Press, 2001).

7 Robert H. Mayer, "Learning to Teach Young People How to Think Historically: A Case Study of One Student Teacher's Experience," *Social Studies* 97, no. 2 (2006): 69-76; and Richard J. Paxton, "The Influence of Author Visibility on High School Students Solving a Historical Problem," *Cognition and Instruction* 20, no. 2 (2002): 197-248.

8 Renee T. Clift and Patricia Brady, "Research on Methods Courses and Field Experiences," in *Studying Teacher Education: The Report of the AERA Panel on Research and Teacher Education*, edited by Marilyn Cochran-Smith and Kenneth Zeichner (Mahwah. NJ: Erlbaum, 2005), 309-424; Pamela Grossman and Susan S. Stodolsky, "Considerations of Content and the Circumstances of Secondary School Teaching," in *Review of Research in Education*, edited by Linda Darling-Hammond (Washington, DC:

American Educational Research Association, 1994), 179-221; and Richard Sawyer and Armando Laguardia, "Reimagining the Past/Changing the Present: Teachers Adapting History Curriculum for Cultural Encounters," *Teachers College Record* 112, no. 8 (2010), 1993-2020.

9 Bruce VanSledright, Liliana Maggioni, and Kim Reddy, "Preparing Teachers to Teach Historical Thinking? An Interplay between Professional Development Programs and School-Systems' Cultures" (paper presented at the annual meeting of the American Educational Research Association, New Orleans, LA, April 7-13, 2011).

10 Sawyer and Laguardia, "Reimagining the Past/Changing the Present: Teachers Adapting History Curriculum for Cultural Encounters," 2016.

11 Ibid.; van Hover, "The Professional Development of Social Studies Teachers," 352-72.

12 VanSledright, Maggioni, and Reddy, "Preparing Teachers to Teach Historical Thinking? An Interplay between Professional Development Programs and School-Systems' Cultures," 21.

13 Ruth Sandwell, "History Is a Verb: Teaching Historical Practice to Teacher Education Students," in *New Possibilities for the Past: Shaping History Education in Canada*, edited by Penney Clark (Vancouver: UBC Press, 2011), 230.

14 VanSledright, Maggioni, and Reddy, "Preparing Teachers to Teach Historical Thinking? An Interplay between Professional Development Programs and School-Systems' Cultures."

15 Keith C. Barton, "'I Just Kinda Know': Elementary Students' Ideas About Historical Evidence," *Theory and Research in Social Education* 25, no. 4 (Fall 1997), 407-30.

16 Sawyer and Laguardia, "Reimagining the Past/Changing the Present: Teachers Adapting History Curriculum for Cultural Encounters."

17 Ibid.

18 The revised curricula were implemented according to the following schedule: 2005 – Kindergarten to Grade 3; 2006 – Grades 4 and 7; 2007 – Grades 5, 8 and 10; 2008 – Grades 6, 9, and 11 (6 and 9 optional); 2009 – Grades 6, 9, and 12. See Alberta Education, "New Social Studies Curriculum Focuses on Citizenship and Identity [Press Release]," (August 15, 2005), http://education.alberta.ca/department/newsroom/news/archive/2005/august/20050815.aspx.

19 "Budget 2005 on Track to Help Alberta Students Achieve Their Education Goals," April 13, 2005, http://education.alberta.ca/department/newsroom/news/archive/2005/april/20050413.aspx.

20 Alberta Education, "Social Studies Program of Studies. Kindergarten to Grade 12: Program Rationale and Philosophy" (Edmonton: Alberta Education, 2005), 9.

21 "Social Studies Program of Studies. Kindergarten: Being Together" (Edmonton: Alberta Education, 2005), 5.

22 "Social Studies Program of Studies: Grade 6" (Edmonton: Alberta Education, 2007), 6.

23 Stéphane Lévesque, *Thinking Historically: Educating Students for the Twenty-First Century* (Toronto: University of Toronto Press, 2008); and Peter Seixas, "Conceptualizing the Growth of Historical Understanding," in *Handbook of Education and Human Development: New Models of Learning, Teaching, and Schooling*, edited by David Olson and Nancy Torrance (Oxford, UK: Blackwell, 1996), 765-83.

24 Peter Lee and Rosalyn Ashby, "Progression in Historical Understanding Ages 7-14," in *Knowing, Teaching, and Learning History: National and International Perspectives*, edited by Peter Stearns, Peter Seixas, and Samuel S. Wineburg (New York: New York University Press, 2000), 199.

25 Penney Clark, ed., *New Possibilities for the Past: Shaping History Education in Canada* (Vancouver: UBC Press, 2011).

26 Alberta is divided into seven regional "professional development consortia" (six anglophone and one francophone, each of which is funded by the Alberta Department of Education). The goal of the regional consortia is to promote "student learning and achievement; school improvement; and parental engagement in the educational process through the provision of professional learning opportunities at the local, regional and provincial levels." See https://education.alberta.ca/department/about/players/consortia.aspx

27 City and teacher names are pseudonyms.

28 Lee S. Shulman, "Those Who Understand: Knowledge Growth in Teaching," *Educational Researcher* 15, no. 2 (February 1986): 4-14.

29 Linda S. Levstik and Keith C. Barton, *Doing History: Investigating with Children in Elementary and Middle Schools*, 2nd ed. (Mahwah, NJ: Lawrence Erlbaum, 2001); Bruce VanSledright, "Confronting History's Interpretive Paradox While Teaching Fifth Graders to Investigate the Past," *American Educational Research Journal* 39, no. 4 (Winter 2002): 1089-115.

30 Ken Osborne, "Teaching History in Schools: A Canadian Debate," *Journal of Curriculum Studies* 35, 5 (2003): 585-626.

31 Sears, "Moving from the Periphery to the Core: The Possibilities for Professional Learning Communities in History Teacher Education."

32 van Hover, "The Professional Development of Social Studies Teachers."

33 Michelle H. Lee, "Seven Principles of Highly Collaborative PD," *Science and Children* 47, 9 (2010): 28-31.

34 Andréa Mueller and Malcolm Welch, "Classroom-Based Professional Development: Teachers' Reflections on Learning Alongside Students," *Alberta Journal of Educational Research* 52, 2 (2006): 143-57.

35 van Hover, "The Professional Development of Social Studies Teachers."
36 Mueller and Welch, "Classroom-Based Professional Development: Teachers' Reflections on Learning Alongside Students."
37 Marjorie Hinds and Marie-Josee Berger, "The Impact of Professional Development on Beginning Teachers' Practices in One Secondary School," *Brock Education* 19, no. 2 (2010): 48-64.

16 On the Museum as a Practised Place: Or, Reconsidering Museums and History Education

BRENDA TROFANENKO

For many, the public museum requires little explanation. As an educational institution, museums are typically seen as the place where exhibitions and displays of objects inform the public about the past, culture, art, and nature. Although public museums have long been aware of their vested educational authority, there remains a general tendency to consider them as sites that disseminate specific knowledge to the public. Furthermore, while within the field of museum studies there is wide recognition of how the museum's educational role serves a particular, though generally unquestioned intent, there is a general lack of agreement about the extent to which museums are responsible for knowledge creation.[1] Over the last thirty years, an extensive literature within museum studies has commented on what has been referred to as the "second museum age."[2] Even with this growing awareness and acknowledgment that education serves a major focus as the "new museology," museums increasingly understand their role as public educators in diverse ways.[3]

Influenced by the growing body of work by museum scholars that is reconceptualizing the relationship between museums and the public, museums have begun to consider how they can advance their educational purpose while retaining their mandates of research, collecting, and display. At this general level, the public museum is dedicated to educating and impressing its public. Yet the public museum is more than a prestigious institution of status, wealth, and influence.[4] Public history museums have a broad commitment to using their various images and narratives to define a collective identity, while at the same time inducing a more critical consideration of history.[5]

However, such lofty ambitions have not been achieved easily in museums. Although many people are urging that the public history museum should provide multiple truths, inconsistent narratives, and contrasting descriptions of the same events, it has, instead, offered an often-unquestioned history that is "taken in and taken home."[6] Even with the long-standing commitment to education, there are few opportunities for public history museums and history educators to critically consider the museum as an educational site. History museums that complement, support, and reinforce what history teachers bring to them are integral to the formation of knowledge in our school-aged youth. We, as history educators, need to consider how we might develop a relationship with museum personnel that draws both from our own pedagogical expertise and from their subject-specific knowledge. The point I wish to make in this chapter is that history museum personnel realize the need to be more responsive to education: this changing role of museums in advancing historical understanding means that we must reconsider what role educators play in their interactions with museum personnel. The intent of this chapter is not to be definitive or prescriptive; rather, it is to raise questions about how teacher education might be supported through public history museums becoming sites of (what Sears calls) "cross-boundary work" that enhance history teachers' and their students' historical understanding. Before I present suggestions about how the relationship between museums and history educators might evolve, I provide a brief history of the educational purpose of public museums, the primacy of objects in the museum, and the relationship between museums and history educators.

"To Diffuse Its Enjoyments": Museums and Public Education

Today's museums had humble beginnings as assemblages of valuable objects that "deserv[ed] to be kept, remembered, treasured."[7] Although museums began as elite, privately sponsored institutions where personal and private collections were served and limited by individual interests, collectors (followed by curators) eventually arranged their collections in the general interest of public education and with the explicit purpose of being seen by visitors. This claim to public education guided museums to purposefully shape the "moral, mental, and behavior characteristics"[8] of those who attended by focusing on "raising and vivifying the common intellectual, diffusing its enjoyments, and broadening its public domain."[9] Here, objects were organized by museum curators, who were seen as "benevolent educators dispensing rational and, more particularly, 'scientific' knowledge,"[10] in such a manner that "the working classes [who] have but little time for study [as] their leisure hours are, and always must be, comparatively brief … may instruct themselves."[11]

The ubiquitous nature of objects and labels sought to reflect a rational, orderly, and systematic way of producing and legitimizing knowledge – a kind of public education – by the museum curator within the museum space. In writing about objects at the Smithsonian Institution in Washington, DC, first director George Brown Goode suggested that an effective "educational" museum might be described as "a collection of labels bearing instructions, each of them illustrated by a carefully selected specimen."[12] The carefully selected object led to the focus on "object-lessons" that aid "abstract thought … [and] may remain much longer in the mind than words or simple images, gained facts, ideas, or reproductions."[13] The displayed object provided a source of knowledge that could offer "a lesson at a glance, a confirmation of actual life as documented and preserved."[14] Beyond the explicit educational purposes of a museum showing the past "as it really was" is a less immediately apparent nationalist purpose: to highlight and promote the wealth and status of the nation. History as defined in a museum would, as Ronald Suny puts it, "help to construct the nation, even as the nation determined the categories in which history was written and the purpose it was to serve."[15] Within the space of the museum, various objects have served as "fragments of the past," selected and displayed in such a way as to deliberately evoke a sense of a particular national past by alluding to some larger, preordained national purpose about which an object provides detail.[16] The object has been decontextualized and then re-contextualized within the confines of what the museum curators have decided is most significant in this national past.

Yet, when visiting history museums, there is a moment when the full measure of the intersection between the past and the nation reveals itself. This relation occurs through displayed objects entwined with narratives that inform the visitor of what has passed and how such events define a nation. Images, objects, and narratives are selected to authenticate history and to represent interconnected and divergent past events, notably nation building and a national identity. When this complexity comes across in a simplified and objective manner,[17] this didactic notion ignores the contemporary debates about how knowledge is interactively produced, consumed, and distributed in a museum.[18]

Current mandates and authority figures of many museums, which continue to posit the bricks-and-mortar museum as a privileged symbol of the past, of culture, and of national identity, seek to simplify the information each object provides the public, when historical inquiry could contextualize that information and support knowledge creation. The fact that objects continue to hold such sway in history museums overshadows the growing tension in the role and place of objects within museums and history. Those who lead history museums grapple with contemporary debates about various issues, including the public relevance, usefulness, and knowledge production of their institutions. Currently, history museum personnel are questioning how objects are used (e.g. virtual exhibitions), how various social media and technologies are employed, and what the museum's role is in representing the past (e.g. thematic versus chronological narratives). These debates highlight the broader question that Steven Conn asks about whether or not museums need objects as they move towards issue-based exhibitions.[19]

Many museum leaders, however, justify their institutions' nationalist focus by arguing that the purpose of a history museum is to define and display a past that is best remembered and preserved for a visible and highly charged collective – the nation.[20] This collective is central to educating the public about the past, and speaks directly to "how people in general see, value, or understand [the past]." Charged with exploring and indeed negotiating many different pasts within its national story, history museums have been caught up in discussions about whose history and what version of history – even within a national history – *ought* to be presented in an exhibit. Conflicts are emerging – not only about whose history should be represented, but why. Recent years have witnessed challenges to the idea that museums should simply support a broad, consensual, and nationalist narrative. Others argue that museums work well as popular but authoritative sites for public education, perhaps because of the simple, or one-dimensional nature, of their narratives.[21] Yet others, such as Hooper-Greenhill, argue that the educational work of museums has expanded to take on a larger social role, as they become more audience-driven, reflexive, and self-aware.[22] Other scholars argue that museums should engage the public in a broader educational mission of nurturing a critical historical consciousness, one that could create a greater public understanding and critique of the museum's purposes, implicit and explicit.[23] The question for these critics – of whom I am one – becomes how to develop a more sophisticated way of understanding, and responding to, the ways in which the public, and indeed history teachers, come to understand disciplinary knowledge.

The Educational Imperative of the History Museum

The public history museum has been able to establish itself as an authoritative entity by its collections of objects and by its exhibition and educational mandates. Part of the problem in merging history teaching and the broad public history education work of museums is that museums remain highly under-examined institutions vis-à-vis their role in history education. New directions in the study of history museums as educational sites have been informed by research that considers how students can develop a critical historical literacy and engage in historical sense making. The more recent studies on historical sense making consider the process of communicating knowledge about the past as "an epistemological and cultural act that conveys deep and sometimes unintended messages about what it means to be historical in modern society."[24] This suggests moving away from history education as a simple technical act of conveying knowledge (the "transmission model" of teaching) towards understanding history education as a cultural act that teaches students metacognitive understanding of their own role in constructing historical knowledge (the "constructivist model"). If we consider history museums as pedagogical sites, then we need to acknowledge them as places where "the contending voices in the debate over what history means, or should mean, in a democracy come together."[25] History museums, then, can become places where individuals participate in the "cultural act" of constructing history and their understanding of how it came to be.

Researchers in history education have begun to examine how the public history museum may be used as a site to understand the past. Some researchers suggest that history museums are learning spaces that strengthen content knowledge, enhance historical thinking skills, and provide learning possibilities and student engagement not easily replicated in school.[26] I suggest that history museums should challenge history teachers and their students to actively engage in historical analysis – not just consume it – and to critically evaluate the constructions of the past presented to them. To engage in the act of historical thinking within a public museum remains, to follow Wineburg's term, "an unnatural act."[27]

Much of the research on museum learning considers pedagogy to be of minimal importance. Instead, examining the knowledge-making capacity in museums more frequently focuses primarily on the complex social and cognitive contexts in which museum learning occurs. Falk, Dierking, and Adams have suggested, however, that an effective educational experience is determined by not only the museum contexts (the objects, the narratives, the exhibition structure, and the physical space of the museum) but also by the public's unique personal, physical, and social attributes.[28] The emphasis on visitors' experience and making of personal meaning that occurs within a museum reflects that there is a continuum of epistemologies between the knowledge gained directly through observation or experience in the world and that which is socially and culturally mediated.[29] Since the 1990s, this constructivist learning theory has dominated museum education. Many of its claims, indeed, are based almost entirely on learning in informal science museum contexts. The examinations, however, ignore the role of the educator, museum curators, and designers as agents of knowledge creation. The focus in this research, as Hein suggests, is "on the learner, not on the subject to be learned."[30]

While acknowledging the socio-constructive theory influence in museums, Viviane Gosselin writes that to know history is to know not only the facts but also the structures of historical thinking and the processes of historical inquiry. She suggests making more public the processes through which curators like herself construct their interpretations of history. In her words, the interpretive strategies pursued by a museum "would better serve the demands of historical inquiry if they were more attuned to the interplay between procedural and substantive knowledge."[31] The point Gosselin stresses is the need to incorporate knowledge from an exhibit with the concepts and vocabulary used by the curators, together with the skills that the public utilizes to make sense of the past. Similarly, others argue that museums need to pay more attention to the public perceptions of what counts as history in order for the museum to effectively articulate a community's past. The history that is often essentialized in the public museum is, in fact, fluid and complex. How history is portrayed and perceived depends on the objects, the exhibit, and the museum itself successfully engaging and working with the attending public.[32]

Bridging Education and Museums

Prior to the 1960s, public museums rarely considered their institutions as part of a democratic process in knowledge creation. The museum held the objects and the museum curator held the authority to influence and direct what would be exhibited. The museum's sanctity as a "public intellectual" endures and continues to direct how the public behaves in the museum by gently discouraging certain behaviours while explicitly supporting others.[33] How often have we witnessed a quiet calm within exhibition spaces where individuals view enclosed displayed objects, read text panels, and saunter slowly around a designated area for the purposes of knowledge engagement, intellectual curiosity, or entertainment? Perhaps we will never know why individuals attend museums (although the discipline of visitor studies actively seeks to understand this), but museums remain institutions enmeshed with elements of control over objects and bodies within designated spaces.[34] The recent change in how public museums are conceived by both the museum community and the public has begun to transform the museum and its relationship with their public. The movement away from the museum as an authoritative institution is reflected in current expectations that museums are accessible and provide services to communities. The creation of new types of museum professionals to facilitate a more inclusive, democratic involvement by the public has prompted several developments. Educational departments have been established within museums, and there has been a rise in the number of museum education professionals. In addition, concern about public programs has increased and some "formerly accepted universal truths have lost the legitimacy they once possessed."[35] Yet new educational directions within museums does not necessarily result in museums engaging in pedagogically sound activities.

Let me provide an example. Prior to returning to Canada, I reviewed funding applications for several US government-sponsored agencies that supported museums, archives, and other cultural heritage institutions. One of the criteria for funding various grant programs, specifically national leadership grants, included involvement by the K–12 community. This translated into two main activities specific to museum education: first, the bulk creation of lesson plans uploaded to a project-specific website; and second, the development of teacher in-service activities (running from three hours to two days in length each year for up to three years). To be fair, many institutions had moved beyond considering their educational mission in terms of field trips. But how these museums defined education and their educational mission raised questions about whether or not museums understood how best to support educators. As the lone educator at the table, I often had to challenge what appeared (at least to me) to be a common thought about how teacher education was construed. Teachers were considered a group who were offered explicit directives about the knowledge provided by a museum without regard for what they brought to learning in museums. In these proposed programs, curators and museum educators maintained their institutionally affirmed authority in highlighting their collections and determining what teachers would learn from such objects. In relegating teachers to the position of passive end users of their programs, the museums ignored the knowledge teachers held regarding pedagogy and ways to best use the museum as an educational site.

This is not to suggest this model remained prevalent through my years of review. In later years, museum proposals acknowledged the value of educators who were using the museum as a site from which to learn. Almost simultaneously, museums were reaching out to educators and educators were requesting collaborative opportunities with museums. Rather than being the last constituents included in a collaborative association, teachers and teacher educators have been included as partners during the pre-planning (as well as planning, implementation, and evaluation) stages. Such an early presence is evident in research projects such as the National Leadership Grant awarded by the Institute for Museum and Library Services to the San Angelo Museum of Fine Arts, which pools community resources to create an interdisciplinary program of art and science. Another example is the UPCLOSE (University of Pittsburgh Center for Learning in Out-of-School Environments) collaborative, which works with museums to ask what families learn about art, culture, and history when visiting art museums. Both of these I consider exemplary research projects.[36]

These projects highlight, as Lubar noted several years ago, that the public "demand[s] to be considered a partner in the creation of meaning."[37] This requires museums to learn how to share authority while ensuring curatorial expertise and knowledge remain. Certainly, as Watson notes, the relationship that museums have with their communities is an unequal one, with much of the power resting with the institution itself.[38] As Ames observes, the terms "partnering" and "collaboration" are commonly used in museums to describe those arrangements from the perspective of the museum.[39] The museum can, without question, determine the degree to which they provide increasing access and availability, and this may never change. But, as Clifford has remarked, unless museums incorporate the public in a truly collaborative arrangement, they will continue to be "perceived as merely paternalistic" as well as exclusive and condescending.[40] Museums and educators need to acknowledge what each brings to the educational project as their relationship changes, even as museums negotiate the continuous tension between ensuring their societal relevance and meeting their various mandates.

Educators need a more nuanced understanding of the museum itself, and although they may not directly influence the "programmed displays of objects ... [or the] highly rationalized installation practices," they ought to understand why such practices continue.[41] Educators need to know what role museums have played in the development of the discipline of history, of the nation state, and of collective memory and identity, and they need to understand the conditions under which knowledge is produced in such institutions. They need to be provided with an opportunity to see how such knowledge is legitimized by particular social practices that occur within the museum. Hall offers an approach that is directed by a specific question about representation: the need to ask not "who we are" or "where we came from," so much as, "how have [we] been represented and how that bears on how we might represent ourselves."[42] I have written previously about understanding "the museum project," and I would argue that it is essential that history educators find ways to understand the museum's role and reflect this in their pedagogical practice.[43]

What I am calling for in this collaboration is the sharing of knowledge and skills in order to generate something of value and usefulness to both museum practitioners and teachers. It involves hearing from history educators what they consider necessary for learning to occur. It will also demand that history teachers reconsider their own agency within museums. Here is where I support Sears' argument in this volume for history educators to not only change their minds about what the discipline is, but also develop a new sense of who they are and what their role is. Their role would draw on their own knowledge base about how best to utilize the museum as a source for learning about the past and about how the past is represented. This requires that history educators be well grounded in theoretical underpinnings of historical understanding and know how to support and develop a critical literary and historical consciousness. What emerges from the collaborative relationship between museums and history educators is not just a better understanding by both constituents about the other's position. It also forces a reconsideration of the distinction between expert and novice by providing a working relationship that takes advantage of each party's educational knowledge.

History educators need opportunities to develop and advance pedagogical knowledge and skills to be "fully engaged with provocative questions ... and clear, well-structured and accessible information" within the physical space of the museum.[44] Exhibitions, gallery spaces, and museum personnel would serve as a starting point for educators to make sense of the museum by considering it as "a practiced place."[45] As such, museums could partner with educators to transcend existing pedagogical and museum practices. At issue is a mutual understanding of the nature of how specific knowledge is constructed through differentiated space and by the articulation of social relations within that space. Collaboration supports a mutual critique of the educator's and museum's own "broad popular understandings of the past, bringing to the forefront ... the problematic relationship between the distinctly modern, disciplinary practices of historiography and the memory practices"; this could occur within the space of the museum with the communities served by the museum.[46]

Perhaps it is naive of me to call for a stronger collaboration without acknowledging the financial issues that dominate both cultural heritage institutions and public education. While the museum's educational imperative can obviously link with public education through aligning exhibits with specific curricular objectives, museums are expected to also connect with broad communities, which increasingly are making their own expectations and demands on the museum. More recently, museums are providing opportunities to engage in debates on issues of public interest and work. This follows the call more than thirty years ago for museums to be both a "temple and a forum," and thereby attract the general public to the museum.[47] New forms of relationships, which involve the sharing of knowledge, have spurred the increasing move towards collaborative opportunities specific to public education. Contemporary exhibitions are no longer imagined merely as a means for the display and dissemination of already existing knowledge.

Museums could support experimental practices for the generation of knowledge, rather than its reproduction. Every exhibition holds narrative strategies and frames through which exhibitions offer up particular positioned readings. If we consider the history educator as critically exploring the history presented – being made – in any one exhibit, then we can consider educators as stewards of knowledge. We need to support history educators as they hone their historical inquiry skills and, as a result, advance in knowledge within the space of the museum. This would manifest a new form of a relationship, and a new conception of a museum, that would rise out of the knowledge and the traditional and contemporary museology theories and practices. Great opportunities. Possible visions. We need to reach out to museums, once more, to share their educational responsibilities, but with a greater commitment to our own theories and practices.

NOTES

1 Susan Crane, "Memory, Distortion and History in the Museum," *History and Theory* 36, no. 4 (1997): 47.
2 Ruth Phillips, "Re-placing Objects: Historical Practices for the Second Museum Age," *The Canadian Historical Review* 86, no. 1 (2005): 83-110.
3 Peter Vergo, *The New Museology* (London: Reaktion Books, 1989).
4 Didier Maleuvre, *Museum Memories: History, Technology, Art* (Palo Alto, CA: Stanford University Press, 1999).
5 James B. Gardner, "Contested Terrain: History, Museums and the Public," *The Public Historian* 26, no. 4 (2004): 11-21.
6 Mieke Bal, "Telling, Showing, Showing Off," *Critical Inquiry* 18, no. 3 (1992): 561.
7 James Clifford, *The Predicament of Culture: Twentieth-Century Ethnography, Literature, and Art* (Cambridge, MA: Harvard University Press, 1988), 231.
8 Tony Bennett, *The Birth of the Museum: History, Theory, Politics* (New York: Routledge, 1995), 60.
9 Edward Edwards, *Lives of the Founders of the British Museum: With Notices of its Chief Augmentors and Other Benefactors, 1570-1870* (London, UK: Trubner, 1870/1969), 7.
10 Annie E. Coombes, *Reinventing Africa: Material Culture and Popular Imagination in Late Victorian and Edwardian England* (New Haven, CT: Yale University Press, 1994), 43-4.

11 Pitt Rivers, A.H. (Lane Fox), "Typological Museums, as Exemplified by the Pitt Rivers Museum in Oxford and his Provincial Museum in Farnham Dorset," *Journal of the Society of Arts* 40 (1891): 115–16.

12 George B. Goode, "The Museums of the Future," in *U.S. National Museum, Annual Report*, (Washington, DC: National Museum, 1889), 427-45.

13 Sue Wilkinson, *A Teacher's Guide to Learning from Objects* (London: English Heritage, 1990), 5.

14 Steven Conn, *Museums and American Intellectual Life, 1876-1926* (Chicago: University of Chicago Press, 1998); and Henrietta Riegel, "Into the Heart of Irony: Ethnographic Exhibits and the Politics of Difference," in *Theorizing Museums*, edited by S. Macdonald & G. Fyfe (Oxford: Blackwell, 1996), 87.

15 Ronald Suny, "History and the Making of Nations," in *Cultures and Nations of Central and Eastern Europe: Essays in Honor of Roman Szporluk*, edited by Z. Gitelman et al. (Cambridge, MA: Harvard University Press, 2000), 296.

16 Rosmarie Beier-de Haan, *Re-staging Histories and Identities* (Malden, MA: Blackwell, 2006), 187-8.

17 Mieke Bal, "Telling, Showing, Showing Off," in *A Mieke Bal Reader* (Chicago: University of Chicago Press, 1991), 173.

18 Simon Knell, *Museums and the Future of Collecting* (London: Ashgate, 2004); and Sharon Macdonald, "Collecting Practices," in *A Companion to Museum Studies*, edited by Sharon Macdonald (London: Routledge, 2006).

19 Steven Conn, *Do Museums Still Need Objects?* (Philadelphia: University of Pennsylvania Press, 2010).

20 David Lowenthal, *The Past is a Foreign Country* (Cambridge, UK: Cambridge University Press, 1985), xxvi.

21 Roy Rosenzweig, "How Americans Use and Think About the Past: Implications from a National Survey for the Teaching of History," in *Knowing, Teaching, and Learning History: National and International Perspectives*, edited by Peter Stearns, Peter Seixas, and Sam Wineburg (New York: New York University Press, 2000), 262-83.

22 Eileen Hooper-Greenhill, *The Educational Role of Museums* (London: Routledge, 1999), xi-ii.

23 Sharon Macdonald, "Museums, National, Postnational and Transcultural Identities," in *Museum Studies: An Anthropology of Contexts*, edited by B. Carbonell (Oxford: Blackwell, 2012) 273-86; and Brenda Trofanenko, "Interrupting the Gaze: On Reconsidering Authority in the Museum," *Journal of Curriculum Studies* 38, no. 1 (2006): 49-65.

24 Peter Stearns, Peter Seixas, and Sam Wineburg, eds., *Knowing, Teaching, and Learning History: National and International Perspectives* (New York: New York University Press, 2000).

25 Ibid.

26 Alan Marcus and Thomas Levin, "Knight at the Museum: Learning History with Museums," *The Social Studies* 102 (2011): 104-9.

27 Samuel S. Wineburg, *Historical Thinking and Other Unnatural Acts: Charting the Future of Teaching the Past* (Philadelphia: Temple University Press, 2001).

28 John H. Falk, Lynn D. Dierking, and Marianna Adams, "Living in a Learning Society: Museums and Free-Choice Learning," in *Companion to Museum Studies*, edited by Sharon MacDonald (Oxford, UK: Blackwell Publishing, 2006), 323-39.

29 George Hein, *Learning in the Museum* (London, UK: Routledge, 1998).

30 George Hein, "The Constructive Museum," *Journal of Education in Museum* 16 (1995): 21-3.

31 Vivienne Gosselin, "Historical Thinking in the Museum: Open to Interpretation," in *New Possibilities for the Past: Shaping History Education in Canada*, edited by Penney Clark (Vancouver: UBC Press, 2011), 252.

32 Sheila Watson, *Museums and Their Communities* (London: Routledge, 2007), 160.

33 Jennifer Barrett, *Museums and the Public Sphere* (New York: Wiley and Sons, 2009).

34 The idea of control of bodies within exhibition spaces has been examined primarily from a standpoint involving Foucault. See, for example, Eilean Hooper-Greenhill, "The Museums in the Disciplinary Society," in *Museum Studies in Material Culture*, edited by S. Pearce (Washington, DC: Smithsonian Institution Press, 1991), 61-72; and Tony Bennett, "The Exhibitionary Complex," *New Formations* 4 (Spring 1988): 73-102. See also Tony Bennett, *The Birth of the Museum: History, Theory, Politics* (London and New York: Routledge, 1995); and Tony Bennett, *Culture: A Reformer's Science* (London: Sage, 1998).

35 Anthony Shelton, "Museums and Anthropologies: Practices and Narratives," in *A Companion to Museum Studies*, edited by Sharon Macdonald (London: Routledge, 2006), 76.

36 For information about these National Leadership Projects, see the Institute of Museum and Library Services, a funding agency sponsored by the US Government, at www.imls.gov.

37 Steven Lubar, "Exhibiting Memories," in *Exhibiting Dilemmas: Issues of Representation at the Smithsonian* (Washington, DC: Smithsonian Institution Press, 1997), 24.

38 Sheila Watson, "History Museums, Community Identities and a Sense of Place," in *Museum Revolutions: How Museums Change and Are Changed*, edited by Simon J. Knell, Suzanne MacLeod, and Sheila Watson (London: Routledge, 2006), 160-72.

39 Michael Ames, "How to Decorate a House: The Renegotiation of Cultural Representations at the University of British Columbia Museum of Anthropology," in *Museums and Sources Communities*, edited by Laura Peers and Alison K. Brown (London, UK: Routledge, 2003), 171-80.

40 James Clifford, "Museums as Contact Zones," in *Routes: Travel and Translation in the Late Twentieth Century* (Cambridge, MA: Harvard University Press, 1997), 208.

41 Carol Duncan, *Civilizing Rituals: Inside Public Art Museums* (New York: Routledge, 1995), 90.

42 Stuart Hall, "Introduction: Who Needs Identity?" in *Questions of Cultural Identity*, edited by Stuart Hall and Paul Du Gay (Thousand Oaks, CA: Sage, 1996), 4.

43 Brenda Trofanenko, "The Educational Promise of Public History Museum Exhibits," *Theory and Research in Social Education* 38, no. 2 (2010): 270-88.

44 Susan Groundwater-Smith and Lynda Kelly, "Seeing Practice Anew: Improving Learning at the Museum" (paper presented at the Australian Association for Research in Education/New Zealand Association for Research in Education Joint Conference, Auckland, NZ, 2003), 6.

45 For a discussion of "practiced places," see Michel de Certeau, *The Practice of Everyday Life* (Berkeley, CA: University of California Press, 1984); Richard Etlin, *Space, Stone, and Spirit: The Meaning of Place* (London: Routledge, 1997); and Doreen Massey and Pat Jess, *A Place in the World? Places, Culture, and Globalization* (Oxford, UK: Oxford University Press/ Open University, 1997), 45-77.

46 Peter Seixas. *Theorizing Historical Consciousness* (Toronto: University of Toronto Press, 2004), 9-10.

47 Duncan Cameron, "The Museum, a Temple or the Forum," in *Reinventing the Museum: Historical and Contemporary Perspectives on the Paradigm Shift*, edited by G. Anderson (Walnut Creek, CA: Altamira Press, 2004), 61-73.

17 Teaching History Teachers in the Classroom

JAN HASKINGS-WINNER

Introduction

Alan Sears notes in his chapter in this volume that student teachers "haven't struggled to define a 'significant' and unexplored (or underexplored) question about the past to study, sat with a pile of diverse sources trying to weigh their relative merits ... or tried to make judgments about the moral actions of historical agents."[1] This, he argues, helps to explain why history teachers often replicate the model through which they studied history: the transmission of information through note taking, lectures, PowerPoint, or perhaps documentaries and Hollywood movies. Sears urges us to take seriously the three-stage nature of teacher education: one that begins before and continues after students begin their formal teacher education program.

Having worked for many years with pre-service and in-service history and social studies teachers, I believe the stage after formal teacher education programs is arguably the most important element of professional learning, and the most difficult to achieve. But it is not impossible! This essay will look at two professional development approaches in Ontario with which I have worked. Each employs a different professional learning model, but both introduce teachers to how they can develop the practice of historical thinking that bridges research and teaching in ways that reflect two of Sears' identified principles for change: "taking the long view of teacher education" and "communities of practice provid[ing] a substantial context for teacher education." For many, this is an introduction into unchartered waters, but it can transform what happens in history classrooms.

The Problem

A teacher in her third year of teaching explained her problem with learning to teach history to me in this way:

> Somehow my professors had me convinced that I just had to love history, communicate my love for history and bring fun anticipatory games to class and kids would be hooked. I held up my end ... but it doesn't work like that ... I wish also we had spent more time on high yield strategies and how to use them in a history classroom.[2]

This is not an uncommon observation from new history teachers, who clearly have a love of history, but cannot seem to translate that enthusiasm into teaching strategies and performance in the classroom that move history teachers from the periphery to the core of their profession.

What happens to history teachers after they graduate from a teacher education program and begin a career? There are many challenges beyond those of pedagogy facing a beginning teacher in the twenty-first century. These challenges include the pace of change, and the expectations for teacher performance held by parents, administrators, school boards, and the ministry of education. Teachers also need to be highly organized and manage classrooms, students, resources, and complex curriculum with multiple expectations for teaching and learning. There is little time provided for teachers to actually reflect on practice, let alone share these reflections. While, as Sears points out, many teachers are missing a deeper understanding of what is involved in knowing and teaching historical thinking, the "closed door paradigm" – where each teacher works behind a firmly closed classroom door – is all too common in education, and limits opportunities for teachers to learn new approaches from each other.

Sometimes the process of doing history and thinking historically can get forgotten, or teachers return to what they think history education is: lectures or the dissemination of facts, and, more recently, the use of technologies such as PowerPoint and smartboards to show pictures that reinforce talking points. I have often heard high school teachers lament that the elementary teachers "don't teach students anything about history" and the high school teachers have to start over when students appear in their classrooms in Grade 10 in Ontario. This is a problem for high school teachers, because the compulsory Grade 10 history course begins with the year 1914. It may be more likely that the elementary school teachers did "cover" the curriculum, but it was quickly forgotten soon after – because student were taught mostly just the facts. As one perceptive student noted, "history was just one damn thing after another."

As a number of history educators have argued in this collection and elsewhere in recent years, the idea that students need to know content or else they do not know history is one that is remarkably persistent. It characterizes the approach of many of the teachers I work with. Often teachers talk as if they are simply filling the empty vessel (students) through methods (board notes, overheads, PowerPoint) that transmit knowledge from the teacher's head to the student's notebook. Too often missing from teachers' pedagogical agenda is the need to teach students to think about and critically assess how history is *done*, and what it means. Teachers often assume that students who struggle with academic subjects prefer the structure of worksheets that contain facts or specific tasks that are defined by right and wrong answers. These worksheets, teachers argue, are "safe" because they offer contained and measurable work. Teachers use them because they seem to provide a clear focus for work, and students know what is expected in terms of behaviour and performance. Again, what is missing is the *doing* of history, and with that omission history becomes a series of events and dates without meaning or relevance that are quickly forgotten!

The Strategy

As Sears notes in this collection, professional development needs to change to reflect better history teaching practice. In my experience, opening the classroom to provide opportunities for teachers to learn together is a more effective teaching and learning experience than professional development offered as a one-day lecture, seminar, or workshop. My own experience suggests the effectiveness of two models of professional development – ones that provide opportunities for teachers to think deeply about teaching history, and reflect Sears' call to rethink the idea that "history teaching essentially involves the passing on of historical information and not the fostering of historical thinking."

Demonstration Classrooms

One successful approach is the demonstration classrooms that are routinely used in some boards of education in Ontario. In Toronto, this model has been expanded to provide teachers in all stages of their careers, and not just beginning teachers, with the opportunity to participate. A second model is summer literacy camp, funded through the Ontario Ministry of Education, which focuses on promoting literacy through subject disciplines and currently includes history, geography, the arts, science and English. In both models, historical thinking has been a key component of the work.

Demonstration classes (sometimes called exploration classes) provide job-embedded professional learning. A demonstration class occurs when a teacher (endorsed by the principal) agrees to host other teachers to watch her or him teach students. The demonstration class is facilitated by an instructional leader or coach, which has been my role. Up to ten teachers may be sitting at the back of the class observing the teacher and students. This approach is a fundamental shift in teacher professional development, as it makes visible the host teacher's actions and thinking.

For two years, I have been an instructional leader in demonstration classrooms working with beginning and experienced teachers as they first observe a history class and then engage in a focused debriefing conversation about the lesson. The planning of a demonstration classroom is expert host teacher's responsibility (in consultation with me, a designated curriculum leader for the school board). The particular lesson of the demonstration classroom focuses on one of the themes identified by the school board, which has a specific goal of improving student engagement. These themes include: historical thinking, use of technology, differentiated instruction or the effective use of collaborative learning in the classroom, and assessment for learning. Teachers can see a menu of the available demonstration classes on the school board website, and, if the focus of the class and the timing are suitable, teachers can book their participation online.

The historical thinking focus makes a particularly important contribution to professional development within the Toronto board, as few history teachers, unfortunately, have any previous experience with teaching historical thinking in general, let alone with the specific formal concepts (significance, evidence, continuity and change, cause and consequence, perspective, and ethical dimension) developed by Peter Seixas, some of which are included in the revised (2013) Ontario curriculum. Many teachers, however, are unhappy with their current approach of "covering" the curriculum through content. During the demonstration, teachers observe the host teacher from the back of the classroom and note the strategies, behaviours, and techniques modelled for them. During the year 2010–11 in Toronto, 31 per cent of all teachers participating in demonstration classrooms had between zero and two years of experience, and over 26 per cent had more than eleven years of experience.[3] The funding for teachers to participate in the demonstration class comes from beginning teacher funding, if applicable. Otherwise, the administration finds the funding for a more experienced teacher to spend the day in job-embedded professional learning.

After each demonstration class, the host teacher and I participate in a focused debriefing of the lesson. This is similar to what often happens in initial teacher education programs; however, as it occurs after teachers receive their professional certification, it is an example of what Alan Sears calls cross-boundary approaches. In this case, it is not a formal evaluation process by the administration. Teachers reflect on what they will do differently in their own practice, after participating in the demonstration class. The focus questions include: "If you were to rate this class out of 10, what would you give it?"; "What worked and why?"; and "What would you do differently next time and why?" At this time, teachers ask questions or discuss what they saw. The rest of the day is spent discussing issues related to the class observed and teachers' interests and needs, including how to integrate historical thinking and assessment for/as learning into their practice, et cetera. Observing teachers are encouraged to invite me back into their classrooms to provide feedback as they develop new ways of approaching the curriculum to focus on historical thinking. This paradigm shift of opening our classroom doors so that others see us teach is significant. It makes our teaching practice more visible.

In some schools, history teachers had the opportunity to see both a Grade 10 and a Grade 7 Canadian history class, where the teacher was using historical thinking concepts as well as assessment for/as learning. These teachers had more time to plan with instructional leaders as part of the process. The challenges for middle school teachers are greater than for high school teachers. They have limited time to meet the curriculum expectations (there are thirty-five expectations in Ontario Grade 7 history alone) and very few minutes to "do history." To prepare for the demonstration class, two instructional leaders (IL; also called a curriculum consultant), myself and the technology IL, spent an entire day with two teachers to plan a fifty-minute lesson. We intended to include two of the historical thinking methods identified by Seixas and included in the curriculum (perspective and evidence) and to use collaborative learning (jigsaw) to engage students and improve learning. This, of course, is not a typical experience for teachers. Prior to the demonstration class, the students had learned about the differences between primary and secondary sources, and they had an anchor chart on the wall that was referred to frequently during the class. The process was beneficial because it introduced students to two benchmarks, and student reflections expressed that they appreciated this approach.

Summer Literacy Camps

The second model of post-teacher education professional learning came in the form of a summer literacy camp funded by the Ontario Ministry of Education. The initiative started after the success of math camps in Ontario and literacy camps have been held since 2010. The Ontario Ministry of Education recognizes that subject-specific thinking needs to be part of the focus on literacy and acknowledges the importance of maintaining disciplinary integrity. This four-day intensive professional learning experience in August brought together Grade 7–10 teachers, consultants, and a few administrators from across the province. Teachers either volunteered or were encouraged by school administrators to attend, and they chose which subject to focus on (history, geography, science, arts, or English). The camp was held at a conference centre on a lake in central Ontario. August 2011 was the second annual summer literacy camp. The theme of literacy camp is "think to learn and learn to think."

There are sessions for all the participants that included keynote speaker Dr Douglas Fisher in 2011. In the small group history sessions, teachers were introduced to historical thinking concepts (HTC) and, using a gradual release of responsibility approach, my co-facilitator and myself modelled a "think aloud" technique using one HTC. A "think aloud" technique makes visible to students how teachers (in this case history teachers) think about the text they are working with. We say out loud what we are thinking. Then, the teachers selected one HTC for which to develop a "think aloud" to share with peers in preparation for taking these techniques back to their respective classrooms. The philosophy of the eduGAINS[4] project of the ministry of education is that literacy is a cross-curricular priority, but it has to be embedded in the heart of the subject discipline. Two of the teachers (of nineteen) who participated in 2011 had some awareness of historical thinking but were trying to figure out how to integrate it into their history courses.

Teachers demonstrated their "think alouds" with peers and were provided with peer feedback. Teachers responded in their workshop feedback that they would "implement the feedback I received!"; that they would "keep at it"; and that they would "develop more 'think alouds' in History class." All nineteen of the teachers at summer literacy camp committed to implementing what they had learned in their practice. In the fall, the ministry of education contacts teachers to follow up on their use of skills developed at the summer literacy camp. There is also an informal online community that shares ideas, challenges, and successes.

How Successful Are They and How Do You Know?

My own classroom experiences showed me that embedding historical thinking into curriculum at the high school level is not a simple task. It took me a whole semester to get my Grade 10 "Applied" (i.e., the non-academic stream in Ontario high schools) students to begin to understand the concept. They did get it, however, and made thoughtful connections as a result of their learning. In my Grade 10 Academic class, my students had been conditioned to "get the facts," and they were initially reluctant to grapple with a historical question. In teaching about Aboriginal land claims (using disputes at Oka, Ipperwash, and Caledonia as examples), I asked, "Was the death of Dudley George worth the gains achieved?" Students struggled, but were finally able to use evidence to support their conclusions and not just focus on finding a single right answer. We were all very pleased – if a little surprised – with our eventual success.

Teachers who are working to develop historical thinking within the practice are changing how they teach, and often what they teach. There are many competing pressures on teachers in the twenty-first century, including changes in assessment and evaluation, changes in technology, differentiation, new pressure for student achievement, as well as changes in the practice of the discipline, combined with limited time and money. All of these initiatives require much rethinking of teacher practice. There is a need for more professional learning; job-embedded learning, particularly through opening classrooms to more observation and feedback, has a great deal to offer in the ongoing education of history teachers, as I have argued.

Our next steps are to continue to engage in those "cross-boundary practices" as suggested by Alan Sears and to encourage teachers to have the opportunities and resources to return to those ideas that kindled their interest in history in the first place. Students need the chance to "do" history by investigating big questions; by making connections between ideas, issues, and themes; and by becoming critical thinkers.

New ways of teaching history are still being developed and explored. The history demonstration classes hosted in 2010–11 had fewer than fifty teachers participate from the Toronto District School Board. An additional nineteen teachers were introduced to this approach during literacy camp in the summer. These strategies are revealing areas where teachers need further exploration and support as they develop better ways to teach history and engage students. Feedback from demonstration classrooms and literacy camp strongly suggests that history teachers want professional learning that connects to the classroom. A few comments from history teachers included: "I experienced history coming alive, which I knew before, but this week was really exciting to see so many History teachers excited about the subject"; and "I experienced the value of collegial learning."

Historical thinking is being incorporated into Ontario policy documents; the question remains: how will this translate to changing classroom curriculum practices? The emphasis on historical thinking involves a steep learning curve for most teachers, but it will allow them to teach history better, and to teach for better historical understanding. As Alan Sears has argued, these new methods and approaches, if followed throughout teachers' professional careers, hold considerable promise for moving history teachers from the periphery (where most currently reside) to the core of their profession. The job-embedded professional development I have described here, meant for both new and experienced teachers, will help them in the process, showing them how to connect research into classroom practice.

NOTES

1 Alan Sears, this volume, p. 12.
2 Personal correspondence with the author.
3 Toronto District School Board, *The Heart and Art of Mentorship. Learning from Students/Learning from Each Other* (Toronto: TDSB, May 2011).
4 Ontario, Ministry of Education, *Literacy GAINS*, http://www.edugains .ca/newsite/literacy2/index.html.

18 Engendering Power and Legitimation: Giving Teachers the Tools to Claim a Place for History Education in Their Schools

ROSE FINE-MEYER

Introduction

The secondary school history and social science department in which I worked had an annual enrolment of approximately one thousand students. The only mandatory history course accounted for a few hundred students; the rest of these history students enrolled in senior-level optional courses. Even more remarkable, in some years we had the highly unusual situation of having more students enrolled in the department than were students in the school. I believe our success as a department was the product of two equally important factors: first, the pedagogical practices taking place in our classrooms; and second, the work we all did as professional historians and teachers to engage students in history research projects within the school and the local community.[1]

What I would like to do in this chapter is to focus on one particular course, one that I developed and had approved for the Grade 12 Ontario curriculum. With its focus on active research into local history, the course facilitated important connections between pedagogical practices that nurtured historical thinking in the classroom and the communities of practice where teachers and students could expand their historical understanding outside the classroom. My school, and in particular the local history course that I developed from my experience in that school, provides convincing evidence in support of Alan Sears' argument in this collection. The key to moving history teachers from the margins to the core of the profession, he asserts, can be found in three principles: changing history teacher's identity from purveyors of facts to participants in a community of historical investigation; recognizing that becoming a history teacher takes an entire professional career; and establishing communities of practice to provide the best, and perhaps the only, way of achieving these aims. I will conclude by suggesting that the focus on local history in the course and in the school not only had the advantage of allowing teachers to nurture historical understanding in their students while participating in the boundary work necessary to keep them at the core of their profession, another considerable advantage to history education more broadly was that the importance of history within the curriculum was constantly being demonstrated to students, parents, the wider community, and to the principal. It was the active engagement of these individuals and groups in the collaborative research projects in local communities that gave history a place of considerable – and highly unusual – importance within in the busy school curriculum.

Reclaiming a Sense of Place

A number of scholars have recently examined the ways in which modern humans are losing a sense of place in their lives due to various factors, such as the ways in which global systems have "homogenized" our cities with common institutions and products that link to common identities, and the fact that we no longer are dependent on local agriculture, energy sources, environments, or people for our survival.[2] Many communities around the world are struggling against global systems, finding empowerment in local associations. David Hutchinson, for example, suggests we are not well equipped to live in a "virtual world" that removes tradition, culture, and communities – once so central to defining a sense of identity and belonging. He suggests that loss of place has affected our education systems, which have been "whittled down to a more prosaic and technical thing unrelated to the specifics of place, ecology and situated personhood," and he suggests following the current movements of locally based food, bio-regionalism, renewable energy, and others to develop schools that are "rooted in place."[3] People identify with the place in which they live and work, but few know or engage in its history. Hutchinson writes that "places shape our consciousness, social identities, behavior and attitudes."[4] Yet schools tend to lock out communities, creating boundaries between the work that is taking place inside classrooms and work taking place outside. As Hutchinson suggests, lacking a sense of place disengages students in the long run because the spaces they inhabit, such as homes, churches, and public parks, have emotional and meaningful connections. Once students enter schools, they often face a giant divide between the work in schools and work in communities, which perhaps explains students' general lack of interest in civic engagement.

The potential of local history to actively engage students in something they know and are interested in is a considerable advantage within a curriculum that many students experience as alienating and irrelevant to their own lives. Scholars, such as John Dewey, advocated educational systems that promoted stronger communication, as well as cooperative and active learning. Dewey argued that in order to deepen the democratic nature of public education students needed to be engaged in the processes of growth and development and "the here and now," thus giving relevance to learning.[5] But local or place-based history has other important advantages for teachers working to nurture historical understanding. By engaging actively in placed-based research projects, students are in the position of "doing history"; using readily available "primary sources," from documents in local archives to architecture, from oral histories to streetscapes, they are learning the principles and practices of historical thinking.

As Alan Sears argued in this collection, place and community can function in other ways for history educators. Etienne Wenger examines "communities of practice" and argues that educational institutions' focus on individual learning processes counters the premise that "we are social beings" who need to actively engage in our world. He notes that learning involves being "active participants in the practices of social communities and constructing identities in relation to these communities."[6] Education that involves the development of processes that link individuals and communities cannot take place only in classrooms focused predominantly on individual learning. There need to be spaces for engagement outside the classroom, and educators need to ensure that students participate in democratic processes by providing ongoing links to communities and professionals outside the school space. By breaking down the barriers to developing blended communities for learning, students engaged in research work develop long-term, sustaining relationships between schools and communities. Teachers and students can draw on the rich and diverse assembly of historical professionals within communities to develop reciprocal relationships that expand their understanding of history, and in the process, of history teaching and learning.

The advantages of local, place-based history have not been lost on history educators. Local history work was popular in the 1970s

Canadian school history curriculum, a product of the post-centennial period.[7] Support from local school boards allowed students to engage in research projects and field studies at historical sites, historical societies, and community fairs. Proud of their educational programs, the Toronto Historical Board (now Heritage Toronto) partnered with local school boards to support joint educational initiatives. The former Toronto Board of Education sponsored educational seminars for teachers that were history lectures held at local historic sites and museums. As well, the Ontario Ministry of Education curriculum guidelines allowed for research projects at historic sites. Attendance at sites was substantial, as funding provided support for student groups.[8] Engagement with local history involved broad-based curriculum work that ensured elementary students attended heritage fairs and high school students studied community history.[9] The current emphasis on global education has removed curriculum work in placed-based history, but that has not dampened community interest in local history, which is evident in the voluminous number of community events and celebrations that occur throughout each year.

The Archives and Local History Course

The course that I developed for Ontario drew on years of research and teaching in the Toronto area, as I worked to find and refine ways of teaching history that actively engaged students in "doing history" especially through research projects within local schools and communities. The *Archives and Local History*[10] course allows students to develop a greater insight into the role of public memory in the preservation of regional and national narratives. The students create an archive in their school that serves as a repository for their research work. The independent and group research supports advanced analytical skills. The course is now in the Ontario curriculum planner and taught by teachers across the province. The feedback from students taking this course has been positive.[11] A teacher in Kapuskasing, Ontario, has been successfully teaching the course for three years. In the first year, she noted,

> We managed to establish the Kapuskasing District high school Archives (we were given a room approximately 20x20) and we spent the good portion of the first term gathering, moving, organizing and discussing the items we found. In fact, as the semester progressed the students became very protective of the archives. An article in the town's newspaper was written about the class and the course. The course is a work in progress, as

is the archive room. The 75th anniversary of the school is occurring in 2011 and the archives will be a central part of the celebration.[12]

The links to national narratives are quite evident in placed-based communities. There is a cemetery outside of Kapuskasing, for example, with graves from the First World War internment camps. In researching the individuals buried in the graves, students are able to link the national story of a world war by engaging in critical thinking skills that examine how public discourse and commemoration can be challenged through critical historical research work. These are skills that they can take forward in their history course work.

The course is shaped by the local community. It begins with an examination of the history of the school: land, people, and buildings, then broadens to explore the larger community and how community memory reflects national understandings. In all areas, the students are linked to professionals: archivists, libraries, educators, elders, academics, genealogists, artists, and historians who demonstrate their role in maintaining and preserving our culture and history. In each unit, the students have an opportunity to discover their past by exploring their community through research projects in placed-based, provincial, and national archives and libraries. As well, students make connections with community members, professional and non-professional. The course is divided into a number of research units that include investigating the history and geography of the school; establishing relationships with historical societies; exploring the history of local sites, parks, religious institutions, cemeteries, community centres, and homes; uncovering Aboriginal history through oral histories and artefacts; and participating in an archaeological dig. The course is designed to allow students to explore how their community has come to define its identity. Students try to deconstruct the reasons behind their community's identities.

Students interview former alumni whose stories are then documented, transcribed, and preserved in the school archives. They engage in a major study of the history of their home by examining the history of the property, the history of the physical building and elements of construction, and the history of the people who lived there. An examination of local houses or buildings includes a trip to the archives or town hall to access primary documents such as fire insurance plans, maps, tax assessment rolls, building permits, city or town directories, and old photographs. The work involves scrutinizing architecture: windows, doors, style of brick, roof, and the land. Students perform interviews with current and previous owners and local historians.[13] Local homes, religious sites, community centres, and retail stores can all be examined in this way. By linking to a community's past, students engage in historical inquiry that is both accessible and meaningful. The final unit involves an archaeological dig. In "digging ourselves up," students discover that we literally walk on top of our past each day. The dig is small, giving students a feel for archaeological work. At the end of the course, students dig in their own backyards. As "trained archaeologists," they do a proper archaeological dig in order to "find" something of their past. What treasures lay waiting in that ground that defines their lives, and the many lives before them? What parts of their own past are lying beneath the very ground that they walk each day ... to their school, to their local community centre, to their park? What will remain of them? In order to answer these questions, students collaborate with professional archaeologists. In the years that I have offered the course, students have found old bottles, hand-forged nails, skeletal keys, bits of pottery and stones, a horseshoe, a barrel ring, and an old brass button. For those who cannot actually find anything, they "find" things that they chose to reflect their research about the history of the place, placed in the ground, and then dug up. Students create PowerPoint presentations that document their work.

The course supports place-based research projects, but history teachers can develop projects with input by a panel of students, parents, and community leaders. Some parts of a school, for example, are shared on a regular basis with the community, such as the school grounds. Therefore, it would make sense to partner with the community to understand, maintain, and preserve the school property. David Sobel argues for a "pedagogy of community," where students are reconnected to their "homeground," where nature, regional, culture, and ecological challenges are explored. Jane Jacobs, social activist, author, and winner of numerous awards, advocated for cities that are liveable, where people of varying ages reside and work within environments that support natural ecosystems.[14] Sustainable and liveable communities are possible if the people who live in them understand, preserve, and celebrate their pasts. I suggest that history teachers engage students in research projects that explore the history of the land in which they live and that support an understanding of Aboriginal history.[15]

Themes and Variations

Having described the course I developed, I maintain that a separate and entire course in place-based history of this kind is not necessary in order to enhance students' historical thinking and their connections to their local communities. A place-based focus can be nurtured within a variety of secondary and even elementary courses. Ontario, for example, has a mandatory Canadian history course that covers the twentieth century, and most students in the province live in homes and attend schools that were built in the twentieth century. Therefore, a study of local houses and community buildings does not stray far from the expectations of the existing curriculum. History teachers can establish a theme each year and create student research teams that examine the history of communities: land, people, and buildings. Partnering with historical societies, archives, town halls, libraries, and elders in the community supports this work. Connecting with individuals and societies actively engaged in the professional work of researching, maintaining, and preserving history allows students to engage in meaningful historical work. Sears argues that teacher education must take the long view by engaging teachers with professional learning communities. Teachers benefit from partnering with a broad range of learning communities to "rethink the role of teaching beyond the classroom and to consider the relationship of teaching to the places where children, youth, and adults actually live and learn."[16]

Place-based approaches can take a variety of forms. A school archive can act as a repository for collaborative student historical research work as well as the memorabilia and ephemera of the school. An archive, created from a small closet or room, becomes a foundation for preserving the school community's history and memory. Materials can be added each year, and senior students can be given responsibility for documenting the holdings as well as maintaining the collection. This has an immediate outcome – linking the past, present, and future together – as students, parents, and others use the archive as a repository for documents that may otherwise have been discarded. It also provides a common space within the school that brings together communities of learners and cuts through the traditional concepts of historical preservation, which often feel remote, isolated, or locked away. This allows for new historical interpretations. The archive can contain trophies, and artefacts from each department in the school such as plaques, old photographs, old lab equipment, music night programs, artwork, and transcripts of oral interviews that the students conduct with alumni.[17] Students can fill the walls of the school with photographs that reflect its history and display placed-based history research projects, artwork, and shared historical events. Teachers can ensure historical research projects continue every year, creating new school traditions and creating new opportunities to engage with different learning communities. Students and local communities can take part in these history research traditions in the same way that they attend annual musical, drama, and sports events. Senior students can act as mentors, and community members can establish permanent ties with the school.

Another research option might involve developing a gardening club. Funds can be raised to acquire proper tools and supplies. Students in history classes can take turns getting out of their classrooms once a month to help with the gardening of the school property. History student groups can begin with a study that researches indigenous trees, plants, shrubs, and flowers that are historically linked to the community and the land in which the school is situated. Aboriginal elders and others in the Aboriginal community known as "knowledge holders" can help direct this work. Archaeological digs can form the basis of studies that trace the remains of people's lives in the past – a past that goes back thousands of years. The students can create explanatory or commemorative plaques to indicate the history of the building, peoples, and land. The students could invite historians, elders, arborists, landscapers, gardeners, archivists, and others to provide advice and support. Students could research the history of local homes, buildings, and community sites and then develop historical walking tours. The tours could be published in the local papers. History teachers can arrange to have community leaders support the research work and share their expertise. These initiatives can take place alongside the curriculum as they support expectations that students will engage in active and critical historical research work. Students receive credit for these research projects, work with others in meaningful and engaging historical work, and make permanent links with the community.

Claiming a Place for History

In this chapter, I have provided an outline of how one course in place-based history – and place-based approaches generally – can facilitate the ongoing professional development of history teachers and the education of students in ways suggested by Alan Sears, particularly by providing more "hands-on" history for students and by providing broad-ranging kinds of "boundary work" for teachers in their local communities. I am also suggesting, however, that developing these initiatives will elevate the status of history education in the school. Increasing the status of history teaching and learning is vital to the continued existence of history as a subject within the high school curriculum.

Peter Seixas asks, "What do young people need to learn in order to make sense of their place in time – in this place, in these times – and what can we do to help them?" He suggests educators must understand the processes and "habits of mind" that allow students to "make sense of who they are, where they stand, and what they can do – as individuals, as members of multiple, intersecting groups and as citizens."[18] I am arguing that work outside the classroom can enhance the same principles and support the same objectives. Timothy Stanley suggests the challenge for history education is to "to construct a narrative that explains how it is we have come to inhabit common spaces and to allow others to see and engage in these narratives." He argues that students need to understand how "personal histories intertwine with those in multiple communities."[19] Engaging students in place-based history research projects allows students to confront historical evidence and to engage in dialogues surrounding a past that they think they know, but that can produce new understandings. Alan Sears in this collection argues that "history teacher education is not about learning new concepts and skills, it is about becoming history teachers: teachers who not only know historical information and can describe historical processes but teachers who are practitioners and shapers of the field itself." Developing collaborative research projects designed primarily to knit together communities of learners can provide opportunities for teachers to model good history practices. New teachers can learn strategies that enable students to develop a greater understanding of themselves as both members of regional communities and members of a global world. In this way, history as a discipline is also enhanced.

Conclusion

At one time history teachers were "keepers of the memory of schools," responsible for knowing, maintaining, and preserving the school's past.[20] People relied on them for their knowledge and expertise, and in the process history teachers made an important place for history in their community. Over time, this has been lost. I have suggested here that now is the time to recapture this role by actively engaging in historical research work within and outside of the classroom and by bridging the gulf that too often exists between communities and schools. These links need to be taught; teacher candidates can develop strategies to effectively maintain a place for history in schools and communities before they enter the school system. By developing place-based research projects, new teachers have a greater opportunity to inspire students and make the meaning and importance of history visible to all members of a school community. Teaching place-based history is an important addition to teaching historical thinking. But I also believe that if we want history taught more effectively, then we need more history to be taught and in more places. Whole communities, as well as individual students, need to be shown how and why history matters. Teaching place-based history does all this.

NOTES

1 The school was situated in the west end of the city of Toronto and had a strong academic focus, a committed and engaged community of parents, and exceptionally dedicated subject department leaders. The school population throughout the period 1980–2003 fluctuated between 1,000–1,300 students.
2 To name a few: David Hutchinson, *A Natural History of Place in Education* (New York: Teachers College Press, Columbia University, 2004); Etienne Wenger, *Communities of Practice: Learning, Meaning, and Identity* (Cambridge, MA: Cambridge University Press, 1998); and Marc Treib, ed., *Spatial Recall: Memory in Architecture and Landscape* (New York: Routledge, 2009). Scholars have also explored specific place-based examinations, such as Bryan Poirier's *The Pedagogy of Place: A Naturalistic Exploration of River as Teacher* (MA thesis, OISE, University of Toronto, 2004). Poirier suggests that students engage in outdoor education as "the natural world contains complexities not found in indoor environments."
3 Hutchinson, *A Natural History of Place*, ix-x.
4 Hutchinson, *A Natural History of Place*, 14
5 John Dewey, *Democracy and Education: An Introduction to the Philosophy of Education* (New York: Macmillan Company, 1916). Dewey famously argued that "we learn by doing" and linked the growth of the child to the here and now: "Children proverbially live in the present; that is not only fact not to be evaded, but it is an excellence," 61.
6 Wegner, *Communities of Practice*, 4. Wegner argued that "communities of practice are formed by people who engage in a process of collective learning in a shared domain of human endeavour." We all belong to communities of practice – in multiple places at one given time – and that changes over time. Shared communities of learning take place within schools and also within all communities.
7 Several Ontario history textbooks in the 1970s had chapters on placed-based history. For example, I.L. Martinello, *Call Us Canadians* (Toronto:

McGraw-Hill Ryerson, 1976) contains a chapter titled "The Study of Local History," in which the author provides a case study for students in any community to follow, suggesting communities of networks and venues for accessing research documents. There are historic maps, sketches, statistics, and stories.

8 Heritage Toronto Archives, *Toronto Historical Board Annual Report* 1972, 27. Proud of their educational programs, the 1972 Toronto Historical Board partnered with the Toronto Board of Education to sponsor educational seminars for teachers, which included lectures held at museums. The Ontario Ministry of Education's curriculum guidelines in the 1970s linked heritage to history curriculum, actively supporting the historic sites. The number of students attending historic sites was quite high, as government funding supported school groups' attendance.

9 Most provinces in Canada have heritage fairs that support student projects. For example the *Ontario Heritage Fairs Association* holds regional fairs across the province each spring that supports place-based research projects. http://www.ohhfa.ca/.

10 The *Archives and Local History* senior-level course is under the umbrella of Interdisciplinary Studies. The code for the course in Ontario is IDC4UI. Teachers use a course outline that contains suggested research projects. The expectation is that the course will be unique to each community.

11 For example, one student, after completing a research project of the student's house, continued part-time work in the field researching other homes in the community. Students stated that they benefited from the advanced analytical research skills and the deeper understanding of their community, and that they welcomed the interaction with communities of learners outside of the classroom.

12 Email correspondence with Dianne Leaist from Kapuskasing District High School, 2009.

13 The Toronto Archives has an excellent "Researching Your House" online guide. See toronto.ca/archives/pdf/researchingyourhouse2004.pdf. For archaeology resources, excavations, and information, see www.pc.gc.ca.

14 Jane Jacobs, *Dark Age Ahead* (Toronto: Random House, 2004). David Sobel, *Place-based Education: Connecting Classrooms and Communities* (Great Barrington, MA: The Orion Society, 2005), 52-70. Sobel provides six strategies for creating place-based schools that include enhancing networks between communities and schools.

15 Often students of history do not fully explore Aboriginal history. Each community has Aboriginal elders, language keepers, and knowledge holders. Students can invite guest speakers, attend Aboriginal centres/sites, and engage in research projects with Indigenous historians.

16 David A. Gruenewald and Gregory A. Smith, *Place-Based Education in the Global Age* (New York: Lawrence Erlbaum Associates, 2008), 351.

17 There are many articles that explore creating an archive. See, for example, Tom Nesmith, "What's History Got to Do with It?: Reconsidering the Place of Historical Knowledge in Archival Work," *Archivaria* 57 (Spring 2004): 1-27; Canadian Council of Archives, *Basic Conservation of Archival Materials* (Ottawa: Canadian Council of Archives, revised edition, 2003); and Sharon Anne Cook, "Connecting Archives and the Classroom," *Archivaria*, 44 (Fall 1997): 102-17.

18 Peter Seixas, "What is Historical Consciousness?" in *To the Past: History Education, Public Memory, and Citizenship Education in Canada,* edited by Ruth W. Sandwell (Toronto, University of Toronto Press: 2006), 20-1.

19 Timothy Stanley, "Whose Public? Whose Memory? Racisms, Grand Narratives and Canadian History," in *To the Past: History Education, Public Memory, and Citizenship in Canada,* edited by Ruth W. Sandwell (Toronto: University of Toronto Press, 2006), 47.

20 Interview with Mel Greif, March 2011. Greif, a retired head of history at an academic secondary school in Toronto and winner of numerous teaching awards, was a mentor and inspiration for this work. His tireless work over thirty-five years, bringing students and their communities together, elevated the status of the department and engaged the community in meaningful and lifelong initiatives.

19 Telling the Stories of the Nikkei: A Place-Based History Education Project*

TERRY TAYLOR AND LINDA FARR DARLING

The Problem

We ask, "How can teachers in a small rural school cultivate students' historical understandings through a project based on local events?" Over two terms, secondary students in the West Kootenays of British Columbia immersed themselves in "place-based education," a multi-disciplinary, community-focused exploration of the local internment of 1,400 Canadians of Japanese descent in 1942–1946. The project unfolded as a partnership between the school, two filmmakers, a rural teacher education program, two arts organizations, two museums, and a national website. Given the scope of expertise and resources, it represented the kind of boundary work across professional communities that Alan Sears has called for in this volume, in order to help bring history teachers inside the circle of practices that occupy historians.

Telling the Stories of the Nikkei responds to a problem rural teachers face in making curriculum come to life in communities far from the cultural and educational resources of larger centres.[1] Rural students can feel isolated from the world and from significant movements, events, and issues, both historic and contemporary.[2] Teachers work to overcome this isolation through many means; their recent efforts have been enhanced by the increasing availability of communicative technologies designed to globalize rural classrooms.[3] Experiences in place-based education are partially intended to engage students with their local communities as vibrant, important sites for local and global learning. David Sobel, one of place-based education's most active proponents, coined the phrase "enlightened localism" to describe education that thoughtfully examines global issues of social justice through a local lens. In this way, for example, questions of tolerance within a diverse society, rights violations, and the limits of free expression can be fruitfully explored through examining relationships, policies, and practices within one's own neighbourhood and community.[4] The spirit of "enlightened localism" permeates our project. The concept leads us to recommend using local historical, geographical, and cultural resources to motivate students to interact with the past. We believe this kind of exploration, guided by informed educators, helps students formulate deep understandings of the ways in which the local and global intersect, leading to a fuller sense of the value of studying history.

The Curriculum

World War II history is integral to BC social studies and secondary history curriculum, and appears across the grades. The internment of Japanese Canadians is first addressed in Grade 4, and revisited through the secondary years. The local connection to these events is powerful. In 1942, at the height of alarm about a possible Japanese invasion of the west coast, over 22,000 Canadians of Japanese descent were stripped of their rights and property and interned in camps throughout British Columbia's interior. The third largest camp and the only one remaining at the end of World War II was New Denver. In 1994, a museum was created at that site as a national memorial to the interned Japanese Canadians. In July 2010, Parks Canada declared the Nikkei Internment Memorial Centre a National Historic Site.

Coauthor Terry Taylor teaches English at Lucerne Elementary-Secondary School in New Denver. Like her social studies colleagues, she is committed to innovative and collaborative classroom practices. In January 2010, Terry and social studies teacher Gary Parkstrom decided to develop a project on the internment using local, distant, and online resources and expertise. They envisioned a multilayered approach using digital storytelling, web-based archival study, and other innovative ways to present the project, "Telling the Stories of the Nikkei: the Japanese Canadian Internment in New Denver." They hoped that an interdisciplinary, place-based approach that included teaching students to create short films would help students appreciate the "local to global" connections found in their community. By making creative use of the contributions of historians, museum curators, teacher educators, filmmakers, and internment survivors, they also hoped (echoing the recommendations of Sears) that a viable community of practice would emerge, one dedicated to better understanding this history and the impact of the Nikkei on Canada.

The Project

Grade 11 and 12 students from Lucerne School in New Denver studied the internment with their social studies and English teachers, along with a student teacher from the University of British Columbia's West Kootenay Teacher Education program. The students toured the Nikkei Centre museum with its original artefacts, and studied archival images and texts online and from the Japanese Canadian National Museum in Burnaby. In addition, they viewed documentaries about the period. They also interviewed local elders who lived in the camp as children. History curriculum based on their investigations was co-constructed by students, teachers, and the UBC student teachers. As culminating experiences of their learning, students created short films in which their historical understandings were expressed artistically, thanks to the guidance of professional filmmakers. Their documentaries, recorded interviews, and animated films were screened at the local meeting hall. The event brought together community members of four generations to hear narratives and see images that brought to life village history, linking its past to significant world events.

The internment camp site was known to students prior to the project, but few had made connections between the textbook explanations of Canada in World War II and the winter of 1942, when 1,400 people, including infants and seniors, arrived with only a few personal belongings in "the Orchard" area of New Denver to live in tents with latrines. The historical investigation, while rooted in one tiny community, also encompasses global themes of injustice, racism, and displacement, ultimately revealing the human capacity for resilience and forgiveness. The experience of studying, then filming, elements of the Nikkei stories led two students to reflect:

> We decided to do a black and white film ... with sad violins, to show how horrible the living situations were for Japanese Canadians. Black and white felt like a powerful way to showing our feelings about the darkness of this time in Canadian history, but also the light and strength of the Japanese-Canadian people who were here.

In this and other responses, teachable moments arose – opportunities to critically engage with the histories discovered through personal accounts, and to question our own "situatedness" as onlookers trying to make sense of events that happened decades ago. As teachers and researchers, we were aware of the presentism that may have coloured our students' first judgments, yet we felt it crucial for their immediate emotive responses to act as catalysts for more thoughtful examination. Further, we argue that pondering important moral questions should be at the heart of social studies, and *Telling the Stories of the Nikkei* became a powerful learning tool for the examination of each student's own ethical framework – including the ideals to which she and her society may be committed.

Engaging Student Teachers

As Lucerne teachers were preparing for the project, plans began to partner with the nearby UBC teacher education satellite program. The Nikkei Centre would serve as the site for inquiry and curriculum development. Student teachers studied World War II history, took field trips to New Denver, and immersed themselves in the artefacts, texts, and images preserved at the museum. They consulted with historians online and at the local college. Student teachers collaborated to develop unit plans, and they integrated lessons on the internment into their classroom teaching during practicum. They brought ideas to their sponsor teachers' classrooms, another layer of collaboration that enriched the curriculum. Their preparation also supported the student teacher assigned to Lucerne School. She was able to get feedback on her lesson ideas from other student teachers and teacher educators with interests in history teaching. In turn, all participants brought stories of the Nikkei, including their own lessons and the student films, into an even larger circle of learning. The preparation of history teachers should always include immersion in the discipline of history and in professional historical practices. Bringing teacher education students into the circle of inquiry was an important element of the project, providing opportunities to constructively engage with the Benchmarks of Historical Thinking (later renamed The Historical Thinking Project).[5] As a result, the possibilities for place-based history education resonated throughout the teacher preparation program. The most visible legacy is the development of a new course focused entirely on place-based education.

Evaluating Lessons Learned for History Education

Historical Significance

Although most Lucerne students had previously visited the Nikkei Museum or the Japanese garden on the lakeshore, the project illuminated these sites' significance. Several student films capture newly discovered understandings of the prevailing Canadian attitudes towards their Japanese enemies in World War II and, by extension, towards all Canadians of Japanese heritage. In particular, the student documentary "Propaganda" investigates racism and prejudice with montages of period posters, proclamations, photographs of confiscated fishing boats, and alien ID cards. Students could link events chronicled at the New Denver site to larger themes and movements of both historic and contemporary Canadian society. Seeing how a particular past "is embedded in a larger, meaningful narrative" is one aspect of students' emerging understandings of historical significance; students begin to realize how a single event can shed light "on enduring or emerging issues in history and contemporary life."[6] As an example, the student film "Never Again" explores the danger of forgetting past injustices and the risk of fear overruling our sense of humanity and fairness. Appreciating the historical significance of the internment challenged students to go beyond the immediacy of their own emotional responses to consider the actions of government and citizenry and come to a fuller understanding of their country at war.

Primary Source Documents

Primary sources formed the project backbone, and interviews with five elders who had been interned as children were the most significant. Several films feature recollections of events that took place almost seventy years ago. Students' belief that these recollections provided evidence for more generalized claims about the internment could have been unsettled more than it was. For students, the power of the elders' anecdotes was undeniable. To their surprise, many memories seemed crystal clear: boarding crowded trains in Vancouver, ice skating with local children on homemade skates, et cetera. Primary source documents, or the "litter of history," were eagerly investigated by young historians, who pored over photographs of tents under snow, tenderly preserved teapots, or babies peeking from government-issued blankets. One film portrays the first winter as it might have appeared to a boy from the coast viewing the strange rural landscape, the deep hole of a latrine, and a rusted toy truck in the ice. Yet, the elders' reflections also revealed the limitations of our memories and the dangers of relying too heavily on anecdotes to piece together the past. As Nobby, one interviewee, points out, asking his mother to share her perceptions of the experience of being interned would have triggered an avalanche of impressions different from his. She would have recollected cold seeping through cracks, the struggle to feed her children with inadequate provisions, and the loneliness of life without her husband, who had been sent elsewhere. Had the project included the voices of those who experienced other aspects of life in World War II, the emerging picture would have looked more different still.

Continuity and Change

Lucerne students take a short walk from school to see "the Orchard" and the wooden structures on site. Several dozen cabins have now been renovated and are permanent residences for New Denver families. The dwellings preserved at the museum look much as they did in 1943, when they replaced the first tents. Japanese surnames on the internees' suitcases in the museum are also painted on mailboxes in the village, since many internees stayed after the war. There are numerous opportunities for students to see that even after seven decades, physical evidence of the internment survives. The project brought details into focus, and students compared "then and now" through wartime photographs of their community. Examining national and regional newspapers of the time, the students could see the inflated rhetoric and the ways in which fear permeated the popular press. They compared wartime editorials to op-ed pieces published after September 11, 2001, and identified both parallels and distinctions. Students came to deeply appreciate continuity and change within their own landscape, and to appreciate continuity and change related to the beliefs and values of Canadians between 1942 and 2010. As an opportunity to further engage with history, the concepts of continuity and change were also introduced to students in terms of understanding the trajectories of their own lives and growing historical imaginations.

Cause and Consequence

There is perennial concern among historians that events of long ago will remain abstractions for today's learners, and their subsequent grasp of causes and consequences will be shallow. And, if some history teachers are as ill prepared to present more than facts and superficial explanations as Sears worries they are, lessons about World War II may be conceptually inadequate. The focus on the internment in New Denver was an attempt to go deeper. It brought home the concept of causes and consequences, allowing students to see the local impact of distant events, and to begin to analyse the implications of the internment not only for the Japanese Canadians who lived through it, but also for their descendants, New Denver residents, and the generations of Canadian citizens who still grapple with creating and sustaining harmonious relations within a diverse society. Several student films focus on the consequences of the internment on the lives of particular families, while one animated short emphasizes the need for vigilance on the part of all citizens in a democracy, so that the freedoms we take for granted do not disappear "in an instant."

Historical Perspectives

Taking historical perspectives meant learning to analyse multiple perspectives on the internment, even from those who lived through the same New Denver experience. Nuances and subtleties began to appear in students' journals and storyboards, as they tried to reconcile their anger at those who forced the relocation with the fatalistic remarks that sometimes came from interviewees. Students' outrage about the treatment of "enemy aliens" was tempered by comments of the Japanese Canadians, who, despite terrible circumstances, found ways to cooperate to improve conditions, and found moments of solace in recreating familiar spiritual rituals in unfamiliar surroundings. Students also heard from elders who experienced aspects of the internment as adventures. "We were just kids," one recounted, "we loved the lake and the games. For our parents, it wasn't funny." One interviewee added another layer of complexity when she told students that her father moved the family back to Japan after the war during the Second Uprooting, but that she "was too homesick for Canada to stay." However rich and interesting the sources, it was essential that the students understood the stories as fragments of a complex and often unknowable past. Historical perspectives are always partial and limited, and it was important to convey to the students that humility must accompany their historical investigations and subsequent claims to knowledge. We can never know all the perspectives, or all the points of view, and aggregating the sum of stories we have heard still leaves us with a flawed and limited historical account.

Ethical Dimensions of History

The films reveal a range of emotions that students felt as they struggled to make sense of what happened. The ethical dimensions of this history became clearer as they discovered posters and cartoons in which Japanese Canadians appear as monsters and devils. Their sense of moral outrage at injustice is palpable. Although these responses to the internment are to be expected from students encountering personal tales and sifting through haunting images and inflammatory rhetoric, it was nevertheless essential that everyone connected with the project appreciated the pitfalls of presentism, or making moral judgments in hindsight without sufficiently grasping the ethos of times past. This was accomplished in various ways, such as connecting world and national events in the students' own lives (i.e., the United States' "War on Terror") with the history of World War II, and critically examining additional accounts of internment experiences as well as wartime records from other civilians.

Conclusion

As an exemplar of place-based history education, our project illustrates the value of bridging across community and school in order to deepen students' understandings, increase civic engagement, and enrich moral and aesthetic imaginations. Further, like any teaching exemplar that might inspire others, the project also tells a cautionary tale. It points out the pitfalls of teaching complex events largely through personal narratives, in this case stories of individuals who lived through the internment. As a lesson for teacher educators who prepare history teachers, the project reveals places to pause to consider the limitations of memory as well as the possible dangers of hastily imposing present-day moral frameworks on the past.

Aspiring place-based history teachers should be encouraged by the capacity of students to investigate what they are genuinely curious about, which often turns out to be what they find on their doorstep. In the case of the Nikkei project, students learned valuable lessons, many from poignant remembrances. The deeper students probed into press accounts of the time and available artefacts and documents, the more convincingly they could argue their case about unfair treatment of Japanese Canadians: "This never should have happened. It was all so unjust. They lost everything." All the films are suffused with earnestness, if not criticality, but we believe such genuine engagement with an issue is a prerequisite for deeper and more critical understanding. As three students wrote,

> Our group wanted to make the audience recognize the freedom that numerous Japanese-Canadians lost during the internment. We portrayed this through claymation, making a cherry blossom fall from the tree to symbolize how alienated they were in their own country.

To students' surprise, elders responded to questions without anger, expressing resignation without blame. One daughter of New Denver internees was raised "not to be bitter." She recalled her father saying, "It's done. It couldn't be helped. It was War." Decades later, internees recalled generous acts on the part of residents who brought vegetables and helped mend their roofs. Several fondly remembered playing ball with local children in "the Orchard," and waking to the beauty of snow on the mountains. They told their stories partly because they want the injustice never to be repeated, and partly to convey the resilience of the human spirit. They have made peace with a difficult past, and forgiven the country that turned on them. That, too, is a powerful lesson for this generation of young Canadians to learn so vividly, and learn so close to home.

*We gratefully acknowledge contributions of filmmakers, Moira Simpson and Catrina Longmuir, funding agencies including The History Education Network and Rix Foundation, the staff and students of Lucerne School, the National Japanese Canadian Museum, the Nikkei Centre, New Denver Kyowakai Society, the interviewees, and residents of New Denver, BC.

Note: The student films, a documentary "Behind the Scenes," and five elder interviews created in the project can be viewed online at http://tellingthestoriesofthenikkei.wordpress.com/.

NOTES

1 J. Edmondson, and T. Butler, "Teaching School in Rural America: Toward an Educated Hope," in *Rural Education for the Twenty-First Century: Identity, Place, and Community in a Globalizing World*, edited by K. Scafft and A. Youngblood Jackson (University Park, PA: Pennsylvania State University Press, 2010), 150-74.
2 P. Theobald and K. Wood, "Learning to Be Rural: Identity Lessons from History, Schooling and the U.S. Corporate Media," in *Rural Education for the Twenty-First Century: Identity, Place, and Community in a Globalizing World*, edited by K. Scafft and A. Youngblood Jackson (University Park, PA: Pennsylvania State University Press, 2010), 17-33.
3 S. Crump and K. Twyford, "Opening their Eyes: E-learning for Rural and Isolated Communities in Australia," in Scafft and Youngblood Jackson, *Rural Education for the Twenty-First Century*, 210-31.
4 David Sobel, *Place-based Education: Connecting Classrooms and Communities* (Great Barrington, MA: Orion Society, 2005).
5 Carla Peck and Peter Seixas, "Benchmarks of Historical Thinking: First Steps," *Canadian Journal of Education* 31, no. 4 (2008): 1015-38.
6 Peter Seixas, The Historical Thinking Project, http://historicalthinking .ca/sites/default/files/Framework.Benchmarks.pdf, accessed 5 October 2011.

20 Conclusion

AMY VON HEYKING AND RUTH SANDWELL

This volume is loosely organized according to the chronology of becoming a history teacher, focusing on three time periods: before, during, and after the formal teacher education and accreditation period of a history teacher's life. This collection grew out of an attempt by Canadian history teacher educators to share the research, reflections, and teaching practices relating to their work in helping student teachers become excellent history teachers in schools, and these approaches are reflected within each of the book's chronological sections. However, as the introductory section sets out, chapters across the volume are bound together by some common and vital themes or issues. The contributors to the volume share the view that if students in our schools are to know history and become engaged citizens in our pluralist democracy, then they must know how to think historically. While there are many conceptual frameworks for historical thinking, many of the contributors to this volume (like other Canadian history education researchers and educators) have particularly benefited from Peter Seixas' work on The Historical Thinking Project. School curricula, teaching resources, and assessments across the country are now framed around the concepts identified by the project as foundational to doing the discipline of history: significance, evidence, continuity and change, cause and consequence, historical perspectives, and the ethical dimension. While there is some variation in the specific definitions of historical thinking across Canada, perhaps most notably in Quebec, there is a general (albeit sometimes contested) consensus that it provides a disciplinary understanding of what history is and what it does.

The contributors also appreciate that teaching for disciplinary understanding requires classroom teachers to teach in ways that are new and unfamiliar. As Sears argues in Chapter 2, most student teachers have not "had to think historically, but rather have been relatively passive observers of others' attempts to do so." The contributors have, as well, taken up the challenge of examining what kind of pedagogical content knowledge our teachers must develop, how that knowledge is best developed, and what kind of experiences teachers need in order to implement that knowledge in classrooms in meaningful ways. In their chapters, they summarize significant research findings, describe their own pedagogical practices with regard to these three goals, and reflect on their profession – acknowledging in the process that efforts to nurture historical pedagogical content knowledge must begin before students enter teacher education programs and must continue throughout their professional careers as classroom teachers. The chapters in this volume also indicate fruitful avenues for further research.

Sears' contribution to the symposium in which these papers were first presented helped all the participants appreciate the complexities and difficulties associated with transforming history teaching practices. As he stresses, many student teachers and practicing teachers have established cognitive frames that have led them to understand history teaching as transmitting historical information. An important first step in transforming teaching practice, therefore, involves challenging those frames. Lévesque (Chapter 7) indicates that student teachers' cognitive frames may be relatively open to teaching for disciplinary understanding. In his study, Lévesque found that compared to the general Canadian population, the relatively small group of student teachers from Ontario and Quebec that he surveyed were more interested in and more informed about history as "disciplined thinking," and more frequently and intensively engaged with history activities. In his words, the student teachers "seem to have a more critical consciousness than most people, at least in the way they represent history in its scholastic form." Potentially, this is encouraging news for history teacher educators, but he tempers his conclusions with the acknowledgment that student teachers face extraordinary challenges in implementing innovative pedagogical approaches when they confront an established classroom culture that values teacher transmission of historical information. In other words, regardless of the relative sophistication of student teachers' disciplinary understanding, they cannot resist or reform the practices of established teaching communities without meaningful and sustained support. Seixas and Webber make the same point in Chapter 9. Lévesque's conclusions indicate the potential value of further large-scale studies of student teachers' cognitive frames in order to determine and assess their prior understandings of history and history teaching. They also raise questions about the nature of teaching communities and the support teachers may require in order to implement instructional practices that nurture students' disciplinary thinking.

Sears' use of Wenger's notion of communities of practice became a helpful framework for contributors to address questions of how best to change teaching practice. As Sears indicates in his chapter, classroom teachers are typically outsiders or at the margins of the community of history practitioners, a community that generally locates history professors and professional historians at the centre. He argues that if history teachers are to teach disciplinary processes – structures and concepts, and not just information – then they must be nurtured as practitioners of history. Similarly, history professors are often marginal members of a teaching community and can and should be challenged to put teaching at the core of their professional enterprise. Sandwell (Chapter 5) echoes his call for those teaching undergraduate history courses to approach their teaching as an opportunity to "do" history, in the same way that they approach their research and writing. Bringing these two communities of practice together requires history teachers and history practitioners to rethink their practice and indeed redefine their identities, but this can be facilitated by practices that cross boundaries of these communities of practice, and that foster dialogue and ongoing engagement with pedagogy for historical thinking.

As Pollock indicates in Chapter 4, Canadian researchers and history teacher educators have drawn on rich and varied research on historical thinking conducted by scholars in the United Kingdom, the United States, and elsewhere. Many scholars over the past thirty years have asked how we can best teach future history teachers how to teach for historical thinking, and the contributors to this volume have all benefited from this work. Pollock's survey of research literature indicates that the historical thinking of student teachers can be enhanced by history courses that specifically attend to this. But the task of cultivating sophisticated pedagogical content knowledge requires attention to at least four relevant facets of this knowledge: the facts and concepts of the discipline, the structure and epistemology of the discipline, the preconceptions that children bring to the discipline, and the elements that they find most difficult. The international research literature examining how best to nurture these facets typically advocates courses or activities that represent what Sears describes as "boundary projects," or projects undertaken by "cross-boundary teams." These are usually history educators and historians working collaboratively with student teachers to nurture their historical reasoning and to provide them with tools to implement more meaningful, authentic instruction in their classrooms. Several of the chapters in this volume build on research in these areas. They describe innovative and promising "boundary projects," and they raise issues for further exploration.

Von Heyking (Chapter 6) outlines the impact of a specially designed Canadian history survey course on undergraduate students' disciplinary understanding and their beliefs about history teaching and learning. This collaboration between a history professor and an education professor provided an opportunity for modelling effective pedagogy. The professors also crafted assignments that allowed student teachers in the course to design teaching resources and learning activities that would require students to interpret primary sources and engage in historical reasoning. The course certainly provoked important epistemological and pedagogical insights for the students, but students struggled in their attempts to design authentic learning tasks. Student teachers, von Heyking concluded, need multiple and sustained opportunities to develop sophisticated historical reasoning and pedagogical decision making. Like von Heyking, Seixas and Webber (Chapter 9) suggest that the structure of teacher education programs can make it all the more difficult for student teachers to develop their historical pedagogical content knowledge. The fact that most programs are after-degree, that student teachers enter programs with a range of academic credentials and limited background in history, and that the curriculum of the programs is overcrowded makes it challenging for student teachers to connect whatever historiographical and epistemological knowledge they may have with their emerging teacher knowledge. Seixas and Webber, however, demonstrate that specific and explicit instruction in the instructional methods provided by The Historical Thinking Project offers powerful tools that student teachers can use to hone their teaching craft.

Many contributors to this volume outline the creative ways that they used history education research to reform their own classroom practices in order to better nurture student teachers' historical pedagogical content knowledge. Kent den Heyer (Chapter 10) develops an alternative reading of historical perspective than that offered by The Historical Thinking Project. In his classroom, he demonstrates the power of challenging student teachers to create multiple or counter historical narrative trajectories as a way of shifting their own perspectives on the past, on historical knowledge, and on curriculum. Gibson (Chapter 12) and Christou (Chapter 13) describe innovative coursework that engaged student teachers in authentic historical research. Their assignments enhanced student teachers' historical thinking and allowed them to experience "the delights and difficulties of historical research." They also introduced them to the possibility of "doing history" with their own students and to authentic strategies that would help in this regard. That the student teachers faced difficulties in engaging in historical research and in developing appropriate primary source learning materials only demonstrates the complexity of sophisticated pedagogical reasoning and the fact that it develops with experience and over time. Case and MacLeod (Chapter 11) reflect on the importance of history teacher educators modelling authentic pedagogical and assessment practices in their courses. Myers (Chapter 14) outlines a structure for student teachers' reflection that helps them to bridge the theory-practice divide in history pedagogy and establish a habit of articulating their growing pedagogical knowledge. All of these contributors stress the possibilities inherent in teacher education programs to help teachers move into classrooms as innovative and thoughtful beginning teachers. But they also demonstrate the importance of a life course approach to teacher development and, in this way, they support Sears' principle that we must take the "long view" of teacher education.

In 1993, Wilson and Wineburg described what they believed would be exemplary professional development for teachers seeking to enhance their teaching for disciplinary understanding:

> It would begin when teachers first learn about teaching in universities, both from their instructors in liberal arts courses and in their teacher education programs. As models of educated persons, these instructors would craft experiences in which prospective teachers engage with ideas, learn the strengths and weaknesses of those ideas, develop a critical perspective on them, and learn that knowledge is ever-changing and growing. Such teachers would then go to work in schools where they, alongside other teachers and students, would explore new ideas in similar ways. Those

schools would be structured to provide the intellectual time and space necessary for teachers to keep abreast in relevant fields. In such schools there would be time to talk, to read, to debate, to question, to argue, or simply – to think.[1]

Contributors to this volume describe ways to provide classroom teachers with those opportunities to talk, read, debate, question, and learn – both from each other and from those at the core of the historians' community of practice.

As Clark demonstrates (Chapter 3), teacher educators in Canada have always struggled to find ways to help teachers bridge a divide between the theory taught in their coursework and the practice of schools. They have also demonstrated a commitment to assisting teachers in their continued development through summer institutes, conferences, and other professional development opportunities. Peck's study (Chapter 15) outlines a potentially powerful model for professional learning. Her program, introducing classroom teachers to the model of historical thinking created by The Historical Thinking Project, was sustained: it consisted of several sessions over a two-year period. It was collaborative in that Peck, as the facilitator and scholar of history education, worked with teachers in teams to develop learning materials and assessment tasks. The professional learning became embedded in teachers' classroom practice because teachers developed materials that they used in their classrooms, and their lessons were observed. The teachers had the opportunity to share samples of their students' work and reshape their materials based on experience and reflection. Haskings-Winner (Chapter 17) also describes an effective job-embedded model for building a community of practice that supports teachers as they implement strategies to help students "think about and critically assess how history is *done*, and what it means." Like Peck's professional learning program, Haskings-Winner's demonstration classes allow teachers to implement new active learning strategies that address historical thinking concepts and then to engage in discussion and debriefing with mentors and colleagues. These are powerful examples of the opportunities that teachers need for dialogue and ongoing engagement with pedagogy for historical thinking in a supportive environment.

Contributors to this volume also stress the potential of "boundary projects" and nontraditional history learning contexts for provoking powerful insights and sophisticated historical thinking for students and teachers. While the museum field trip is a long-standing hall-mark of school history instruction, Trofanenko (Chapter 16) outlines how contemporary museums' more democratic approaches to knowl-edge creation – their willingness to share their decisions about how the past is represented – has implications for the learning opportuni-ties that museums could offer. Museums and history educators have a significant opportunity, in using these sites to develop pedagogies that enhance historical thinking, to work collaboratively and cross boundaries of communities of practice. The local history course that Fine-Meyer (Chapter 18) developed for Ontario high school students prompted her students to engage in original historical research, but also brought her into a community of local historians and history practitioners. Taylor and Farr Darling's (Chapter 19) project is a mod-el of collaboration among communities of practice. Their project of-fered high school students an extended opportunity to work with museums, historic sites, and student teachers to research the experi-ence of those Canadians of Japanese descent who were interned in their community during World War II. The project was clearly fo-cused around concepts of historical thinking. The students communi-cated their findings in films that they created under the mentorship of filmmakers and presented at a community gathering. As they con-clude, "our project illustrates the value of bridging across commu-nity and school in order to deepen students' understandings, increase civic engagement, and enrich moral and aesthetic imaginations." This is powerful historical understanding indeed.

Over the years, there have been many initiatives to shift history teaching to reflect disciplinary understanding and to provide students with opportunities to do "hands-on" history. The Canadian contribu-tors to this volume have learned from and contributed to international scholarship that insists historical thinking must play a central role in history teaching if our students are to develop the knowledge and skills they need to make sense of a complex world and engage criti-cally and actively in pluralist democracies. Over the past decade, Canadian school curricula have been reformed to reflect procedural and conceptual frameworks for historical understanding. Scholars and educators have collaborated to create research-based teaching resourc-es for use in classrooms. But teacher education – before, during, and after formal teacher education programs – remains key to implement-ing and sustaining new instructional practices. The critical, creative, and collaborative research projects and teaching practices outlined in this volume will make a significant contribution to developing teachers' facility with the disciplinary practices of history and their abilities to foster their students' historical understanding.

NOTE

1 Suzanne M. Wilson and Samuel S. Wineburg, "Wrinkles in Time and Place: Using Performance Assessments to Understand the Knowledge of History Teachers," *American Educational Research Journal* 30, no. 4 (1993): 761-2.

Bibliography

Adler, Susan A. "The Education of Social Studies Teachers." In *Handbook of Research on Social Studies Teaching and Learning,* edited by James P. Shaver, 201–21. New York: Macmillan, 1991.

Adler, Susan A. "The Education of Social Studies Teachers." In *Handbook of Research in Social Studies Education,* edited by Linda S. Levstik and Cynthia A. Tyson, 329–51. New York: Routledge, 2008.

Ames, Michael. "How to Decorate a House: The Renegotiation of Cultural Representations at the University of British Columbia Museum of Anthropology." In *Museums and Sources Communities: A Routledge Reader,* 171–80. London, UK: Routledge, 2003.

Angvik, Magne and Bodo von Borries, eds. *Youth and History: A Comparative European Survey on Historical Consciousness and Political Attitudes among Adolescents.* Hamburg: Körber-Stiftung, 1997.

Antonelli, Fabrizio. *From Applied to Applause.* Toronto: Ontario Secondary School Teachers' Federation, 2004.

Ashton, Paul and Paula Hamilton. *History at the Crossroads: Australians and the Past.* Sydney: Halstead Press, 2010.

Axelrod, Paul. "Normal School." In *The Routledge International Encyclopedia of Education,* edited by Gary McCulloch and David Crook, 406–7. London: Routledge, 2008.

Bain, Robert B. "Into the Breach: Using Research and Theory to Shape History Instruction." In *Knowing, Teaching, and Learning History,* edited by Peter N. Stearns, Peter Seixas, and Sam Wineburg, 331–52. New York: New York University Press, 2000.

Bain, Robert B. "'They Thought the World Was Flat?': Applying the Principles of *How People Learn* in Teaching High School History." In *How Students Learn: History, Mathematics, and Science in the Classroom,* edited by John

Bransford and Suzanne Donovan, 179–213. Washington: The National Academies Press, 2005.

Bain, Robert and Jeffrey Mirel. "Setting Up Camp at the Great Instructional Divide: Educating Beginning History Teachers." *Journal of Teacher Education* 57, no. 3 (May/June 2006): 212–19.

Bal, Mieke. "Telling, Showing, Showing Off." *Critical Inquiry* 18, no. 3 (1992): 556–94.

Banks, James A., and Walter C. Parker. "Social Studies Teacher Education." In *Handbook of Research on Teacher Education*, edited by W. Robert Houston, 674–86. New York: Macmillan, 1990.

Barca, I. "Prospective Teachers' Ideas about Assessing Different Accounts." *International Journal of Historical Learning, Teaching and Research* 1, no. 2 (2001). http://centres.exeter.ac.uk/historyresource/journal2/barca.pdf.

Barrett, Jennifer. *Museums and the Public Sphere*. New York: Wiley and Sons, 2009.

Barton, K.C. "'I Just Kinda Know': Elementary Students' Ideas about Historical Evidence." *Theory and Research in Social Education* 25, no. 4 (1997): 407–30.

Barton, K.C. and L.S. Levstik. "Why Don't More History Teachers Engage Students in Interpretation?" *Social Education* 67, no. 6 (2003): 358–61.

Barton, K.C. and L.S. Levstik. *Teaching History for the Common Good*. Mahwah, NJ: Lawrence Erlbaum Associates, 2004.

Barton, K.C. "Primary Sources in History: Breaking through the Myths." *Phi Delta Kappan* 86, no. 10 (2005): 745–53.

Beier-de Haan, Rosmarie. *Re-staging Histories and Identities*. Malden, MA: Blackwell, 2006.

Belanger, Elizabeth. "How Now? Historical Thinking, Reflective Teaching, and the Next Generation of History Teachers." *The Journal of American History* 97, no. 4 (2011): 1079–88.

Ben-Peretz, Miriam, Sara Kleeman, Rivka Reichenberg, and Sarah Shimoni. "Educators of Educators: Their Goals, Perceptions and Practices." *Professional Development in Education* 36, no. 1–2 (2010): 111–29.

Bennett, Tony. *The Birth of the Museum: History, Theory, Politics*. New York: Routledge, 1995.

Berry, Amanda. *Tensions in Teaching about Teaching: Understanding Practice as a Teacher Educator*. Dordrecht: Springer, 2007.

Blume, Robert. "Humanizing Teacher Education." *The Phi Delta Kappan* 52, no. 7 (1971): 411–15.

Bohan, C., and O. L. Davis. "Historical Constructions: How Social Studies Teachers' Historical Thinking is Reflected in their Writing of History." *Theory and Research in Social Education* 26, no. 2 (1998): 173–97.

Boix-Mansilla, Veronica. "Historical Understanding: Beyond the Past and into the Present." In *Knowing, Teaching, and Learning History: National and International Perspectives,* edited by Peter N. Stearns, Peter Seixas, and Sam Wineburg, 390–418. New York: New York University Press, 2000.

Borko, Hilda. "Professional Development and Teacher Learning: Mapping the Terrain." *Educational Researcher* 33, no. 8 (2004): 3–15.

Britzman, Deborah. *Practice Makes Practice: A Critical Study of Learning to Teach,* 2nd ed. Albany, NY: State University of New York Press, 2003.

Britzman, Deborah, Donald Dippo, Dennis Searle, and Alice Pitt. "Toward an Academic Framework for Thinking about Teacher Education." *Teaching Education* 9, no. 1 (1997): 15–26.

Brouwer, Neils, and Fred Korthagen. "Can Teacher Education Make a Difference?" *American Educational Research Journal* 42, no. 1 (2005): 153–224.

Bruner, Jerome. *The Process of Education.* New York: Vintage, 1960.

Burstein, Joyce H. "Do As I Say and As I Do: Using the Professor-in-Residence Model in Teaching Social Studies Methods." *The Social Studies* 100, no. 3 (May/June 2009): 121–7.

Calam, John. "Culture and Credentials: A Note on Late Nineteenth Century Teacher Certification in British Columbia." *BC Historical News* 14, no. 1 (Fall 1980), 12–15.

Calam, John, ed. *Alex Lord's British Columbia: Recollections of a Rural School Inspector, 1915–36.* Vancouver: UBC Press, 1991.

Calkin, J.B. *Notes on Education: A Practical Work on Method and School Management.* Truro, NS: D.H. Smith, 1888.

Carson, Terrence R. "Closing the Gap between Research and Practice: Conversation as a Mode of Curriculum Research." *Phenomenology and Pedagogy* 4, no. 2 (1986): 73–85.

Carson, Terrence R. "The Time of Learning: A Dilemma for Teacher Education's Response to Diversity." Paper presented at the CATE Invitational Conference on Research in Teacher Education, Winnipeg, MB, November 2007.

Carter, D.S.G. "Knowledge Transmitter, Social Scientist or Reflective Thinking: Three Images of the Practitioner in Western Australia High Schools." *Theory and Research in Social Education* 18, no. 3 (1990): 274–317.

Cary, Lisa. "The Refusals of Citizenship: Normalizing Practices in Social Educational Discourses." *Theory and Research in Social Education,* 29, no. 3 (2001): 405–30.

Case, Roland. "Beyond Inert Facts." In *The Anthology of Social Studies: Issues and Strategies for Elementary Teachers,* edited by Roland Case and Penney Clark, 33–47. Vancouver: Pacific Educational Press, 2008.

Case, Roland and Penney Clark, eds. *The Anthology of Social Studies: Issues and Strategies for Secondary Teachers*. Vancouver: Pacific Educational Press, 2008.

Charland, Jean-Pierre. *Les élèves, l'histoire et la citoyenneté. Enquête auprès d'élèves des régions de Montréal et de Toronto*. Québec: Presses de l'Université Laval, 2003.

Clark, Penney. "The Historical Context of Social Studies in English Canada." In *Challenges and Prospects for Canadian Social* Studies, edited by A. Sears and I. Wright, 17–37. Vancouver: Pacific Educational Press, 2004.

Clark, Penney. "'A Nice Little Wife to Make Things Pleasant': Portrayals of Women in Social Studies Textbooks." *McGill Journal of Education* 40, no. 2 (2005): 241–65.

Clark, Penney, ed. *New Possibilities for the Past: Shaping History Education in Canada*. Vancouver: UBC Press, 2011.

Clark, Penney, and Roland Case. "Four Purposes of Citizenship Education." In *The Anthology of Social Studies: Issues and Strategies for Elementary Teachers*, edited by Roland Case and Penney Clark, 18–29. Vancouver: Pacific Educational Press, 2008.

Clifford, James. *The Predicament of Culture: Twentieth-Century Ethnography, Literature, and Art*. Cambridge: Harvard University Press, 1988.

Clifford, James. *Routes: Travel and Transition in the Late Twentieth Century*. Cambridge: Harvard University Press, 2007.

Clift, R. T., and P. Brady. "Research on Methods Courses and Field Experiences." In *Studying Teacher Education: The Report of the AERA Panel on Research and Teacher Education*, edited by Marilyn Cochran-Smith and Kenneth Zeichner, 309–424. Mahwah, NJ: Erlbaum, 2005.

Conn, Steven. *Museums and American Intellectual Life, 1876–1926*. Chicago: University of Chicago Press, 1998.

Conrad, Margaret, Jocelyn Létourneau, and David Northrup. "Canadians and Their Pasts: An Exploration in Historical Consciousness." *Public Historian* 31, no. 1 (2009): 15–34.

Cook, Sharon Anne. "Connecting Archives and the Classroom." *Archivaria*, 44 (Fall 1997): 102–17.

Coombes, Annie E. *Reinventing Africa: Material Culture and Popular Imagination in Late Victorian and Edwardian England*. New Haven: Yale University Press, 1994.

Costa, Arthur L., and Richard A. Loveall. "The Legacy of Hilda Taba." *Journal of Curriculum and Supervision* 18, no. 1 (Fall 2002): 56–62.

Costa, A.L., and B. Kallick. *Assessment Strategies for Self-Directed Learning*. Thousand Oaks, CA: Corwin, 2004.

Coulter, Rebecca Priegert. "Getting Things Done: Donalda J. Dickie and Leadership Through Practice." *Canadian Journal of Education* 28, no. 4 (2005): 669–99.

Counsell, Christine. "Disciplinary Knowledge for All, the Secondary History Curriculum and History Teachers' Achievement." *The Curriculum Journal* 22, no. 2 (June 2011): 201–25.

Crane, Susan. "Memory, Distortion and History in the Museum." *History and Theory* 36, no. 4 (1997), 44–63.

Crump, S., and K. Twyford. "Opening Their Eyes: E-learning for Rural and Isolated Communities in Australia." In *Rural Education for the Twenty-First Century: Identity, Place and Community in a Globalizing World*, edited by K. Schafft and A. Youngblood Jackson, 210–31. University Park, PA: Pennsylvania State University Press, 2010.

Dalongeville, Alain. *L'Image du Barbare dans l'Enseignement de l'Histoire*. Paris: L'Harmattan, 2001.

Darling-Hammond, Linda, Deborah Holtzman, Su Jin Gatlin, and Julian Vasquez Heilig. "Does Teacher Preparation Matter? Evidence about Teacher Certification, Teach for America, and Teacher Effectiveness." *Education Policy Analysis Archives* 13, no. 42 (2005): 1–48.

Darling-Hammond, Linda, Ruth Chung Wei, Alethea Andree, Nikole Richardson, and Stelios Orphanos. *Professional Learning in the Learning Profession: A Status Report on Teacher Development in the United States and Abroad*. Stanford: National Staff Development Council and The School Redesign Network at Stanford University, 2009.

den Heyer, Kent. "History as a Disciplined Ethic of Truths." In *New Possibilities for the Past: Shaping History Education in Canada*, edited by Penney Clark, 154–72. Vancouver: University of British Columbia Press, 2011.

den Heyer, Kent, and Laurence Abbott. "Reverberating Echoes: Challenging Teacher Candidates to Tell Entwined Narrations of Canadian History." *Curriculum Inquiry* 41, no. 5 (2011): 605–30.

Denos, Mike, and Roland Case. *Teaching about Historical Thinking: A Professional Resource to Help Teach Six Interrelated Concepts Central to Students' Ability to Think Critically about History*. Vancouver: Critical Thinking Consortium, 2006.

Dewey, John. *Democracy and Education: An Introduction to the Philosophy of Education*. New York: Macmillan Company, 1916.

Dickie, Donalda. *The Enterprise in Theory and Practice*. Toronto: W.J. Gage, 1940.

Dickie, Donalda J. "Education via the Enterprise." *The School* 21, no. 9 (1940): 3–6

Dickie, Donalda J. "Democracy and the Enterprise." *The School* 31, no. 6 (1943): 464–69.

Dickinson, A.K., Peter Lee, and Peter Rogers, eds. *Learning History*. London: Heinemann, 1984.

Dierenfield, Robert. "Let's Practice What We Teach." *Journal of Teacher Education* 10, no. 2 (1959): 207–10.

Donald, Dwayne T. "The Curricular Problem of Indigenous: Colonial Frontier Logics, Teacher Resistances, and the Acknowledgement of Ethical Space." In *Beyond "Presentism": Reimagining the Historical, Personal, and Social Places of Curriculum,* edited by J. Nahachewsky and Ingrid Johnston, 22–39. Rotterdam: Sense Publishing, 2009.

Donovan, M. Suzanne, and John D. Bransford, eds. *How Students Learn: History in the Classroom.* Washington, DC: The National Academies Press, 2005.

Doppen, Fran. "The Influence of a Teacher Preparation Program on Preservice Social Studies Teachers' Beliefs: A Case Study." *Journal of Social Studies Research* 31, no. 1 (2007): 54–64.

Duke, D. "Looking at Schools as a Rule-Governed Organization." *Journal of Research and Development in Education* 11, no. 4 (1978): 116–26.

Duncan, Carol. *Civilizing Rituals: Inside Public Art Museums.* New York: Routledge, 1995.

Earl, L.M. *Assessment as Learning.* Thousand Oaks, CA: Corwin, 2003.

Edmondson, J., and T. Butler. "Teaching School in Rural America: Toward an Educated Hope." In *Rural Education for the Twenty-First Century: Identity, Place and Community in a Globalizing World,* edited by K. Schafft and A. Youngblood, 150–74. University Park, PA: Pennsylvania State University Press, 2010.

Edwards, Edward. *Lives of the Founders of the British Museum: With Notices of Its Chief Augmentors and Other Benefactors, 1570–1870.* London: Trubner, 1870/1969.

Engle, Shirely H. "Late Night Thoughts about the New Social Studies." *Social Education* 50, no. 1 (1986): 20–2.

Epstein, Terrie L. "Sociological Approaches to Young People's Historical Understanding." *Social Education* 61, no. 1 (1997): 28–31.

Evans, Richard W. "Teacher Conceptions of History." *Theory and Research in Social Education* 17, no. 3 (1989): 210–40.

Falk, John H., Lynn D. Dierking, and Marianna Adams. "Living in a Learning Society: Museums and Free-choice Learning." In *A Companion to Museum Studies,* edited by S. Macdonald, 323–39. London: Routledge, 2006.

Fallace, Thomas D. "Historiography and Teacher Education: Reflections on an Experimental Course." *The History Teacher* 42, no. 2 (2009): 205–22.

Fallace, Thomas D. "Once More Unto the Breach: Trying to Get Preservice Teachers to Link Historiographical Knowledge to Pedagogy," *Theory and Research in Social Education* 35, no. 3 (2007): 427–46.

Fallace, Thomas, and Johann N. Neem. "Historiographical Thinking: Towards a New Approach." *Theory and Research in Social Education* 33, no. 3 (2005): 329–46.

Farley, Lisa. "Radical Hope: Or, the Problem of Uncertainty in History Education." *Curriculum Inquiry* 39, no. 4 (2009): 537–54.

Fehn, Bruce, and Kim E. Koeppen. "Intensive Document-Based Instruction in a Social Studies Methods Course." *Theory and Research in Social Education* 26, no. 4 (1998): 461–84.

Fragnoli, Kristi. "Historical Inquiry in a Methods Classroom: Examining our Beliefs and Shedding our Old Ways." *The Social Studies* 96, no. 6 (2005): 247–51.

Francis, Daniel. *The Imaginary Indian: The Image of the Indian in Canadian Culture.* Vancouver: Arsenal Pulp Press, 1992.

Friedland, Martin L. *The University of Toronto: A History.* Toronto: University of Toronto Press, 2002.

Friesen, Gerry. "The Shape of Historical Thinking in a Canadian History Survey Course in University." In *New Possibilities for the Past: Shaping History Education in Canada*, edited by Penney Clark, 210–23. Vancouver: UBC Press, 2011.

Gaffield, Chad. "The Blossoming of Canadian Historical Research: Implications for Policy and Content." In *To the Past: History Education, Public Memory and Citizenship Education in Canada*, edited by Ruth Sandwell, 88–102. Toronto, University of Toronto Press: 2006.

Gaffield, Chad. "Towards the Coach in the History Classroom." *Canadian Issues/Thèmes Canadiens* (October/November 2001): 12–4.

Gardner, Howard. *Changing Minds: The Art and Science of Changing Our Own and Other People's Minds.* Boston: Harvard Business School Press, 2006.

Gardner, Howard. *The Development and Education of the Mind: The Selected Works of Howard Gardner.* London: Routledge, 2006.

Gardner, James B. "Contested Terrain: History, Museums and the Public." *The Public Historian* 26, no. 4 (2004): 11–21.

Gibson, Susan E. *Teaching Social Studies in Elementary Schools: A Social Constructivist Approach.* Toronto: Nelson Education, 2009.

Gidney, Robert D. *From Hope to Harris: The Reshaping of Ontario's Schools.* Toronto: University of Toronto Press, 1999.

Goode, George B. "The Museums of the Future." In *U.S. National Museum, Annual Report*, 427–45. Washington, DC: National Museum, 1889.

Gosselin, Viviane. "Historical Thinking in the Museum: Open to Interpretation." In *New Possibilities for the Past: Shaping History Education in Canada*, edited by Penney Clark, 245–63. Vancouver: UBC Press, 2011.

Gradwell, Jill M. "Using Sources to Teach History for the Common Good: A Case Study of One Teacher's Purpose." *The Journal of Social Studies Research* 43, no. 1 (2010): 59–76.

Grant, J. "The Canada Studies Foundation: An Historical Overview." In *The Canada Studies Foundation*, edited by J. Grant et al., 9–35. Toronto: The Canada Studies Foundation, 1986.

Grant, S.G. *History Lessons: Teaching, Learning, and Testing in US High School Classrooms*. Mahwah, New Jersey: Laurence Erlbaum Associates, Publishers, 2003.

Grant, S.G., and Cinthia Salinas. "Assessment and Accountability in the Social Studies." In *Handbook of Research in Social Studies Education*, edited by Linda Levstik and Cynthia Tyson, 219–36. New York: Routledge, 2008.

Grossman, Pamela, and Alan Schoenfeld. "Teaching Subject Matter." In *Preparing Teachers for a Changing World: What Teachers Should Learn and Be Able to Do*, edited by Linda Darling-Hammond and John Bransford, 201–31. San Francisco: Jossey-Bass, 2005.

Grossman, Pamela, and Susan S. Stodolsky. "Considerations of Content and the Circumstances of Secondary School Teaching." In *Review of Research in Education*, edited by Linda Darling-Hammond, 179–221. Washington, DC: American Educational Research Association, 1994.

Groundwater-Smith, Susan, and Lynda Kelly. "Seeing Practice Anew: Improving Learning at the Museum." Paper presented to the Australian Association for Research in Education/New Zealand Association for Research in Education Joint Conference, Auckland, NZ, 2003.

Hall, Stuart, and Paul Du Gay. *Questions of Cultural Identity*. Thousand Oaks, CA: Sage, 1996.

Hammerness, K., Linda Darling-Hammond, and John Bransford. "How Teachers Learn and Develop." In *Preparing Teachers for a Changing World: What Teachers Should Learn and Be Able to Do*, edited by Linda Darling-Hammond and John Bransford, 358–89. San Francisco: Jossey-Bass, 2005.

Hein, George. *Learning in the Museum*. London, UK: Routledge, 1998.

Hinds, Marjorie, and Marie-Josee Berger. "The Impact of Professional Development on Beginning Teachers' Practices in One Secondary School." *Brock Education* 19, no. 2 (2010): 48–64.

Hirschkorn, Mark, Alan Sears, and Elizabeth Sloat. "The Missing Third: Accounting for Prior Learning in Teacher Education Program Admissions." In *ATEE Annual Conference 2011 Riga: Teachers' Life-cycle from Initial Teacher Education to Experienced Professional*. Riga, Latvia, 2012. [in press]

Hoolihan, K.A. "'Willing to Listen Humbly': Practice Teaching in Alberta Normal Schools, 1906–44." *Historical Studies in Education* 9, no. 2 (Fall 1997): 237–50.

Hooper-Greenhill, Eileen. *The Educational Role of Museums*. London: Routledge, 1999.

Hutchinson, David. *A Natural History of Place in Education*. New York: Teachers College Press, Columbia University, 2004.

Idrissi, Mostafa Hassani. *Pensée Historienne et Apprentissage de l'Histoire*. Paris: L'Harmattan, 2005.

Johnson, F. Henry. *A Brief History of Canadian Education*. Toronto: McGraw-Hill, 1968.

James, Jennifer H. "Teachers as Protectors: Making Sense of Preservice Teachers' Resistance to Interpretation in Elementary History Teaching." *Theory and Research in Social Education* 36, no. 3 (2008): 172–205.

Korthagen, Fred A.J. "Situated Learning Theory and the Pedagogy of Teacher Education: Towards an Integrative View of Teacher Behavior and Teaching Learning." *Teaching and Teacher Education* 26, no. 1 (2010): 98–106.

Kosnik, Clare. "The Effects of an Inquiry-Oriented Teacher-Education Program on a Faculty Member: Some Critical Incidents and My Journey." *Reflective Practice* 2, no. 1 (2001): 65–80.

Kosnik, Clare, and C. Beck. *Teaching in a Nutshell: Navigating Your Teacher Education Program as a Student Teacher*. New York: Routledge, 2011.

Laurier, Michel D. "Évaluer des Competences: Pas si Simple..." *Formation et Profession* (Avril 2005): 14–7.

Laville, Christian. "Place et Rôle de l'Enseignement de l'Histoire, Principalement dans l'Enseignement Secondaire, pour la Formation de l'Homme du XXᵉ siècle." *Bulletin de la SPHQ*, 17, No. 2, (April 1979): 30–5.

Laville, Christian. "Historical Consciousness and History Education: What to Expect from the First for the Second." In *Theorizing Historical Consciousness*, edited by Peter Seixas, 165–82. Toronto: University of Toronto Press, 2006.

Lee, Michelle H. "Seven Principles of Highly Collaborative PD." *Science and Children* 47, no. 9 (2010): 28–31.

Lee, Peter. "From National Canon to Historical Literacy." In *Beyond the Canon: History for the Twenty-First Century*, edited by Maria Grever and Siep Stuurman, 48–62. New York: Palgrave Macmillan, 2007.

Lee, Peter. "Understanding History." In *Theorizing Historical Consciousness*, edited by Peter Seixas, 129–64. Toronto: University of Toronto Press, 2004.

Lee, Peter. "'Walking Backwards into Tomorrow': Historical Consciousness and Understanding History." *International Journal of Historical Learning, Teaching and Research* 4, no. 1 (2004). http://www.heirnet.org/IJHLTR/journal7/lee.pdf.

Lee, Peter, and R. Ashby. "Progression in Historical Understanding in Students Ages 7-14." In *Knowing, Teaching, and Learning History: National and International Perspectives*, edited by Peter Stearns, Peter Seixas, and Sam Wineburg, 199–222. New York: New York University Press, 2000.

Lee, Peter J., and Alaric K. Dickinson, eds. *History Teaching and Historical Understanding*. London: Heinemann Educational Books, 1978.

Létourneau, Jocelyn. "Remembering Our Past: An Examination of the Historical Memory of Young Québécois." In *To the Past: History Education, Public Memory and Citizenship in Canada*, edited by Ruth Sandwell, 70–87. Toronto: University of Toronto Press, 2006.

Létourneau, Jocelyn. "Young People's Assimilation of a Collective Historical Memory: A Case Study of Quebeckers of French-Canadian Heritage." In *Theorizing Historical Consciousness*, edited by Peter Seixas, 109–28. Toronto: University of Toronto Press, 2006.

Lévesque, Stéphane. *Thinking Historically: Educating Students for the Twenty-First Century*. Toronto: University of Toronto Press, 2008.

Levstik, Linda S., and Keith C. Barton, *Doing History: Investigating with Children in Elementary and Middle Schools*, 4th ed. New York: Routledge, 2011.

Levstik, Linda S., and Keith C. Barton. *Researching History Education: Theory, Method, and Context*. New York: Routledge, 2008.

Loughran, John, and Amanda Berry. "Modelling by Teacher Educators." *Teaching Teachers* 21, no. 2 (2005): 193–203.

Lowenthal, David. *The Past Is a Foreign Country*. Cambridge, UK: Cambridge University Press, 1985.

Lunenberg, Mieke, Fred Korthagen, and Anja Swennen. "The Teacher Educator as a Role Model." *Teaching and Teacher Education* 23, no. 5 (2007): 586–601.

Maleuvre, Didier. *Museum Memories: History, Technology, Art*. Palo Alto, CA: Stanford University Press, 1999.

Mansilla, Veronica B., and Howard Gardner, "Disciplining the Mind," *Educational Leadership* 65, no. 5 (2008): 14–9.

Martineau, Robert. *L'Histoire à l'Ecole, Matière à Penser*. Montréal: L'Harmattan, 1999.

Martineau, Robert. *Fondements et Pratiques de l'Enseignement de l'Histoire à l'Ecole: Traité de Didactique*. Québec: Presses de l'Université du Québec, 2010.

Mayer, Robert H. "Learning to Teach Young People How to Think Historically: A Case Study of One Student Teacher's Experience." *Social Studies* 97, no. 2 (2006): 69–76.

McDiarmid, G. "Understanding History for Teaching: A Study of the Historical Understanding of Prospective Teachers." In *Cognitive and Instructional Processes in History and the Social Sciences*, edited by Mario Carretero and F.J. Voss, 159–85. Hillsdale, NJ: Lawrence Erlbaum Associates, 1994.

McDiarmid, G., and P. Vinten-Johansen. "A Catwalk across the Great Divide: Redesigning the History Teaching Methods Course." In *Knowing, Teaching, and Learning History: National and International Perspectives*, edited by Peter Stearns, Peter Seixas, and Sam Wineburg, 156–77. New York: New York University Press, 2000.

Meuwissen, Kevin W. "Maybe Someday the Twain Shall Meet: Exploring Disconnections Between Methods Instruction and Life in the Classroom." *The Social Studies* 96, no. 6 (2005): 253–8.

Milewski, Patrice. "Teachers' Institutes in Late Nineteenth-Century Ontario." *Paedagogica Historica* 44, no. 5 (2008): 607–20.

Moisan, Sabrina. "Historical Thinking in Quebec History Education." *THEN/ Hier E-bulletin*, 19, no. 3 (2011): 3.

Moniot, Henri. *Didactique de l'Histoire*. Paris: Nathan, 1993.

Morton, Desmond. "Canadian History Teaching in Canada: What's the Big Deal?" In *To the Past: History Education, Public Memory, and Citizenship in Canada*, edited by Ruth Sandwell, 23–31. Toronto: University of Toronto Press, 2006.

Mueller, Andréa, and Malcom Welch. "Classroom-Based Professional Development: Teachers' Reflections on Learning Alongside Students." *Alberta Journal of Educational Research* 52, no. 2 (2006): 143–57.

Osborne, Ken. "Fred Morrow Fling and the Source Method of Teaching History." *Theory and Research in Social Education* 31, no. 4 (2003): 466–501.

Osborne, Ken. "Teaching History in Schools: A Canadian Debate." *Journal of Curriculum Studies* 35, no. 5 (2003): 585–626.

Osborne, Ken. "To the Past: Why We Need to Teach and Study History." In *To the Past: History Education, Public Memory and Citizenship in Canada*, edited by Ruth Sandwell, 103–31. Toronto: University of Toronto Press, 2006.

Osborne, Ken. "'To the Schools We Must Look for Good Canadians': Developments in the Teaching of History in Schools since 1960." *Journal of Canadian Studies* 22, no. 3 (1987): 104–25.

Pace, David. "The Amateur in the Operating Room: History and the Scholarship of Teaching and Learning." *The American Historical Review* 109, no. 4 (October 2004): 1171–92.

Patterson, Robert S. "History of Teacher Education in Alberta." In *Shaping the Schools of the Canadian West*, edited by David C. Jones, Nancy M. Sheehan, and Robert M. Stamp, 192–207. Calgary: Detselig, 1979.

Paxton, Richard J. "The Influence of Author Visibility on High School Students Solving a Historical Problem." *Cognition and Instruction* 20, no. 2 (2002): 197–248.

Peck, Carla. "'It's Not Like [I'm] Chinese and Canadian. I Am In Between': Ethnicity and Students' Conceptions of Historical Significance." *Theory and Research in Social Education* 38, no. 4 (2010): 574–617.

Peck, Carla, and Peter Seixas. "Benchmarks of Historical Thinking: First Steps," *Canadian Journal of Education* 31, no. 4 (2008): 1015–38.

Pendry, Anna, Chris Husbands, James Arthur, and Jon Davison. *History Teachers in the Making: Professional Learning.* Buckingham, UK: Open University Press, 1998.

Phenix, Philip. "Key Concepts and the Crisis in Learning." *Teachers College Record* 58, no. 3 (1958): 137–43.

Phillips, Charles E. *The Development of Education in Canada.* Toronto, W.J. Gage, 1957.

Phillips, Robert. *History Teaching, Nationhood and the State: A Study in Educational Politics.* London: Cassell, 1998.

Phillips, Ruth. "Re-placing Objects: Historical Practices for the Second Museum Age." *The Canadian Historical Review* 86, no. 1 (2005): 83–110.

Popkewitz, Thomas. "Knowledge, Power, and Curriculum: Revisiting a TRSE Argument." *Theory and Research in Social Education,* 26, no. 1 (1998): 83–101.

Portal, Christopher, ed. *The History Curriculum for Teachers.* London: Falmer Press, 1987.

Raths, James. "Teachers' Beliefs and Teaching Beliefs." *Early Childhood Research and Practice* 3, no. 1 (2001): 385–91.

Riegel, Henrietta. "Into the Heart of Irony: Ethnographic Exhibits and the Politics of Difference." In *Theorizing Museums*, edited by S. Macdonald and G. Fyfe, 83–106. Oxford: Blackwell, 1996.

Rosenzweig, Roy. "How Americans Use and Think about the Past: Implications from a National Survey for the Teaching of History." In *Knowing, Teaching, and Learning History: National and International Perspectives*, edited by Peter Stearns, Peter Seixas, and Sam Wineburg, 262–83. New York: New York University Press, 2000.

Rugg, Harold, and Ann Shumaker. *The Child-Centered School: An Appraisal of the New Education*. Yonkers-on-Hudson, NY: World Book Company, 1928.

Rüsen, Jörn. "Historical Consciousness: Narrative Structure, Moral Function and Ontogenetic Development." In *Theorizing Historical Consciousness*, edited by Peter Seixas, 63–85. Toronto: University of Toronto Press, 2006.

Rüsen, Jörn. *Rekonstruktion der Vergangenheit*. Gottingen: Vandenhoeck and Ruprecht, 1986.

Sandwell, Ruth W. "History Is a Verb: Teaching Historical Practice to Teacher Education Students." *In New Possibilities for the Past: Shaping History Education in Canada*, edited by Penney Clark, 224–42. Vancouver: UBC Press, 2011.

Sandwell, Ruth W. "The Internal Divide: Historians and their Teaching." In *Bridging Theory and Practice in Teacher Education*, edited by Mordechai Gordon and T.V. O'Brien, 17–30. The Netherlands: Sense Publishers, 2007.

Sandwell, Ruth W. "Reading Beyond Bias: Using Historical Documents in the Secondary Classroom." *McGill Journal of Education* 38, no. 1 (2003): 168–86.

Sandwell, Ruth W. "School History Versus the Historians." *International Journal of Social Education* 20, no. 1 (2005): 9–17.

Sandwell, Ruth. "'We Were Allowed to Disagree, Because We Couldn't Agree on Anything': Seventeen Voices in the Canadian Debates Over History Education." In *History Wars and the Classroom: Global Perspectives*, edited by Tony Taylor and Robert Guyver, 51–76. Charlotte, NC, Information Age Publishing, 2012.

Sawyer, Richard, and Armando Laguardia. "Reimagining the Past/Changing the Present: Teachers Adapting History Curriculum for Cultural Encounters." *Teachers College Record* 112, no. 8 (2010): 1993–2020.

Sears, Alan. "Children's Understandings of Democratic Participation: Lessons for Civic Education." In *Civic Education and Youth Political Participation*, edited by Murray Print and Henry Milner, 143–58. Rotterdam/Boston/Taipei: Sense, 2009.

Sears, Alan. "Historical Thinking and Citizenship Education: It Is Time to End the War." In *New Possibilities for the Past: Shaping History Education in Canada*, edited by Penney Clark, 344–64. Vancouver: UBC Press, 2011.

Sears, Alan. "Making Room for Revolution in Social Studies Classrooms." *Education Canada* 49, no. 2 (2009): 4–8.

Segall, Avner. "Critical History: Implications for History/Social Studies Education." *Theory and Research in Social Education* 27, no. 3 (1999): 358–74.

Segall, Avner. "Teachers' Perceptions of the Impact of State-Mandated Standardized Testing: The Michigan Educational Assessment Program

(MEAP) as a Case Study of Consequences." *Theory and Research in Social Education* 31, no. 3 (2003): 287–325.

Segall, Avner. "What's the Purpose of Teaching a Discipline Anyway? The Case of History." In *Social Studies: The Next Generation*, edited by Avner Segall, Elizabeth Heilman, and Cleo Cherryholmes, 125–39. New York: Peter Lang, 2006.

Segall, Avner, and William Gaudelli. "Reflecting Socially on Social Issues in a Social Studies Methods Course." *Teaching Education* 18, no. 1 (2007): 77–92.

Seixas, Peter. "Beyond 'Content' and 'Pedagogy': In Search of a Way to Talk about History Education." *Journal of Curriculum Studies* 31, no. 3 (1999): 317–37.

Seixas, Peter. "The Community of Inquiry as a Basis for Knowledge and Learning: The Case of History." *American Educational Research Journal* 30, no. 2 (1993): 305–24.

Seixas, Peter. "Conceptualizing the Growth of Historical Understanding." In *Handbook of Education and Human Development: New Models of Learning, Teaching, and Schooling*, edited by David Olson and Nancy Torrance, 765–83. Oxford, UK: Blackwell, 1996.

Seixas, Peter. "A Discipline Adrift in an 'Integrated' Curriculum: History in British Columbia Schools." *Canadian Journal of Education* 19, no. 1 (1994): 99–107.

Seixas, Peter. "A Modest Proposal for Change in Canadian History," *Teaching History* 137 (December 2009): 26–30.

Seixas, Peter. "Review of Research in Social Studies." In *Handbook of Research on Teaching*, edited by Veronica Richardson, 545–65. Washington, DC: American Educational Research Association, 2001.

Seixas, Peter. "Student Teachers Thinking Historically." *Theory and Research in Social Education* 26, no. 3 (1998): 310–41.

Seixas, Peter, ed. *Theorizing Historical Consciousness*. Toronto: University of Toronto Press, 2006.

Seixas, Peter. "What is Historical Consciousness?" In *To The Past: History Education, Public Memory, and Citizenship Education in Canada*, edited by Ruth W. Sandwell, 11–22. Toronto: University of Toronto Press, 2006.

Seixas, Peter, Daniel Fromowitz, and Petra Hill. "History, Memory and Learning to Teach." In *Understanding History: Recent Research in History Education. International Review of History Education, Vol. 4*, edited by Rosalyn Ashby, Peter Gordon, and Peter Lee, 116–34. London: RoutledgeFalmer, 2005.

Seixas, Peter, and Carla Peck. "Teaching Historical Thinking." In *Challenges and Prospects for Canadian Social Studies*, edited by Alan Sears and Ian Wright, 109–17. Vancouver: Pacific Educational Press, 2004.

Seixas, Peter, and Tom Morton. *The Big Six: Historical Thinking Concepts.* Toronto: Nelson Education, 2012.

Sheehan, Nancy M., and J. Donald Wilson. "From Normal School to the University to the College of Teachers: Teacher Education in British Columbia in the 20th Century." *Journal of Education for Teaching* 20, no. 1 (1994): 23–37.

Shelton, Anthony. "Museums and Anthropologies: Practices and Narratives." In *A Companion to Museum Studies*, edited by Sharon Macdonald, 64–80. London, UK: Routledge, 2006.

Shemilt, Denis J. *History 13–16: Evaluation Study.* Edinburgh: Collins Education, 1980.

Shemilt, Dennis. "The Caliph's Coin: The Currency of Narrative Frameworks in History Teaching." In *Knowing, Teaching, and Learning History: National and International Perspectives*, edited by Peter N. Stearns, Peter Seixas, and Sam Wineburg, 83–101. New York: New York University Press, 2000.

Shulman, Lee S., *The Wisdom of Practice: Essays on Teaching, Learning, and Learning to Teach.* San Francisco: Jossey-Bass, 2004.

Sikula, J., T. Better, and E. Guyton, eds. *Handbook of Research on Teacher Education*, 2nd ed. New York: Simon and Schuster Macmillan, 1996.

Slekar, Timothy D. "Case History of a Methods Course: Teaching and Learning History in a 'Rubber Room.'" *The Social Studies* 96, no. 6 (2005): 237–40.

Smaller, Harry. "Teachers' Institutes: Instituting Proper Teaching." *Ontario History* 80, no. 4 (December 1988): 275–91.

Sobel, D. *Place-based Education: Connecting Classrooms and Communities.* Great Barrington, MA: Orion Society, 2005.

Stanley, Timothy. "Whose Public? Whose Memory? Racisms, Grand Narratives and Canadian History." In *To the Past: History Education, Public Memory, and Citizenship in Canada,* edited by Ruth Sandwell, 32–49. Toronto: University of Toronto Press, 2006.

Stearns, Peter, Peter Seixas, and Sam Wineburg, eds. *Knowing, Teaching, and Learning History: National and International Perspectives.* New York: New York University Press, 2000.

Swartz, Ellen. "Casing the Self: a Study of Pedagogy and Critical Thinking." *Teacher Development* 8, no.1 (2004): 45–65.

Swennen, Anja, Mieke Lunenberg, and Fred Korthagen. "'Preach What You Teach!' Teacher Educators and Congruent Teaching." *Teachers and Teaching: Theory and Practice* 14, no. 5–6 (2008): 531–42.

Taba, Hilda, Mary C. Durkin, Jack R. Fraenkel, and Anthony H. McNaughton. *A Teacher's Handbook to Elementary Social Studies: An Inductive Approach,* 2nd ed. Reading, MA: Addison-Wesley, 1971.

Tatto, Maria Teressa. "The Influence of Teacher Education on Teachers' Beliefs About Purposes of Education, Roles, and Practice." *Journal of Teacher Education* 49, no.1 (1998): 66–77.

Theobald, P., and K. Wood. "Learning to be Rural: Identity Lessons from History, Schooling and the U.S. Corporate Media," in *Rural Education for the Twenty-First Century: Identity, Place and Community in a Globalizing World,* edited by K. Schafft and A. Youngblood Jackson, 17–33. University Park, PA: Pennsylvania State University Press, 2010.

Torff, Bruce, and Katherine Byrnes. "Differences across Academic Subjects in Teachers' Attitudes About Professional Development." *The Educational Reform* 75, no. 1 (2011): 26–36.

Torney-Purta, Judith. "Psychological Perspectives on Enhancing Civic Education through the Education of Teachers." *Journal of Teacher Education* 34, no. 6 (1983): 30–34.

Trofanenko, Brenda. "The Educational Promise of Public History Museum Exhibits." *Theory and Research in Social Education* 38, no. 2 (2010): 270–88.

Tupper, Jennifer, and Michael Cappello. "Teaching Treaties as (Un)usual Narratives: Disrupting the Curricular Commonsense." *Curriculum Inquiry* 38, no. 5 (2008): 559–78.

Tutiaux-Guillon, Nicole. "La Conscience Historique des Jeunes: Deux Enquêtes," *Historiens et géographes* 396 (November 2006): 255–7.

van Hover, Stephanie. "The Professional Development of Social Studies Teachers." In *Handbook of Research in Social Studies Education*, edited by Linda S. Levstik and Cynthia A. Tyson, 352–72. New York: Routledge, 2008.

van Hover, Stephanie, and Elizabeth Yeager. "'I Want to Use My Subject Matter to …': The Role of Purpose in One U.S. Secondary History Teacher's Instructional Decision Making." *Canadian Journal of Education* 30, no. 3 (2007): 670–90.

VanSledright, Bruce. *The Challenge of Rethinking History Education: On Practices, Theories, and Policy.* New York: Routledge, 2011.

VanSledright, Bruce. "Confronting History's Interpretive Paradox While Teaching Fifth Graders to Investigate the Past." *American Educational Research Journal* 39, no. 4 (2002): 1089–1115.

VanSledright, Bruce. "Fifth Graders Investigating History in the Classroom: Results from a Researcher-Practitioner Design Experiment." *Elementary School Journal* 103, no. 2 (Nov 2002): 131–60.

VanSledright, Bruce. *In Search of America's Past: Learning to Read History in Elementary School.* New York: Teachers College Press, 2002.

VanSledright, Bruce. "Narratives of Nation-State, Historical Knowledge, and School History Education." *Review of Research in Education* 32, no. 1 (2008): 109–46.

VanSledright, Bruce. "What Does It Mean to Think Historically … and How Do You Teach It?" *Social Education* 68, no. 3 (2004): 230–33.

VanSledright, Bruce, Liliana Maggioni, and Kim Reddy. "Preparing Teachers to Teach Historical Thinking? An Interplay between Professional Development Programs and School-Systems Cultures." Paper presented at the Annual Meeting of the American Educational Research Association, New Orleans, LA, April 7–13, 2011.

Virta, A. "Student Teachers' Conceptions of History." *International Journal of Historical Learning, Teaching and Research* 2, no. 1 (2001). http://centres.exeter.ac.uk/historyresource/journal2/barca.pdf.

von Heyking, Amy. *Creating Citizens: History and Identity in Alberta's Schools, 1905–1980.* Calgary: University of Calgary Press, 2006.

von Heyking, Amy. "Fostering a Provincial Identity: Two Eras in Alberta Schooling." *Canadian Journal of Education* 29, no. 4 (2006): 1127–56.

Watson, Sheila. "History Museums, Community Identities and a Sense of Place." In *Museum Revolutions: How Museums Change and Are Changed*, edited by Simon J. Knell, Suzanne MacLeod, and Sheila Watson, 160–72. London, UK: Routledge, 2006.

Watson, Sheila. *Museums and Their Communities.* London, UK: Routledge, 2007.

Wenger, Etienne. *Communities of Practice: Learning, Meaning, and Identity, Learning in Doing.* Cambridge, UK: Cambridge University Press, 1998.

Wenger, Etienne, Richard A. McDermott, and William Snyder. *Cultivating Communities of Practice: A Guide to Managing Knowledge.* Boston: Harvard Business School Press, 2002.

Wesch, Michael. "Anti-teaching: Confronting the Crisis of Significance." *Education Canada* 48, no. 2 (2008): 4–7.

Westhoff, Laura M., and Joseph L. Polman. "Developing Preservice Teachers' Pedagogical Content Knowledge about Historical Thinking." *International Journal of Social Education* 22, no. 2 (Fall 2007/Winter 2008): 1–28.

Wideen, Marvin. "Teacher Education at the Crossroads." In *Changing Times in Teacher Education: Restructuring or Reconceptualization?*, edited by Marvin F. Wideen and Peter P. Grimmett, 1–16. London and New York: RoutledgeFalmer, 1995.

Wilkinson, Sue. *A Teacher's Guide to Learning from Objects.* London: English Heritage, 1990.

Wilson, S.W. "Research on History Teaching." In *Handbook of Research on Teaching*, edited by Veronica Richardson, 527–44. Washington, DC: American Educational Research Association, 2001.

Wilson, Suzanne M., and Samuel S. Wineburg. "Peering at History Through Different Lenses: The Role of Disciplinary Perspectives in Teaching History." *Teachers College Record* 89, no. 4 (Summer 1988): 525–39.

Wilson, Suzanne M., and Samuel S. Wineburg. "Wrinkles in Time and Place: Using Performance Assessments to Understand the Knowledge of History Teachers." *American Educational Research Journal* 30, no. 4 (1993): 729–69.

Wineburg, Samuel S. *Historical Thinking and Other Unnatural Acts: Charting the Future of Teaching the Past.* Philadelphia: Temple University Press, 2001.

Wineburg, Samuel S. "On the Reading of Historical Texts: Notes on the Breach between the School and the Academy." *American Educational Research Journal* 28, no. 3 (1991): 495–519.

Wineburg, Samuel S., and Daisy Martin. "Tampering with History: Adapting Primary Sources for Struggling Readers." *Social Education* 73, no. 5 (2009): 212–16.

Wineburg, Samuel S., and Suzanne M. Wilson. "Models of Wisdom in the Teaching of History." *The History Teacher* 24, no. 4 (1991): 395–412.

Wright, Ian, and David Hutchison. *Elementary Social Studies: A Practical Approach to Teaching and Learning,* 7th ed. Scarborough, ON: Pearson Education Canada, 2010.

Yeager, Elizabeth, and O. L. Davis. "Classroom Teachers' Thinking about Historical Texts: An Exploratory Study." *Theory and Research in Social Education* 24, no. 2 (1996): 146–66.

Zeichner, Kenneth M., and B. Robert Tabachnick. "Are the Effects of University Teacher Education 'Washed Out' by School Experience?" *Journal of Teacher Education* 32, no. 3 (1981): 3–11.

Contributors

Roland Case is executive director of The Critical Thinking Consortium (www.tc2.ca) – a non-profit association of fifty school districts and educational organizations in Canada and the United States. He is a retired professor of social studies education at Simon Fraser University in Vancouver. Roland has edited or authored over one hundred published works. Notable among these are the two-volume *The Anthology of Social Studies* (Pacific Educational Press, 2008, 2013) and several series of award-winning critical thinking resources published by The Critical Thinking Consortium. His most recent article is "The Unfortunate Consequences of Bloom's Taxonomy" (*Social Education*, 2013). In addition to his public school and university teaching, Roland has worked with over 18,000 educators worldwide to support the infusion of critical thinking into teaching. Roland was the 2006 recipient of the Distinguished Academics Career Achievement Award.

Theodore Christou is Assistant Professor in the Faculty of Education at Queen's University in Kingston. His research and teaching concern the history and philosophy of education. Theodore is a published poet and an advocate for humanities subjects in teacher education.

Penney Clark is Professor in the Faculty of Education, University of British Columbia and Director of The History Education Network (THEN/HiER). She is Associate Director of the Centre for the Study of Historical Consciousness, UBC, and a board member for The Historical Thinking Project. Her research is in the areas of history of education and history teaching and learning. She has written on the history of education in *The History of the Book in Canada* series, *Historical Studies in Education*, *Papers of the Bibliographical Society of Canada*, *History of*

Education (UK), *History of Education Quarterly*, the *Journal of Canadian Studies*, and the *Canadian Journal of Education*. Her most recent work on history teaching and learning is her edited volume, *New Possibilities for the Past: Shaping History Education in Canada* (UBC Press, 2011). She is coeditor (with Roland Case) of two social studies anthologies used widely in teacher education courses.

Kent den Heyer is Associate Professor in the Department of Secondary Education, University of Alberta, where he teaches in the undergraduate and graduate studies programs. His research explores curriculum theory, the intersections of empire logics and social studies in North America, and the educational implications of the work of the French philosopher Alain Badiou. Recently published work appears in *Curriculum Inquiry*, *Journal of Curriculum Theorizing*, *Educational Theory*, and *Theory and Research in Social Education*.

Catherine Duquette is Professor of Didactics of History at the Université du Québec à Chicoutimi. She earned her PhD in Didactics of History at Université Laval, Québec. Member of the Centre de recherche interuniversitaire sur la formation et la profession enseignante (CRIFPE-UQ) and the The History Education Network (THEN-HiER), her research interests include how students – elementary and high school – learn historical thinking, the relationship between historical thinking and historical consciousness, and the assessment of historical thinking. She has contributed to books on history education, and published papers in both academic journals such as the *Cartables de Clio* and professional journals such as *The Beaver*, *Traces*, and *Enjeux de l'univers social*.

Linda Farr Darling is the first Eleanor Rix Professor of Rural Teacher Education at the University of British Columbia, an endowed position that combines collaborative interdisciplinary research, teacher preparation for small and remote schools, and examination of rural educational and social policy. Her research interests centre on the links between schooling and the sustainability of rural communities. Linda and coauthor Terry Taylor have worked together on various teaching and writing projects that focus on the history of the West Kootenay region of British Columbia and the role of place-consciousness in both K-12 and teacher education.

Rose Fine-Meyer teaches in the Master of Teaching and Initial Teacher Education programs at the Ontario Institute for Studies in Education,

University of Toronto. Her research examines how widespread social movement activism has influenced the work of teachers, how the second wave women's movement affected educational change in Ontario, and the ways in which activist teachers' curriculum choices contributed to peace education. She has developed interdisciplinary curricula that incorporate place-based history in schools and has written a number of supplementary resources for history and social science classrooms. On a community level, she has developed a local women's history talk series, herstoriescafe.com, which has been instrumental in linking diverse history education communities and was recognized in 2012 with a Heritage Toronto's Community Award. She is the recipient of the Governor General's award for Excellence in the Teaching of Canadian History and the Queen Elizabeth II Diamond Jubilee Medal.

Lindsay S. Gibson is a PhD candidate in the Centre for the Study of Historical Consciousness in the Department of Curriculum and Pedagogy at the University of British Columbia, where he is currently completing his dissertation research. He also works as a member of the Instructional Leadership Team in School District No. 23 (Kelowna, British Columbia), where he previously taught secondary school history and social studies for eleven years. He has been working with The Historical Thinking Project since 2008 as a presenter and is part of the Executive Committee. Lindsay also works as presenter, writer, and editor for a variety of The Critical Thinking Consortium (TC²) history education projects.

Jan Haskings-Winner is Assistant Curriculum Leader of Canadian and World Studies at Malvern Collegiate Institute, in the Toronto District School Board. She has taught for over twenty-five years in Malaysia, northern Ontario, central Ontario, and Toronto in a variety of schools and communities, including maternity homes, rural schools, and inner city schools. She has been the president of OHASSTA and has been on the executive for six years. She has been seconded to teach in the Pre-Service Teacher Education program at OISE/UT and currently teaches additional qualification courses with Queen's University and Lakehead University.

Stéphane Lévesque is Associate Professor of history education at the University of Ottawa, Ontario. In 2011, he was Visiting Professor of digital history at Umea University in Sweden. Dr Lévesque is the director of the Virtual Historian Laboratory (VH Lab), the first CFI research centre in Canada to study the online learning of history (www.virtual historian.ca). His research focuses on students' historical thinking, historical consciousness, and new media and technology in education. He is a board member of the Virtual Museum of Canada, Canada's History Society, and The History Education Research Network/Histoire et éducation en réseau (THEN/HiER). Dr Lévesque served as an educational expert for the Canadian government on the establishment of the Canadian Museum for Human Rights as well as curriculum expert for the Ontario Ministry of Education. He is the author of *Thinking Historically: Educating Students for the Twenty-First Century* (UTP, 2008) and *Enseigner la pensée historique* (Critical Thinking Consortium, 2013). In 2006, he was nominated by the Council of Ontario Universities for the award for Excellence in Teaching with Technology.

Genie MacLeod is a writer, editor, and researcher from Vancouver, BC. She has worked as a program assistant and documentarian at Christianne's Lyceum of Literature and Art and as a researcher and digital resource editor at The Critical Thinking Consortium. She holds a bachelor's degree in English literature and Latin from the University of British Columbia and a master's degree in English literature from the University of Oxford.

John JC Myers began his teaching career as a high school history and social studies teacher in Toronto. Over the decades, he has taught and worked with classes from Grade 3 to adult in four provinces and three countries. He is currently a curriculum instructor, teaching history methods courses in the Department of Curriculum, Teaching and Learning at the Ontario Institute for Studies in Education (OISE), University of Toronto. Among his interests are classroom assessment, small group processes in the classroom, and the nature of change in education. He has published widely in each of these areas.

Carla L. Peck is Associate Professor of Social Studies Education in the Department of Elementary Education at the University of Alberta, and editor of *Theory and Research in Social Education*. Her research interests include students' understandings of democratic concepts, diversity, identity, citizenship, and the relationship between students' ethnic identities and their understandings of history. She is the principal investigator of a Social Sciences and Humanities Research Council (SSHRC) grant investigating elementary students' and teachers' conceptions of ethnic diversity in four Canadian provinces. She is also a coinvestigator on a SSHRC-funded project on high school students' conceptions of democratic participation. Dr Peck was awarded the Canadian Education Association's Pat Clifford Award for Early Career Research in Education (2010) and the 2011 English language Article Award from The History Education Network/Histoire et éducation en réseau. She has published journal articles on citizenship education and history education in the *Canadian Journal of Education*, *Curriculum Inquiry*, and *Citizenship Teaching and Learning (CTL)*, as well as several book chapters.

Scott A. Pollock has been teaching history, social sciences, philosophy, and law at the secondary level for the past eleven years. He completed his MEd at the University of Western Ontario and is working towards a PhD at OISE/UT. His research areas of interest include historical thinking, teacher thinking, gender and education, and pre-service teacher education.

Ruth Sandwell is Associate Professor in the Department of Curriculum, Teaching and Learning at the Ontario Institute for Studies in Education (OISE), University of Toronto. She teaches and writes in the area of history teaching and learning, and also publishes in the field of Canadian rural history, the social history of energy, and the history of education. She is editor of a collection of essays, *To The Past: History Education, Public Memory and Citizenship Education in Canada*, (Toronto, University of Toronto Press: October: 2006). She is a founding codirector and educational director of the of the online history education project: The Great Unsolved Mysteries in Canadian History, www.canadian mysteries.ca.

Alan Sears is Professor of Social Studies Education at the University of New Brunswick. His research and writing are in the areas of citizenship education, teacher education, history education, educational history, and policy studies in education. He is editor of the journal *Citizenship Teaching and Learning* and coeditor of the recent book *Globalization, the Nation-State and the Citizen: Dilemmas and Directions for Civics and Citizenship Education*, published by Routledge.

Peter Seixas is Professor and Canada Research Chair in the Department of Curriculum and Pedagogy at the University of British Columbia, Director of the Centre for the Study of Historical Consciousness, and a member of the Royal Society of Canada. He taught high school social studies in Vancouver over the course of fifteen years and earned a PhD in history from the University of California at Los Angeles. He is the author of numerous articles on history education in Canadian and international journals, editor of *Theorizing Historical Consciousness* (Toronto: University of Toronto Press, 2004), coeditor, with Peter Stearns and Sam Wineburg, of *Knowing, Teaching, and Learning History: National and International Perspectives* (New York: NYU Press, 2000), and coauthor, with Tom Morton, of *The Big Six Historical Thinking Concepts* (Toronto: Nelson, 2012). He also directs The Historical Thinking Project, the aim of which is to promote critical historical literacy.

Terry Taylor is the Superintendent of Schools in SD #10 (Arrow Lakes). She also teaches for UBC's West Kootenay Teacher Education program. Terry is a passionate educator committed to celebrating and nurturing the rich innovations of rural schools. Creativity, the role of the arts in education, and literacy are some of her interests. In partnership with coauthor Linda Farr Darling, she births brilliant place-conscious learning initiatives for K–12 students, and builds capacity with teachers and teacher candidates.

Brenda Trofanenko is an associate professor and Canada Research Chair in Education, Culture, and Community at Acadia University in Wolfville, NS. She is also a visiting professor in the Graduate School of Library and Information Sciences and in the Russian, East European, and Euroasian Centre at the University of Illinois at Urbana-Champaign. Her research interests focus on exploring how public institutions – specifically museums and archives – define specific subject disciplines and community and individual identities. She has published articles in scholarly journals including the *Journal of Curriculum Studies, Anthropology and Education Quarterly,* and *Discourse: Studies in the Cultural Politics of Education,* and several edited books. She is editing workshop papers for two journals: *Museum Management* and *Curatorship* and *Education, Pedagogy, and Cultural Studies.* Her current research agenda is examining the role of public institutions in defining collective memories of distressing events, how youth respond to such events, and how memory serves as a community membership.

Amy von Heyking is an associate professor in the Faculty of Education at the University of Lethbridge in Alberta. Her research interests include history teaching and learning, and history of school curriculum. Her academic publications include articles in *Historical Studies in Education*, *Canadian Journal of Education*, and *History of Education Quarterly*. She authored chapters in *New Possibilities for the Past: Shaping History Education in Canada* (UBC Press, 2011) and *Britishness, Identity and Citizenship: The View From Abroad* (Peter Lang, 2011). She is the author of *Creating Citizens: History and Identity in Alberta's Schools* (University of Calgary Press, 1996).

Graeme Webber is originally from British Columbia. He began his undergraduate degree in history at Cornell University and finished it at Queen's University. After completing his bachelor's of education at the University of British Columbia, he followed his wife to Edmonton where he spent a year as a middle school librarian. He currently works as a Grade 7 teacher in Spruce Grove, Alberta.